James A. Herne

The American Ibsen

The University of Maine.

James A. Herne

The American Ibsen

John Perry

Nelson-Hall
Chicago

LIBRARY OF CONGRESS CATALOGING IN PUBLICATION DATA

Perry, John, 1937–
    James A. Herne: The American Ibsen.

    Includes bibliographical references and index.
    1.   Herne, James A., 1839–1901—Biography.
2.   Dramatists, American—19th century—Biography.
PS1919.H75Z8   812'.4   77–17931
ISBN 0–88229–265–X   (cloth)
ISBN 0–88229–561–6 (paper)

Manufactured in the United States of America.

To Mom

contents

acknowledgments

This biography started one afternoon in July, 1968, when I found a copy of *Shore Acres and Other Plays* in a New York City book store. Nine years have passed—and numerous revisions. First written as a doctoral dissertation at Southern Illinois University called "James A. Herne: A Life in the American Theatre," it has continued to grow. The present text involves several additional years of research, which nearly doubled the original manuscript. Although I cannot mention everyone who enabled me to complete this book, certain individuals and institutions deserve special mention.

For three years, Dr. Archibald McLeod, Chairman of the Department of Theatre at Southern Illinois University, now emeritus, served as my dissertation advisor. His interest and assistance started it all.

Dr. David Potter, Professor of Speech at Southern Illinois University, who served as my interim dissertation advisor, also deserves thanks, especially for his continued encouragement of my writing.

The progress of the research was greatly aided by Mrs. Glendon Blodgett, Reference Librarian, The Lynn Public Library, Lynn, Massachusetts; Dr. Edwin Cady, Department of English, Duke University; Mrs. Leona Darrow, Librarian, Syracuse University Library; Mrs. Frances Hartgen, Curator, Special Collections, The University of Maine Library; Dr. Richard Moody, Director, Indiana University Theatre; Paul Myers, Curator, Theatre Collection, New York Public Library at Lincoln Center; Louis A. Rachow, Librarian, The Walter Hampden Memorial Library in New York City; Virgil Regalbuto, Special Collections, Queens College of the City University of New York; Dr. Neda M. Westlake, Curator, Rare Books Collection, The University of Pennsylvania Library, and Geraldine Duclow, Theatre Collection, Free Library of Philadelphia.

Finally, I am most grateful for the cooperation and assistance of the following institutions: Albany Public Library; Boston Public Library; The British Library, London, England; Brooklyn Public Library; Chicago Public Library; Cornell University Library; District of Columbia Public Library; The Houghton Library, Harvard University; Memphis Public Library; Metropolitan Toronto Central Library; Montana State University Library; The Free Library of Philadelphia; The University of Pittsburgh Library; Oregon Historical Society; San Francisco Public Library; Stamford Public Library; Troy Public Library; The University of Southern California at Los Angeles Library, and the Humanities Research Center, The University of Texas at Austin.

1 the dog
of montargis

I DON'T SUPPOSE anybody cares where I was
born," James A. Herne once said. "I don't care
much about it myself. I really had no choice in the
matter. In order to live, I had to be born somewhere, that's all."[1]

For the record, however, Herne was born James A'Herne in
Cohoes, New York, on February 1, 1839, at a rather inauspicious
time in American history. Martin Van Buren was President. The
lingering effects of the financial panic of 1837, which included
bank failures, overcrowded poorhouses and flour riots in New
York City, were helping to ruin Van Buren's hopes for re-election
in 1840. A diary kept by Philip Hone blamed conditions on "the
effects of . . . a want of sound moral and political principle on the
part of the mass of the people, and bad government and a crush-
ing down of everything good and great to subserve party objects
on the part of the rulers."[2] Such criticisms, of course, sound familiar enough, nearly a hundred and fifty years later.

The year 1839 was also that in which American patroon
Stephen Van Rensselaer died, leaving new spoils to John Jacob
Astor, the former trader and son of a butcher who had already
accumulated $30,000,000 with his son and Pierre Lorillard—
whose 1834 death had led newspapers to coin the word millionaire. In 1839, too, Francois Gouraud was privately exhibiting a
collection of Daguerre's photographs, and Edgar Allan Poe was
defending his newly-published *The Conchologist's First Book*.
Accused of copying from other sources, Poe had retorted, "All
school books are made in the same way."[3]

These were the headliners. The common people studied

1

scripture, sang "Home Sweet Home" and busied themselves with domestic duties. Father was king—most of the time. The Reverend J. N. Danforth declared: "Home is the place of the husband and the father. He is the monarch of that little empire, wearing a crown that is the gift of Heaven, swaying a sceptre put into his hands by the Father of all, acknowledging no superior, fearing no rival, and dreading no usurper."[4]

The A'Herne home was one of these little patriarchial empires. James feared his father, Patrick A'Herne, "a small, wiry irascible man"[5] from the south of Ireland, who drank heavily, ruined his children's books and toys and solved parental problems with "a frequent use of the strap." Yet he was an honest, hardworking fellow, a former Roman Catholic who had turned to the Dutch Reformed Church in later life. His "narrow-minded"[6] religious bigotry was one reason for Herne's later hatred of any organized faith that preached love and patience, while practicing hate and intolerance.

Shortly after James' birth in Cohoes the A'Hernes moved to Albany, a city filled with the expanding industry and commerce of the Erie Canal and the Hudson River. The canal traffic glided past the endless warehouses, shops, and smokestacks that lined the winding towpath. Those same colorful cargo and packet boats later inspired young James to run away—a brief indulgence of wanderlust rewarded by Patrick's stinging whip.

On another occasion, after getting drunk one night, Patrick attacked the eldest son Charles, who turned the tables and thrashed his father. Charles then stormed from the house, and never returned. This sobered Patrick, who stopped drinking and stopped beating the children. Shortly after, he was promoted in his job at a hardware store, and the family moved to a more respectable neighborhood in West Troy.

Puritanical in his attitude toward theatre, Patrick A'Herne believed that actors were "doomed to hellfire."[7] Lucky it was that he didn't peer into the darkened gallery of the Albany Museum one night during the 1850's, where his sons James and Charles perched on the edge of their seats watching the great tragedian Edwin Forrest. Both boys were awed by the mystical world of canvas and grease paint with its "curious combination of dust, stale air, dampness, tobacco, and a faint odor of leaking gas jets."[8]

Remembering the experience, James later wrote, "My destiny was sealed." Forgotten were his other dreams of becoming a private coachman or a sailor on the high seas. "I cast all former ambitions to the wind, and resolved to be an actor. A good many years had to elapse before I would be old enough to be eligible for the stage,—I think I was at that time thirteen,—and I must cherish my dream in secret, both from a wholesome dread of being laughed at by my brothers, and being again sailorized by my father."[9]

One person, however, understood James' acting ambitions— his mother, Ann Temple A'Herne, "a tall, handsome woman, with great dignity and sweetness of manner."[10] (She later became the model for the character of Ann Berry in Herne's play, *Shore Acres*.) A woman who had to work and sacrifice, she didn't have time or money to waste on such contemporary amusements as *Godey's Ladies Book,* or Currier & Ives lithographs, or stylish fashions of silk, satin, and ermine. Hers was a plain life, like the lives of many other nineteenth century women who placed their families above themselves. But she admired education and understood James' love of theatre.

Nevertheless, James' formal education ended at thirteen. His father thought that schooling was a waste, one of life's frills for the rich, which only soured plain working men on work. So the tall boy with clear blue-gray eyes, light-brown hair, and a misshapen left thumb, (the result of a Fourth of July mishap), surrendered the romantic literary worlds of Scott and Dickens for the mundane world of sorting nails, filling potato sacks and lugging lumber in the hardware store where his father worked.

An apprenticeship at a Cohoes brush factory followed, which wasn't much better. However, the wealthy owner sensed James' drive and tried to persuade Patrick to allow the boy to continue his education, even offering to finance it. But this didn't work. Although others also found the A'Herne boy bright, his father quipped: "James has a head like a forty-shilling pot."[11] Meanwhile, the youth saved his earnings—around $165—to purchase a theatrical wardrobe, then invaluable to an aspiring actor.

"Time seemed only to increase my longing for Thespian glory."[12]

Then came James' barnstorming break, with an acting troupe called the Coney and Webb Company that visited West Troy. Webb played the handsome hero, while Coney impersonated the vicious villain—with a broad Cockney accent. Herne saw them perform at the old Green Street Theatre in a production of *The Butcher of Ghent and his Dog.* (It was on this same stage that Adah Isaacs Menken first presented *Mazeppa,* the spectacle that brought her fame and fortune.) James later met Webb, who had split with Coney and needed cash. In exchange for his $165, Coney cast James as the Seneschal in *The Dog of Montargis,* a rehash of *The Butcher of Ghent.* This bargain seemed to please all concerned.

Nineteenth century theatre audiences loved animal performers, especially dogs. "The stars supported the dogs and the stock company supported the stars, sometimes very indifferently,"[13] wrote Herne. These canines performed stage miracles: they saved children from roaring fires, rescued damsels in distress, and found lost wills. But dog stars, like human stars, needed cues. Without cues, their super feats fell flat. This infuriated Coney, who screamed from the wings, "Give the bloody dog 'is blawsted cue, hey beg-ga-a-a-r-r!" Then the actor cried, "This darkness is impenetrable! If I had but a lanth-o-r-n!"[14] A tail-wagging dog soon trotted across stage, holding a lantern in its mouth. Wild applause followed.

Webb, a good-natured fellow who knew the trade's tricks, was troubled by fast-fading funds, especially when the sheriff confiscated his "star" dog for a hotel bill. At one point an uncle of James' played angel, donating $100 and a gold watch to the troupe. But even this didn't help. James was soon forced to return to Troy, unemployed.

Destiny plays strange games, however, and the next day James Connor, manager of Troy's Adelphi Theatre, visited Albany. He was looking for actors to appear with J. B. Roberts, Mr. and Mrs. Howard, and their charming daughter Cordelia, in *Uncle Tom's Cabin.* Business looked prosperous. So they hired James as an actor, and his uncle became treasurer of the Adelphi. Both jobs were secured on Webb's recommendations.

James later said: "No *part* ever rivalled in importance the first part essayed by the old stock actor; no triumph ever equalled his first 'call' before the curtain, no stage door ever creaked just like his *first* stage door; every door had its personality—that of the stage door is very marked. I can hear the squeaking of the old Adelphi stage door now, as I pulled it open for the first time.

"No transformation scene has ever approached in magnificence my first view of that company of actors assembled in the greenroom, tawdrily dressed for the stage. No magician's *presto* —*agramento—chango* was ever half so mysterious to me as was the 'first music!' 'second music!' 'everybody down!' of my first call boy. All the perfumes of Arabia could never banish the delicious scent, musty to a degree, which permeated that old-time theatre.

"The sky wore a rosy hue in those days. Twenty years old— an actor, and six dollars a week—why, I had reached the summit of earthly bliss. My dream was realized. Not a wish remained unsatisfied."[15]

Coney suggested that James slightly alter his last name for the stage. James A'Herne was easily persuaded, and a period replaced the apostrophe on playbills, creating James A. Herne.

Young Herne's experiences at the Adelphi gave him a broad foundation of roles in popular farces, melodramas, and some of the classics—mainly Shakespeare. Although he was early used for "general utility business" or as a "boot-jack," he rapidly advanced, and later played Horatio in *Hamlet*, Michael Cassio in *Othello*, and Tressel, Buckingham, and Oxford in *Richard III*. Sometimes he even played romantic lovers.

Herne didn't approach acting seriously during this period— something he later resented in novice actors. He learned lines leisurely and relished "guying"—improvising lines and stage business for laughs, a common practice when directors didn't exist and actors tried to dominate American stages. This practice sometimes led to stardom, always an actor's dream. Herne told many stories such as this one about his old stock company days:

"I had played with Sothern, and he had introduced all sorts of things. I was apt and I absorbed a lot of things unconsciously, —a lot of things they call gags. Among them was a scene where Dundreary comes on reading a letter from his brother Sam, in which occurs the expression, 'I shook dice for the drinks and got stuck.' 'Well,' muses Dundreary, 'Sam's dead. Sam has been stabbed. He shook dice for the drinks. He's dead.' Then he turns over and reads,—'stuck for the drinks. Oh!' When I played with Owens I commenced introducing these things into the play. You never saw such a wild man. I got on the stage and pulled out this letter, and I commenced to read. I could see Owens in the wings. He swore and ripped and tore, but he could not get me off. Now, to-day such things would not be tolerated."[16]

Herne also "winged" lines easily. This offended some senior actors. Tragedian J. B. Roberts, for example, once noticed Herne memorizing his lines for Bassanio in *The Merchant of Venice* just a few hours before show time:

"Jimmy," said he, turning to the manager in dismay, "look there; that young man's reading Bassanio. My God, he'll make a mess of the casket scene to-night."

"Oh, he'll be all right," said Connor.

"All right,—and reading Shakespeare at rehearsal!"[17]

Herne returned to the brush factory in Cohoes at season's end. His uncle, who lived in the town, presented the acting company there, printing playbills with the line from *Hamlet*, "The actors have come, my lord!" Thus, for a few evenings, Cohoes played host to a potpourri of plays, including such potboilers as *Black Eyed Susan* and *Sketches of India*.

The factory system dismayed Herne. It offered a dead-end future. Besides, Herne wanted to act at the New Gayety Theatre in Albany. And that's what happened—almost miraculously. After buying two ostrich feathers and a dress wig in New York City, he joined the company and was soon playing Eugene deLorem in *Love's Sacrifice*.

The Gayety Theatre opened in 1859 "when Albany could not boast of any place of regular entertainment, and theatricals were at a rather low ebb," according to Henry Dickinson Stone. A former carpet and upholstery shop, the theatre had an "elegant and commodious" design that included "two tiers of boxes, several private boxes and a parquette."[18] A small dramatic company soon graced the boards of the small 500-seat theatre, even mounting the spectacular melodrama, *The Last Days of Pompeii*, on its 7-by-9-foot stage. During its brief two-year life, the Gayety presented such stars as J. E. Murdock, E. A. Sothern, John

T. Raymond, Helen Western, Adah Isaacs Menken, Henrietta Irving, F. S. Chanfrau, and the rabid secessionist, John Wilkes Booth.

During February, 1861, young Booth played Pescara in *The Apostate,* nearly killing himself. H. P. Phelps wrote that "while playing the last act, in falling, the actor's dagger fell first and he struck upon it, the point entering the right arm-pit, inflicting a muscular wound, one or two inches in depth, from which the blood flowed freely."[19] Booth recovered, and played the same role several nights later. He finished out that week with *Julian St. Pierre, Othello, The Stranger, Richard III,* and *Charles de Moor.* He had played six parts in six plays in one week—with a severe wound.

In April of the same year, Booth's leading lady attacked him at Stanwix Hall with a dirk-knife, slashing his face. It seemed that dark shadows already hovered above the youthful actor of twenty-three, who was to become a hated symbol of evil four years later.

The young Herne's first benefit at the Gayety led him to confess his theatre calling to his father. The reaction? Patrick offered to serve as combined press agent and chief ticket seller. He did surprisingly well on both counts. Tickets were "Gallery, twenty-five cents," "Dress Circle, fifty cents," and "Parquette, seventy-five cents." Patrick, who didn't differentiate between theatre and hardware, soon sold the first batch and returned for more. "My soul," Herne said, "you are selling tickets!"

"Oh, yes," said Patrick, "they're selling like hot cakes. I tell all my friends that you are going to the war, and they buy one or two tickets. Of course, I'm selling them for what I can get for them. They couldn't have cost you over two cents apiece. I'm getting a shilling and fifteen cents for them, which gives you a big profit, and you won't have any left on your hands."

Herne later recalled: "I was dumb with astonishment. Words had no value. I had a big house, but they were all my father's friends; and but for the fact that I had the house free, and that the actors volunteered, I would have been in debt."

The benefit was a performance of *St. Marc, The Soldier of Fortune,* and a success. After curtain calls, Herne asked Patrick for his opinion, receiving the answer, "The fools are not all dead yet."[20] But his mother was delighted. It was the first time she had ever been in a theatre.

Then the Civil War convulsed America for four years. Edwin Booth, manager of the Winter Garden in New York, remarked that "while at Antietam dead men lay rotting on the blasted fields . . . , the theatres were crammed to their flag-drapped roofs."[21] In Albany, however, the Gayety closed; like many of the smaller playhouses it was unable to attract audiences and support a company.

Herne avoided the war, "appearing under the flag by proxy, while the money to pay for his substitute was earned before the footlights."[22] (He later translated the human agonies of war into a script, *Griffith Davenport*, America's finest nineteenth century military drama.) James' brother, John, who was fourteen, lied about his age to enlist as a drummer. He emerged four years later as a captain, the youngest commissioned officer in the Union army. John paid a price, however, for such honor—invalidism until his death. Herne's father enlisted as a private in the Union army, serving in John's company. He died, as did half a million others.

John, strangely enough, also became an actor. He was James' business manager for several seasons and also became a minor player with Edwin Booth and Tommaso Salvini during their notable co-performances in *Hamlet* and *Othello*.

Herne was lucky—in the beginning. Acting success came early. John T. Ford, manager of the Atheneum Theatre in Washington, D.C., and the Holliday Street Theatre in Baltimore, hired him for "utility business." Although Herne earned more at the Gayety Theatre, he liked these bigger, bustling cities, and accepted every role Ford offered, including romantic ones.

"I never was fitted for the romantic roles of the old drama," Herne later admitted, "although I played many of them. My choice was for strong character parts such as are found in the dramatizations of Dickens' novels, which first gave me an insight into everyday life and character. The pathos of Peggotty, the droll humor of Captain Cuttle, and the fierce animal passion of Bill Sykes appealed to my youthful mind, and started me on my studies of humanity."[23]

When the Atheneum Theatre burned in 1862, Ford built

Ford's New Theatre on its site, the place where John Wilkes Booth was to assassinate Abraham Lincoln.

The New Theatre opened on August 27, 1863, with *The Naiad Queen! or The Mystery of the Lurlieberg*. Herne bathed in glory that night. Besides playing Rupert the Fearnought, he also delivered the opening address. It was quite an honor. Herne read well, which was why Ford chose him. At one time when Edwin Booth played *Hamlet,* he had overheard Herne reading some passages from the lofty tragedy and inquired about the interpretation. Where had he heard it? From which tragedian? None, replied Herne, except himself.

Like most theatre managers, Ford faced endless turnovers in his casts. He tried to prevent this situation by featuring the actors' names in bold print on playbills. This apparently worked with Herne, who stayed for three years. Managing two showplaces also helped Ford to give his actors greater job stability, reduce production costs, encourage familiarity between his actors, and enable them to know their theatre environments very well.

Herne's knack of "winging" lines brought roles that pushed him to the front ranks, but he still made mistakes. After successfully playing *Ben Bolt,* he started specializing in sailor parts. In the casting for *Mat of the Iron Hand,* a comedian received the sailor's role. This shook Herne, who asked the stage manager:

"Mr. Hall, by what precedent do you cast Mr. Bishop for this part in 'Mat of the Iron Hand'?"

"By what precedent that I believe he'll play better than any one in the theatre."

"But Mr. Hall, that part belongs to me; I played Ben Bolt, and here are the original casts of 'Mat of the Iron Hand': Bowery Theatre, F. Eddy; Chatham Street Theatre, John R. Scott; Chestnut Street Theatre, Philadelphia, William R. Goodall, and so on."

Hall looked at Herne. He reached for the book in Herne's hands and browsed over the casts. In a quiet manner, he replied, "I don't see James A. Herne here anywhere."[24] And James A. Herne didn't play the sailor in *Mat of the Iron Hand.*

Herne, who was footloose at the time, got involved with the "wrong" crowd in Baltimore. Ford, who liked him, even promised to advance his career—if he'd just settle down. But the young actor preferred to carouse around town. What did he have to gain? More responsibility? That could come later. Nat C. Goodwin, an acquaintance of Herne's for many years, wrote that "in his early days he was prone to much dissipation, even to ruffianism; but he always drank and fought before the world. He was honest even when violently inclined. He never sneaked up back alleys to fight a foe, but met him in the open—no hiring of rooms in which to get drunk but at the open door where all could see him. And even in those days everybody loved the man."[25]

One night in Baltimore, Herne staggered home with Owen Fawcett and John T. Raymond, who later played the celebrated Colonel Mulberry Sellers in Mark Twain's *The Gilded Age*. They spied an old German saloonkeeper cleaning up, sauntered into his bar, then measured it. The old man scratched his head and looked. Herne finally said: "There's no use making any fuss. We are United States officials, with orders to appropriate your property for an arsenal."[26] This turned the saloonkeeper's face red. He thrashed his arms. He pleaded. He prayed and even offered free drinks. Then he stumbled up the stairs, calling to his wife. Herne and his cronies almost made it to the bar, but the German quickly returned, shooting his shotgun. Herne and Fawcett reached the street unscratched. Raymond didn't. Screaming, he ran into the arms of a policeman.

The next morning, Ford rescued his three thespians from the jug. Raymond had to eat his meals standing for several weeks, and practical jokes became much less popular for awhile.

2 lay on, macduff!

FALL, 1864. HERNE was strutting and fretting and tearing a passion to tatters at the Walnut Street Theatre in Philadelphia. He was a very versatile actor at a time when "not-so-versatile" actors stayed street fixtures. Labor unions were nonexistent. Theatre managers measured success through boxoffice receipts. And actors hustled.

One asset, however, helped compensate some male players: strength—pure masculine energy. Edwin Forrest, America's leading tragedian, followed a rigid physical-culture program to keep his biceps bulging for heroic roles. When Fanny Kemble saw him during one of her American trips, she exclaimed, "What a mountain of a man!"[1] Yet, he was only five feet ten inches tall.

Herne venerated Forrest, saying his "voice always reminded me of the master tones of a cathedral organ when a genius was at the keys. I think he was the best actor I ever saw."[2] Only one thing about Forrest was "a grievous disappointment" to Herne, who felt that he failed to exploit combat scenes, reducing them to "a few simple blows."[3]

One Herculean tragedian who didn't relegate combats to a few simple blows was McKean Buchanan. Herne played Macduff to Buchanan's Macbeth at the Walnut Street Theatre. During one swashbuckling rehearsal sequence, the star informed Herne: "I pride myself on this fight. It's original with me, and I don't want it shortened by a blow. I have duplicates of these swords; at night I'll place one in the right second entrance and one in the left second entrance and continue the fight to the end."

Curtain time arrived. Herne heard the ringing words, "Lay

11

on, Macduff, and damned be he who first cries hold! Enough!"
The audience broke into applause. Deep breaths followed.
"Guard your head," yelled Buchanan.

Herne followed this advice, stiffening his arm. The sword
cut air. "Whang!" It snapped. Buchanan dashed for the wings
where the reserve sword waited, but Herne decided to revise
Shakespeare's honored tale of torment. Tracking down his foe,
he cried:

"I've stabbed you. Fall!"[4]

Buchanan lunged a few times, spit at Herne, and slashed
feebly with his sword. Then he rolled over and died. Macduff
killed Macbeth. A theatre first, and Buchanan never forgave
Herne.

Such was America's star system—at its worst.

Mrs. John Henry probably inaugurated America's star system. She was followed by James Fennell in 1796 and Thomas Ab-
thorpe Cooper in 1803. All succeeded. Many other repertory performers soon joined their ranks. As W. B. Wood put it, "The extraordinary pretension of some of these was provokingly amus-
ing."[5] George Frederick Cooke's phenomenal 1910 tour of the
United States compounded the problem. So-called British stars
flooded American stages with garish handbills, puffy print, and
lots of brass. These rakes made fortunes, sometimes demanding
—and getting—half of the gross receipts.

Leading managers like Lester Wallack knew their playhouses' facilities, including the strengths and weaknesses of
their actors. This enabled them to avoid certain plays. Many stars
voiced indifference to fellow players. W. B. Wood remarked, "The
star is the light of everything; the centre about which all must
move. He has his own times, his own pieces, his own play of
business, and his own preferences of every sort."[6] Tall stars
wanted tall companies, and short stars wanted short companies.
There were always new grievances.

Rehearsals often were haphazard affairs. The stars didn't
arrive until several hours before curtain time. Other principal actors couldn't study scripts or block lines because the star held the
book. Actors sometimes had to learn more than 500 lines of dialogue within twenty-four hours. Mary Anderson wrote: "They
had frequently to memorize their parts while standing in the

wings during the performance, awaiting their cues—'winging a part,' it was called. Rapid study, a hurried rehearsal daily, the rearranging of their costumes for the ever changing plays, left them no free time to reflect upon the characters they were to enact."[7]

On stage, stars like McKean Buchanan used gimmicks. One stunt was especially infuriating to other actors. The stars would retreat upstage center, forcing the others on stage to turn their backs to the audience. This would focus full attention on the star. To the snubbed performers famed playwright Dion Boucicault recommended, "Simply turn your back upon the bellowing artist, and in ignoring him, cause the public to do likewise."[8] Herne eclipsed even this solution, of course, when he killed Buchanan's Macbeth.

John Wilkes Booth's assassination of Abraham Lincoln shook Herne as it did millions of others. He knew Ford's Theatre, and traced the killer's frantic escape—his heavy steps through the wings, out the rear door, and down the dark, narrow cobblestone street. Herne had known John Wilkes Booth in Philadelphia, but Booth had tried to kill him after a quarrel, an incident that ended their friendship. Herne drank, played practical jokes, and chased women during his youth, but he didn't mix freely with people. A manic-depressive, he once said he "could travel from New York to California without speaking to a single soul on the way."[9]

Herne was not long in Philadelphia before he joined the Susan Denin Company, which was touring the western states. Susan Denin captured his attentions for a while, as did a handful of other actresses, including Maggie Mitchell and the Western sisters, Lucille and Helen. The last two were more serious romances.

Lucille and Helen Western ("The Star Sisters") broke into show business during the late 1850's. Their comedian father, George Western, pulled strings at such reputable houses as New York's Bowery Theatre, the National Theatre in Boston, and the Boston Museum to launch their careers.[10] Both were very young—Lucille fifteen and Helen thirteen.

Herne's daughter Julie believed her father had first met Lucille Western at Ford's Holliday Street Theatre in Baltimore, where they played together in a melodrama called *The Flowers of the Forest*. She wrote: "Herne was in love with her, and she—in her way—very much in love with him. But James A. Meade, her husband, was very much in the picture, and he had no intention of retiring. It was Herne who withdrew."[11]

Both Ford and Herne were impressed with Lucille Western's acting, especially in *Camille,* an interpretation they ranked higher than those of Matilda Heron, Susan Denin, and even Charlotte Cushman. Lucille Western's big break arrived when she bought rights to *East Lynne* by Mrs. Henry Wood, (Ellen Price), for $100. This play was first presented at Ford's Theatre in October 1862, with Herne as Sir Francis Levison, another successful role. Lucille Western appeared more than 1,000 times throughout the country in *East Lynne,* along with other public favorites such as *Leah, the Forsaken, Lucrezia Borgia,* and *The Child Stealer,* a real chiller.

Meanwhile, Lucille's sister Helen was deserted by her husband in Paris, leaving the nineteen-year-old actress with a "feeble-minded" child. This forced Helen to make a provincial tour of France in *The French Spy*. This was followed by a Canadian and American stint in which Helen played at the Bowery Theatre and Lucille at Niblo's Gardens, both in New York.

Herne then toured with Susan Denin, and it wasn't until he played the Walnut Street Theatre that Lucille Western again entered his life. She opened with *Leah, the Forsaken* in November 1864, then played opposite Herne's Armand in *Camille*. Her repertoire also included a six-role play called *Satan in Paris,* in which Herne portrayed Count Henri de Beau Soleil.

The ties between Herne and the Western sisters soon became very close.

During the summer of 1866, Herne supported John McCullough and other stars at the Theatre Royal in Montreal. Here he met Helen, marrying her on July 12, 1866, following a whirlwind romance.[12] They played several seasons together, with Herne as Helen's leading man. George C. D. Odell noted that Herne played opposite Helen in 1866: "Helen Western, supported by James A. Herne (then, or subsequently her husband), began on May 28th, in *Satan in Paris* and *Jenny Lind*. On the 30th, she acted Louis and Fabian dei Franchi in *The Corsican Brothers,* Herne appearing as Chàteau Renaud."[13] During the 1868–69 season, however, Herne also was supporting actor to Lucille Western at Brooklyn's Academy of Music in *East Lynne* and *Oliver Twist*.

While married to Helen, Herne purchased a farm at Topsfield, Massachusetts. They lived there for a year before their divorce in 1868. Columnist Amy Leslie called theirs "one of the most tragic romances of the American stage."[14] Why? Herne fell in love with Lucille Western, forgetting Helen, who died of pneumonia in December 1868 in Washington, D.C. Herne seldom discussed his marriage to Helen. Yet, her mother remained a friend of Herne's for years, and his daughters of a later marriage called her grandma.

It is not definitely known whether Herne and Lucille ever legally married. The two always signed their contracts "Lucille Herne and James A. Herne,"[15] which doesn't prove much. One thing is certain: Herne traveled first class as Lucille Western's leading man, a position previously held by actor E. L. Davenport. The scandal that touched their lives did not adversely affect box-office receipts. Such diverse places as the Academy of Music in New York City, McVicker's Theatre in Chicago, the Boston Theatre, the Theatre Royal in Montreal, and the Salt Lake Theatre played host to them.

In 1868, Lucille and Herne headed for California in a stagecoach, the actress' first trip west. The rough mountain roads, rocky canyons, and thoughts of bandits and Indians terrified her, a fear difficult to grasp in today's world of safe, comfortable, fast-moving vehicles. Such journeys, now made in days and hours, then took many weeks.

Until the age of steam, travel was arduous and dangerous for actors who journeyed on flatboats, horses, mules, stagecoaches, and sometimes their own two feet. Cross-country transportation didn't boom in the United States until the 360-mile Erie Canal opened in 1825 at a staggering cost of more than $7,000,000. The canal reshaped America's destiny. Thriving cities and villages sprang up along its banks. Commerce and transportation was vastly improved when this gateway to the frontier was opened.

It didn't take long for minstrels, mimes, and strolling players to appear to peddle their miracles wherever people collected along the towpath. A few actors wrote of their impressions of Clinton's ditch as the Erie Canal was called. Among them were Edwin Forrest and Joseph Jefferson III.

Like many travelers, Forrest found canaling a memorable experience. Upon arriving in Buffalo he wrote home, "I made this journey for the purpose of recreation, in viewing the romantic beauties of our country, and the development of art and industry which are so rapidly leading to wealth and happiness."[16]

Several years later, Joseph Jefferson III and his family traveled on the Erie Canal, agreeing to pay their fare by giving canalside performances at Utica and Syracuse. It was an idea the captain liked. The packet *Pioneer* had a flat roof, caboose stovepipe, and sleek shape, "painted white and green and enlivened with blue window blinds, and a broad white strip running from bow to stern."[17] Young Jefferson was impressed. He thought the craft looked like Noah's Ark.

Railroads, of course, eventually made canals impractical. The first chartered railroad to haul passengers and freight was the Baltimore and Ohio, whose first 24 miles of track opened in 1830. The first railroad to span the continent opened in 1869, four years after the Civil War ended.

On tour, Lucille Western led a private life shrouded in mystery. She seldom wandered in the hotel corridors during tours and she ate meals in the seclusion of her room. She wore a shoulder-length black lace veil in public, a device which served to heighten her mystique. The effect was apparently very successful, because she made half a million dollars.

Unfortunately Lucille Western's fame and fortune soon vanished. New faces like Clara Morris (whose career also stumbled, forcing her to play in cheap houses, while show biz called her "the shopgirl's Duse"), Mary Anderson, and Fanny Davenport attracted the public's fancy for a few years. Lucille died on January 11, 1877, of pneumonia, with her final husband, Arthur Cambridge, at her side. James A. Meade, her first husband, also attended the funeral.

In 1869, however, Lucille Western was still the star whom some called "The Pearl of the American Stage." That year the

Western Company played in Salt Lake City between March 15 and April 17. Their repertoire included such favorites as *Dombey and Son, Our American Cousin, Rip Van Winkle,* and *Oliver Twist,* the play that almost caused their ejection from Salt Lake City.

What shocked the Mormons? Lucille had glued a piece of raw beef to the cheek that Bill Sykes (Herne) brutally beat in the climactic murder scene as he dragged the screaming actress across the stage by her hair. When she faced an astonished audience, they thought they saw raw flesh. One Mormon eyewitness later wrote: "The picture was so revolting that several women in the audience fainted—everybody was shocked. . . . President Young was very angry over it. The picture was abhorrent; there is no knowing what the physical results were; it was rumored afterwards that a number of children were birthmarked as a result of it."[18]

Brigham Young, who liked light plays, didn't forbid another performance of *Oliver Twist,* but let his bishops know the company wasn't wanted in town. At the opening ceremonies of the Salt Lake Theatre, Young stated: "If I had my way, I would never have a tragedy played on these boards. There is enough tragedy in everyday life, and we ought to have amusement when we come here."[19]

Brigham Young hated tragedy but promoted theatre. The Mormons built a little Social Hall soon after settling in Salt Lake City, and by 1862 the impressive Salt Lake Theatre opened. With a seating capacity of 3,000, it was America's largest theatre west of Chicago. As one visiting correspondent commented: "It is said that the character of a people can be correctly estimated by the theatres and saloons to be found in their midst. The Latter Day Saints are fond of theatrical shows; and, in fact, of amusements of any kind. One of the largest theatres in the union is to be found here, and generally a good stock company of artists."[20]

Brigham Young saw theater as an educational force that would uplift people's lives. He encouraged his followers to attend shows and even to embrace the art themselves if so moved. Two of his daughters were later so moved, and it was said that Young himself fell in love with Julia Dean Hagre, the theatre's leading lady, one summer. Julie Dean Hagre, unfortunately, declined his marriage proposal, which left the prophet standing in the wings without a cue.

The Western Company vacated Salt Lake City after a performance of *Foul Play*. Lucille Western was "indisposed" and the actors mutilated the script; Herne, scheduled to perform Shaun the Poet in *Arrah Na Pogue* the following day, collapsed.[21] Flags didn't fly when the troupe said farewell, especially after the *Oliver Twist* fiasco.

Herne's Bill Sykes shocked audiences everywhere, and helped to establish his acting reputation. Many critics likened its fierce intensity to E. L. Davenport's famous portrayal of Sykian depravity. John Maguire recalled, "I have seen great performances of certain characters by great actors, but no such indelible impression on my memory was ever made by any other like that of Bill Sykes by James A. Herne."[22] Following one New York performance, a startled child approached Lucille Western, saying, "I hate that Mr. Herne, he's such a brute; he always makes you cry."[23]

Katharine Corcoran, (Herne's later wife for whom he wrote his dramas, including *Margaret Fleming*), also shivered while sitting through *Oliver Twist* as a child. She cheered and feared for Lucille Western while booing Herne's savagery. It appeared Herne made manifest the words of Ferdinand in John Webster's *The Dutchess of Malfi*, "A good actor many times is curs'd for playing a villain's part!"

Herne played *Oliver Twist* because of its box-office appeal. Adaptations of Dickens' novels were the rage, along with Washington Irving's *Rip Van Winkle*, the Cooperesque sagas, and Harriet Beecher Stowe's *Uncle Tom's Cabin*. All had great audience appeal. A second interest, however, motivated Herne's portrayal of such characters as Caleb Plummer, Dan'l Peggoty, Captain Cuttle, and Bill Sykes: Dickens' detail—his sense of reality coupled with his delightful atmosphere of fantasy, and support of common folks. "Dickens seemed real to me," Herne later said. "I knew the people in his books. I'd met them, or people like them. Scott's stories were exciting, but his people were strangers. Dickens made me an actor."[24]

Herne also said: "Charles Dickens was a great man. His

characters are not always typical, and some of them are grotesque, but, oh! so representative, so full of humanity, so full of
the great personality of the man, so positively 'art for truth's
sake.' I feel that I owe much to Charles Dickens. I feel that reading his books, and loving them, and acting some of his characters, have helped materially in my dramatic development."[25]

As late as 1896, the *Boston Sunday Post* commented,
about Herne's play, *Shore Acres*: "Those familiar with the writing of Charles Dickens cannot but notice a similarity between
his character sketches and those of Mr. Herne.... Where Mr.
Herne surpasses Dickens is his ability to condense into dramatic form a narrative of considerable length and complexity."[26]

Dickens certainly exerted a lifelong influence on Herne's
work, a span of time reaching beyond four decades.

After leaving Salt Lake City, Herne returned to New York's
Grand Opera House on the corner of Twenty-third Street and
Eighth Avenue. Playbills listed him as the manager, under
proprietor Colonel James F. Fisk, Jr.,[27] who opened the theatre
on June 2, 1869, in a building formerly called Pike's Opera House.
This theatre palace seated 3,500 and cost $1,000,000,[28] a wallop-
ing figure for those days. It also offered an innovation: instead
of a permanent repertory company, Fisk decided performers
would perform only one play in a continuing run, a standard
Broadway practice today.[29]

Fisk's opener was *East Lynne*, starring the ever-popular Lucille Western, supported by Herne.[30] The lively actress remained the entire summer, playing all her famed roles, contrary
to Fisk's original one-play policy. In August she revived the spectacular melodrama *The Sea of Ice* with Herne as Carlos, the Ad-
venturer, afterwards the Marquis de Monie, the Man of Gold.[31]
It played for three weeks, a long run.

Then Lucille Western revived *Patrie*, another mistake like
Oliver Twist in Mormonland. The critics howled about this potboiler, one in the *Spirit of the Times* calling the first act foul
and the second vapid, suggesting it be "thrown aside as waste
lumber." He added, "At the end of the fourth act the action is
so manifestly completed that many persons on Monday night rose
to leave, thinking the performance closed." This reviewer, however, was more favorable in his remarks about one cast member.

"Mr. Herne played a most remarkable Captain Rysoor. . . . It is pleasant, though, to add that Mr. Herne surprised his friends by the unexpected vigor and power he threw into the heroic scene. (This critic obviously missed *Oliver Twist*.) His elocution, however, hardly redeems his constraint and awkwardness of manner."[32]

James F. Fisk, Jr. was a shrewd businessman. The Grand Opera House was New York's only privately endowed theatre. Fisk managed his expenses by renting the second floor to the Erie Railroad Company for $75,000 a year and receiving additional revenues from ground-floor shops. This enabled him to speculate on shows. Shakespeare's *The Tempest* cost a staggering $30,000.[33] *The Twelve Temptations,* a song and dance musical extravaganza with a cast of 200, was capitalized for $75,000,[34] an unbelievable figure then.

One theatre, however, didn't satisfy Fisk's exuberant nature. He also leased the Academy of Music at Irving Place and Fourteenth Street, the largest theatre in New York. Then he bought the Boudoir Theatre on West Twenty-Fourth Street, altering its name to Brougham's Theatre after hiring famous actor John Brougham as manager. But within two months Fisk fired "the genial John," and renamed the playhouse the Fifth Avenue. Under the later managerial genius of Augustin Daly, the Fifth Avenue Theatre gained national recognition.

Fisk was notorious for firing managers. Although he wanted to be esteemed as a theatre producer, he lacked the theatre sense possessed by practical men like Herne. By the end of the 1869–70 season Fisk abandoned both the Academy of Music and the Fifth Avenue Theatre because of bad attendance. Although political "bigwigs" such as Boss Tweed attended plays, the general public resented Fisk's shady reputation and blacklisted him.

Fisk just puttered with theatre. He was actually a stock market speculator, thought to control the purse strings of Tammany Hall, New York City's ruling political machine. His payroll included corrupt judges, ambitious politicians, and anyone else who would accept bribes. His attempt to corner the American gold market with Jay Gould led to "Black Friday" in 1869, a financial catastrophe that ruined many and caused a nationwide depression. Yet Fisk donated a fortune to charities, the needy, and various theatre enterprises. His managers all received generous salaries. Herne made $10,000 per year[35] as manager of the Grand Opera House, an inflated wage that indicated his professional standing many years before Bostonian culturalists "discovered" him after the production of his play *Margaret Fleming.*

Most managers paid actors meager wages during this period. Actress Olive Logan wrote in 1870:

> "The salary of a leading actor or actress ranged from $40 to $60 a week. But 1 know one leading actress in New York who gets $100 a week, and two who get $75 each.
>
> These, however, are peculiar cases; all three being actresses specially attractive for youth, beauty and talent.
>
> 'Walking gentlemen' or lady will get from $20 to $35 a week; 'old man' or 'old woman' from $25 to $40; while other players of a lower grade of talent than these will get all the way from $25 to $10 a week."[36]

Some stars shared the theatre receipts. Because of their magnetic drawing power they seldom collected less than $1,000 a week. Joseph Jefferson, famed impersonator of Rip Van Winkle, received the highest salary that had ever been paid an American actor—$500 a night. But he was an exception among exceptions. Most performers scraped and struggled from week to week, earning $3 or $4—if and when they found work.

Besides low salaries, performers suffered another hardship. They had to provide their own wardrobes. This was a difficult problem for actresses because styles changed; yet managers demanded new costumes for each season's new plays. Rich women often attended the theatre to applaud the exquisite costumes, not the actresses. Clare Morris complained, "Precious time that should be given to the minute study, the final polishing of a difficult character, is used instead in deciding the pitch of a skirt, the width of a collar, or open sleeve-strap, or no sleeve at all." Male leads also were expected to supply a wardrobe of "elegant morning suits, dress suits, overcoats, shooting jackets, hats, gloves, canes and boots."[37]

Time failed to alter theatre's fashion show. In 1899 Herne said, "If a play is staged handsomely, and the women dress magnificently, they are satisfied. You would be surprised to know how many people go to the theatre, consciously or unconsciously, to see beautiful dresses and fine stage settings."[38] Even Herne once purchased such things as ostrich feathers and a dress wig in New York.

On January 6, 1872, James F. Fisk was shot by a former friend and rival in romance, Edward S. Stokes. Fisk died, and the incident became one of New York's most publicized and scandalous murder cases. A regiment of soldiers escorted Fisk's casket to the train station, while a band of 200 played. Such a tribute marked a glorious end to a life of magnificent contradictions.

Herne knew about Fisk's Machiavellian schemes, later recalling that Fisk and Gould met regularly in a room next to his office at the Grand Opera House. Even then Herne distrusted big business as a swindler of the common people. Big business also represented special privilege and monopoly—two evils he later preached against as a Georgist single taxer.

Herne had severed his ties with Fisk sometime in 1869. In November he and Lucille Western presented *Oliver Twist* at Niblo's and at Brooklyn's Park Theatre. Then in May 1870 the Western Company returned to Montreal's Theatre Royal, performing such plays as *Rip Van Winkle* through July. Another road show followed that fall. The *Pittsburgh Post* reviewer stated, "that (*Oliver Twist*) was well played we need not say, for Lucille Western, supported by Mr. Herne and the excellent Opera House Company could hardly play it otherwise."[39]

Herne and Western, however, finally split. Lucille married Arthur Cambridge, another actor. Herne then went to California where he met Katharine Corcoran, the young actress who became his wife and great inspiration.

A new technological age had emerged from the Civil War. The first telegraph wire reached San Francisco in 1861. Two years later, John D. Rockefeller, a kingpin among later profiteers, dipped his fingers in oil; and in 1865 Samuel Van Syckle constructed his first oil pipeline. The Atlantic Cable became a reality in 1866, the Bessemer Steel Company (later U. S. Steel) started flexing its muscles, and in 1869 the transcontinental railroad opened. As Howard Mumford Jones has written: "The Civil War did not directly 'cause' inventions like these; but it dramatized ingenuity, it accustomed people to mass and size and uniformity and national action, it got them used to ruthlessness, it made clear the dominant place of energy in the modern state."[40]

The time's changing temper also affected the theatre. Railroad ties and telegraph wires stitched together isolated towns and hamlets. More money floated, which meant more cash for theatre tills. The result was a larger theatre audience. America's road show soon arrived—full blast.

3 the city of canvas

L ONG AGO VIRGIL wrote in *The Aeneid*: "Accursed thirst for gold! What does thou compel mortals to do?" The California goldrush would have provided the classical poet with a classical answer to his question—anything!

Once gold was discovered at Sutter's Mill in 1848, people descended like locusts on this drowsy, desolate part of California, with its sand dunes, scattered missions, and Indian settlements. Sailors abandoned ships; soldiers abandoned camps; youth abandoned homes. In a few short months the California soil crawled with gold-maddened miners.

Reaching California took time, patience, and lots of grit. Money also helped. The affluent boarded steamers and sailed around Cape Horn. Some less affluent souls chose to cross the steaming, disease-infested jungles of Panama, among them the noted tragedian Junius Brutus Booth and his son Edwin. Others bitten by goldfever came overland via the Platte route, the Santa Fe Trail, and other southern routes, their ranks often much reduced by starvation, Indian attacks, and freezing weather, by the time they reached the coast.

San Francisco mushroomed into a major port city during the early gold rush days. Almost overnight the town exploded from 100 to 100,000 inhabitants—gamblers, swindlers, businessmen, murderers, dreamers, and miners. A democratic smorgasbord. Many drifted north to the Sacramento region by riverboat or on foot and started diggings. They were a brawling, brawny breed with high hopes. Few struck gold. Some abandoned mining to become farmers. As one observer wrote, "Only such men as can endure the hardship and privation incidental to life in the mines are likely to make fortunes by digging for the ore."[1]

Prices were outrageous: boots sold for $200, picks for $20, and a butcher knife for $40. Even potatoes were $1 each and a loaf of bread was 50 cents. Lumber cost $500 to $600 per thousand board feet, the reason why flour, tobacco, and cook stoves were lined up in shelters in the muddy ditches of San Francisco, and why so many slept in tents. Only a few could afford cabins. Undertakers charged $100 for a crude pine coffin, which was sometimes returned after friends dumped the occupant into a grave. Some Forty Niners even slept in coffins to save housing expenses.

Still the gaudy gambling saloons flourished amidst the fluctuations of poverty and plenty—as always. Among these hedonist haunts were the famous Parker House, Denison's, the Eagle, the United States, and the big El Dorado, whose owner paid $40,000 a year rent and once witnessed a $20,000 loss in a single card game. The banks handled more than $250,000 a day, with stacks of Spanish ounces or doubloons, gold coins, five-franc pieces, and sacks of gold dust. Strains of music (one woman playing a genuine Stradivarius) accompanied games of monto, rondo, roulette, and "chuck-luck."

Women, of course, were scarce in San Francisco. "There weren't many," wrote one actor. "A woman walking along the streets was as much of a sight as an elephant or giraffe."[2]

Lawlessness ran rampant in California, leading the *San Bernardino Semi-Weekly News* to observe in 1864 that "a horde of the worst kind of characters now infest the lower portion of the State, and there is little or no safety for travellers, when a murder . . . can be committed in broad daylight, on a frequently travelled road, and within a short distance from town."[3] This was the reason why vigilante committees had been formed in San Francisco a decade earlier to act against riffraff, cutthroats, and "shoulder strickers" (bullies). But vigilante justice and lynchings were horrifying solutions to some. One visitor wrote: "When a criminal was due to be hanged, the sandhills of San Francisco swarmed with human beings. They seemed to cluster together like bees on a tree branch, and for the purpose of seeing a criminal convulsed and writhing in the agonies of violent death! This desire seemed to pervade all classes of Americans in the city."[4]

Some people felt vigilante committees a necessary evil. It is difficult to imagine living under the conditions described by Hubert Howe Bancroft:

> That the first decade of the Americanization of California represents the nadir of racial prejudice, lawlessness, and unrestrained frontier violence would be difficult to dispute. How many individuals lost their lives as a result can only be estimated. For what it is worth, Hinton Helper, in his *Land of Gold*, put the total figure of deaths by murder, hanging, suicide, accident, starvation, and attack by Indians at 16,400 for the years 1849–54. Bancroft, who studied the criminal records for 1855 for California states that 583 persons met death by violence during the twelve month period. Of these, 373 were whites, 133 Indians, 32 Chinese, and 3 Negroes. He admits that the killing of additional hundreds of Digger and Mission Indians went unrecorded.
>
> The official records for 1855 indicate that 47 people were executed by mobs, 9 by legal tribunals, 10 by sheriffs or police officers, and 6 by collectors of foreign miners' licenses. Most of the remainder of deaths of miners resulted from claims of gambling disputes. These figures for 1855 represent an improvement over previous years. The district attorney for San Francisco, for example, asserted that, between 1850 and 1853, 1200 murders took place in that city alone.[5]

Yet San Francisco, a city overflowing with cultural contradictions, hungered for learning. By 1850 it claimed fifty printers. Only five years later, San Francisco housed more newspapers than London and published more books than all the rest of trans-Mississippi. It supported three public libraries, twenty-four public grade schools, and a public high school.[6] And it also became a western theatre center.

California's first theatre was Sacramento's Eagle, built in 1849 for approximately $80,000. It was a canvas structure with sheet-iron roof and packing-box stage. Entrance to its pit of rough-board benches was through the bar, and access to the "dress circle" was up a step ladder veiled on the underside with canvas in deference to the ladies. The theatre's physical comforts didn't include heat or ventilation. Candles and whale-oil provided lighting, and one orchestra was entirely composed of "a very cheezy flageolet, played by a gentleman with one eye."[7]

Local rains and floods complicated matters. Actor Walter M. Leman wrote about one show: "The water rose six inches deep in the pit before the doors opened, and the play had progressed but an act or two when the seats ceased to afford a dry foundation. Half the town was submerged, and the few second floors then to be found in the city of canvas, afforded sleeping apartments for but a portion of its unhoused inhabitants. Fortunately, the actors were better bestowed, for the stage was their domicile by day and night."[8]

Such rude theatres as the Eagle soon were refined, many becoming extravagant "opera houses" with embroidered plush draperies, frescoed ceilings, carpeted aisles, and upholstered boxes. In many cities, one man dominated the theatre renaissance: Horace Tabor in Leadville, Alexander P. Arkeny in Portland, J. H. McVicker in Chicago, and Thomas Maguire in San Francisco.

Thomas Maguire was a former New York cab driver who couldn't read or write—a quiet, impeccably dressed fellow with a cigar always dangling from his lips. For twenty years he ruled the San Francisco stage. In 1870 the city presented him with a $1,000 plate service covered with silver medallions of his favorite stars, including Charles Kean, Edwin Forrest, and Adah Menken. Unfortunately, Maguire went bankrupt in 1882 and the New York Actors' Fund supported him in his last years.

When Maguire arrived, San Francisco had four places of amusement listed in the 1850 city directory. One of them, Robinson and Evrard's Dramatic Museum, presented farces and variety shows. Its proprietor, "Doc" D. C. Robinson, was a former associate of P. T. Barnum. The other three listings were Rowe's Olympic Circus, the Athenaeum, and an arena for bull fights. Not much in the way of entertainment, and one reason why Maguire decided to build the Jenny Lind Theatre—named after the famous singer, who made a renowned American tour under Barnum's auspices but never reached California.

There were three Jenny Lind theatres. The first two burned. The third one was built by Maguire of imported Australian yellow sandstone at a cost of $150,000. (The city fathers later bought it for $200,000, converting the historic building into the city hall.[9]) Maguire later constructed more San Francisco theatres—several managed by a young eastern director, James A. Herne.

Herne first toured California in 1868, performing in such melodramas as *The Dream of Destiny* and *Dombey and Son* at San Francisco's Metropolitan Theatre. He returned East, remaining there until around 1874, when Maguire offered him stardom at the Bush Street Theatre. The penniless Herne reached California via Panama. His total wardrobe consisted of what he wore —a pair of trousers, linen duster, and straw hat—an outfit that startled Maguire, who expected a more glamorous figure. Herne was quickly ushered into a nearby hotel, where Maguire purchased clothes for his new star. *Then* San Francisco was permitted to meet him.

Herne, like Tom Maguire, was a self-educated pragmatist who radiated a constant flow of energy—two reasons why they got along. One reporter wrote about Herne's appearance: "Although usually rough in his manners and exterior, he can be a thorough gentleman. He is noted at times for practical jokes. He is a man above the medium height and squarely built; has brown hair, brown eyes, florid complexion and an unintelligent, smoothly-shaven face."[10] Amy Leslie was more complimentary, writing in 1900: "Herne is still a handsome man, though I can remember when he stood straight as an arrow, brawny and spirited, with an odd, unruly crop of brown hair, fine blue eyes and about as neat a foot and hand as are usually given to the ruder sex."[11]

Herne eventually became Maguire's stage manager at the New Theatre, formerly called the Alhambra. To bolster attendance Maguire extensively remodeled the building, adding gilt, fresco paintings, fresh upholstery, a dress circle, orchestra, and balcony with 850 seats.[12] Herne also acted in Maguire's company. His bills included *Divorce* and *Rip Van Winkle or The Sleep of Twenty Years,* a triumph held over for a second week, an unusual record in San Francisco or anywhere.[13] The reason was Herne's performance. David Belasco later wrote: "I have seen three *Rips,*—that of Jefferson, that of Robert McWade, and finally that of James A. Herne. This last was a wonderful characterization, with all the softness and pathos of the part. I was a *Dwarf*, to Herne's *Rip*, in the Maguire's Opera House days. But *Fate* chose to thrust forward Jefferson as the only *Rip* that ever was or ever could be. I *happen to know better*. Jefferson was never the Dutchman; he was the Yankee personating the Dutchman. But James A. Herne's *Rip* was the real thing."[14]

Herne had hardly stretched his Rip Van Winkle legs and stroked his beard at Maguire's before he became Solon Shingle in *The People's Lawyer or Who Stole the Barrel of Apple Sass*, the play that brought fame to John C. Owens.[15]

At this time David Belasco enters the picture, but even his dedicated biographer, William Winter, couldn't pinpoint exact dates. Belasco did portray the dwarf in *Rip Van Winkle* and Fagin in *Oliver Twist*. His Fagin really shocked—like Herne's Bill Sykes. One day, according to Julie Herne, he told Herne about some new stage business he had worked up. But he wouldn't reveal the details. So Herne watched from the wings. During the prison scene, when Fagin goes mad, Belasco started pulling out his red hair, an effect that floored the audience. Herne soon learned the trick: young Belasco had used a duplicate wig for the scene—one that needed refurbishing after each performance.

Maguire and Herne kept the New Theatre running from week to week but audiences diminished. Things looked bright for a while when Maguire presented the original production of Herne's first play, *Charles O'Malley, The Irish Dragoon*, based on Charles Lever's novel.[16]

But the playhouse's final curtain dropped on December 3, 1874. Its last play was the sensational *Carlotta, The Queen of the Arena*, with Herne cast as Bambrine, King of the Arena. The *San Francisco Chronicle* concluded: "As it has too often happened recently at Maguire's, it has not been sufficiently rehearsed, and, consequently, was less effective than it should have been.... Of the performance it is better to say nothing until an extra representation has effaced the memory of last night's imperfections."[17] According to Winter this production was directed by David Belasco.

Few accounts exist of Herne's expertise during this period. Mrs. Thomas Whiffen, Herne's leading lady at Maguire's, later recalled Herne. "He was an inspiring man to work with and we both learned a lot from his direction. (Her husband, Thomas Whiffen, was Herne's chief comedian.) He had formerly played with Lucille Western, a very famous and intelligent actress who had created many big parts, and it was my good fortune to step into her shoes, so to speak. I'm afraid I did not fit them very well, but Mr. Herne taught me all the older actresses' business."[18]

Herne's reputation must have travelled beyond California, because his company was invited to perform at the grand opening of Portland's New Market Theatre.

After farewells, Herne's company boarded a boat—railroads didn't exist in the region yet—and sailed on a hazardous journey. Mrs. Whiffen wrote: "I shall never forget that trip for it was one of the most trying sea voyages I had ever experienced. That coast is very rough and dangerous, dotted with many lighthouses, warning ships away from treacherous rocks and promontories. It took us five days and a half to make the trip, which is made in two days now."[19]

Portland was a small city surrounded by water and hills. Alexander P. Arkeny, industrialist, steamboat captain, gold miner, lumber tycoon, trailblazer, and Wells Fargo Express investor, added a touch of class with his New Market Theatre.

The financial panic of 1873 postponed the theatre's grand opening, but expectations grew. Seats were hawked (some for $7.50), and a newspaper suggested auctioning them, an idea Arkeny rejected. But spectators weren't disappointed with the opulent playhouse. Boxes flanked its huge stage (60 by 140 feet, with a 35 foot ceiling). It also featured a horseshoe parquet, red upholstered benches, statuary, chandeliers, marble counters, arched stalls, a $400 hand-painted drop curtain, and even a third-floor cafe.

Tired but anxious, Herne's company arrived on the north-bound steamer *Idaho*, ready for the March 24, 1875, opening. Anyone holding a ticket was admitted. The *Oregonian* wrote: "This new and popular place of amusement was crowded last evening by a refined and appreciative audience on the occasion of the presentation of the familiar drama 'Rip Van Winkle.' Under the glamour of a hundred gas jets, the theatre presented a scene of dazzling brilliancy, the equal of which has never before been witnessed in this city. The play was very acceptably rendered by the new company, and failed in no essential particular to afford satisfaction to the large audience. The scenery was complete and perfect in its working, and added greatly to the effect and success of the play."[20]

The following day the *Oregonian* commented on Herne's portrayal of Rip. "He does not suffer the interest to drag for a moment, while in some of the more pathetic scenes the genuine feeling with which he invests the part touches the hearts of the most apathetic."[21]

Rip Van Winkle was followed by *Dombey and Sons* and *The Irish Doctor*. Ticket prices were sold for "dress circle and orchestra $1; reserved seats, 25 cents extra; gallery 50 cents; children half-price."[22] Other repertoire pieces included *Lighthouse Cliffs* (which Belasco and Herne adapted), *Charles O'Malley*, *The Octoroon*, *Rag Picker of Paris*, and *The School of Reform*.

Herne remained in Portland for about a month, each week adding more plays to his repertoire, *The Clockmaker's Hat*, *Handy Andy*, and *Rosina Meadows, or City Temptation Uninvited* among them. Then attendance sagged, and Herne drifted north to the Puget Sound region for the summer, not returning until fall, when he starred in *David Garner*.

Meanwhile, Arkeny continued to endow the New Market Theatre with a sense of class and quality. Ruffians weren't welcome. Neither were troublesome actors. Several reasons for the public's failing interest were Arkeny's strict rules, which he posted:

Theater rented subject to the following Rules, which are a part of all contracts:

No smoking, no kerosene, coal oil or any burning fluid allowed to be used as light in any room or part of the Theater, except Candles and Gas, red and blue lights for stage-use from iron pans.

All persons belonging to the troupe or engaged about the stage will enter by the rear stairway and pass out the same way. No person belonging to the troupe will be allowed to pass through the Dress Circle to and from the stage, other than the Manager.

No scenes to be painted out or altered, taken or removed from the Theater without the written consent of the Proprietor.

No person allowed on the stage of the Theater, other than those belonging to the troupe.

All persons are required to leave the Theater after the performance is closed.

All gentlemen who use Tobacco will be particular to use the spittoons in order to ensure cleanliness on the stage.

In no case will permission be granted to any person or persons to sell any candies, nuts, fruit, &c. in the Theater under forfeiture of contract.[23]

These were tough rules, but trouping in the frontier west was tougher. Danger from bushwhackings lurked everywhere. Swift and harsh was justice—even for women. A Spanish woman named Juanita was hanged in 1851 beyond the Yuba River at Downieville in California after she murdered a well-liked gambler. Miners in Sacramento even pelted with vegetables the notorious cigar-smoking Lola Montez—former mistress of Bavaria's King Ludwig I during her "El Olle" dance.

The hot-tempered Montez retaliated by trampling bouquets, jeering, and insulting her audience. While the orchestra ducked cabbages, the management ducked out. Wooden chairs crashed through windows, benches were broken, and stage props were plundered. Lola fled to the Orleans Hotel, followed by a mob with pots and pans. After another fearful confrontation from her balcony she mellowed, apologizing the next night, "Two or three individuals insulted me grossly by sneering and laughing at me," she told her audience. "I was more sensitive, perhaps, than most artists upon such an occasion, for the reason that I am persecuted and followed by certain persons and their agents, because I made political enemies in Europe who follow and annoy me upon every occasion."[24]

Why did performers like Lola Montez continue to perform under such conditions? For money. Actors who could beat the heat and bear the cold received high dividends—sometimes $300 a night.

Herne didn't comment on the difficulties of his Northwest adventures, but Walter M. Leman, who played in Downieville with McKean Buchanan, wrote, "We had to leave our concord wagon, and go down into town in the saddle, for no wheeled carriage could descend the grade." They played in "the upper story of a cloth-and-paper house having no stage. . . . The spectators seemed to enjoy the thing as much as the players, and there was a deal of fun if not of tragic fitness."[25]

Charles Warren Stoddard, an actor of the time, reported: "We were billed for the evening at a small mountain town some twenty miles distant before us, in a substantial wagon, with our 'call-boy' as driver, rode the entire orchestra; there were eight of us, ladies and gentlemen, in the second division of our caravan, and the 'dramatic combination' concluded with a clumsy affair overloaded with trunks and baskets of all sizes, the while being surmounted by three of the most unpromising votaries of the art that it has been my lot to meet."[26]

The ability to improvise also helped actors. The Chapmans played on a stage made of a behemoth tree from Calaveras. Farther north at Grass Valley near the forks of the Feather River (where Lola Montez once lived), Alonzo Delano scratched in his *Pen Knife Sketches; or, Chips off the Old Block* that they had "a real theatre in the mountains, where three years ago not a single civilized dwelling stood, except here and there a miner's tent; where the scenes of real life were enacted by a few weary, hungry, toil-worn, watchful miners, who worked in fear by day, and watched with arms in hand by night, lest the wily savage pounce upon them in their helplessness, and turn the comedy of life into real, appalling, and bloody tragedy."[27]

What melodrama could upstage such stuff?

4 monstrosity in art

WHILE HERNE TROUPED in the Northwest, Maguire made more plans, big plans that soon involved Herne. He owned a piece of property in San Francisco opposite St. Ignatius College. It was a centrally located site that also intrigued Elias Jackson, alias "Lucky" Baldwin, successful gambler, livery-stable owner, hotelman, and speculator supreme who had made millions from the Comstock Lode.

Baldwin was a self-made man of sharp contrasts. Legend says that a hotel in Virginia City ejected him from its lobby one day; but the next day he returned a millionaire, and received the red carpet treatment. Even Baldwin's funeral made news, because his last will and testament prohibited a religious service. Old friends eulogized him instead, and a band played sections from *La Bohème, Aïda,* and other operas.

Baldwin's story was actually quite simple. He wanted to build a mammoth six-story Victorian hotel on Maguire's property to increase his social status. Maguire wanted another theatre. They struck a deal that satisfied both ex-hostler and ex-hack driver. Baldwin would provide funds for and have control of the new hotel they would build, while Maguire would manage the theatre in the building.

Construction of the hotel began in February 1875. A sprawling gingerbread mansion with a huge ornamental dome flanked by several smaller ones, it had 495 rooms and many shops. One critic called the theatre a "beautiful temple of the drama."[1] Frescoes, velvet draperies, and prismatic crystal gasoliers adorned the place. Its barroom with a unique collection of paintings, was

34

the largest in San Francisco. Its restaurant served gourmet foods.

The price of this imposing edifice was $2,750,000, and represented Baldwin's bid for respectability. The building became a San Francisco landmark. Fire destroyed it on November 24, 1898, but many nostalgically recalled its sumptuous high style and the "four-in-hand coaches that rolled between the hotel and the ferries and trains. Drawn by high-spirited, high-stepping horses, groomed and harnessed to perfection, tossing their heads and champing their bits as they cantered along the streets."[2]

Baldwin and Maguire surely weren't San Francisco's chief custodians of extravagance—not by a long shot. Many "muck-a-mucks" flaunted their newly-acquired sacks of wealth. They enjoyed billiards, banquets, balls, French fashions, archery, receptions, roller-skating, concerts, weddings, lectures, musical festivals, and ostentatious houses—the eternal monuments of worldly wealth. Frescoes, oriental carpets, marble, Chinese brocades, silver balustrades, and antique furniture they adored—the more garish the better. Among these princely palaces on Nob Hill were the Charles Crocker home ($2,300,000), and the Mary Hopkins castle ($3,000,000). By 1879 around 6,000 young bloods roamed across San Francisco, personifying Victorian excess.[3]

Meanwhile, Maguire needed a manager for his theatre, to satisfy the whims of San Francisco's aesthetes. He rehired Herne as stage manager, and Herne hired David Belasco as his assistant-prompter.

The Baldwin Academy of Music, as Maguire's theatre was called, opened on March 6, 1876, with the Irish tragedian Barry Sullivan as *Richard III*. Even a new national melody was composed for the occasion.[4] "A fashionable and full dress audience"[5] attended the gala opening, the *Daily Alta California* saying, "it was the universal opinion that a more handsome theatre does not exist to-day in the United States." Their reviewer then described the lavish showplace:

> The prevailing color of the house is a rich deep crimson, bordered with gold; plate-glass mirrors at the sides reflect again and again the beauties of the auditorium. The impression on first entering is that one is standing in some magnificent parlor. The crown of the whole, however, lies in the

dome of the auditorium. The concave ceiling, directly over
the stage, and which breaks away from a gorgeous lambre-
quin, is in blue and white tints, representing the clouds and
sky, in which are seated two symbolic figures, representing
Music and Drama, with cherubins playing around them.
They are as correctly drawn and vigorously colored as a
well wrought oil painting. In a second section of the vault,
more directly over the gallery, is a second emblematic group,
consisting of a fewer number of figures, but as highly artistic as the first one. The proscenium boxes are eight in
number. They are upholstered in crimson rep and satin, the
papering being of a crimson ground figured with various
golden forms. By a novel arrangement of the partitions, any
two of the boxes may be thrown into one. The carpeting and
furnishing of these boxes are rich and tasteful. At the back
of the dress circle are twin mezzanine boxes, richly carpeted
and decorated. Above the stage is a copy of one of the few
authentic portraits of Shakespeare. The drop curtain consists of two rich, crimson silk draperies, which part in the
middle and are drawn up to the sides, revealing a well ar-
rayed stage 50 feet in breadth, 35 feet deep and 36 feet
high.[6]

However, there were several drawbacks to the theatre.
Among them were insufficient aisles in the orchestra circle and
a narrow entrance. "Last night being about the wildest night
that has been experienced in San Francisco, there was a terrible
crowding in the vestibule because of almost the entire audience
waiting for carriages."[7] Sections of the theatre also needed finishing. Lime, mortar, and lumber still showed several days before
the opening.[8]

The underportion of the stage also remained unfinished, and
it very nearly killed Barry Sullivan. William H. Crane, who
played the Grave Digger in *Hamlet,* later recollected that it was
"suspended from the stage floor and there was nothing on the
sides and a sheer drop of twenty feet or more to the ground. A
floor cloth which covered the stage had been placed partly over
the opening of the trap, and Sullivan stepped on this by accident,
falling into the grave. He knocked me over. I had Yorick's skull
in my hands at the time. This I threw quickly on the stage, and
it was caught by Louis James, who was playing Laertes. I just
managed to save myself and Sullivan from falling off the narrow,

shelf-like platform. He never thanked me even for saving my own life."[9]

Perhaps this was one reason the *Free Press* asked that licenses be withheld from those theatres failing to provide ample exits, suggesting that Baldwin's Academy of Music was a magnificent firetrap whose management also ignored its actors' safety. Baldwin sued for libel, receiving $20,000 in damages.[10]

Meanwhile, Sullivan's *Richard III* was highly praised. The *San Francisco Chronicle* called the production "one of the most brilliant events in our theatrical annals."[11] The *Chronicle* said, "The acting, apart from that of the star, was of level excellent, and does not call for special comment."[12] The *Daily Evening Bulletin,* however, thought the audience wasn't "in a particularly demonstrative mood," failing even to acclaim Sullivan with "hearty applause."[13]

Sullivan followed *Richard III* with *Hamlet.* Herne played the ghost of Hamlet's father. Belasco portrayed two roles: Bernardo and the second actor. Two other members of Baldwin's Company also deserve mention: James O'Neill and William H. Crane.

James O'Neill portrayed Laertes in *Hamlet.* Before arriving in San Francisco he had alternated with Edwin Booth in the roles of Othello and Iago, and of Brutus, Cassius, and Anthony in *Julius Caesar*; he also played Romeo to Adelaide Neilson's Juliet and Macbeth opposite Charlotte Cushman. All were topflight performers. Many even considered O'Neill to be Booth's eventual successor as America's foremost tragedian. But in 1883 he appeared at Booth's Theatre in *The Count of Monte Cristo* and continued playing the role for nearly sixteen years. His performances brought him fame and fortune; they also eroded his mind and soul, turning him into an alcoholic. O'Neill once lamented: "If I could not feel the part anew each time I acted it, I could not do myself justice. Perhaps you can imagine the tremendous mental effort that was required after I had acted the character so long that I came to hate every thought of it."[14]

James O'Neill, of course, sired Eugene O'Neill, three-time winner of the Pulitzer Prize and eventually the recipient of the Nobel Prize, for distinguished contribution to dramatic literature.

William H. Crane also became one of the country's favorite

actors. His credits later included *Our Boarding House, The Senator,* and *David Harum,* based on the phenomenally best-selling novel.

Herne and Crane once clashed at Baldwin's during the staging of *A New Way to Pay Old Debts.* Crane, listed as the servant Order, said he wanted first comedian billing and refused to perform otherwise.

Herne smiled and said: "You're a long way from home."

Crane snapped: "I wouldn't care if I was in China. You had no right to cast me for Order."

David Belasco finally played Order, and Crane sat out front with his wife on opening night, fuming. Appalled even more by Belasco's wretched performance, he rushed backstage and accused Herne, "You had your nerve to cast me for that part."

"But you didn't play it," replied Herne, who always remained unruffled. "It was not that you were cast for the part, but seeing Belasco play it that has upset you."[15]

Type-casting "stuck like glue" in the old resident repertory system, performers seldom wandering from their assigned characters—unless they became famous—a practice that hampered their growth and versatility. Yet it simplified production, as works constantly changed. The general types included: Leading Man, Light Comedian, First Old Man, Second Old Man, Walking Gentleman, Heavy Man, Utility Man, First Walking Lady, First Old Woman, and Singing Chambermaid. In *Footlight Flashes* (1866), comedian William Davidge outlined each type:

"The Leading Man, is the personifier of the principal characters in tragedy, as well as some of the more serious ones in comedy; as, Mr. Oakley, in the 'Jealous Wife,' Lord Townley in the 'Provoked Husband,' etc.

"The Light Comedian, is the representative of the fine gentleman of the old school, as Charles Surface, in the 'School for Scandal,' and others of a more modern date, who stand prominently forward in the play.

"The First Old Man, clearly defines itself. They are such parts as aged characters where they assume a similar significance with the principles of other lines of business; if not, they are only Second Old Men.

"The Walking Gentleman, is he who enacts all the young

men in all sorts of pieces,—youths for whom the young ladies of the drama have a preference, despite the opposition of their parents.

"The Utility Man, must appear in any thing for which he is cast, the stage manager being the judge of his fitness for the positions in which to place him.

"The Leading Lady, plays all the prominent characters of the drama of the serious kind. Such is however the power of their influence in a theatre, that they not unfrequently absorb many of the comic parts likewise.

"The First Walking Lady, is she who must play the parts in both tragedy and comedy that are not claimed by the leading, and the second lady, and has also charge of some very prominent ones in farces.

"First Old Woman takes the same relation in the allotment of parts as the First Old Man.

"The Singing Chambermaid is not necessarily obliged to enact chambermaids only, but appears in all the Subrettes, and is called singing chambermaid, to specify her musical capability, and in distinction to those who are not in possession of that accomplishment."[16]

Native American playwrights didn't usually create realistic characters in realistic environments. Why? Managers wouldn't produce such works, and audiences wouldn't attend their performances.

Other things, such as huge auditoriums, complicated the problem. The Metropolitan Theatre's curtain opening was sixty feet, making many realistic conventions impossible. Seating capacities reached several thousand. When the Academy of Music opened in Philadelphia, comedian Charles Mathews suggested that spectators bring a telescope and each actor a speaking-trumpet. Dion Boucicault called this "monstrosity in art."[17]

The "wing and drop" system also added troubles. Few managers would invest in new scenery. They preferred cheaper stock sets.

Most actors supported the oratorical tradition; restrained acting was beyond their capabilities. So, they, too, clung tight to tradition.

All these factors worked against Herne's "fidelity to truth"

ideas. This was why it took him nearly forty years to make his
mark. As Theodor Herzl wrote, "Whoever would change men
must change the conditions of their lives."

It was Baldwin's theatre that changed Herne's life and career. Involvement with the Western sisters had failed to fulfill
his long-range needs. He needed someone to provide shape, direction, and purpose—a devoted companion. The theatre offered the
emptiness of illusion, like the bottle. Herne resembled *Alice in
Wonderland's* rabbit—dashing so fast he couldn't catch himself,
until he met Katharine Corcoran, following her audition at
Baldwin's.

Herne's daughter Chrystal later wrote: "Mother was the
spark that was needed to light up the fires of genius that were
smouldering in father's soul. . . . My mother seemed to be the one
thing needed to make my father's life well rounded and full to
overflowing."[18] David Belasco also agreed that Katherine Corcoran transformed Herne's erratic ways. "No one ever owed more
to a woman than he to little 'K.C.' "[19] As late as 1960, John
Herne wrote about his parents, "James A. Herne was a great
actor, all by himself, drunk or sober but it was his leading lady,
Katy Corcoran, who made him into a great dramatist."[20]

Katharine Corcoran Herne was born on December 8, 1856,
in Ireland. (Nearly two decades separated the Hernes in age, yet
they were very compatible.) Her family soon migrated to America, settling in New York City. When the Civil War erupted, her
father enlisted. He was captured and thrown into Libby Prison.
He eventually escaped, but the brutal treatment received there
led to his death. This left the family destitute, forcing the children into an orphanage. Although her mother regained their custody after finding factory work, they sometimes sold newspapers
and flowers, shoveled snow, and even begged. It was a story
snatched from the pages of Dickens. An uncle finally used his influence to get her a widow's pension, then took the family to
California.[21]

Katharine loved the theatre and as a young girl began
studying with Julia Melville, a respected San Francisco actress,
who arranged a reading at Baldwin's under the pretext of testing
her protégée's projection. Herne stood quietly in the wings—impressed. Several days later, the aspiring young actress received

a contract. Herne often remarked that while watching K.C. that afternoon he decided to marry her.[22] She was lovely. One reporter later noted she had "brown hair, gray eyes and a pale, sad face, a slight figure, and [was] below the medium height." He also observed she "dresse[d] with elegant taste on and off the stage, and [was] noted for her quiet, lady-like demeanor on the street."[23]

K.C.'s first assignment at Baldwin's was as Peg Woffington in *Masks and Faces*. A contract followed this benefit. Belasco offered an alternate story, later saying the play was Augustin Daly's *Divorce*, although his biographer, William Winter, wasn't certain. Belasco wrote:

> The manuscript arrived, but we had no one to play the woman's part, when a young girl came into the theatre and asked to see Mr. Herne. Her name was Katharine Corcoran. When she was ushered in we saw at a glance that we had found the heroine of 'Divorce.' It required a *petite* woman, full of fascination, charm, intensity, and with the power to weep. Of course, we did not know her capacities, but she seemed full of promise. She was engaged at once. When the time came for rehearsals she went quietly through them— an alien not particularly welcome to the company. 'Who is she?' they all asked, and the leading man came to Herne and myself, and laid before us the numerous complaints he was receiving. As it was very obvious that Herne was in love with her, and so likely to be prejudiced, Maguire turned to me. 'She is going to make a sensation,' I said; 'I'll stake my life on it.' And she did, becoming one of the big elements in our support and quite winning the players. It was not long before she and Herne were married.[24]

But things slowed at Baldwin's Academy of Music. Even Barry Sullivan failed to boost attendance in March 1876. The *Daily Alta California* blamed the Lenten season and stormy weather, unaware of California's impending panic and severe depression.[25] By spring in 1877, Maguire's losses tallied $50,000. This figure led management to replace him with a rival, John McCullough, who upstaged Maguire with a deficit of $28,000 more in less than three months. Although Maguire had lost the Opera House, the New Theater, and Baldwin's, he waited for another chance. Then Baldwin appointed him lessee of the Academy for two years—rent free—in exchange for the property.

Herne survived during this period by touring with Belasco and K.C. along the Pacific Slope. According to Belasco their small company landed in Eureka, on the east shore of Humboldt Bay. At Pratt's Opera House they played *The Marble Heart,* followed by *The Two Orphans.* Then Herne decided to stage *Robert Macaire.* But they had no script. So they collaborated, rewriting it from memory. A few hectic rehearsals followed, and the play pleased Eureka's playgoers.

After the triumphant *Robert Macaire,* the troupe became local celebrities for awhile, and Belasco accepted a benefit. All needed cash, so Herne warned, "While it will be your personal benefit, of course, you are gallant enough to understand that we shall all share in any profits that may accrue."[26] And all shared the spoils.

Then the elated Belasco made a mistake. He threw a celebration that devoured all the benefit's profits. The dejected company packed their bags and returned to Baldwin's, where they reorganized with K.C. as leading lady.

William Winter mentions Belasco's *Not Guilty,* a hacked version of Watts Phillips' spectacle that opened at Baldwin's on December 24, 1878, with Herne as Joe Triggs and James O'Neill as Robert Arnold. Although it was flaunted as "The Grand Production of the Magnificent Musical, Military, Dramatic, and Spectacular (*sic*) Christmas Piece, which has been given for eight successive Christmas seasons in Philadelphia." Belasco admitted being the "stock dramatist," a position that paid $12.50 a performance for both play adaptation and stage management, a task that took two weeks. This work included a battle scene with hundreds of extras, horses, and cannon. The *San Francisco Evening Bulletin* called the scene "about the most realistic ever produced on the stage."[27]

On February 15, 1879, the following ad appeared in the San Francisco *Chronicle:* "The management of Baldwin's Theatre has the honor to announce that in consequence of the immense stage room required for the production of the great play, *Within an Inch of His Life,* the Grand Opera House has been taken for a special dramatic season commencing Monday, February 17th."[28]

Belasco and Herne had dramatized Emile Gaboriau's French

novel, *La Corde au Cou,* played as *Almost a Life* in New York and Philadelphia.[29] Although they promoted this as "the most powerful play ever acted," Belasco later admitted that "a week of strenuous days and sleepness nights"[30] was necessary to produce it. Herne played Count de Clairnot and K.C. became Dionysia Chandore. (Audiences liked fancy French names and exotic titles.)

Gaboriau enjoyed wide popularity in the United States, which almost assured a profitable engagement for the play at Baldwin's. So Belasco and Herne decided to admit plagiarism, promoting the play as Gaboriau's *Within an Inch of His Life.* Their hunch paid dividends. Praise followed, and Herne laughed backstage at the gullibility of critics who venerated French literature.[31]

Belasco later claimed full credit for the authorship of *Within an Inch of His Life,* although the manuscript isn't written in either his or Herne's hand. (Notations in the margins, however, were in Herne's handwriting, but he directed it.) Julie Herne thought her father probably read the original in translation, or Belasco helped him revise a rough draft. Neither playwright could read French. Trouble followed. The *San Francisco Call* printed a letter from Stephen Maybell, a Workingmen's Party agitator, who claimed authorship. This led Belasco to retaliate the following week with this caustic letter:

> The gentleman claiming the dramatization of my play from Emile Gaboriau's novel, "Within an Inch of His Life," must be under an illusion. I met him a short time ago, when he informed me that he was in poor circumstances, and asked me to try and secure him a position as property man or scene-shifter at the Baldwin. Such a thing I told him was impossible, but as I was working on my new play, I could give him some copying to do. This he did, and for which I *paid* him. This, dear sir, explains his strange illusion and which you will do me the favor of stating. Yours respectfully,
>
> David Belasco,
> Prompter of Baldwin's Theatre.[32]

Within an Inch of His Life supplied audiences with the usual melodramatic trappings: cardboard characters, plot complications and twists, pulsating action, and a last-minute explosive reversal of fortune, all salable ingredients.

The plot involves Jules De Dardeville, who loves the Countess De Clairnot, who is married to Count Clairnot. Dardeville discovers the enchanting Dionysia Chandore. Words flare. Then the chateau flares. The count is shot. Dardeville plays scapegoat. The revengeful Countess' testimony consigns him to the gallows. But truth outs. Cocoleau, an idiot, saves the day by confessing he did it for the Countess De Clairnot. Curtain.

The *News Letter* ridiculed the production. "A murder is committed, of course. All other crimes are so extremely venial now-a-days that it is almost impossible to hallow up an audience with anything else. As a matter of course James O'Neill, whatever his alias for the night may be, is suspected of having committed it and is thrown into prison. The number of times that he has been suspected and thrown into prison—in mimic play—since his advent in the *Celebrated Case* is something inconceivable. He never knows his lines anymore excepting in a prison scene, and in that it has almost become possible for him to speak extremporaneously. Mr. Lewis Morrison plays the part of an idiot, who, in the last act exclaims: 'I must speak or I shall go mad,' which is a specimen of the refreshing ingenuousness of an idiot."[33]

The melodrama's most thrilling moment? Probably "the terrible fire spectacle" that Belasco contrived by fanning red and yellow lighted strips of silk with a bellows, an effect that startled audiences. Tension mounted until the authorities mounted the stage to investigate, finding only silk strips—more Belasco theatre magic.

Belasco and Herne then tried to surpass the sensationalism of *Within an Inch of His Life,* and almost landed in jail.

Salmi Morse was a "tall, rabbinical-looking Hebrew, scrupulously dressed in black, with reverent gray hairs, mild, benignant eyes and somewhat heavily moulded features,"[34] according to the *Call.* His dream was to have his religious play, *The Passion,* produced. It was a work he swore took twenty years to research in the Holy Land. He even carried parchment scrawled with esoteric Chaldean, Roman, and Arabic symbols found in a Maltese monastery. San Francisco's Roman Catholic archbishop sanctioned the work, supposedly adding several passages.

Belasco chose *The Passion* as his *magnum opus* of scenic splendor. He studied paintings of The Last Supper and Salome's dance in Mechanic's Mercantile Library for hours and contracted hundreds of extras: 200 singers, 400 men, women, children, and infants for the ensembles, plus sheep for the Joseph and Mary scene. O'Neill expanded his spiritual consciousness by giving up smoking and swearing, whiskey and other indulgences. Belasco carried a Bible under his arm. And "the boards of the stage became Holy Land."[35]

The Passion finally opened on March 3, 1879. Everyone sensed catastrophe, and O'Neill later confided to a friend: "I was uncertain up to ten minutes before I went to the theater whether I should not give up the whole thing. My wife threw herself upon her knees at my feet and pleaded with me to send word that I would not go on. She said the people would kill me."[36]

Opening night passed smoothly. An intense religious aura filled the theatre. Belasco's scenic wonders, the "Passion" music of Bach, and O'Neill's transcendent portrayal of Christ created a spellbinding atmosphere. Although the critics voiced moral outrage and some factions sent threatening letters, Maguire scheduled a second performance. Religious censorship often proved profitable.

The following evening's events electrified everyone. Cast, crew, and audience—including hardened miners—knelt in prayer at O'Neill's entrance onstage. His thorn-crowning made women faint. Some spectators stormed from the theatre, attacking Jews, pawnshops, and other holdings. Eight days passed, and audiences dwindled, mainly because of the play's controversial theme. Maguire replaced *The Passion* with *The Miner's Daughter*, which promptly flopped. Maguire then made an even greater mistake and revived *The Passion* on April 15, its day of doom.

Following the performance, two policemen served warrants on O'Neill and other cast members, dragging them to jail in their costumes. Belasco escaped by hiding in the cellar. (Winter later said he avoided a fine through the sheriff, a local friend.) Herne's involvement isn't known. The trial received national coverage, and O'Neill was fined $50, the other cast members—including the apostles—$5 each, all for performing *The Passion*.

Reactions differed. A "Betsy B" wrote in *The Argonaut* that when the play deviated from Biblical verse, it became "a lot of meaningless drivel." She also called the pageant scenes "blasphemous, desecrating, unholy."[37] San Francisco's Board of Supervisors finally passed a new city ordinance: "It shall be unlawful for any person to exhibit, or take part in exhibiting, in any theatre, or other place where money is charged for admission, any play or performance or presentation displaying or intended to display, the life or death of Jesus Christ, or any play, performance or representation, calculated or tending to debase or degrade religion."[38] The *News Letter* retaliated: "We expect next to hear of an ordinance for the burning of all old women who keep cats or have a mole on their noses."[39]

O'Neill long remembered *The Passion*, insisting "there was nothing irreverent or theatrical about the performance. Its intense solemnity throughout was most impressive. To my mind there was nothing sacrilegious in *The Passion*. . . . If anything, it was in the line of biblical education."[40] Belasco said years later: "I have produced many plays in many parts of the world, but never have I seen an audience awed as by 'The Passion Play.' The greatest performance of a generation was the *Christus* by James O'Neill."[41] Herne said: "The most sublime play I ever saw in my life, was 'The Passion.' . . . If ever a man was exalted by his work, that actor was exalted by coming so closely in spiritual touch with Jesus Christ. I have never seen or read anywhere anything which so ennobled and dignified the Christian religion as did that play and that actor's work."[42]

An Eastern manager planned a production of *The Passion*, but pressure groups forced its withdrawal. *The Passion's* creator, Salmi Morse, fared less well—his body was found floating in the Hudson River on February 23, 1884.

San Franciscans soon forgot Salmi Morse, returning to their church pews, saloons, and other social pastimes. Events moved fast, and new gossip caught their ears—especially theatre talk:

Did you hear what happened at The Alhambra? The doorkeeper was almost killed by a madman with a six-shooter.

Remember that blonde actress? Her soldier boy killed her.

Why? He found her with another soldier boy. Serves her right.

Want a good laugh? A former fan of Booth's brought a watermelon for him to the stagedoor of the California Theatre. He put it in the wings and left to hitch his horse. The watermelon? It started rolling, hitting Iago. Then it tumbled over the footlights, knocked down the clarinet player and smashed into the drums. Everybody went crazy. They had to drop the curtain.[43]

Madmen, murderers, and watermelons were just a few tales sifted through San Francisco's dizzy social scene, a scene including Baldwin's, where Belasco and Herne concocted another patchwork melodrama called *A Woman's Life*. This time Herne played a smuggler who carried Violet Skeptic (K.C.) to his cave of cohorts. Critics called it threadbare.[44] *A Scrap of Paper* wasn't much better. One critic concluded that K.C. "ignored repose, that most difficult art in the profession."[45] But critics praised the special effects—as usual.

Belasco and Herne needed a hit, a big one. They considered reviving an earlier work, writing a new melodrama, and plagiarism. They finally decided to convert Bronson Howard's smash *The Banker's Daughter* into *The Millionaire's Daughter*. Belasco played Timothy Tubbs; Herne, Ulysses S. Danripple, N.Y., U.S.A.; and K.C., Mabel St. Everard. It was a very expensive production, one that used $30,000 of lace from Maguire's home.

Things looked good—for a while. Then the West Coast representative of A. M. Palmer, New York producer of the Howard play, filed a plagiarism suit. The *San Francisco Chonicle* suggested that Belasco and Herne vindicate themselves regarding "the extraordinary similarity between the plot and incidents of the two dramas."[46] The investigation, however, failed to furnish enough evidence of plagiarism. Belasco later told Winter: "The chief real resemblances are the title and the Duel Scene. We did call my play 'The Millionaire's Daughter' because of the success of Howard's piece: the Duel Scene, however, I took from 'The Corsican Brothers.' Howard, probably, took his from the same source; nobody acquainted with the theatre could very well help knowing that scene."[47]

Herne had gone from the Ghost in *Hamlet* to Joe Triggs, Count de Clairnot, and Ulysses S. Danripple. He also played the

Peeping Tom in his adaptation with Belasco called *Marriage by Moonlight*, later *Moonlight Marriage* (originally Watts Phillips' *Camilla's Husband*, which played the Royal Olympic Theatre, London, in November 1862). The romance was written for Baldwin's star, Rose Coghlan.

The story concerns Lady Clarissa, an affluent aristocrat obligated to marry on her eighteenth birthday. The Marquis hears his son Harold ringing wedding bells. But the plot thickens. Lady Clarissa is secretly married to a young artist who mingles with gypsies. This complication the Marquis removes, having the youth arrested for stealing. But justice triumphs. As the curtain falls, the lovers miraculously reunite. Presumably they live happily ever after.

But Rose Coghlan was bored with San Francisco and accepted a contract from Lester Wallack, who also offered to purchase *Marriage by Moonlight*. Herne refused because he planned an Eastern tour with K.C. and himself as leads.

Maguire also had problems—financial ones. Repaying his heavy debts—including those from his gambling habit—devoured the profits. Belasco and Herne finally requested a benefit, presenting both *The Moonlight Marriage* and *Rip Van Winkle*. As Belasco recalled: "That benefit was urgently needed! Maguire was, among other things, an inveterate gambler and would often stake every dollar the treasury contained. Then, if luck went against him, he'd come and tell us salaries could not be paid, because he had lost! The salaries *were* paid,—out of 'Lucky' Baldwin's pocket. But he had grown tired of backing a losing game and, besides, he and Maguire had had some special row,— I don't now remember what it was about,—and Baldwin had withdrawn his support. Expenses were very high: Miss Coghlan's engagement had 'run on' and her $500 a week was a heavy drag: Herne and I had an interest, and we simply had to have some ready money to keep us going,—so I suggested a double-barrelled 'benefit' as a way of getting it."[48]

The benefit replenished both Belasco's and Herne's pocketbooks and purpose. Zola's *L'Assommoir* ran through July with Herne as Bibi-La-Grillade, K.C. as Nana, and James O'Neill as Coupeau. Steele MacKaye's *Won at Last* followed; then *Musette*,

La Cigale, and other spectacular splashes by one of America's most enchanting actresses, Lotta Crabtree.

What magnetism Lotta possessed! Both princes and paupers adored her. After attending a performance in New Orleans, the Grand Duke Alexis presented her a set of bracelets and a necklace set with diamonds and turquoises, inviting her aboard a Russian warship where they dined. Many managers gave her gifts, and even Brigham Young favored her. Audiences longed to see and touch her garments. This innocent Lotta, who puffed black cigars and rode insanely through the night, lived in seclusion with her mother, a shrewd businesswoman who bought plays for pennies and made millions from them with Lotta.

Every manager in San Francisco wanted to contract Lotta. She represented living gold dust. Maguire finally secured her talents for seven performances at the staggering price of $2,000. The play was *Musette,* an inferior work, but no one cared. Audiences wanted to see Lotta, not the play.[49]

The machinery moved smoothly at Baldwin's—too smoothly. Something had to bend or break, and it did. Other San Franciscans wanted *Musette,* and one of the two original scripts vanished. Lotta's mother—who paid $5,000 for the play—searched frantically, finally locating the script half a block from the theatre in a hotel room rented by a former Baldwin manager. Mrs. Crabtree blamed Belasco and Herne, but nothing happened.[50]

A new play then captured Belasco's and Herne's interest. At first called *Chums,* it was later renamed *Hearts of Oak* and eventually made Herne $100,000, a fortune he later lost while trying to revolutionize the American theatre.

5 babies, beans, and buckwheat cakes

S TAGE STARS MADE news during the 1870's—as always. Without the virtues of film, radio, and television, Mainstreet U.S.A. relied on gossip and newsprint for the latest details. The *San Francisco Chronicle*, for example, ran a column that faithfully reported the inside stories about show biz: John E. Owens' decision to quit amateur farming, Edwin Booth's daughter's crack-shot expertise, and Tony Pastor's $17,000 profit from his four-week bonanza in San Francisco.[1] And at Maguire's, Belasco and Herne were mounting a new play called *Chums*.

Chums was a frantic fling to bolster sagging attendance at Maguire's—something the public didn't know. Originally the play was written as a starring vehicle for James O'Neill and Lewis Morrison. But Belasco and Herne soon dreamed bigger dreams— a national tour with a grand finale in New York. Meanwhile, Maguire's made a good tryout place.

Chums was a melodrama about honor and duty among simple folks on the Massachusetts coast. (Herne's later sea plays, *Drifting Apart*, *Shore Acres*, and *Sag Harbor* were all variations on this theme.) The play's plot was pirated, as both authors admitted on the program. Its original source was an old English melodrama called *The Mariner's Compass*, first presented at Astley's Theatre, London, in 1865, and then at the New Bowery Theatre in New York the same year.

Chums' plotline focuses on Terry Dennison, "the sailor miller" (played by Herne) who raises both Chrystal, "the sweetheart," and Ned Fairweather, a fine fellow. When Terry, who long loves Chrystal, proposes, she accepts. Duty forces her decision, although she loves Ned, who goes to sea. Two years pass. When Ned returns, he finds Chrystal with "a sunbeam"—little Chrystal—which doesn't soothe his ardor. Melodrama's creaking conventions then let Terry overhear the following conversation, which turns him seaward also:

> *Ned.* I tell you I will not give you up ... Oh, that lie! That lie! Better the truth—the fearful truth at once, than to let him marry a girl whose whole love was given to his dearest friend. It was not a sacrifice—it was a *crime.*
>
> *Chrystal.* ... Would you have me go to Terry Dennison and tell him that I loved you before I married him—that I—(*He turns as if divining what she would say.*) Yes! That I love you still! And out of my weakness I will pluck strength to cry out. "Terry! Husband—friend! Come to me—help me—save me from myself!"[2]

This confession nearly destroys Terry, who asks Chrystal not to marry Ned for five years, a promise she gives. Time flies —six years. The blinded Terry, who everyone thought was lost at sea, returns on the exact day when Chrystal and Ned marry and sits on his own tombstone in the church graveyard. He's finally invited into the house by little Chrystal, where he reveals all, then dies. Tears flood the stage.

Chums opened on September 9, 1879. The audience, apparently satisfied with its 50 cents worth of escapism, cheered and applauded, calling both actors and playwrights before the curtain following each act. Prospects backstage looked roseate, larders of food flashing through everyone's mind. The *San Francisco Chronicle's* reviewer even said the play had "some of the most realistic scenery ever seen upon a stage."[3]

Belasco's scenic wonders had triumphed again. He used real water for a rain scene instead of shot poured across a drum's face. A working gristmill and a shipwreck also helped. And one bit of bewitchery had audiences chattering like squirrels for days. A cat ran across the stage to a fireplace, stretched itself, then drank milk from a dish. Years later the "Bishop of Broadway" revealed his method:

> One day I was in a friend's house and the cat at the fireside stretched herself. "There," I thought, "that is the domestic

touch I want in 'Hearts of Oak' ". For a cat before the
hearth is always a comfortable touch, and a cat never looks
quite so comfortable as when she stretches herself. But how
could I make a cat stretch herself to order every night on
the stage? It would be a great touch if I could do it, but
how?

However, I did it, and this is how: I got a black cat and
had a stage man fasten her in a box which was a little too
short for her. Then I put her in the cellar, where I fed her
in the morning, but gave her no food during the day. Then
just before the curtain went up the cat was brought up in
her box, which was placed as a part of the stage hidden by
the table but near the fire; and at exactly the right point in
the play I would open the box. Of course the cat, stiff from
being kept in the box all day, would walk over to the fire,
stretch herself and hungrily begin lapping up the milk in
the saucer. That cat was always greeted with laughter and
applause and every night brought down the house. And yet
it was only a little thing, you see.[4]

Belasco became a master of dazzling, inventive, and mind-
bending stage tricks, his work eventually labelled "Belascoism,"
a term that the anti-illusionists ridiculed. He spent a fortune on
naturalistic techniques. In *The Governor's Lady* (1912), he re-
constructed a Child's restaurant with everything from salt shak-
ers to table napkins. In *Tiger Rose* (1917), real pine needles
were scattered on stage to heighten audience sensory involvement, and for *The Easiest Way* (1908) he purchased the interior
of an old boardinghouse, rebuilding it on stage—running faucets
and all. Belasco's *magnum opus* was probably a scene in *The Girl
of the Golden West* (1905), with its kerosene lamps, banjos, con-
certinas, and bones. Critic William Winter, spellbound by the effects, wrote that "the audience heard the wild moaning and
shrill whistle of the gale, and at moments, as the tempest rose
to a climax of fury, could see the fine-powdered snow driven in
tiny sprays and eddies through every crevice of the walls and
the very fabric of the cabin quiver and rock beneath the impact
of terrific blasts of wind."[5] This fantastic feat involved a backstage crew of thirty-two technicians.

Chums didn't have a snowstorm, but it settled for a genuine
old-fashioned dinner, including steaming potatoes, baked beans,
buckwheat cakes, and a meat pie. Belasco jokingly admitted his

indebtedness to this banquet, which "was practically the only square meal (they) had during the day."[6]

Naturally, there was a baby in *Chums*. It received even more attention than Belasco's trained cat and the meat pie. The child delighted audiences. She cooed and grinned and did amazing things—always the same way. Her movements were hard to believe.

Show business had taught Belasco and Herne a lot about babies. Herne once told William Dean Howells, "A child is a great attraction in a play—a *baby* a power."[7] But babies are unpredictable. So Herne inserted this note in the stage directions: "All this business can be elaborated as the baby gets used to the stage and to the people. Whatever the baby does must be acted upon by the actors and taken advantage of, as it is impossible to set down in so many lines just what the baby will or will not do, so watch out for the star's humor."[8] One mystified critic cried, "Why, that baby would draw at Booth's theatre—the severest test to which any star can be subjected."[9] Twenty years later another critic remarked: "No Herne play is complete without a baby and a good dinner."[10]

By *Chum's* fifth act, the baby grew into little Chrystal, played by one of the most popular child stars on the Pacific slope, Maude Adams, who traveled with her actress mother, Annie Adams (Mrs. Asenath Kiskadden). Maude Adams, of course, became a legendary American actress, the original Peter Pan.

Maudie was about seven when she joined Baldwin's. She was bright and engaging. Everyone loved her. "From the time Maude Adams created the role, it became one of the most vital parts of the play," recalled Belasco. "*Chums*, in short, scored an immense success, and 'Little Maudie' for the time being was the heroine of the town."[11] Belasco also fondly remembered: "When we were beginning rehearsals of a new play at the Baldwin I would take Maudie on my knee and bit by bit would explain to her the meaning of the part she had to play. I can see now, with her little spindle legs almost touching the floor, her tiny face, none too clean, perhaps, peering up into mine, and those wise eyes of hers drinking in every word. I soon learned to know that it was no use to confine myself to a description of her own work; until I had told the whole story of the play to Maudie, and treated her almost as seriously as if she were our leading lady, she would pay no attention."[12]

Maude Adams wasn't the only child star of the nineteenth century American and English theatres. Dozens of such moppets existed. *Horizon, East Lynne, Alice in Wonderland, The Prince and the Pauper, Little Lord Fauntleroy,* and the perennially popular *Uncle Tom's Cabin* all included them. Even the spectacular musical *The Black Crook* featured a child prodigy, James G. Speaight, an accomplished violinist and orchestra conductor at seven, who also played in *The Naiad Queen* and led the Boston Theatre's orchestra in 1873.

Young boy players also rivaled adult actors in their popularity. Critics called Master Betty the Infant Roscius, Lawrence Hutton acclaiming him "the most remarkable and successful Phenomenon in the whole history of the stage."[13] Some considered young Betty greater than David Garrick, and Mr. Pitt adjourned Parliament to attend his Hamlet at Drury Lane. John Howard Payne, composer of "Home Sweet Home" and dozens of plays, including *Brutus,* had also been a child star. And Thomas Burke portrayed Tom Thumb at five. His other roles included Richard III, Shylock, and Sir Giles Overreach—in addition to playing violin solos, singing, and conducting the orchestra. Joseph Ireland claimed that "as a prodigy, both in music and the drama, he has been unapproached by any child who has trodden the American stage."[14]

Other stars who started their careers as children included Kate and Ellen Bateman, Mary McVicker, Clara Fisher, Fanny Davenport, Matilda Heron, Lotta Crabtree, Susan Denin (with whom Herne traveled), and Madame Ristori (who made her first entrance at two months in a basket). Joseph Jefferson fought with broadswords on the Park Theatre's stage at the seasoned age of six.

Through the years Herne lost track of his stage children. But many remembered him. "He taught me every gesture, every inflection of the voice, every move I made," said one. "I was taken ill during our first week's engagement in Washington. Mr. Herne could not do enough for me. He used to sit by my bed side, read stories to me, and he never visited me without bringing a big bunch of roses."[15]

The debonair **Herne** during the 1860's. The University of Maine.

Herne as a young man.
The University of Maine.

A family portrait of the Hernes. The University of Maine. 1899.

The Hernes at Herne Oaks. New York Public Library.

Herne Oaks. The University of Maine.

Herne and daughters at Herne Oaks. New York Public Library.

Herne and son John.
Theatre Collection,
Free Library of Philadelphia.

A scene from *The New South*. Herne in background as Sampson. New York Public Library.

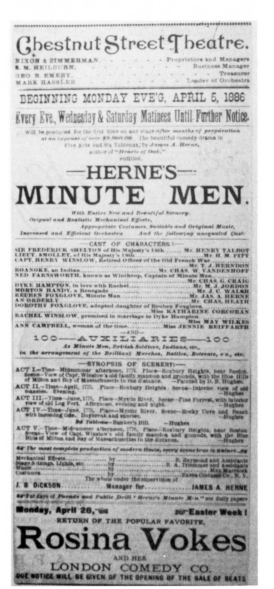

The Minute Men program at Philadelphia's Chestnut Street Theatre.
New York Public Library.

K.C. as Dorothy Foxglove in *The Minute Men*.
The University of Maine.

Walnut St. Theatre

Messrs. AL. HAYMAN, KLAW & ERLANGER, - Directors
MR. FRANK HOWE, JR., - Manager

Week Beginning Monday Evening, October 2, 1899.
Matinee Saturday Only.

LIEBLER & CO. PRESENT

THE ZANGWILL PLAY
"Children of the Ghetto."

AN ORIGINAL HEBREW DRAMA BY MR. ISRAEL ZANGWILL,
Founded on his world-famous novel of the same title, treating of Jewish life and
customs in the Ghetto of London.

STAGED BY MR. JAMES A. HERNE.

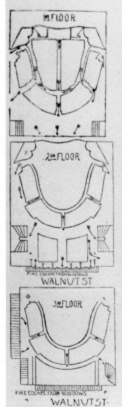

CAST OF CHARACTERS.

"REB" SHEMUEL, the Ghetto Rabbi . . . . WILTON LACKAYE
DAVID BRANDON, a young man from the Cape . . . . FRANK WORTHING
MELCHITSEDEK PINCHAS, a HEBREW POET . . . . . WILLIAM NORRIS
MOSES ANSELL, a pauper alien . . . . ADOLPHE LESTINA
SIMON WOLF, free thinker and labor leader . . . . . JOHN D. GARRICK
GUEDALYAH, the green grocer, a Zionist . . . . GUS FRANKEL
MICHAEL BIRNBAUM . . . . EMIL HOCH
President of a synagogue and married to Malka.
EPHRAIM PHILLIPS . . . . FRANK CORNELL
A business man, married to Malka's daughter, Milly.
SAM LEVINE . . . . FRED LOTTO
A commercial traveller, engaged to Malka's daughter, Leah.
SUGARMAN, the Shadchan, a marriage broker . . . . . CHARLIS STANLEY
SHOSSHI SHMENDRIK, a shy carpenter . . . . RICHARD CARLE
FATHER SOL, oldest inhabitant of the Ghetto . . . . . PHINEAS LEACH
BARNEY AURATO, a millionaire from Australia . . . . . ARTHUR SOMERS
FISHMONGER . . . . A. GHAISTLY
PURSE TRICKSTER . . . . JOHN D. GARRICK
CLOTHES DEALER . . . . O'FREDERICK HOFFMANN
SHOWMAN . . . . GUS V. DEVERE
SCHNORRER (BEGGAR) . . . . WILLIAM SINGERMAN
BOY SALESMAN . . . . MASTER BUCKLEY
THE PIOUS PARTISAN . . . . FRANK BAILEY
CAKE SELLER . . . . H. F. DOLAN
THE BUTCHER . . . . C. E. ODLIN
THE CHAZAN (CANTOR) . . . . L. GREENBURG
B. ROTMAN } THE CHORISTERS . . . . } S. SWARTZ
S. SCHULTZ } . . . . } N. TRUCKS
MRS. BELCOVITCH, an imaginary invalid . . . . . MADAME COTTRELLY
BECKY, her buxom daughter . . . . ADA CURRY
MRS. JACOBS, wife of "Reb" Shemuel . . . . LOUISE MULDENER
MALKA, a business woman and head of her clan . . . . . ADA DWYER
MILLY PHILLIPS } Malka's daughters . . . . . . { LAURA ALMOSNINO
LEAH } { ROSABEL MORRISON
WIDOW FINKLESTEIN, owner of a grocery . . . . . . SADIE STRINGHAM
ESTHER ANSELL, 12 years and very old for her age . MABEL TALIAFFERO
THE SABBATH FIRE WOMAN . . . . ISABEL PRESTON
An Irish woman who tends the Ghetto fires and candles on Friday nights and
Saturdays, it being unlawful for a Jew to touch fire on the Jewish Sabbath.
MRS. MONTMORENCY, a grandchild of the Ghetto . . . . JENNIE BUCKLEY
HER FRIEND, a fashionable visitor to the Ghetto . . ZELLE DAVENPORT
BEGGAR WOMAN . . . . MARY STONER
HANNAH JACOBS, "Reb" Shemuel's daughter . . . . . BLANCHE BATES
Policeman, Beggars, Dancers, Lamplighter, Peddlers, Congregation,
Rioters, Pedestrians, Children, etc., etc.

SYNOPSIS OF SCENES.

The action takes place in the Jewish settlement in East London, a gen-
eration ago, and covers a period of a hundred days.
ACT I—THE LETTER OF THE LAW.
At Milly's, in Zachariah Square.
(On the Feast of Chanukah.)
ACT II—THE SPIRIT OF LOVE.
At the Ball in the People's Club.
(On the Feast of Purim. Seventy-two days later.)
ACT III—THE LETTER AND THE SPIRIT.
At "Reb" Shemuel's Friday evening, on the great Sabbath.

The Zangwill Play program.
Theatre Collection,   Free Library of Philadelphia.

Herne revealed his method for training child actors in *The Arena*. "In the first place I select the child, and then I tell the mother to go home and teach the child the lines, but not to try to teach it to act or to read. Then when it comes to me I mold it a little, but chiefly let it alone. Of course, I teach it where to go and when to speak its lines, but for the rest I let nature take its course for the most part. Children are very easy to handle when you know how to handle them rightly. Another thing: In all my plays, where there are children, they are given real children's parts. We do not have a child speaking the lines of a man of twenty. I have had more experience with children on the stage than any one else. There is no trouble in getting children, and when they are handled properly there is no trouble in making them appear effectively."[16]

Although the baby and the cat and the real mill attracted curiosity seekers, *Chums* closed within two weeks, Belasco later lamenting that receipts were only $17.50 one night. But good fortune favored Baldwin's. Gen. Ulysses S. Grant, the former President, stopped at San Francisco on September 21, 1879, on his return to the United States from a world tour. A celebration followed. He was greeted by a fleet led by the S. S. *State of California,* and 500 singers waited at the docks. Following a reception at the Palace Hotel (owned by Baldwin), a carnival ball was given in Mechanics Pavilion. Fireworks thundered throughout the gala night.

Every theatre in San Francisco tried to exploit Grant's visit. All declared a General Grant week, hoping he'd attend their house of magic. Baldwin's was lucky. Grant saw scenes from *Romeo and Juliet* and Sardou's melodrama, *Diplomacy*. The Baldwin Grand Orchestra also played a grand march in his honor. On September 25, the *San Francisco Chronicle* reported: "The General attended the Baldwin last night and manifested much more interest in the stirring scenes of *Diplomacy* than he usually displays at theatrical entertainments, and was frequently observed to converse quite animatedly with Mrs. Grant during the program of the play. At ten minutes past 11 the Presidential Party took its departure, amidst a perfect storm of cheers."[17]

Baldwin's then announced the revival of *Marriage by Moonlight* for four nights and a matinee honoring Grant. This still didn't satisfy Belasco and Herne, who worried about *Chums'* failure. They finally agreed on a Chicago staging, and Maguire arranged a farewell benefit. "Everybody volunteered; Maguire (the manager of the Baldwin) gave us the use of the theatre; the actors gave their services; the orchestra gave theirs; the newspapers gave the 'ads.'" recalled Belasco. "All that came in was clear gain, and I got a little more than $3,000. That was our working capital."[18]

Benefits were used to reward popular and successful actors, retirees, and guest stars during the nineteenth century. Even employees (chorus leaders, ushers, ticket takers, etc.) sometimes benefited from so-called "Ticket Nights." Receipts were split between them and the manager, not a bad managerial investment, because friends and relatives often packed the house.

Lester Wallack, however, who despised benefits, wrote in his autobiography, "They were degrading, and as I thought begging, appeals from actors and actresses who already received what they conceived as an adequate return for their services, and who had no reason to call upon the public for something extra."[19] He increased wages at Wallack's Theatre to discourage the practice, and other managers followed suit. Benefits soon disappeared in the American theatre.

Belasco's benefit, however, didn't help much. The company played Salt Lake City and other towns but disbanded before reaching Chicago, even their scenery having been confiscated. Neither J. H. McVicker nor R. M. Hooley, the two most important Chicago managers, would stage *Chums*.

"We were in a dreadful way," said Belasco, in telling William Winter this story: "We had gone to the old Sherman House and taken the smallest, cheapest rooms we could get, and Alvin Hurlbert, the proprietor, had let our bills run. But at last they had run so long we had to make an explanation,—and I did the explaining. It wasn't an easy thing to do,—though I'd done it before, in the early, wild days in the West. But Hurlbert was very kind: "I believe in you, my boy,' he said, 'and it's all right,'—so we had a little more time to hustle in. And we *hustled!*"[20]

Belasco and Herne now renamed *Chums, Hearts of Oak* (the name of the sailors' chorus line in *The Mariner's Compass*). Then they scoured Chicago and finally found a beer garden called the

Coliseum, owned by John Hamlin. Business was bad. So Hamlin agreed to staging *Hearts of Oak* on one condition: he'd provide the theatre, and they would provide everything else. This deal sounded pretty good. "We got credit in one place or another," said Belasco, "and did it,—a production costing thousands, on credit, and without a dollar of our own in it. We had a big success, although Hamlin's Coliseum wasn't much of a place."[21]

Herne agreed. "It was in horrible shape," he said. "There was not a whole gas globe in the place. The theatre was very dirty, and Hamlin had a queer orchestra,—one that you would have supposed would have emptied any theatre."[22]

Things soon changed. New globes were installed over the lamps, palms and other plants beautified the lobby, and Herne perfumed the place. Then he hired a reputable orchestra. Hamlin also helped. He knew a physician with local influence who brought friends. Meanwhile, Herne drove around town handing out tickets. When people saw carriages lining the street near Hamlin's in mid-November they grew curious, and more tickets started selling.

Hearts of Oak opened at Hamlin's Theatre on November 17, 1879, promoted as "Herne's and Belasco's American Play, in Five Acts and Six Tableaux."[23] Reviews were mixed. The *Chicago Tribune* called the play "one of the best and strongest productions that the theatregoers of Chicago have ever been given a chance to witness."[24] But one wonders.

Belasco and Herne then took *Hearts of Oak* on a brief tour, returning to Chicago in March 1880. But instead of reviving the play at Hamlin's they chose Hooley's Theatre. This infuriated Hamlin, who staged his own version. Belasco and Herne sued him, but since *The Mariner's Compass* was unprotected in America, the judge concluded that Hamlin could present the play whenever he wanted, providing he didn't use the title *Hearts of Oak*. Hamlin fumed over the loss of the title but eventually received a lucrative return from the play, profits that helped him build the Grand Opera House in Chicago.

Herne apparently didn't know that any part of *Hearts of Oak* was pirated originally. "Now I've got a damned lawsuit on my hands," he stormed at Belasco.

"I don't see why I should have told you anything about the

old play," snapped Belasco. "And, anyway, I don't see what you
have to complain about. You ought to be mighty glad you've got
a half-interest in something worth a lawsuit to protect—and you
haven't got the suit on *your* hands anymore than I have on
mine."[25]

After *Hearts of Oak* became a big success, Herne brought
suit against another company that produced a version called
Oaken Hearts. Its star, Frederick Ward, told the story in his
autobiography:

> Mr. James A. Herne had made an adaptation of an old
> English play, 'The Mariner's Compass,' and called it 'Hearts
> of Oak,' playing it with considerable success in the eastern
> cities.
>
> Mr. David Dalzell, who was the husband of Miss Dickie
> Lingard, prepared another version of the same play and
> called it 'Oaken Hearts.'
>
> I was engaged to play the leading part, Mack Dawson.
> We opened at Pope's Theatre, St. Louis, early in May. Dur-
> ing the week Mr. Herne, through his manager, Mr. Bert,
> sought an injunction restraining our production of the play.
> Miss Lingard, Mr. Dalzell, Mr. Frank Pierce and myself
> were summoned as witnesses in the case. It was practically
> proved at the first hearing that 'The Mariner's Compass'
> under existing laws, was common property in this country,
> but the case was adjourned to the following week for a fur-
> ther hearing. The witnesses were ordered by the court to
> appear at the adjournment, but were privately told by the
> attorneys that there would probably be no further proceed-
> ings; so upon the conclusion of our engagement in St. Louis,
> the company went to Chicago and opened at Hooley's
> Theatre.
>
> During the week Frank Pierce and I were arrested by
> a United States marshal and taken back to St. Louis to
> answer to a charge of contempt of court.
>
> The marshal was a good natured fellow and did not
> submit us to any indignity, but it was a very embarrassing
> position; however, on appearing before the judge the follow-
> ing morning, we explained the circumstances, apologized for
> any disrespect, and were released.
>
> No further legal proceedings were taken, the play not
> proving worth an expensive legal battle. 'Hearts of Oak'
> continued a success for Mr. Herne, but 'Oaken Hearts'
> ceased as a dramatic attraction.[26]

Belasco and Herne played *Hearts of Oak* almost everywhere,

but until the Fifth Avenue Theatre made an offer New York had turned its back. Belasco's and Herne's excitement was short-lived because the critics crushed their brainchild, advertised as a "powerful, realistic home drama." The *Times* called it "a dull, long-winded, ultra-sentimental drama of a kind long deceased, and, we had hoped, not liable to resurrection."[27] The *Tribune* cushioned its blow, but agreed that the work was lacklustre. Critic William Winter (who would later write Belasco's two-volume biography) condemned the real water, boiled potatoes, baby, fishing folk, and idiomatic language. He also called Herne a "phlegmatic and monotonous actor, neither brilliant in quality nor fire in touch."[28]

One newspaper did defend the troupe. The *Spirit of the Times* explained that the cast had arrived in New York exhausted and that rehearsals weren't possible because the theatre had booked a concert. The Belasco-Herne company mounted the set, rehearsed, and familiarized themselves with the theatre's environment overnight. Then the paper launched a few barbed criticisms against Herne: "It is called James A. Herne's *Hearts of Oak*. The dialogue, situations, new scenes, and characters are the work of James A. Herne. It was produced successfully in California by James A. Herne. It has been played to crowded houses by James A. Herne's company. The hero is James A. Herne. Under these circumstances, one must suppose that James A. Herne is either more or less than mortal if he ever, except upon compulsion, permits the drama to be condensed to reasonable length."[29]

At the public's expense, *Hearts of Oak* gradually improved through performance. Its ultimate success, of course, was probably due to the realistic scenic effects and baby. As one writer observed: "No woman can hear of a real baby on the stage that does all the familiar baby-business—coos, crows, jumps, plays 'bo-peep,' pulls hair, sucks its fists, plays with its feet, reaches for everything, makes friends with everybody."[30]

Could Belasco and Herne be regarded as theatre magicians? Regarding one bit of baby business Belasco said: "I bought a bottle of oil of peppermint, and told Mrs. Herne, who played the mother of the child, to dip a piece of cloth in the peppermint and rub the baby's gums with it several times. Then, just before she went on the stage and held up a big stick of candy the child naturally, with the taste still in his mouth, thought it was more peppermint, reached for the candy and became all animated at once."[31]

Hearts of Oak offered the public something new beyond the usual trappings of asides, contrived situations, and bathos. It lacked a "real" villain. It also lacked a conventional hero. This placed it several notches above the typical American melodrama. Herne was caught between two forces: the old popular school of Boucicault and his growing conviction that drama should truthfully mirror the lifestyle of common people. But Gilded Age audiences loved gilded gibberish. They loved romance. They loved oratory. They loved pasteboard plays that didn't make intellectual demands. Herne later wrote: "Seriously, melodrama is valueless to the progress of dramatic art. Seen under the analytical microscope, it is false to almost every aspect and color of life, and eternally comic to the judicious, in its absurdities of perspective and proportion, its grotesqueries of calcium and characterization. Like crimps and crinoline, or the difficult stock tie of our periwig-pated grand parents, the melodrama has outlived its day of usefulness."[32]

Although Herne didn't restructure *The Mariner's Compass*, he made alterations, searching for a sense of quiet realism. Arthur Hobson Quinn, who was familiar with both plays, said in his *History of the American Drama* that Herne eliminated a comic subplot and toned down the melodramatic elements such as the scene in which the heroine throws her wedding ring into the sea. He also added Owen Garroway, a sailor suggested by Dickens' Dan Peggotty, and the homelike supper and real baby. Concerning the original ending of *The Mariner's Compass,* Quinn wrote: "The violent reactions of Silas when he returns to find his wife just married to Ruby, the attempted suicide of Hetty in the mill race, her rescue from the mill wheel by Ruby, who dies in the act, and the final picture of the returned husband clasping his dripping wife in his arms, are replaced by two scenes, quiet in action and touching in their human appeal."[33]

Unlike other nineteenth century melodramas, Herne inserted some low-key, colloquial dialogue in *Hearts of Oak*. Take the following scene, between little Chrystal and the blind Terry in the graveyard, that creates tension and subtlety of character with its simple, economical use of words:

> *Little Chrystal.* (*A pitying look crossing her face.*) Oh! I know, you're an orphan, ain't you?
> *Terry.* (*Holding out his hand.*) Come here—little one—take my hand—(*She draws a little away.*) Don't be frightened. I won't harm you, my child. (*She gains courage and slowly crosses to him.*) I'm very fond of little children—come—take my hand, won't you? (*She draws closer and closer and finally takes his hand.*)
> *Little Chrystal.* There, I've got it. (*laughs*) I ain't a bit afraid now. Come! (*She tries to pull him to his feet*).
> *Terry.* (*Rising*). Where?
> *Little Chrystal.* Just a little ways—over by my flowers.
> *Terry.* (*Moving with her towards the monument.*) Have you been picking flowers?
> *Little Chrystal.* Yes.
> *Terry.* Will you give me some?
> *Little Chrystal.* Yes. (*As they get to the monument.*) Now sit down![34]

Today, such dialogue doesn't shatter conventions. But Herne wasn't writing today. It was 1879—a long time ago—even before Ibsenism grappled with the threadbare traditions of the American stage. In 1899 Herne frankly admitted about *Hearts of Oak*: "It was as true as I knew how to make it when I wrote it, and it was expressed in as good art form as I then knew. Of course, I see now that it was crude and often silly."[35]

Before *Hearts of Oak* had become famous, Belasco and Herne split, after a very bitter quarrel. The cause still is not clearly known. William Winter is the main source of information, but he hated Herne and all realists. So his credibility remains questionable, especially after his abusive assault on Herne in his 1918 biography of Belasco: "As a playwright he (Herne) was deficient in the faculty of invention and in the originality of characterization.... (He) localized his plays in America and, to a certain extent, treated American subjects, but he made no addition to American Drama, and his treatment of the material that he 'borrowed' or adapted never rose above respectable mediocrity."[36] (More about Winter and his war against realism in Chapter 12.)

What is known of the quarrel is quite sketchy. When *Hearts of Oak*'s novelty started wearing, Mrs. John Drew, (Louisa Lane), manager of the Arch Street Theatre in Philadelphia, contracted for the play. Belasco and Herne argued. Accusations and counter-accusations followed. Herne offered to buy Belasco's share for $1500, or vice versa, knowing, Belasco told Winter, "that I had not drawn any of my share of the profits, while there were any; that I had been living and keeping my family, in San Francisco, on $50 a week (I was allowed that and talked to all the time about 'the barrels of money 'Dave' would have at the end of the season'!), and also knowing that I didn't have fifteen hundred cents!"[37]

Belasco supposedly agreed to sell his share for $1500, Herne giving him a promissory note that wasn't paid for years. Meanwhile, the play hit the jackpot, earning Herne more than $100,000, while the broken Belasco returned to Maguire's where he played bit parts for $25 a week.

Belasco's later biographer, Craig Timberlake, wrote that "in his 'Life Story' Belasco set forth his version of the affair, which was later expanded by the devoted William Winter. Both accounts appeared many years after Herne's death and Herne's wife did not see fit to defend her husband against Winter's unflattering estimate of his abilities and alleged behavior on the occasion. She may have concluded justly that Herne's subsequent efforts as a playwright and actor, and the high regard in which he had been held by such prominent literary figures as William Dean Howells and Hamlin Garland, obviated the necessity of any statement in his behalf."[38]

Julie Herne said that by the late 1870's, Herne had acquired a firm reputation on the West Coast. Even Winter admitted he was "well established in popular favor,"[39] which meant Herne wielded some influence with Maguire and other area theatricalists. Belasco, on the other hand, was a mediocre actor who served as prompter and assistant and was known better for his flair for scenic effects.

Julie said "Dave" often ate supper with the Hernes, sometimes staying far into the night—as did Hamlin Garland. (The fourteen-year age difference between Belasco and Herne deserves thought. Herne was very quiet, Belasco the opposite.) The sympathetic K.C. asked Herne to read Belasco's plays and make suggestions. A series of collaborations followed, although Herne disliked Belasco's carpentership, leading him to provide the frameworks and backstage knowhow.

Then came *Hearts of Oak*, which still carried Herne's trademarks. *Within an Inch of His Life* and *Marriage by Moonlight*, both romantic melodramas, lack the simple rhythms of *Hearts of Oak* with its humble seafolks. Such a thread doesn't exist either in Belasco's numerous later works, including *Madame Butterfly*, *The Rose of the Rancho*, and *The Return of Peter Grimm*. In *Hearts of Oak* Herne contributed the second-act supper scene, the character Owen Garroway—which he later played—and the last-act Terry Dennison scene. Belasco told Winter that Herne "introduced *a lot of good work* on it . . . a lot of *Rip Van Winkle* stuff."[40] Winter embellished this statement, saying "the play was a patchwork of hackneyed situations and incidents, culled and refurbished from such earlier plays as 'Little Em'ly,' 'Rip Van Winkle,' 'Leah the Forsaken,' and 'Enoch Arden.' "[41] This was probably true—although Herne added a new tone: simplicity.

Several other confusions exist regarding the Belasco-Herne history of *Hearts of Oak*:

Julie Herne said Belasco and Herne made $800 in Salt Lake City and weren't broke when they hit Chicago. Did Belasco confuse figures?

Six months after Belasco sued Herne, he produced *May Blossom* (1884) at the Madison Square Theatre in New York. Although an adaptation of (Elizabeth Cleghorn) Gaskell's *Sylvia's Lovers*, it looked a lot like *Hearts of Oak*. Even the star, Georgia Cayvan, told K.C., "I feel as though we were sisters, for we are both playing the same part."[42]

Herne did appoint Belasco as director at the Arch Street Theatre production of *Hearts of Oak*. The program's bottom line clearly read, "the whole under the direction of Mr. David Belasco, late stage manager of the 'Baldwin Theatre' "[43] Herne may have been making amends for removing Belasco's name from the New York program, but it is not known why his name was removed in the first place.

One thing is definitely known. Herne's *Hearts of Oak* succeeded throughout America advertised as "a play for the millions; replete with thrilling and exciting scenes and situations: a beautifully, interesting, simple story, simply told; no villainy, no adultery, no morbid sentiment, no jarring word; and organization complete in every detail; a wholesome play, superbly mounted and magnificently acted."[44] Reviewers seemed to agree.

Daily Memphis Avalanche: "It is remarkable that the minor parts in the play afford most attraction to the audience. Owen Garroway, for instance, is a secondary factor in the plot, but as personated by James A. Herne, he is decidedly the best and most thorough characterization." This critic also called the baby "the only six month's infant on earth who can wipe her own nose," and concluded "The cat also 'caught on' from its first appearance. It did the walking business in a first-class feline manner."[45]

Pittsburgh Post: "It has been many a day since a piece has been put on the stage here as well as this one. The storm scene at sea when the vessel is saved, the real rain, the mill interior and the last scene were excellent. It is rare indeed that a travelling company mounts its plays as this is, and it is most commendable."[46]

St. Paul Daily Globe: "The mounting of the piece is the finest ever seen upon the St. Paul stage,"[47] and the *St. Louis Globe Democrat* called it an "absolute revelation."[48]

Life wasn't all glitter and gold for Herne. Scenery ripped. Special effects failed. Trains arrived late. Blizzards and rain made travel hazardous. And audiences always were unpredictable. One time Herne was still hoisting scenery into the opera house at curtain time. He gave the audience an option: either wait or attend a matinee the following Tuesday. The audience chose to wait with a few catcalls, the show starting at 9:30. When the scenery collapsed after the first act, some playgoers decided to return the next evening.

Theatre made a hard taskmaster. Perhaps Junius Brutus Booth, Jr., expressed it best to young Mary Anderson: "So you still like to fret and strut upon the boards? Wait till the novelty wears off! I would rather plough all day than act half the night."[49]

6 the
dramatic junoration
of the age

ERNE FINISHED A new play called *The Minute Men of 1774–75* while touring with *Hearts of Oak*. It was his first solo creative effort. He wondered where to send the script, whether managers would consider the play's message too radical, and whether their theatres' technical equipment was equal to the demands of the script. After considering dozens of playhouses he sent the script to the Chestnut Street Theatre in Philadelphia, which accepted it.

The Chestnut Street Theatre, with its long, respectable heritage, reaching back to 1794, wasn't an "unworthy scaffold" for any dramatist. Called "incomparably the finest home of the drama in America,"[1] it was competently managed by Thomas Wignell and Alexander Reinagle. By 1886, it still remained a first-class showplace.

Herne cast K.C. as Dorothy Foxglove, the adopted daughter of Reuben Foxglove in this Revolutionary War melodrama—it was her favorite role, next to *Margaret Fleming*. While Herne toured she studied lines, writing him: "Now, if the play only makes a hit, your reputation as a dramatist will be firmly set, and a thousand-fold stronger. How I glory in it!... I am practicing my voice every morning and altogether I am doing nicely. I seem to get stronger every day."[2]

Harry M. Pitt appeared in *The Minute Men* as Lieutenant Smollet of the 18th Grenadiers. Ten years later Herne wrote in *The Dramatic Mirror*: "I wrote *The Minute Men* to fit H. M. Pitt. I had never seen him act but I got people to tell me about his methods and the way he played certain parts. If Mr. Pitt had

walked into a tailor's shop and walked out again with a perfectly
fitting suit of clothes, the analogy between the clothes and the
part I wrote for him couldn't have been closer."[3]

Pitt also played Percy Seward in *Drifting Apart* and then
portrayed the Earl of Dorincourt in *Little Lord Fauntleroy,* and
the lead in Pinero's *Sweet Lavender*. But his career faltered.
Years later Herne found him in Buffalo, a local stock company
actor, trying for a comeback. He died shortly afterwards—another tragic theatre life.

Although *The Minute Men* was scheduled to open on April
5, 1886, production snags postponed its premiere until the next
day.[4] The critics seemed pleased with the performance. The
Philadelphia Inquirer noted that it "won vociferous applause"
but suggested "a judicious pruning that will take out about half
an hour of dialogue."[5] The *Public Ledger* praised its six tableaux, reporting that after the Bunker Hill depiction both the
scene designer and Herne appeared out front. Herne spoke
briefly, asking:

"Is our piece a success?"

The audience responded: "Yes, yes."[6]

Everyone concluded that *The Minute Men* would enjoy a
long stay in the City of Brotherly Love. But the conclusion was
wrong.

This was Herne's pivotal play. Even with its claptrap plot,
flat characters, and cornball theme, *The Minute Men* "was one
of the pioneers in the field of American historical dramatic literature."[7] This realistic thread in Herne's work later extended
through *Drifting Apart, Margaret Fleming, Shore Acres, Griffith Davenport,* and *Sag Harbor*. His earlier "San Francisco"
scripts were either collaborations with David Belasco, or adaptations of novels and plays, written by others.

The many crosscurrents of nineteenth century American
romanticism influenced *The Minute Men,* especially from the
works of James Fenimore Cooper, a boyhood reading favorite.
The suggestion of other sources also glimmered through its
pages: George Eliot's *Silas Marner* (one speech is almost completely lifted from the novel), Richard Doddridge Blackmore's
Lorna Doone, Dickens' sense of caricature, and the numerous
American frontier Indian dramas.

Other literary influences on *The Minute Men* are guesswork. Herne could have read or discussed Henry Wadsworth Longfellow's *The Song of Hiawatha*, Washington Irving's *Sketch Book* and *A Tour of the Prairies*, Henry Thoreau's *Walden*, Charles Brockton Brown's early *Edgar Huntley, or Memoirs of a Sleep Walker*, and stacks of cheap novels and folk stories besides exposure to a rich oral tradition. Two sources, however, appear definite: James Fenimore Cooper's *Leatherstocking Tales* and the Indian dramas whose American popularity peaked during the 1840's.

James Fenimore Cooper was America's leading nineteenth century romantic writer. He popularized the mythical noble Indian savage and the raging battle between nature and civilization in his novels; but he gathered information on Indian culture secondhand. He admitted to one friend, "You have the advantage of me, for I never was among the Indians. All that I know of them is from reading and hearing my father speak of them."[8] Cooper's chief source was the definitive book on American Indians, Rev. John Heckewelder's *An Account of the History, Manners, and Customs of the Indian Nations Who once Inhabited Pennsylvania and the Neighboring States* (1819). This Moravian missionary lived among the Delaware and Mohegan Indians and immortalized them on paper.

Cooper paradoxically believed that Indians were inferior to white Christians. Most *Last of the Mohicans* fans overlook the cruelty of Magua, while romanticizing the epic nature of Chingachgook and Uncas. They also neglect reading Cooper's later novels, which portrayed Indians as uncivilized barbarians. Cooper even wrote in the preface to the 1850 edition of *Leatherstocking Tales*: "It is the privilege of all writers of fiction, more particularly when their works aspire to the elevation of romances, to present the *beau-ideal* of their characters to the reader. This it is which constitutes poetry, and to suppose that the red-man is to be represented only in the squalid misery or in the degraded moral state that certainly more or less belongs to his conditions, is, we apprehend, taking a very narrow view of an author's privileges."[9]

Cooper's featherweight characters were "clothes on sticks"[10] as James Russell Lowell expressed it. They were cardboard types who voiced typified sentiments. His white males were genteel snobs, his women paste, his Indians wooden. Mark Twain growled that *"The Deerslayer* is simply a literary *delerium tremens,"* adding that "its conversations are—oh! indescribable; its love scenes odious; its English a crime against the language."[11] Lowell poeticized in *A Fable for Critics,* "His Indians, with proper respect be it said/Are just Natty Bumpo daubed over with red," and his women "all sappy as maples and flat as a prairie."[12] Even Francis Parkman, author of *The Oregon Trail,* complained that Cooper's Indians were "for the most part either superficially or falsely drawn; while the long conversations which he puts into their mouths are as truthless as they are tiresome."[13]

Influenced by Cooper's *Leatherstocking Tales* when he wrote *The Minute Men,* Herne introduced new, unconventional ideas that audiences questioned.

James L. Ford wrote that A. M. Palmer "inaugurated the modern American drama"[14] with two plays, *The Banker's Daughter* (1871) by Bronson Howard and *My Partner* (1879) by Bartley Campbell. He added that before this, American dramatists existed to satisfy the whims of stars and money-grubbing managers. In 1879 an outraged *Atlantic Monthly* critic charged that American drama "is of no-country and no time," but admitted, "You must please the public, to be successful."[15]

This situation posed a dilemma for Herne throughout his career. Even Pierre Corneille had warned, "The sole end of the drama is to please the audience," and the venerable Dr. Samuel Johnson had added with his pithy poem, "The drama's laws the drama's patrons give and we that live to please must please to live."

Herne attempted to solve this artistic problem by giving his audience what it wanted—almost.

The Minute Men's major concession was in plot. It carried many of Cooper's literary genes: breath-taking escapes, last-minute rescues, savage villainies, poetic justice, and pale-faced colonists, all sketched against a wide panorama of early America's struggle for independence.

The plot was essentially a patriotic tale of Dorothy Foxglove, lost daughter of a British commander, raised by Reuben

Foxglove. (Her locket, of course, reveals Dorothy's identity.) Stitched between raging battles, tableaux, and intrigues is her romance with Roanoke the Indian, who is also the misplaced son of a colonial officer.

Imagine the following action sequence from the Indian attack in this thriller. The set showed both an exterior and interior view of the besieged cabin to heighten audience involvement:

> (*Twelve Indians appear bearing large pine trunk as a ram—it is very heavy. Two others creep around from behind house placing brush, etc. When the ram is near enough, the men swing it backwards and forwards several times to give it an impetus*) Fire! (*Six Indians fall. The balance drop the ram and disappear. Four are killed of the six who fall, the other two regain their feet and stagger off badly wounded*) Good boys—load! Here, Dorothy—(*Gives her gun. Places eye to loop*) Give me a gun! Quick! (*She gives him Soldier's gun. At that instant an Indian darts out from L. with pine knot lighted. Reuben fires. The Indian falls*) Another gun! Quick! (*Before they can get it to him, another Indian rushes on, snatches torch from dead one and fires the house. A tremendous yell and the Indians swarm around the fire*) They have fired the fort! We're lost! (*All stand aghast*)[16]

Is this the dreadful end of the colonists? Guess again. Everyone escapes through an underground tunnel while the incoming tide relentlessly fills the passage. Meanwhile, the Indians sharpen their tomahawks outside the fort. Inside, the gunpowder's lit. A terrific blast. Smoke. The cabin collapses. Indians scream. Confusion. More screams. A quick curtain.

The settings for *The Minute Men* are Dorchester Heights and its general environs during the Revolutionary War's prologue. (Cooper's time location was the earlier French and Indian Wars.) The Battles of Bunker Hill, Lexington, and Concord become tableaux. Even George Washington sits majestically upon his steed in the last glorious scene.

The tableau was a fascinating nineteenth century theatre convention, lately revived in films with a new label—frozen action. At the conclusion of choice scenes, cast members and extras assumed statuesque poses copied from famous paintings. Herne used "plates" of John Trumbull's painting of Bunker Hill for his depiction of that historic battle. The tableau also served another practical purpose: because of space problems, stage-houses couldn't mount titanic clashes without spending much time and money. Even then, most battles failed because they lacked that "sense of detached reality" that modern films offer.

Victorian "parlor entertainments" also used the tableau. So did New York's "free and easies" in Bowery cellars. Then during the 1890's, "Living Pictures" became the rage: reproductions of famous paintings and sculptures of the human torso posed in "flesh colored" tights. As Henry Collins Brown writes in *The Golden Nineties*: "Some of the pictures were very like the originals, others required imagination. 'Paul and Virginia' flying from the storm were quite good if they were not kept too long standing each on one leg. The 'Dying Gladiator' was often the victim of a conqueror who lacked biceps, and there were other lapses from strict realism observable to the captious."[17]

Herne was extraordinarily faithful to strict realism. He even designed costumes from plates for period authenticity, and experimented with subtle lighting effects. Act I in *The Minute Men* begins shortly after a thunderstorm, and the stage directions specify that lighting "must have that grand effect the sun gives shining through a peculiar sky after a rain, rendering one portion of the scene nearly dark, the other lighted by a peculiar but very effective brightness. . . . During the Act the sun sets and twilight appears—the sky and entire scene must change with the setting sun."[18] The fourth act opens at sunrise, and Herne used a subtle interplay of colors for atmosphere, indicating it "must be very fine or not done at all."[19] He insisted that scenery, lighting, and costumes all be "true to history."[20]

This became the famous Herne credo: art for truth's sake in the drama.

Such technical trend-setting ideas placed Herne in the forefront of late nineteenth century stage reformers. Only a handful of directors, such as Steele MacKaye, David Belasco, and William Gillette—Herne's friend—bothered to study light mood values. Belasco even designed a miniature theatre with tiny bulbs that worked electrically and held filters.

Both the weakest and strongest points of *The Minute Men* were its characterizations.

The play's male figures unfortunately are rather two-dimensional. Dyke Hampton, "a dark, sinister man about forty-five years," was a villain whose evil cunning matched Magua's in *The Last of the Mohicans.* He's the only "true villain" Herne ever created. Hampton, however, offers one redeeming quality, a madness for the pristine-pure, pulchritudinous Rachel Winslow (daughter of Captain Henry Winslow) who loves her hero, Ned Farnsworth. When Hampton is finally captured he confesses: "Only this—I love your daughter. To force her to my arms I did it all. No punishment you can inflict will equal the torture of losing her."[21] True love—if somewhat twisted.

The starched officers (both colonial and British) were all pressed from the same mold. Lieutenant Smollet of the 18th Grenadiers, however, seems likable, even though he's British. But the hero, Ned Farnsworth, is a rubber stamp hero. Consider the following confrontation with Dyke Hampton that made audiences chew their nails and hug their seats in 1886:

> *Ned.* (*Springing through door*) You lie, you hound—you lie!
> *Rachel.* (*Rushing to him*). Ned!
> *Captain and Dyke.* (*Astonished*). Ned?
> *Ned.* Yes! Ned Farnsworth! (*Dyke staggers back, thunderstruck*) Do you know me now, you craven cur? The boy your coward hand struck to the earth—from whom has sprung the avenging man to pay you back ten-fold the blow you gave, and who will not rest till your foul carcass swings from the gallows tree![22]

Such dialogue is as flat and lifeless as the characters who mouthed it. Dyke Hampton, of course, escapes. The chase continues throughout the melodrama, until Ned's soldiers finally nab him. Then, a happy ending.

The most intriguing male character in *The Minute Men* is Roanoke the Indian. Herne's decision to exhume the dramatic relic of the savage and noble Indian, thirty years after its popularity had paled, prompts a question. Why? This native type had long since been discarded. Henry Nash Smith says: "The theme of communion with nature in the West proved too flimsy to sustain a primitivisitic literature of any magnitude. The spiritual meaning which a former generation had believed it found in nature became more and more inaccessible after the middle of the century. The static ideas of virtue and happiness and peace drawn from the bosom of the virgin wilderness ... proved quite irrelevant for a society committed to the ideas of civilization and progress, and to an industrial revolution."[23]

Maj. Robert Rogers (of Rogers' Rangers fame) wrote the earliest American Indian play, *Ponteach*, staged in London after its author's demise. A rash of Indian melodramas followed, from James Nelson Barker's Pocahontas play *The Indian Princess; or, La Belle Sauvage* (1808) to George Washington Parke Custis' version of the romantic legend, *The Indian Prophecy* (1827). The most famous of all Indian dramas was John Augustus Stone's *Metamora; or, The Last of the Wampanoags* (1829), which starred the great Edwin Forrest. The inimitable John Brougham eventually burlesqued this in 1847 with *Metamora; or, The Last of the Pollywogs*. Serious dramatists finally abandoned the Indian tradition, James Rees remarking in 1846 that they "had of late become a perfect nuisance."[24]

A word about tandem titles may be in order. A rash of these spread across American stages during the early nineteenth century. Maybe dramatists thought two titles would lure twice the audience, especially if the second one were intriguing enough. A few examples should suffice as illustration: *She Would Be a Soldier; or, The Plains of Chippewa* (1819); *Adeline; or, The Victim of Seduction* (1822); *The Benevolent Lawyers; or, Villainy Detected* (1823); *The Widow's Son; or, Which is the Traitor?* (1825); *Tancred; or, The Siege of Antioch* (1827); *The Gentlemen of Lyons; or, The Marriage Contract* (1838); and *Moll Pitcher; or, The Fortune Teller of Lynn* (1855).

Herne realized that the Indian figure still exuded a sense of nobility and grandeur, and that this provided a structural means of blending past and present. The character of Roanoke also made the perfect solution to love's laments: Roanoke was really a white man, a lost white man raised by noble savages who taught him the transcendent purity of nature. Yet, he remained genteel—under the skin, an inversion of Cooper's "tried-and-true" method of revealing the Indian girl as upper-crust, to please readers.

Roanoke represented ideal young Indian manhood: "a tall, handsome young Indian, of 25 years or so, face as light as a man heavily tanned and sunburned. He must be strong as an

arrow and lithe as a willow. He is fully and picturesquely cos-
tumed (see plate), carries a rifle and game."[25] The perfect
Cooperesque Indian brave.

More relevant to Herne's dramatic growth were two
minor figures in *The Minute Men*: Ann Campbell and Reuben
Foxglove, both early portraits of Herne's Yankee characters
that later brought him fame and fortune in *Shore Acres*. Their
homespun humor, provincial views, and Down-East drawls appealed to audiences. Take Reuben's endless puns that Herne
lifted from public places and beer halls:

"Roanoke, you've begun the week well, as the feller said
who was to be hanged on a Monday."[26]

"Roanoke—there's a good deal o' man in yeou—as Jonah
said to the whale's belly."[27]

"It's more blessed to give than to receive, as the mate
said when he flogged the cabin boy."[28]

Herne's most important social contribution to American
dramaturgy in *The Minute Men* was his radical feminist idea
mirrored in Dorothy Foxglove, a feminist image later rekindled
in his mature work, *Margaret Fleming*. Unlike Cooper's pallid
heroines, Dorothy is a product of early American pioneer stock,
neither the genteel type nor conventional Victorian clinging
vine. She values the work ethic, spirited nationalism, and family
life, even though her roots are English. The stage directions call
her "the quintessence of roguish and witching comedy."[29]
Herne later dubbed her "a glorious character."[30]

Attractive, self reliant, and resourceful—all described the
character of this nineteen-year-old heroine. These were objectionable qualities in an age when women were expected to slave
over a steaming stove, care for their babies, and mind their men.
It was an age when even the "shadow of flirtation"[31] violated
social etiquette, and chaperones glued themselves to young ladies, "especially to theater parties."[32] English novelist Anthony
Trollope voiced the age's temper regarding womanhood when he
preached, "The best right a woman has is the right to a husband, and that is the right to which I would recommend every
young woman...to turn her best attention."[33]

In *The Minute Men,* Dorothy wants a husband, but she's
no paper doll. When Lieutenant Smollet tries to arrest her and

Reuben, she grabs his gun saying, "If you attempt to move but as I dictate, I'll send a bullet through your brain."[34] Hardly proper talk from a proper Victorian miss. Dorothy also handles weapons with expertise, gallops through hostile lines to warn the colonists, and rallies the soldiers at Lexington Common (through Herne's liberal use of literary license). And she expresses opinions. Her remark that liberty is "cheaply purchased by the best blood of our country"[35] is strong stuff, a far cry from the usual saccharine verbiage of nineteenth century damsels, which eventually helped strangle the lifelines of romantic literature. To top it off she marries Roanoke the Indian, quite the social taboo.

This innovation, however, audiences opposed. It contributed to the play's failure, and in a later version Herne married Dorothy to Captain Smollet, the British officer. Audiences liked the revised ending.

K.C.'s portrayal of Dorothy Foxglove demanded much. She not only had to satisfy the audience's thirst for simple, identifiable types but had to treat the script's intentions honestly—which meant presenting a red-blooded feminist. The reviewer of the *Philadelphia Inquirer* admitted she had a "varied and difficult part to fill and she fills it with admirable fidelity to nature."[36] Forty years and several thousand American plays later, Arthur Hobson Quinn reaffirmed this in *A History of the American Drama*: "Whenever Dorothy Foxglove enters there seems to be blown into the action a breath of inspiration."[37]

Following its brief Philadelphia run, Herne took *The Minute Men* to Miner's People's Theatre on New York's Bowery—that crowded, continuous tenement of 300,000 souls, mostly immigrants, striving for a new life. This mile-long strand once ran through Peter Stuyvesant's property. At night the Bowery became "the most brilliantly lighted thoroughfare on this planet," with its saloons, stores, rum-shops, eateries, dime-museums—and vice, a "great electric lantern"[38] illuminating humanity's melting pot: shop-girls, newsboys, sailors, street walkers, tramps, and criminals. And what infamous resorts! Owney Geoghegan's "free-and-easy," with its raw whiskey and roughneck rogues, next door to the Windsor Palace. Down the street,

pianist Will H. Fox once played with boxing gloves at Com-
bossy's Crystal Palace. An opium den lurked in the cellar of
Paddy Martin's saloon. By 1898 the New York police recorded
ninety-eight amusement places on the Bowery, calling fourteen
respectable.[39] The old song made sense: "The Bowery, the
Bowery!/They say such things and they do strange things/On
the Bowery, the Bowery!/I'll never go there any more!"

But the Bowery also housed the old Bowery Theatre (renamed the Thalia in 1879) that burned down six times. This
great classical edifice helped reshape the face of American theatre during the 1830's when manager Thomas S. Hamblin decided to democratize the institution and offer "native talent" instead of British imports. Hamblin changed the building's name
to the American Theatre, Bowery, reopening it in 1831 with William Dunlap's *The Glory of Columbia*. The following month he
received an "American Eagle" to mount on his pediment.

Hamblin found melodrama both sensible and profitable.
There were far fewer aristocrats than common people, and the
general public preferred extravagant action and sets. The cost
of stars could be reduced because melodrama could run longer.
(This also made it financially feasible to construct new sets for
new plays, instead of relying on worn stock drops and wing
pieces.) Hamblin also dropped the traditional afterpiece, reasoning that it was anti-climactic.

Hamblin's idea worked. *Mazeppa; or, The Wild Horse of
Ukraine*, ran forty-three consecutive performances in 1833, an
unbelievable achievement. His system encouraged another reform: the elimination of "scene stealing." Plays with long runs
enabled actors to develop ensemble methods, thus improving the
performances as a whole.

The Miner engagement wasn't Herne's first skirmish at the
Bowery. He had played a benefit at the Bowery Theatre in
1871 with Lucille Western. The theatre's conditions then were
startling. Alvin F. Harlow quotes a playgoer's impressions during the 1870's:

> The house was a study more interesting than the stage. We
> idled about behind the seats of the balcony, with audible
> steps among thick-strewn peanut-shells. In the front lobby
> we met a man whom somebody had just "gone through,"

the check-taker and usher calmly comparing guesses concerning the offender.... Steadily sloping upward from the
footlights was lifted, row above row, the close-packed,
stamping, shrieking, cat-calling, true Bowery crowd.

... Besides the proper and prevailing peanut, the spectators refreshed themselves with a great variety of bodily
nutriment. Ham sandwich and sausage seemed to have prec-
edence, but pork chops were also prominent, receiving the
undivided attention of a large family party in the second
tier, the members of which consumed chops with a noble
persistence through all of the intermissions; holding the
small end of the bone in the hand and working downward
through the meaty portion. The denuded bones were most of
them playfully shied at the heads of acquaintances in the
pit; if you have never seen it done, you can hardly fancy
how well you can telegraph with pork bones when the aim
is true; and if you hit the wrong man, you have only to look
innocent and unconscious.

The Bowery audience was by no means content with inarticulate noise; besides the time-honored modes of encouraging the players, there was full and free communication in
speech, sometimes a set colloquy with the actors—which the
audience counted on and waited for with great expectancy.
This the actors well understood, and when the Irish patriot
had a line of particularly overpowering moral import, his
sure way to make a point with it was to come down front,
declaim it vociferously and end by saying, "Is that so,
boys?" or "Don't you, boys?" and then the acclaim and out-
cry were so loud and long that all babies in the house cried
out, which caused another terrible din, with uncomplimen-
tary remarks about the infants and "Cheese it!" again—a
cry which, though a highly plastic expression, yet from the
variety of its frequent application during the evening, must
have come in sometimes with great irrelevance.[40]

Imagine Herne—or any actor—performing under such
wretched conditions. But they did. When Frances Trollope visited
the United States in 1831, she noted "It requires some courage"[41]
to attend the nearby Chatham Theatre. But she went. Among the
sights was "a lady performing the most maternal office possible,"[42] nursing a baby in public being a not uncommon practice,
even during theatre performances.

The Bowery also housed the Atlantic Gardens, founded in
1856 on the former site of the Bull's Head Tavern, whose most
celebrated patron had been Edwin Booth. For a while Tony

Pastor's famed Opera House on the Bowery became New York's leading variety showplace. But in 1883 Henry Miner remodeled the worn building, renaming it Miner's People's Theatre, the place where Herne's *The Minute Men* played in September 1886.

Miner really pushed *The Minute Men,* spending an extravagant $9,000 on the production. Such an investment required loud drum beating, a Miner specialty. One newspaper ad hyperbolized: "A tale of humanity, of love and hate, joy and despair, hope and disappointment with comedy and pathos happily and powerfully blended and commingled, interspersed with Thrilling Incidents, Stirring Situations, Deadly Ambuscades, Hair-Breadth Escapes, Brilliant Marches, Battles, Retreats, etc. . . . The Dramatic Junoration of the Age."[43]

Miner speculated, offering Herne $25,000 for half-interest in *The Minute Men.* Herne should have agreed. The play soon folded on the Bowery.

The Minute Men's next bivouac was the famed Boston Theatre, where one critic called the work "beautifully picturesque" and added, "Mr. Herne has carefully avoided being too patriotic in his speeches, and there is little of bombast or pathos in the text."[44] But failure followed Herne, who returned to New York City, finding temporary refuge at the Brooklyn Theatre and the Novelty Theatre in Williamsburg.

It seemed indifference existed everywhere. In Chicago, Herne leased the Casino, another second-rate house, and played *The Minute Men* at popular prices. But bills mounted, draining profits that had accrued from *Hearts of Oak.* Herne eventually shelved *The Minute Men* after losing his fortune and revived *Hearts of Oak.*

During the Chicago run of *The Minute Men* Herne's affection towards children surfaced again when he presented a special youth matinee that sold out. Suddenly came more bad luck—in the form of a fierce snow storm. Herne opened the doors to all, whether holding tickets or not, and even sent the overflow home in cabs and horse-cars. His wife K.C. worried about the disastrous possibilities of a fire, and this led to a delightful Herne curtain speech, informing the crowd of youngsters that all was make-believe. Then he concluded:

"However, if anything should happen to frighten you, I

want you to promise me that you won't scream and try to run out of the theatre, but form in line, and march out in good order, just as you do when you are having a practice fire drill at school."[45]

All's well that ends well. Shouts and whistles greeted the play's end, and Herne's young audience safely left the theatre, happily accompanied by an orchestral march.

The ghastly number of nineteenth century theatre fires justified K.C.'s concern. Showplaces were wooden matchboxes, with inflammable sets, poor ventilation, stuffed boxes and galleries, inadequate exits, hazardous open-flame stage lighting, and often ridiculously dangerous special effects. Theatre owners didn't help much. They ignored safety, sinking funds into showy prosceniums and facades. Few theatres survived a lifetime without at least one fire. Maguire's Jenny Lind, the Bowery, and even P. T. Barnum's American Museum all burned more than once.

But the theatre companies seldom folded their scorched tents and called it quits. They usually swept the ashes from the theatre's wings and started over. Take the prop man from *The Streets of New York* whose bags of powder pre-exploded in the flies. His first conscious words after landing on stage were, "Was it a hit?"[46]

Famous words that summarize the story of nineteenth century American theatre, with its irrepressible, if often penniless, progress toward the formation of a national theatre art.

7 turn your glasses upside down

B Y THE 1880'S, Herne had been in show business for two decades, running the gamut from melodramatic potboilers to *Drifting Apart*. But it was a chance meeting with a struggling young idealist-realist from the farmlands of South Dakota named Hamlin Garland that changed his life, leading him to finish the play that Arthur Hobson Quinn later called in *The Literature of the American People* "unequalled in realism by any other known American drama of its century."[1] This was *Margaret Fleming*, Herne's most famous play.

Hamlin Garland arrived in Boston one drizzly day in the autumn of 1884. His worldly wealth included a $20 suit (mostly cotton with a purplish Prince Albert frock), a broadbrimmed black hat, an imitation leather valise, a pasteboard trunk that held a few books and clothes, and $130, which needed stretching until spring. It wasn't long before he championed such radical movements as Henry George's single tax, women's rights, literary realism, and the explosive theories of Charles Darwin and Herbert Spencer. He eventually wrote hundreds of essays, articles, plays, poems, and books including *Main-Travelled Roads* (1891), *Roadside Meetings* (1930), and *A Son of the Middle Border* (1917), which received the Pulitzer Prize for Biography.

Garland was awed by Boston, the city Oliver Wendell Holmes dubbed "the hub of the intellectual universe." It was America's literary capital, the home of Emerson, Hawthorne, Longfellow, Lowell, Whittier, and Howells. Cultural landmarks lined its "maze of narrow streets" of "low brick buildings"[2]: the Public Library, the Parker House, Music Hall and Tremont Temple, Faneuil Hall, the Boston Museum, and Howard Atheneum.

79

Charming town houses with polished brass doorplates lined the Back Bay's Commonwealth Avenue. The drawing-room windows of Howells' retreat looked "out on this noble thorough- fare with its centre esplanade of trees and statues,"[3] its "tier upon tier of windows and roofs, topped with the gilded dome, ris- ing in serried lines, broken by spires and tall chimneys."[4] As Garland later recalled: "I was a bewildered plainsman, a scared rustic in the midst of a gigantic metropolis."[5]

But all life wasn't as comfortable as the Back Bay in Boston. "Within cannon-shot of Beacon Hill," wrote Benjamin Orange Flower, "are hundreds of families slowly starving and stifling; families who are bravely battling for life's barest neces- sities, while year by year the conditions are becoming more hope- less, the struggle for bread fiercer, the outlook more dismal."[6] *The Arena* published an article called "Destitution in Boston with Striking Illustrations and Practical Suggestions" that detailed the hovels of "white slaves." It decried the tenements "in which from one hundred and fifty to two hundred persons—men, women, and children—are herded together like cattle, and sleep in heaps upon the landings of the stairs." It described rooms "re- sembling the dark back bin of a pig-pen," and children with "scarcely a rag on them" who hadn't "tasted bread for three days, nor meat for weeks."[7]

Boston was a city of paradox whose upper-crust aristo- crats locked their gates and peered through opera glasses at commoners.

Culture thrived in this Puritan fortress, however, espe- cially such intellectual movements as transcendentalism, so- cialism, Christian Science, Swedenborgianism, suffragism, na- tionalism, Unitarianism, vegetarianism, and phrenologism. Such diverse intellectual activity was Boston's heritage. As early as 1719 a traveler had observed: "There are five Printing Presses in Boston, generally full of Work, by which it appears that Hu- manity and the Knowledge of letters flourish more here than in all the other English plantations put together, for in the City of New York there is but one Bookseller's Shop, and in the Planta- tions of Virginia, Maryland, Carolina, Barbadoes, and the Islands none at all."[8]

Garland migrated to "the Athens of America" for several

reasons: to study, to teach, and to escape the mundane routine of midland America. For $6 a week he rented a room on Boylston Place, "a dismal blind alley whose only advantage was its nearness to the Public Library,"[9] a wretched nook from which he "could see only a gray rag of mist hanging above a neighboring chimney."[10] He studied ten hours a day in Bates Hall at the public library, then walked home to save carfare, cramming another four hours of study in his chilled room. Though often starving, he began the outline for a book called *The Evolution of American Thought.*

Garland's exhaustive self-education lacked direction at first, but one source led to another. He already knew Chambers' *Encyclopedia* and Green's *Short History of the English People.* He had earlier outlined Taine's *History of English Literature,* scratching notes on the walls and ceiling of his Dakota shanty. Beadle's dime novels, the Old Sleuth's stories, Edward Eggleston's *The Hoosier School-Master,* and Henry George's *Progress and Poverty* were other books familiar to him. But Boston expanded Garland's knowledge. It unveiled the evolutionist Charles Darwin, Herbert Spencer, Ernst Haeckel, Hermann Helmholtz, and John Fiske. Garland soon quoted Darwin in his notebook: "Man expresses his passions in common form with the brute. In fact man betrays his animal origin as clearly in his brute actions as in brute formation." Garland added: "Therein Mr. Darwin confirms what I have argued for years. And I am glad to have such a man upon my side. Expression can be reasoned out and systematized for it has certain obvious laws at its root."[11]

Herbert Spencer, however, became Garland's intellectual beacon through his manifesto in *First Principles*: "Evolution is an integration of matter and concomitant dissipation of motion; during which the matter passes from an indefinite, incoherent homogeneity to a definite, coherent heterogeneity; and during which the retained motion undergoes a parallel transformation."[12] Meaning what? Forms change from simple to complex through evolution. Such a scientific system reinforced Garland's embyronic ideas of two solid American beliefs: progress and democracy. It also, of course, trampled upon another solid American belief—religion. Spencer replaced divine law with natural law, divine order and harmony with natural order and harmony.

His theories helped Garland explain the evolution of novels, which he called "the epic of the age,"[13] ideas he had derived from the German writer Friedrich Spielhagen.

Another Spencerian seduction was its adaptability. As Donald Pizer writes, "Because of the vastness of the over-all conception, in application and interpretation it tended to become like a large apple shared by several boys—each searches for a favored spot, one takes a bite here, another there, but no one swallows it whole."[14] Spencer's social theory satisfied everyone from Robert Ingersoll to Henry Ward Beecher. As Richard Hofstadter says in *Social Darwinism in American Thought*: "Some part of his success probably came because he was selling the guardians of American society what they wanted to hear. Grangers, Greenbacks, Single Taxers, Knights of Labor, trade unionists, Populists, Socialists Utopian and Marxian—all presented challenges to the existing pattern of free enterprise, demanded reforms by state action, or insisted upon a thorough remodeling of the social order."[15]

Garland swallowed a mouthful of Spencerianism, applying it to the entire spectrum of Western literature. "I became an evolutionist in the fullest sense," he wrote, "accepting Spencer as the greatest living thinker. Fiske and Galton and Allen were merely assistants to the Master Mind whose generalizations included in their circles all modern discovery."[16]

Other early influences on Garland were Eugene Veron's *Aesthetics*, which he concluded "helped me more than any other work on art,"[17] Hippolyte Taine's theory of "race, milieu and moment," and H. W. Posnett's *Comparative Literature* (1886), which related scientific principles to literature. Walt Whitman's democratic individualism also snuggled in one corner of Garland's mind.

New Bostonian friends also helped, especially Moses True Brown, John J. Enneking, Charles E. Hurd, and Benjamin Orange Flower.

Moses True Brown, director of the Boston School of Oratory, hired Garland as an assistant, then appointed him Professor of American Literature. When a socialist student coaxed friends to attend a lecture by Garland at her Hyde Park home, impressionistic painter John J. Enneking and Charles Hurd, literary editor of the *Boston Evening Transcript,* showed up. It was Hurd who introduced Garland to Flower, Howells, and other members of Boston's literati.

Hurd pushed Garland's career by publishing his early articles and short stories in the *Evening Transcript,* including a favorable review of Howells' *The Minister's Charge,* which led to a thirty-year friendship between Garland and "the Dean of American letters." He also exposed Garland to the works of James Whitcomb Riley, Joseph Kirkland, Henrik Ibsen, and Bjørnstjerne Bjørnson.

Benjamin Orange Flower published Garland's work in his left-wing magazine *The Arena,* which American intellectuals, social reformers, and radicals clamored to read. *The Arena* embraced the splinter ideas of the times including, "advocacy of governmental relief of unemployment by a public works building program; the right of labor to organize and to strike; municipal slum-clearance and construction of low-cost housing units; federal or state control of the liquor traffic; reform of the prison system with an extension of industrial training; and governmental ownership of natural monopolies. In addition, the *Arena* antedated the muckrakers by ten years in its attacks on corruption in the trusts; and also championed such diverse movements as feminism, the eradication of child labor, and modernization of the nation's school system"[18] These were controversial ideas that competitive magazines like the *North American Review* and *Forum* avoided.

Flower's reputation grew when *The Arena*'s circulation soared to 100,000, which meant there was lots of public interest in what he was publishing. The maverick editor also endorsed the works of naturalists such as Garland, Frank Norris, Jack London, Stephen Crane, Upton Sinclair, and James A. Herne.

When Garland first met Flower, the energetic journalist's age and attitude amazed him. "I was surprised to find him of my own age, a small round-faced smiling youth with black eyes and curling hair. He was a new sort of reformer, genial, laughing, tolerant. Nothing disturbed his good humor, and no authority could awe him."[19] They fast became friends.

Garland devoured the works of authors that Boston's intellectuals recommended, everyone from Victor Hugo, Sir Walter

Scott, and Charles Dickens to Alexis de Tocqueville, Leo Tolstoy, Hermann Sudermann, and Emile Zola. "I learned a little of everything and nothing very thoroughly," he later admitted. "With so many peaks in sight I had no time to spend on digging up the valley soil."[20]

Garland's main criticism of American literature was its failure to deal with the quiet desperation of common people, especially farmers. He complained that "for two centuries our colonial authors wrote as if from the most violent distaste of their surroundings, finding pleasure and poetic exaltation only in Rome or Egypt or in the memories of their former English homes."[21] The age of aristocratic, romantic, and anti-democratic sentiment belonged to the buried past, he argued, an age when people "studied books and not men, the past and not the present."[22] He asked: What about local-color studies? What about the real America? What about the common person instead of Byronic romantics?

One day in early 1889, Garland and Hurd sat in the overworked and underpaid editor's office. One topic led to another. Then Hurd suggested: "By the way, Garland, you ought to know Jim Herne. He's doing much the same sort of work on the stage that you and Miss Wilkins are putting into the short story. Here are a couple of tickets to his play. Go and see it and come back and tell what you think of it."[23]

The play Garland saw was *Drifting Apart*, advertised as "a story of the Gloucester fishermen."[24] Garland's luke-warm interest in this show soon turned hot. He wrote in *The Literary World*: "knowing nothing of Mr. Herne or his play, I went with little curiosity and no special interest, intending to go out after a couple of acts. I stayed through the whole play, more stirred to thought as well as feeling than I have been for years. I said, 'Here is a play which, with all its faults, deals with the *essentials* of American domestic life.' "[25]

Drifting Apart was running at the Grand Opera House, according to Julie Herne. Garland, however, wrote: "They were playing at that time on a second-rate stage in the South End and their surroundings were cheap and tawdry."[26] Perhaps Garland confused theatres; the Grand Opera House was not at that time either very grand or very well known. An editorial in the *Evening Transcript* once observed that "plenty of people in Boston have never been to the Grand Opera House at all; there are those who only know dimly that it's south, somewhere on Washington Street."[27]

Drifting Apart played the Grand Opera House because its 1888 fall road tour had failed. First-class theatres in New York, Chicago, and Boston wouldn't touch the play. They called Herne a moralist, stitching the work between farces and tank plays (melodramas such as *A Dark Street* and *Lost in New York* in which the villain dumped the hero or heroine in a water tank). Although Herne had managed around 250 performances, the receipts barely paid expenses. The Hernes sold their bonds, and K.C.'s jewelry, even mortgaged property to meet payrolls.

Drifting Apart was a temperance drama without the usual hackneyed harangues that rivaled Bible-belt preachers. It told a simple story without a hero or villain. Benjamin Orange Flower called it "probably the most powerful temperance sermon ever produced on the boards of a theater."[28]

Sailor Jack Hepburn (Herne) drinks too much. He marries Mary Miller (K.C.). Time passes. One Christmas eve Jack visits the local fishing village, returning home drunk and ashamed. He then flees to sea aboard the *Sprite*, which is shipwrecked later. A trading ship in the China Seas rescues the bedraggled sailor, but Chinese pirates attack them, enslaving Jack, who eventually escapes. Years pass. He finally returns to Mary who is marrying Percy Seward, the "son of a rich mother whom he loves; a good fellow but a trifle sentimental."[29] Percy's mother cringes when little Margaret enters and Jack cries, "My child."[30] She evicts both Jack and Mary. In a shocking fourth-act curtain, Mary and the child die of starvation, and Jack goes mad, carrying Mary's limp body from their squalid garret. Imagine Herne delivering these powerful lines:

> *Jack.* (*Who has not moved, stares wildly around and sees Mary's body and goes to her*) Why Mary girl, what is the matter with you, child? Oh I see—well—well—I'll not go out tonight; let the watch go. Come let's fill the stockin's, perhaps in a year there may be another stockin' hangin' here. Ha! ha! ha! there

Caesar, you stop here with them—Mary be sure you keep askin' me the time o'day. Ha! ha! ha! Why, what place is this? I won't stay here, come Mary, let's go. (*He lifts her and supports her in his arms; her dead body is limp, but he is strong*) Let's go home, back to the old home in Gloucester—(*Kisses her*) Poor child—I have so loved—so wronged you. But I'll make amends—I'll drink no more, come. Mother, be sure you put plenty of onions in the stuffin'—Mother—see—here's Mary—she's not well, poor girl—quick, food. She's starvin', I tell you—come Mary, we'll go home—home—home—(*Moving towards door with dead body of Mary, Hester and Silas horrified but unable to stay him*)[31]

This startling scene, however, was really a dream. Jack awakens. Sleigh bells are ringing, the Christmas fire is crackling, and crickets are chirping. Everyone is celebrating, singing the temperance tune "Turn your glasses upside down" as the final curtain falls.

Just another melodramatic potboiler? Read Herne's speech again. In 1889 this play rattled cherished theatre traditions. The dream sequence, the child's starvation, and Jack's madness shook audiences everywhere. K.C. later thought "that the audience resented the discovery that their emotions had been harrowed by what was after all unreality, while the tragedy was too keen for it to be appreciated for its own sake."[32] Garland and William Dean Howells agreed.

Even Garland shuddered during the "true-to-life" fourth act, later writing in *The Arena*: "Mrs. Herne's acting of Mary Miller was my first realization of the compelling power of truth. It was so utterly opposed to the 'tragedy of the legitimate.' Here was tragedy that appalled and fascinated like the great fact of living. No noise, no contortions of face or limbs, yet somehow I was made to feel the dumb, inarticulate, interior agony of a mother. Never before had such acting faced me across the footlights. The fourth act was like one of Millet's paintings, with that mysterious quality of reserve—the quality of life again."[33] A "wailing little melody"[34] played during this climactic scene heightened its terrible reality.

This transitional drama also offered a humorous subplot in which Herne satirized the period's popular theatre through two young lovers, Hester and Silas. Both dream of stardom—Hester as an actress, and Silas as a musician. One scene, a spoof of local acting companies, mirrors both Herne's deep frustration and his swing towards naturalistic dialogue:

Hes. Oh! Yes—Idol shattered. I knew it was some kind of a image—I only heard it once—it was in the theater up at the Town Hall, Lampey's Unequalled Dramatic Alliance from the Boston Museum, every member a star, in a carefully selected repature.

Percy. Repertoire!

Hes. I guess so. Six days only, three grand performances daily, mornings at ten, afternoons at two, evenings at eight, admission ten cents, a few very choice seats reserved at five cents extra, change of bill at each performance—special provisions for families from the country desiring to eat lunch in the theater—

Percy. Why! Of course, they could not eat lunch without provisions—see?

Hes. (*Looks at him*) Don't interrupt me—lemonade, popcorn, candies and peanuts, served by gentlemanly attendants—no whistling, stamping or catcalls allowed—did you ever see Lampey's Constellation?

Percy. Never heard of it before.

Hes. Why, you live in Boston, don't ye?

Percy. Yes—born there.

Hes. And—ye—never—heard—of—Lampey's Constellation?

Percy. Never!

Hes. Don't ye ever go to the Museum?

Percy. Oh Yes! Frequently.

Hes. Well—They're from the Museum.

Percy. I dare say—a very long way from it. (*laughs*)

Hes. You needn't laugh. Lampey's great. I've seen all the constellations that come here—I've seen *Peck's Bad Boy, Uncle Tom, Ten Nights in a Barroom, Alvin Joselyn* and all of them and I like Lampey's in "Alonzo the Brave" better than any of them—but then mebbe you can see more actin' in Boston than we do down here.[35]

All ends well for the stagestruck couple, who finally receive the usual Barnum ballyhoo on their playbill: "Town Hall, Gloucester, extraordinary attraction. Engagement at enormous expense of the young, beautiful and talented comedienne, Miss Hester Barton, assisted by the incomparable musician and pharmacopoeist, Mr. Silas Cummings."[36]

Drifting Apart was first called *Mary, the Fishermen's Child,* but K.C. suggested *Storm Signals.* A compromise produced the name *Drifting Apart.* The play opened "for the first

time on any stage, for two weeks"[37] at the People's Theatre on
May 7, 1888, with a cast featuring H. M. Pitt and Maude Jef-
fries, who later starred in Wilson Barrett's *The Sign of the
Cross.*

Herne encouraged K.C. to criticize *Drifting Apart.* Would
it work? What about its form and content? Were the characters
real? She reacted honestly, sometimes too honestly—but softened
all with solid support. In one *Drifting Apart* letter she said: "I
believe that it will go, but I would not advise you to risk a dollar
upon it. Yet there is a greater chance for its success than there
was for the *Minute Men.*" K.C. thought Herne placed too much
emphasis on theatrical effects—Herne's weakness and link with
past traditions. The opening scene between Mary and Percy
lacked originality, and the comedy was "the kind that goes, but
not to my mind," meaning it was situational and lacked character. But she did commend the fourth act "I don't know how else
you could make the child die. It is very beautiful—her dream a bit
old, that is for the child, and maybe a bit too long for acting pur-
poses. Entrance of Jack and Mary sending him out again, good.
His return and ending of act *very dramatic,* the one *great* touch
in the whole work."

K.C. recognized the bases of audience appeal. So she concluded, "Of course, the great thing in the play that warrants one
looking for its success [is] the temperance moral it contains and
the charm in it that you do not realize that it is a lecture until
you have gone away and begin thinking of it."[38]

K.C. gradually liked *Drifting Apart* and wanted to play
Mary. In one letter she said: "Oh, God grant that this play will
be a success! I am very anxious, too, dear. I share your feelings.
I know too well the tumult that is in your poor heart, and all for
us! I will work as hard as I can with you, dear, and if this play
fails, well, we'll go to California and work hard together to re-
trieve what is lost. I shall begin at once preparations for Mary.
Send me the part or bring it to me that I may study it at my
leisure." And again: "My own darling: I am perfectly *wild* over
this part. Oh, if I can only act it as I feel it should be acted! I
have not yet begun to study the *words* of the Fourth Act, but
the spirit of it is upon me strong. It is great for acting. I am
positively ill I cried so over it this morning. I am going out for

a walk and when I return I will give a few hours more to Mary. You see, I do not—cannot—study the lines. I read them and do a great deal of thinking. Oh, Jim, *if* I can only play the part. There are so many exquisite things in it."[39]

There were other temperance plays before *Drifting Apart*. After the American Temperance Society was formed in 1826 the "drink problem" grew popular on stage. In 1850 P. T. Barnum opened his "lecture room" (a theater in disguise) at his American Museum with *The Drunkard or the Fallen Saved* by William S. Smith, a reformed alcoholic. *Ten Nights in a Bar Room or What I Saw There* (1850), by W. W. Pratt, also touched the public's pulse—and purse—inspiring its author to become a preacher.

The difference between *Drifting Apart* and other temperance plays was its realistic tone. Many years later, it still held up and Hollywood director-producer D. W. Griffith liked it. During the spring of 1919, K.C. and Griffith met to discuss filming Herne's plays. Griffith said, "We'll do *Drifting Apart* for James A."[40] But Griffith filmed *Way Down East* instead, using in it the pantomime and stage business of Mary Miller's fourth act scene from *Drifting Apart,* a betrayal K.C. always remembered.

Garland promoted *Drifting Apart*. He wrote that instead of "the conventional business of last wills, lost heirs, seductions, intrigue and sensational claptrap,"[41] it offered a sense of quiet realism. Garland was impressed, especially by the realism in atmospheric touches: rag rugs, old furniture, and Jack's quaint shaving scene. Herne's directions read: "Clock and ornaments on mantel, kettle steaming and singing on hob, cricket chirping on hearth. Within all warm and cozy, without storm howling; candles on mantel, lamp holly branches ready for Jack, dog and cat lying on hearth."[42] Even puffs of snow drifted inside the open door. The dog was Herne's own Scotch collie shepherd.

Drifting Apart intrigued Garland, particularly the New England local color and its present time setting. He later wrote: "There could be no progress, no native output, so long as the past lay like a brazen wall across the way of the young dramatist. The free untrodden paths do not lie in the direction of the past."[43] *Drifting Apart* studied plain, everyday people, not nobility or the romantic escapades of another Hawkeye or Davy Crockett. It emphasized colloquial speech rhythms, even though a few "purple patches" of melodrama remained.

Garland didn't know about *Hearts of Oak,* Herne's earlier New England fishing village play, with a plotline similar to *Drifting Apart.* Both Chrystal and Mary were orphans who married the men who befriended them, and both first acts ended with a terrific storm and shipwreck. A child influenced the resolution of both works. But *Hearts of Oak* remained a "romantic melodrama," while *Drifting Apart* was a "domestic tragedy" dealing with drink. *Drifting Apart* also included the radical dream sequence and deeper characterizations. Julie Herne thought the fourth-act death scene was the equal of *Margaret Fleming*'s sensational third act, which the romantic critics blasted.

Garland wanted to meet the Hernes, writing them a letter that said in part, "By such writings as that in the first and last acts of 'Drifting Apart,' you have allied yourself with the best local-color fictionists of New England and deserve the encouragement and support of the same public."[44] Several days later, Garland received this reply from Herne:

> Your kindly conceived and earnestly written letter lies before me. I have read and reread it, and each perusal has added strength to the already firm conviction I had in the ultimate success of my play. By success, I mean that by which the managers measure—'financial,' for be the play or player never so fine, when there is no cash, there are no open doors. Your letter demonstrates the fact that as you saw my work, others will see it also, not so readily, nor so clearly—but they will see it. My task, and a difficult one at first, is to secure the attendance of the fine auditor—the others will follow— the masses never like to think for themselves—the opinions and criticisms of a man like you—carry great weight—they are repeated. . . . It was, as you say, a daring thing to present such a subject in such a delicate form, but I have received many letters concerning it—none perhaps that I prize so much—for none bear such evidence of having given the subject deep thought. They are written from the heart, yours from the head and the heart. You say you would like to know more of me. I can only repeat that

the desire is mutual. It will, however, be impossible for me to meet you during my present engagement. The past week has been devoted to nine performances of 'Drifting Apart' and six rehearsals of next week's production, 'The Minute Men' (please see that play), no small task you will admit but, when my season is ended and I return home, I will feel honored if you spend a few hours and dine with Katharine C. (Mrs.) Herne, myself, and our three babies.[45]

Probably both Garland and Herne exaggerated each other's importance. Garland idolized Edwin Booth but lacked stage connections. So he "was almost frenziedly eager"[46] to meet the Hernes, who might unlock a few backstage doors. On the other hand, Herne wanted recognition from the realists, thinking Garland could also open doors. Hurd had published Garland's criticisms—most without pay—in the *Evening Transcript*, and another handful appeared in magazines. But *Main-Travelled Roads*, Garland's first book, wasn't published until 1891, the same year Herne produced *Margaret Fleming* in Boston.

Both writers profited from their chance encounter. Garland's theatre commitment became firm, and Herne was encouraged to finish *Margaret Fleming*. It is possible to speculate about *Margaret Fleming's* eventual production and Herne's meteoric rise to fame if he hadn't met Garland. Would Shakespeare have won success without the Burbages, or Eugene O'Neill without the Provincetown Players? In 1912, William Dean Howells wrote: "So far as one influenced the other I do not think Mr. Garland owed more to Hearne (*sic*) than Hearne to him in practising in their art the veritism which they both preached.... I have no doubt the author of these books did very greatly help to stay the dramatist in his allegiance to the thing that was, while on his part Hearne doubtless helped his younger friend to clarify his native dramatic perception."[47]

Garland promoted *Drifting Apart* among his literary friends. Hurd published an editorial in which Garland called American theatre "a reign of horse-play and spectacle" and its audience "that hydra-headed, myriad-tongued monster." He asked for support, but it was never realized because the public wanted farces, musicals, and European melodramas, more than the new serious, American works. Garland concluded, "Their play is far from perfect, but it has moments when it rises above any other American play."[48]

Garland then wrote a letter to *The Literary World* editor called "Truth in the Drama." It applauded Herne's life-like characters, fidelity to truth, and treatment of New England native types. "My plea is that when any man or woman produces a play with the serious intent of *Drifting Apart,* or the love for common things as in *The Old Homestead,* it is the duty of the *literary* public to study carefully and express kindly their exact feeling with regard to it. There is no other way for encouraging good work and suppressing bad work."[49]

William Dean Howells finally saw *Drifting Apart,* reviewing it in *Harper's* the following year. Although he thought Herne depended on mechanical tricks for some effects, he admitted that "upon the whole he has produced a play fresh in motive, pure in tone, high in purpose, and very simple and honest in method." The scene where Jack "small talks" the two women while dressing for Christmas in an adjoining room charmed the novelist. He praised both performances. "Mrs. Herne has the flashes of power that transcend any effect of her husband's exquisite art; but this art is so patient, so beautiful, so unerring, that upon the whole we must praise him most."[50]

And that's what Hamlin Garland did. He praised James A. Herne—to everyone.

8 those ashmont days

HERNE KEPT HIS word. At season's end Garland received an invitation to Ashmont, an invitation he long remembered.

The Hernes had moved to 3 Beale Street, in Ashmont, Massachusetts, in early summer, 1881. Their square-framed home with its mansard roof and vine-covered porch looked like several dozen others. Maples shaded the front lawn, tall evergreens the driveway. In the rear "was an orchard, bordered with shrubs and flower-beds, as well as a vegetable plot and a strawberry bed," wrote Julie. "The soil was rich, and in the summer the 'back garden' was a riot of bloom, and the air was sweet with the scent of roses, honeysuckle, and syringa; in the autumn the trees were laden with luscious fruit."[1]

At Ashmont Herne wrote six plays. It was also the place where he finally met with Hamlin Garland, and the place where he entertained many of Boston's literati. Here two of his four children were born: Chrystal on June 16, 1882, and Dorothy on September 17, 1885. (His first child, Julie, was also born in Boston but at the Adams House on October 31, 1880.) Both Chrystal and Julie became notable actresses. Dorothy, who played Little Lena in *Margaret Fleming*, married critic-author Montrose J. Moses, who wrote about Herne in *The American Dramatist*:

"There are some men born to see clearly, to be zealous for the vital principles of life, the unchangeable, constant truth of the ages; the thoughts and ideas which elevate in the effort to live our highest and best. These are the thoughts which were

93

usually upon the lips of Mr. Herne. . . . [He] represents the most original strain in the American Drama of his day."[2]

Julie wrote that her father "never was so happy in his life as he was at Ashmont."[3] She recalled the parlor with its flowered, velvet carpet and carved black walnut furniture upholstered in red plush, the upright piano, huge Bible, and K.C.'s portrait as Peg Woffington above the white marble mantel piece. And who could forget Herne's study with its cozy fireplace, tall bookcases, and flattop desk where he mapped routes, corresponded with managers, and devised promotional materials.

Herne later wrote to Garland: "Yes, those Ashmont days were indeed glorious days. They laid the foundation of what success we have since achieved, by strengthening and encouraging us in our work, and making us steadfast to a purpose that we felt was the true one. And we believe that you, too, got something in your work and for your future out of them. They are gone, but not forgotten. They change, but cannot die."[4]

Garland's first reaction to the vine-covered home on Beale Street was one of disappointment because it wasn't a palace or Victorian gingerbread mansion with cupolas and ornamental frills. It was just "a small plain, frame cottage such as a village carpenter might build."[5] K.C. answered the door, reminding him of Mary Miller in *Drifting Apart* with her long, brown chestnut hair and inner radiance. She ushered Garland into the library, where the three girls, Julie, Chrystal, and Dorothy, waited anxiously. He passed the test, and thereafter they always greeted him first.

Herne seemed like the character of Dan'l Peggotty in person. Garland wondered: Was this a star without pompous puffing, falseface, or arrogant notions? He soon learned that Herne seldom spoke when with strangers. "It was only when in the presence of old comrades or very intimate friends that he gave up his attitude of smiling and interested reticence." As friendship developed, Herne became a wag storyteller and master dialectician who "could imitate almost any nationality and could dramatize at a moment's notice any scene or dialogue his wife demanded of him."[6] He also mastered the ventriloquist's art.

Herne's "small boy's passion for practical jokes" sometimes angered K.C. There was the time he and the girls greeted her at the train station with Herne dressed like a tramp, mumbling in an Irish brogue, "Evening, Ma'm. Sure and the little ladies would not leave me in peace. I had to leave me garden half weeded for they insisted on meeting your train."[7] This failed to amuse K.C., who walked home, Herne trailing close behind, a bit concerned.

Another time he played a trick on his neighbor Benjamin Heath, a retired detective. Heath later told the humorous story in the *Boston Herald*:

"He was a practical joker and an all-round terror when he started out to have fun at somebody else's expense," said Mr. Heath, "but we all loved him. I was his next door neighbor on Beale Street, Dorchester, for a long time, and we became fast friends. But he 'did' me at last—or, rather, he 'did' the public at my expense—and I spent about two years trying to get even with him. He was always on the alert and never gave me an opening. What he did was this: He had advertisements printed in the Boston papers to the effect that I had then in bloom at my house some of the most wonderful night blooming cereus, which I was desirous should be seen by all lovers of flowers, and especially by experts in floriculture. My name and address were given as large as life in the advertisement.

"The first we knew about it was on the evening after this appeared in the papers. I was sitting with my family on the plazza of our house on Beale Street where we saw a great crowd of people coming round the corner, heading our way. We wondered what it was all about. And concluded that the people were going to give a surprise party to some one in the neighborhood. We were quite right in that conjecture, and the surprise party was all our own. The strangers stopped at our gate and inquired if this was Mr. Heath's house, and could they see his wondeful night blooming cereus. They were inclined to be indignant when I said I had no such plants. They thought I had them, but didn't want to show them. I had to explain to about 10,000 people that the advertisement was a hoax. Then we got sick of it, locked up the house, and refused to answer the bells. People came from everywhere to see those blooms. I recall one later party from one of the colleges. Herne used to lean over his gate and chuckle.

" 'You seem to have a good many callers, Mr. Heath,' he would say, in the most aggravating and insinuating manner.

"He never admitted the trick, but as soon as I saw that advertisement I knew who was responsible for it."

"He died before I got even with him," Heath remarked sadly.[8]

Herne sometimes annoyed K.C. in little ways. When she'd talk too much, he'd quietly rise, shrugging his shoulders. This meant "here we go again." Garland recalled that she usually laughed—usually, but not always. "Indeed he was a little afraid of her keen wit, and often when she loosed her verbal arrows he quite frankly dodged."[9]

That first night at Ashmont always highlighted Garland's memories. The Hernes first dubbed him "Professor," then altered this to "Dean," a name that stuck for years. Their meeting became "a session of Congress, a Methodist revival, and an Irish comedy. . . . My head rang with their piquant phrases, their earnest and cheerful voices. These extraordinary theatrical folk brought to me a whole new world—a world of swift and pulsating emotion, a world of aspiration, and the story of brave battle for an art."[10]

Garland became a Herne fixture as David Belasco had been in San Francisco, often bicycling out to Ashmont. The Hernes introduced Garland to Stuart Robson and William H. Crane, William Gillette, and Mary Shaw; he reciprocated by introducing them to Boston's literati: E. A. Chamberlain of the *Evening Transcript*, Mildred Aldrich of the *Journal*, and William McCracken, author of *The Rise of the Swiss Republic*. Many others followed. Ideas crackled like cellophane wrappers at 3 Beale Street. "No one ever leaves this house as he came," commented one visitor. "We all go away with something new and vital to think about."[11]

Garland exposed the Hernes to Europe's most controversial playwrights: Emile Zola, Bjørnstjerne Bjørnson, Henrik Ibsen, Hermann Sudermann, Ivan Turgenev, Leo Tolstoy, and Fyodor Dostoevsky; they also accepted Garland's evolutionary theories and literary manifesto and Henry George's Utopian ideas. "In their home oft-quoted volumes of Spencer, Darwin, Fiske, Carlyle, Ibsen, Valdes, Howells, give evidence that they not only kept abreast but ahead of the current thought of the day," Garland wrote in *The Arena*. "Spencer is their philosopher, and Howells is their novelist, but Dickens and Scott have large space on their shelves."[12]

Garland disliked Dickens, and several decades passed before his prejudice mellowed. He finally confessed in 1934: "As a student of fiction in Boston, I ridiculed his exaggerations and deplored his characters—for that was the fashion among the younger critics. Today . . . I feel something resembling awe as I confront the throngs of Dickens' characters."[13] Howells also loathed Dickens' "Gothic tendency to grotesque and monstrous decoration,"[14] but years later he repented after rereading *Great Expectations*. "For the most part I was charmed with him because he could thrill me, and make me hot and cold; because he could make me laugh and cry, and stop my pulse and breath at will," wrote Howells. "In all that vast range of fiction, there is nothing that tells for the strong, because they are strong, against the weak, nothing that tells for the haughty against the humble, nothing that tells for wealth against poverty."[15] Herne agreed. Among his earliest roles were Dan'l Peggotty and Bill Sykes—among his earliest play adaptations had been the novels of Dickens.

K.C. also liked Dickens and most other writers, especially Sidney Lanier. Her enormous appetite for ideas amazed Garland. "But to see her radiant with intellectual enthusiasm, one has but to start a discussion of the nebular hypothesis, or to touch upon the atomic theory, or doubt the inconceivability of matter. She is perfectly oblivious to space and time if she can get someone to discuss Flammarion's super-sensuous world of force, Mr. George's theory of land-holding, or Spencer's law of progress."[16]

K.C. had an open mind in a closed society. Her hobbies included cooking, French, painting, and the latest scientific theories of child raising; she also studied astronomy and accepted the theory of reincarnation. This intrigued Garland, who studied psychic phenomena, attended seances and meetings of the Society of Psychical Research, and then wrote a book called *Forty Years of Psychic Research* (1938). The Hernes and Garland tried "table tipping" without success. Herne just laughed, calling it ridiculous.

The Garland-Herne stand on religion was unorthodox. Herne admitted. "I do not believe I, James A. Herne, will exist as an in-

dividual after I leave here."[17] The more conventional K.C. wrote
Herne in 1885, "I am beginning to realize for the first time in my
life what a great benefaction Christ was to the world, and how
noble and yet simple were the truths that He taught, and how by
that greatest of all methods, Example, He impressed upon the
people the God-like laws of humanity."[18] When Herne said
Christ never existed, she answered so what—his ideas mattered
most.

K.C.'s Christ, however, wasn't a tradition-tied Christ but a
deep, individualized experience. She once expressed this view to
friends at York Harbor who replied, "But Mrs. Herne, if you
sweep the churches away...."

"Sweep them away!" cried K.C. with a rhetorical slash,
"And let us begin all over again with the religion of Jesus Christ
in our hearts!"

The ladies soon left. K.C. overheard these departing
remarks:

"Did she really say, 'Sweep them away?'"

"Yes, she did, my dear, I heard her. She said, 'Sweep the
churches away.'"[19]

These ladies reported to their friends in Boston that K.C.
encouraged free love. It was possibly a distortion of truth to be
expected from such good church women.

Garland, raised on the agnosticism of Robert E. Ingersoll,
supported the Hernes. "The faith in which we had been reared
had already grown dim, and under the light of Ingersoll's re-
morseless humor most of our superstitions vanished. I do not
think my father's essential Christianity was in any degree diminished; he merely lost his respect for certain outworn traditions
and empty creeds."[20]

That's what bothered both Garland and the Hernes—all
the outworn traditions and empty creeds.

The Hernes soon shared Garland's guilt complex. His family still lived in a desolate prairie shanty in South Dakota, a hopeless place of hardship. Had Garland been right to leave them?
His father, like other fathers described in *Main Travelled Roads*,
"rose early and toiled without intermission until the darkness fell
on the plain, then tumbled into bed, every bone and muscle ach-
ing with fatigue, to rise with the sun next morning to the same

round of the same ferocity of labor."[21] His mother was worn and wasted, suffering from a stroke. K.C. assured him, "You'll work it out, I am sure of it."[22]

Herne also had troubles. The fortune of $100,000 from *Hearts of Oak* had vanished fast. He told Garland: "The managers all admit the good points of my play. In fact they say it is too good. 'The public doesn't want a good play,' they say. 'It wants bad plays. Write a bad play, Jim. Not too bad but just bad enough,' is their advice. Meanwhile I must play in theaters which are not suited to my way of doing things and am obliged to insert into my lines tricks and turns which I despise."[23]

Henry James expressed a similar sentiment in a remark about *The American*. "Oh, how it must not be too good and how very bad it must be! *A moi*, Scribe; *à moi*, Sardou, *à moi*, Dennery!—Reduced to its simplest expression, and that reduction must be my play."[24]

Garland finally told Herne: "There is a public for your plays if we can reach it. You can do better work than any you have done and no play can be 'too good.' I want you to write a play in which there are no compromises at all."[25] So Herne rewrote *Drifting Apart*—for the third time—and Garland criticized it, scene by scene, rejecting those sections managers liked most. Yet "he never suggested"[26] a line in any of Herne's dramas; he just commented on results.

Herne hit the road again in *Hearts of Oak*, while polishing the script for *Drifting Apart*. He also completed the first draft of *The Hawthornes* (later *Shore Acres*) and worked on *Margaret Fleming*. He worked on three plays while both managing and starring in a show. K.C. wrote him sympathetically, "How you have energy enough to perform the manifold duties that you have burdened yourself with after playing that exacting part twice a day is honestly wonderful to me, for that alone is enough to tax the strength and vitality of an ordinary man."[27]

The nineteenth century road show was an ordeal modern unionized actors cannot conceive. Performer George Barton Berrell recorded the conditions of these shows in his copy-books during the 1870's. Berrell once rode on eleven railroad lines in fifteen days. (Most lines were locally owned, and each had a different track gauge. So passengers had to change trains very fre-

quently.) The wooden railroad cars were heated by open iron
stoves that sometimes overturned and caused fires; when the
stoves didn't overturn, passengers would either freeze or roast.
Congestion, stifling air, and low seatbacks added to the dis-
comfort.

Layovers at train stations were far removed from the romantic Victorian paintings of such scenes that hang in art galleries. "At Terre Haute we were compelled to lay over a little
more than five hours," complained Berrell. "The station was cold,
disagreeable and dirty; the benches were divided into narrow
little seats, affording a fellow no chance to stretch himself, and
sleeping in an upright position is anything else but comfortable,
and we were at a loss for something to do to pass away the time.
A lunch counter in the depot afforded some coffee and very stale
sandwiches, tough pies and last spring chicken, at treble the
value of the same, and the disposal of this, and a cigar afterwards, caused an hour to pass by almost unheeded."[28]

Exhausted actors, shifting from one "tank town" to another and forced to sleep in shoddy hotels, sometimes fell asleep
during rehearsals. Winging lines resulted. Berrell wrote, "The
part I am cast for in *Lorle* is a long one, and we have been so
pushed with study and travel, that up to the present moment I
have not even had time to read over the lines."[29] Once he rehearsed *Camille, King John,* and *As You Like It* in one morning.

Herne continued rewrites on *Drifting Apart* through the
following summer, corresponding with Garland, whose literary
judgment he trusted. Two letters support this:

June 4, 1889: "Thank you for your offered aid in rewriting 'Drifting Apart,' but let me try first what I can accomplish.
I rewrote the parts of Percy and Mary on Sunday—worked hard
all day. I never did such hard work—or rather I never found
writing such hard work. It didn't seem to come, I had to think it
all out—all day and 7 pages—and my day's work is usually 30
pages. Katharine C. says it is fine work, but I'm going over it
again. If I do make fine work of it, it will be a reflection of Hamlin Garland and his mentorship. I never saw my faults, conspicuous as I know they must be to others. I could not see them, until
you made them so clear. I shall take the 1st and 3rd acts with me

and when I have them as perfect as I can get them I'll ask you to read them."[30]

August 5, 1889: "I will do no more with 'Drifting Apart' until I see you. I have done about all I can with it. After I have heard you fully and get closer to your ideas, I will then scribble a little more on it, and try to get it nearly right by the time it gets to the stage again. I've finished 'The Hawthornes'—'rough finished'—and you'll like some of it."[31]

Garland's brother, Franklin, also caught theatre fever and, when a retired leading lady reduced to the "Kerosene Circuit" offered him a tentative job, Hamlin turned coach for his brother. Three nights a week, from seven until nine, the brothers met in a cutlery where Franklin was bookkeeper, and rehearsed *East Lynne, Leah the Forsaken,* and *The Lady of Lyons.* "At last, emboldened by his star's praise, he cut loose from his ledger and went out on a tour which was extremely diverting but not at all remunerative," recalled Garland. "The company ran on a reef and Frank sent for carfare which I cheerfully remitted, crediting it to his educational account."[32]

Franklin never returned to ledger keeping. Herne offered him "the small but excellent character bit of the Old Fisherman" in *Hearts of Oak* at $20 a week and "ostensible charge of the stage" while he learned "the artistic, mechanical and commercial parts of the dramatic profession from the back door to the front."[33]

Hamlin Garland became Herne's unpaid, self-appointed press agent. The next season he attended the opening of *Drifting Apart* in Troy, sharing the road's "ups and downs" in Brooklyn and Buffalo. As the train rumbled along he and the Hernes studied *Drifting Apart,* trying to pinpoint its failures and structural weaknesses. They worried whether the western audiences would accept the play. Hopes wavered from stand to stand. Years later Garland remembered: "I experienced the desolating effect which the sounds of slow-dropping seats in a half-filled auditorium had on a manager. The deep discouragement of watching streams of people pass the open door was another scarring experience."[34]

Herne joked about the empty seats, but sometimes lines of worry etched his comic mask. "He was the Irish bard whose songs are compounded of laughter and the wailing keen," Garland wrote. "His face is one of the saddest and sweetest I have ever seen,"[35] another Ashmont visitor observed. His daughter Chrystal said, "There was a deep core of sadness in him which was part of the heritage of his genius."[36]

Herne was caught in a proletarian paradox. Common people refused to accept reality on the stage because its harsh lights exposed psychological scar tissue. They preferred the soft glow of romanticism. It lied a lot better. Meanwhile the intellectuals avoided theatrical lures. As the *Atlantic Monthly* commented in 1869, "The Boston which makes itself known in civilization—letters, politics, reform—goes as little to the theatre as fashionable Boston."[37] And the fashionables much preferred the scintillating wit of English drawing-room comedies or well-made French and German dramas of intrigue. Intellectually, Herne was committed to writing realistically of and for the common people —whether they flocked to attend his plays or not.

Garland and Herne were an odd-matched pair. Though close friends their ideas and temperaments differed. "There was about Garland a directness and forthrightness that amounted almost to brusqueness. He had no small talk and abhorred trivialities. When the conversation did not interest him, he would get up and walk away," recalled Herne's daughter Julie. "His humor was grim and ironic rather than genial."[38] In 1895 *The Atlantic Monthly* accused Garland of "Napoleonic self confidence" and of being "self-willed and contemptuous of those better trained than himself."[39] Friend Joseph Edgar Chamberlain wrote that he "wore a rather long, brown beard, that gave him a sort of apostolic appearance. His grave, meditative manner heightened this apostolic effect."[40]

Garland's reform motives seem blurred, and there is a question whether he was genuinely committed to social change or to literary recognition. Did he use people for personal gain? And why didn't he follow his own advice? Garland had urged Herne to write a work without compromise, one exposing the painful truths of life. Yet, he reshaped his short stories for

Richard Watson Gilder, editor of the conservative and prestigious *Century*. In October 1889 he altered a "maternity scene" in "Ol Pap's Flaxen" for Gilder. He also changed an offensive speech in "The Test of Elder Pill." When Gilder rejected "A Prairie Heroine," Garland responded that he'd "submit to any reasonable change." He had colloquialized the speech in "A Stop Over at Tyre" and then agreed to "soften down the lingual sins of Albert."[41]

Although Garland urged realism in theatre reform during the '90's, time drenched his flame. As a member of the Pulitzer Prize Drama Committee in the 1920's, he attended O'Neill's *Desire Under the Elms*. His judgment: "It is cast in the present vogue for illicit love, brutal speech, cynical philosophy and pretentious realism. . . . Without its morbid sexual scenes it would have no box office appeal. It failed to move me save to a disgust."[42] He also concluded that *What Price Glory* "pleased the audience by its profanity, its irreligion, its utter lack of heroism and especially by its open sensuality." Comparing it to Maxim Gorki and Eugene O'Neill he added: "The formula of these plays is quite simple. Scrape together in one spot all the panderers, harlots, drunkards, thieves and cowards of the army, and report their filthy jests, curses and embraces, and women will crowd to see it and applaud it. This military play is not military, it is merely the life behind the lines."[43]

Garland eventually resigned from the Pulitzer Prize Drama Committee. He rationalized: "My judgments did not agree with those of the other members of the committee. They placed too much importance on novelty and on 'daring situations' —that is to say, on animalism, and on dialogue which in the natural course of evolution we should leave to the barroom and cow-camps."[44]

In an assessment of Garland perhaps Lewis O. Saum struck nearest the truth when he wrote: "Literary critics and historians have claimed both too much and too little for the son of the middle border. On the one hand, they admiringly present him as a wrathful man heaping artistic scorn and indictment upon the prevalent cruelty of the American system. On the other hand, they impatiently dismiss him as one who fled the uninspiring

Midwest kitchen because he could not stand the heat, subsequently betaking himself to the Rocky Mountain realm of comfortable romance."[45]

Garland's "veritism" was an impressionistic view of life, influenced by Boston's famed painter, J. J. Enneking. In one Gilder letter he confided, "I aim to be true to the life I am depicting and deal not with abnormal phases so much as with representative phases."[46] He reaffirmed this in an *Arena* article on Ibsen, concluding that realism "has only one law, to be true, not to the objective reality but to the objective reality *as the author sees it*."[47]

Such ambiguous ideas soon plunged Garland into the sprawling abyss of adventure yarns, including such romantic romps as *The Spirit of Sweetwater, Her Mountain Lover, The Light of the Star,* and *The Trail of the Goldseekers.* When C. Hartley Grattan reviewed Garland's *Roadside Meetings* for *The Nation* in 1930, he remarked: "There is something tragically ironic in his deference to Gilder, Johnson, and Alden when one considers that he was supposed to be a radical. But the situation reveals the important fact that Garland never quite knew where he was going. He wanted to be truthful in his own stories, but he got himself confused by thinking about 'wholesome' realism."[48] Bernard I. Duffey commented: ". . . for Hamlin Garland reform and realism were never in themselves *primary* literary or intellectual pursuits. They were accessory for a time to his campaign for intellectual and literary success: *To the extent that they served his end, he used them; but he seemed from the beginning never to hesitate over any necessary compromises.*"[49]

The great difference between Garland and Herne became apparent as each faced demands for compromise. Garland grew conservative and relished literary lionization. Herne remained unchanged by fame and fortune. Even reporters remarked about his unaffected attitude backstage, a far cry from the preoccupation with self that attacked many star performers. Garland was also amazed by Herne's unchanging nature: "He was intellectually young. He seemed of my own age rather than a generation ahead of me."[50]

Even Garland's energetic endorsement of Henry George's single-tax theory seems suspect. He told Flower in 1890 that

Progress and Poverty had "opened a new world to him, a world of hope and inspiration, when all life seemed hopeless and chaotic."[51] But he also wrote Gilder the same year: "The single-tax with me means international copyright, the Sermon on the Mount, and vacations for everybody."[52] Perhaps this latter remark was only a jest?

Garland gradually divorced himself from Herne, although he continued to admire the playwright's persistence. But Herne's *Griffith Davenport* (1899) went too far for Garland, who offered "novel adaptation" as his major criticism. Another objection seems more reasonable—Herne's honest depiction of the slavery question in *Griffith Davenport*. Garland couldn't sanction suicide on stage, or accept a black slave slashing his own throat in preference to bondage. This act certainly rattled his prediction in *Crumbling Idols* that future literature would deal "with the wholesome love of honest men for honest women, with the heroism of labor, [and] the comradeship of men."[53] Maybe in Garland's romantic West it would, but not in Herne's troubled South.

Garland's earlier years were dynamic ones. He supported everything from farm reform to women's rights, and he helped Herne dig roots among Boston's literati. As he affirmed in 1893: "The conservative tries to argue that fundamentals cannot change; that they are the same yesterday, to-day, and to-morrow. If that were true, then a sorrowful outlook on the future would be natural. Such permanency would be death. Life means change."[54]

Life means change. Perhaps the radical Garland of the 1890's should be remembered, not the later despairing writer who lamented in *A Son of the Middle Border*: "The ravening years—how they destroy." [55]

9 a miserable lot of twaddle

IAGO, MACBETH, HAMLET, and Lear were all Shakespearean showcases for America's top tragedian, Edwin Booth, that prince of players whom Hamlin Garland called "my chief exemplar of noble speech."[1] During his Boston lean years, Garland paid 35 cents to perch in the first balcony of the Boston Museum and inhale Booth's liquid diction. He wrote detailed notebook impressions (6,700 words on *Hamlet*) called "Edwin Booth as a Master of Expression"[2] and even sent Booth his *Macbeth* analysis. Booth sympathetically replied:

"I am very 'poor in thanks' and know not how to express the gratification which your mention of those seldom noticed effects of tone, eye and gesture have given me. It is more encouraging to know that such delicate lights and shades are appreciated and not wasted (as I have often feared they were) than in loudest applause bestowed on the bolder effects of one's art work. But as this seems to come too near the praising of myself, I will say no more than I thank you sincerely for the pleasure you have given me in the knowledge that the more careful part of my labor is not lost."[3]

Booth inspired Garland to write more notebook impressions on theatre such as: "The drama is following the lead of the novel and from the romantic is becoming realistic. The present is being studied."[4] Play scratchings also started. Then came *Drifting Apart* and the Hernes.

Playwriting became one joint product of the Garland-Herne friendship. Garland mailed a single-tax work, *Jason Ed-*

wards (later altered to *Under the Wheel* from a line in Turgenev's *Fathers and Sons*), to Gilder, saying: "Mr. Howells calls it a great play and Mr. Herne agrees from the actor's standpoint. Their opinions make me courageous enough to send it to you.... The publication of this book or play would help the production and the production would help the sale of the publication."[5] Garland followed up, "You couldn't do me more good than by the publication of my drama—which is at least an American play."[6] But Gilder didn't bite. Benjamin Orange Flower published the play in the July 1890 issue of *The Arena,* causing the excited Garland to write Herne: "B. O. Flower and I are getting chums. He's one o' my kind. Don't smoke, chew, drink... he's indefatigable.... He's concentrated moral purpose. And behind him stands that brother of his pouring out money wherever needed."[7]

According to the *Standard,* Garland planned to publish a fifty-page paperback of *Under the Wheel* for 25 cents or less. He preferred it "rather to be widely read than to be a paying production." The *Standard* added, "He has other plays, with reform tendencies in preparation."[8] Meanwhile, Herne continued to help.

Under the Wheel was a social protest play with one intent —to preach Georgism. (See the following chapter for Herne's connection with Henry George and the single-tax movement.) In the play's Barta Press preface, Garland wrote: "I do not insist on the infallibility of my belief. I simply say I am satisfied that the destruction of all monopoly on land by a simple governmental levy upon the social or site-value of land is the heroic cure for most—if not all—of the disease and deformity of our social life."[9]

Under the Wheel's plot concerned Jason Edwards, a Boston laborer, who is crushed in the awesome vise of rising costs and falling wages, deceived by the false hopes of a "road leading to the West, to wealth, health, and freedom."[10] He goes to Boomtown and free land but truth soon reveals social corruption. The roving reporter Reeves (who loves Edwards' artistic daughter) pleads Garland's case: "I say, if this is free land, what in the devil would you call high-priced land? The settler pays for his free land all that makes life worth living; these families have purchased their bare and miserable acres with blood and

sweat and tears. Free land! Bah! For a century there has been
no free land in America."[11] And that's the story—almost. Lack
of rain coupled with a fierce hailstorm ruins Edwards' farm.
Crushed again by the deterministic forces of nature, he agrees
to live with his daughter and Reeves, who affirms Garland's romantic prophecy, "A fair chance for every man—it's coming!"[12]
Then the climactic clincher: Edwards' sudden paralysis, which
proves Garland's playwriting pluck. Yet, Garland pontificated
too much, his great flaw. He didn't heed Herbert Jhering's
words, "The didactic piece that sets out to activate the spectator, only ends by making him passive once more."

Another Garland flaw was his resistance to romanticism,
a temper he couldn't reconcile with realism. After seeing Beatrice Cameron in Ibsen's *A Doll's House,* he told Herne, "No
more of Shakespeare's hash!"[13] He also blustered about Shakespeare in *The Arena.* "Had he done his work with keener perception and with less regard for traditions, he would have been
greater, because he would thus have embodied more of the loves
and aspirations of his fellow-men and less of the intrigues and
crimes of the crowned brigands, whose lives were crimes, whose
deaths were public blessings, and he would have been greater,
and his relationship to democratic America closer than it is."
Then Garland uttered a classic hypocritical statement, "He was
painfully anxious to please my Lord This or That, who could be
of living and very material use to him,—or to the Queen, who
could help him keep the wolf from his door. Witness his abject
dedications."[14] One might ask Garland about Gilder and
Flower. Wasn't he painfully anxious to please them?

Garland based his second polemic, *A Member of the Third
House,* on a scandal in the Massachusetts legislature involving
railway monopoly. (He attended the hearings, collecting notes.)
This time even Flower gasped, writing Garland: "I think it is
immense, one of the finest dramatic creations I have ever read.
I am not, however, certain that you do not lay yourself and your
publishers liable notwithstanding your preface, because you
graphically portray so many individuals that will be readily recognized, then passing from that without changing your characters you picture individuals which in the first part of the play
are well known personages as being criminals."[15]

Garland finally gave an "author's reading" on October 30, 1890, at Boston's Chickering Hall, where Herne later staged *Margaret Fleming*. He charged 50 cents. Like Garland's early stories, the script was diluted. He "changed three acts" and took "the vim out of the dialogue because making it so much vaguer,"[16] as he confessed to friend Howells.

The critics' comments were contradictory—as usual. The following review snatches support George Bernard Shaw's contention that critics "become so accustomed to the formula that at last they cannot relish or understand a play that has grown naturally, just as they cannot admire the Venus of Milo because she has neither a corset nor high heeled shoes:"

"It has sufficient action to conform to the demands of the stage;" "reportorial in style, lacking in humor and movement;" "a conventional instinct for situation, but no power for developing character;" "a powerful play full of peculiarly dramatic situations."[17]

A Member of the Third House was never published, Garland stacking it in his "Development Bureau." It later became a novel, an unfortunate end because Garland had playwriting talent. Walter Fuller Taylor writes that "Garland possessed unusual dramatic force. In sheer power, none of the commercial plays of the era can be seriously compared with it; nor did Garland's generation produce, in any other literary form, a more striking treatment of the victim-of-society theme."[18]

Political plays like *A Member of the Third House* and *Under the Wheel* offered poor production prospects during the 1890's because of their controversial topics. Caspar H. Nannes remarks in *Politics in the American Drama* that *A State of the Union* (a 1946 Pulitzer Prize winner that ran 765 performances) wouldn't have survived a week during the 1890's. "The plays of the 1890's reveal the widespread political immaturity of the audience to whom the playwrights were appealing," he says. "Though there were plays on the Cuban situation, woman suffrage, and prohibition, none of them came to hard grips with these problems. The plays about the Cuban rebellion were primarily ones using the explosive international question as an excuse for presenting a melodramatic plot. These plots, with very little effort, could substitute any other situation and be as effective theatrically. In contrast to such plays as *Watch on the Rhine* (1941) and *There Shall be No Night* (1940), melodramas like *The Last Stroke* indicate an almost childish immaturity in their approach to grave problems."[19]

This was Garland's complaint. He dealt with grave political problems to some extent in his dramas, but failed to attract audiences.

Playwriting intrigued Garland. He dramatized Howells' *A Modern Instance* and labored on adaptations of "Rise of Boomtown," "Ol' Pap's Flaxen," and other early unpublished stories. Several other Herne collaborations followed: *Fall River*, which Herne told Howells "did not come out right,"[20] *Mrs. Crisp* with K.C., and *Marrying a Title*.[21] He also wrote several Hollywood scenarios in later years.

Herne's reactions to Garland's playwriting skill were mixed. He respected Garland's literary background and analytical knowhow but questioned his grasp of dramatic movement. Herne jokingly said Garland's idea of a play was "a scene in which two people discuss, for instance, the purchase of a ton of coal. One says, 'I think we are running short of coal.' The other replies, 'We have enough to last until next week.' To him, this is realism. To me it is not drama."[22]

Garland's work often presented aesthetic contradictions. When he gave the Hernes *A Member of the Third House* to criticize, K.C. questoned his philosophy:

"Mr. Garland, does this play express your idea of drama? Is it an example of what you think a play ought to be?"

"Yes," replied Garland with great solemnity for he was always very serious about his work. "I think that it pretty well represents me."

"Well," said Katharine. "It is a very fine play and in it you have embodied all the dramatic principles that James A. and I have been fighting for and which you said you didn't believe in."[23]

Many of Herne's contemporaries as dramatists were, like Garland, novelists turned playwrights. He had reputable company: Mark Twain, Bret Harte, and Henry James. All four would have cherished Truman Capote's conclusion that "in the theater one is a molecule that has to be joined to other molecules to produce a living, breathing thing. I've done it, but I don't really accept it. That's why I'm not partial to the theater. I just don't function well in team sports."[24]

Mark Twain, for instance, hated theatre; or so he said. This feeling grew when he wrote drama reviews for the *San Francisco Morning Call,* six reviews a night, seven nights a week. "There has never been a time from that day to this, forty years, that I have been able to look at even the outside of a theater without a spasm of the dry gripes,"[25] he wrote in *Mark Twain in Eruption.* But this was a typical Twain overstatement.

On other occasions Twain passionately defended American actors. When a minister refused George Holland burial, friends removed his body to the Church of the Transfiguration, "the little church around the corner." Twain despised organized religion, and wrote, "Was it not pitiable, that spectacle? Honored and honorable George Holland, whose theatrical ministry had for fifty years softened hard hearts, bred generosity in cold ones, broadened bigoted ones, and made many and many a stricken one glad and filled it brim full of gratitude, figuratively spit upon in his unoffending coffin by this crawling, slimy, sanctimonious, self-righteous reptile!"[26]

Theatre attracted Twain throughout his life. He dramatized *The Prince and the Pauper* and *Tom Sawyer,* the play Augustin Daly refused before its novelization, although he had earlier produced a version of Twain's *Roughing It.* He tried to persuade Howells to collaborate on Thomas Carlyle's life of Oliver Cromwell and his brother's life; he corresponded with a leading Viennese playwright at the Burg Theater and wrote an updated version of *Hamlet.* He also completed the unproduced *Simon Wheeler, The Amateur Detective* and considered dramatization of *Huckleberry Finn* and *A Connecticut Yankee.*

Twain's theatre "hit" was *The Gilded Age,* a melodrama bordering on burlesque about a heroine who murders a villain but is rescued by Colonel Mulberry Sellers' witness stand "stump speech." This role brought fame and fortune to actor John T. Raymond, whom Twain disliked. It opened at New York's Park Theatre in 1874, running 119 performances, a smash. Brander Matthews called it "a rickety contrivance; it creaked in its joints; its plot was arbitrary and violent and unconvincing."[27] The play earned around $150,000, split between Twain and Raymond. Twain even hired an agent who traveled with the road show, reporting receipts each day on a postcard, and each day apparently, Twain danced around his dinner table counting profits.

The Gilded Age's astonishing success inspired Twain to write a sequel. His collaborator was William Dean Howells. Twain wrote America's "dean" of realistic literature: "Your refined people and purity of speech would make the best possible background for this coarse old ass, and when you are done, I could take your manuscript and rewrite the Colonel's speeches and make him properly vulgar and extravagant. . . . Shall we think this over, or drop it as being nonsense?"[28]

Howells thought it over and collaborated, a big mistake. Although he was Twain's editor and friend, their botched-up play, *The American Claimant, or Mulberry Sellers Ten Years Later* was called "a mistable lot of twaddle with neither dramatic construction nor reason"[29] by *The Theatre* and "so remote from human sympathy that probably, it cannot be long lived"[30] by the *Tribune*. Even Howells conceded defeat, finally writing Twain: "It is a lunatic that we have created, and while a lunatic in one act might amuse, I'm afraid that in three he would simply bore. . . . As it stands, I believe the thing will fail, and it would be a disgrace to have it succeed."[31]

Howells and Twain also approached Herne about collaborating on *The American Claimant*. Howells wrote Twain on January 28, 1890: "I have given Herne the play, and talked the matter over with him. He is very hopeful of something from us; and he knows just how we're fixed regarding this."[32] He followed up on February 7: "Herne is immensely pleased with main points of play—fire extinguisher, phonograph, telephone scene, drunken scene; but we both think the materialization must all come out, and Sellers kept sane, and broadened, deepened, softened—made everything Raymond could do and all he couldn't do. If you can get the play back from Burbank, I'll sketch a new plot keeping all the good that's now in it, and involving your notion of rich international marriage. Then Herne will be sure whether he wants it. I like him better and better. He was wonderfully intelligent about the piece, and could edit it splendidly, and play it to break your heart with joy."[33]

Twain responded on February 11: "All right—I've written B'bank. Herne's is a fine straight-forward utterance. Put it where you can find it (when) if a time comes for making a contract."[34]

The "straight-forward" utterance Twain mentioned was Herne's frank letter to Howells, in which he said, "Just as soon as I am at liberty to announce the fact that 'W. D. Howells and Sam'l Clemens 'Mark Twain' are writing a play for Jas. A. Herne' I will begin to arrange for a proper opening and there will in my mind be no difficulties in getting that."

But Herne rejected claptrap like *The American Claimant*, even with the magic Howells-Twain insignia. "As I explained in part to you, a play for me must be more than a 'farce.' it must be a play of human interest—the more scope for the portrayal of *all* the emotions the more grasp of opportunities for grasp of character." This was why Howells told Twain he'd decided to restructure Sellers, creating a more three-dimensional figure.

Herne continued: "I dare say you are aware that I have always done my own plays and at my own expense. I have of late been unsuccessful."[35] Herne meant he couldn't afford to take a long-shot chance. As he told Howells in another letter: "I'm not in the position of Mr. Howard—to say to a manager, 'I'll write you a play to be ready such a time' and have the manager say—'Very well, the time is so and so and I'll book it for these months.' I've got to *show* my play."[36]

Herne offered Howells and Twain three options: (1) A weekly-salary contract including a percentage of the profits for his "creative share in the undertaking."[37] For this he'd book times, engage the company, arrange business, and superintend the entire production. (2) Stage the play, paying Howells and Twain a royalty and "an equitable division" of profits with him "positive head of the working organization." The cost would be about $3,000. (3) Purchase the play, offering Howells and Twain royalties on receipts."[38] The three, however, didn't reach an agreement. Herne's association with Howells did continue through most of the 1890's, including association with Howells' later play, *The Rise of Silas Lapham*.

Bret Harte wrote more theatre twaddle. His infatuation with the theatre's till first spawned *Two Men of Sandy Bar* (1876), produced by Stuart Robson, who gave him a $3,000 advance and guaranteed $20 a performance. This western romp corralled Harte's favorite characters: John Oakhurst, Colonel Starbottle, and a newcomer, Hop Sing, the Chinese laundryman. Its critical reviews were obituaries. Joseph Francis Daly later wrote, "Stuart Robson took the chief part, and perhaps his unnatural enunciation—which was not only not Western, but not anything known to civilization—killed it."[38] The *New York Times* also helped dig the play's grave when its reviewer said, "The piece is utterly aimless, is without coherency of plot, definiteness of purpose, or actions, and lacking in any sort of artistic symmetry in its model, or characterization in the *dramatic personae*. Its sentiment is maudlin and mushy, its plot shallow, its pathos laughable, and its wit lachrymose."[39]

Hop Sing, in *Two Men of Sandy Bar,* amused Mark Twain, who criticized the critics' harsh criticism. He also charged, "Bret killed off his own chances in New York by having charged loudly and publicly before the opening that the newspaper critics never said a favorable thing about a new play except when the favorable thing was bought and paid for beforehand." Twain agreed to co-author a play based on the "perfectly delightful Chinaman" and "divide the swag"[40] with Harte. They called it *Ah Sin*.

Harte and Twain both hungered for success. But madness was their method. According to Twain, "Bret came to me at Hartford and we talked the whole thing out. Then Bret wrote the piece while I played billiards. Of course, I had to go over it and get the dialect right. Bret never did know anything about dialect."[41] But Twain exaggerated again. He told Howells the work "nearly killed"[42] him.

The Harte-Twain association wasn't productive for long. Twain accused Harte of offending his wife, calling him "a born bummer and a tramp" and "a loafer and an idler"[43] in a letter. Thus ended their brief encounter, even before opening night.

Ah Sin finally limped onto Broadway, minus Harte. Its audience included "Sothern, Boucicault and Brougham and all the literary lights in town."[44] A Harte-Twain play made big news. The evening's highlight was Twain's now-famous curtain speech, full of exaggerations such as: "The construction of this play was a work of great labor and research, also of genius and invention —and plagiarism. . . . I never saw a play improve as this one did. The more he cut out of it the better it got right along. He cut out, and cut out, and I do believe this would be one of the best plays in the world today if his strength had held out, and he could have gone on and cut out the rest of it."[45]

Harte finally scored on Broadway with Charles Frohman's staging of *Sue* (1898), based on "The Judgment of Bolinas Plain." It starred Annie Russell, who also triumphed in the London run. Perhaps Frohman pigeonholed *Sue*'s claim to fame in his opening-night cablegram: "Well received. Fine acting. Press praises."[46]

Henry James' drama addiction also dawned early, long before the "sawdust and orange-peel phase"[47] of his literary life. He once scrawled the names of plays and players on New York billboards, saving pennies to attend matinees at Barnum's "lecture room" in the famed American Museum. Theatre attendance was a family tradition. In his autobiography James remembered much: "the painted portrait, large as life, of the celebrity of the hour, then 'dancing' at the Broadway Theatre, Lola Montez, Countess of Lansfeldt, of a dazzling and unreal beauty and in a riding-habit lavishly open at the throat . . . the Ravels, French acrobats, dancers and pantomimists (at Niblo's, and Franconi's circus) that blazed with fresh paint and rang with Roman chariot-races."[48]

James also suffered from the dilemma regarding how to reconcile drama and theatre, those perennial irreconcilables. He once moaned: "The whole odiousness of the thing lies in the connection between the drama and the theatre. The one is admirable in its interest and difficulty, the other loathsome in its conditions."[49] James also boasted: "It has been long my most earnest and definite intention to commence at playwriting as soon as I can. This will be soon, and then I shall astound the world."[50]

James didn't astound the world. The world astounded James

with its general indifference to his drawing-room dramas, *Daisy Miller*, *The American*, and the catastrophic *Guy Domville*.

James' earliest play, *Daisy Miller*, was an expansion of a well-received short story. Daniel Frohman, manager of the Madison Square Theatre, thought it had "too much talk and not enough action."[51] So James drew on a Garland technique and held a reading at the St. James Theatre in London. But luck seemed stacked against him. Even Shaw complained the work was "out of fashion."[52] James eventually dissected the script, producing the novelette, *Daisy Miller*.

The American (1891), which ran seventy performances in London, was James' "tribute to the vulgarest of the muses,"[53] meaning theatre. James, who loved English culture, carefully copied all the Oscar Wilde twists and turns of witty repartee, which were all the things Herne despised. James also managed a happy ending for this unhappy story about an honest American entangled with sophisticated European socialites, a frequent theme for James.

James' audience according to *Echo* was "one of the most cultured ever brought together in so small a space."[54] Among their ranks: John Singer Sargent, George Frederick Watts, George du Maurier, Frank Harris, W. E. Norris, Arthur Wing Pinero, George Meredith, and Augustin Daly, the latter always searching for good comedies. Unfortunately, *The American* wasn't one.

Guy Domville (1895) doused James' dramatic drive—almost forever. (In 1908 *The High Bid* was played at Edinburgh by Forbes-Robertson and his wife.) Its opening-night audience at the St. James Theatre in London hissed and shouted. When the lead exclaimed, "I'm the last, my lord, of the Domville's," someone screamed, "It's a bloody good thing y'are." And when the star later approached the footlights, one fellow assured, "T'aint your fault, gov'nor, it's a rotten play."[55]

Guy Domville ran for one month. The disillusioned James wrote his brother William, "Produce a play and you will know, better than I can tell you, how such an ordeal—odious in its essence!—is only made tolerable and palatable by great success; and in how many ways accordingly non-success may be tormenting and tragic, a bitterness of every hour, ramifying into every throb of one's consciousness."[56]

Howells certainly agreed, and in *The Story of a Play*, one of Howells' characters complains: "It's a compromise all the way through—a cursed spite from beginning to end. Your own words don't represent your ideas, and the more conscience you put into the work the further you get from what you thought it would be. Then comes the actor with the infernal chemistry of his personality. He imagines the thing perfectly, not as you imagined it, but as you wrote it, and then he is no more able to play it as he imagined it than you were to write as you imagined it. What the public finally gets is something three times removed from the truth that was first in the dramatist's mind."[57]

Howells really cared about American drama. He published numerous essays on dramatic theory and criticism, wrote about three dozen plays, mainly farces that enjoyed immense popular success outside New York City, and he strongly supported Herne's *Margaret Fleming*. Booth Tarkington recalled that Howells' plays "began to be acted everywhere within a week or two of their publication, and a college boy of the late eighties and 'golden nineties' came home at Christmas to be either in the audience at a Howells farce or in the cast that gave it."[58]

Broadway buffs, however, didn't buy Howell's one-act farces. As Augustin Daly told him, "One-act pieces bring no profit & give little lasting reputation to author, actor or manager."[59] Several Howells plays were professionally staged: Ellen Terry and Beerbohm Tree produced *The Mousetrap* in London; Lawrence Barrett added *Yorick's Love* and *A Counterfeit Presentment* to his repertory; Alessandro Salvini (Tommaso's son) starred in *A Foregone Conclusion*; and the Actors' Guild produced *The Rise of Silas Lapham*.

During the mid–90's, Howells and his cousin, Paul Kester, rewrote *The Rise of Silas Lapham* into a full-length "problem" play about a paint manufacturer with a conscience. But Howells' confidence failed. He once told Augustin Daly, "You know that I can't deal exclusively in tragedy, and I think I could make my play in some parts such a light affair that many people would never know how deeply they ought to have been moved by it."[60]

Herne admired Howells' novel and wrote Hamlin Garland in 1889: "Should you and Mr. Howells conclude to write a play or plays, particularly should you induce Mr. Howells to work with you on a dramatization of Silas Lapham—and put it before the public—will you give me the stage management of it? I know I can do grand work for you in that line, and at the same time benefit myself through winning the endorsement of—and perhaps the acknowledgment of being worthy to be enrolled in—in a measure—in the army of the realistic workers of the day."[61]

But Herne presumed too much. *The Rise of Silas Lapham* wasn't a well-crafted play. Howells also presumed too much and collaborated with Paul Kester. Kester, a swashbuckling hack whose romances such as *The Countess Roudire, Guy Mannering, The Musketeers, When Knighthood was in Flower,* and *Zamar* flooded New York stages during the 90's, couldn't cut serious ice. Howells finally wrote his sister, "Paul gets it together, and then I revise." He added: "It seems promising, but it all depends upon how Herne sees it. He asked for it, however, and there is a good prospect of his taking it."[62]

On June 8, 1898, Herne wrote Howells that new characters and dialogue were needed before he'd stage *Silas Lapham.* He thought the novel would make "a very great play," but "while there is a great play in the book—the book is not a play." Herne also reminded Howells: "And a play from your pen—*must* be a success—artistically and financially. You can't afford to have any other." Howells' reputation was involved, and a poor play could damage it severely. Herne added, "Since reading your manuscript, I am more than ever convinced that my theory of the impossibility of *dramatizing* a great book is correct. What one must do in order to make a play of a great book is *freely adapt* it."[63]

Howells didn't agree. He wrote Kester: "I am writing to Mr. Herne that I cannot undertake the radical reconstruction he looks to with the uncertainty of succeeding at last. I do not know whether to suggest that you would do the work."[64]

Howells appreciated Herne's reputation and competency. The country didn't have a better director-playwright. Yet his ego interfered. Again, on July 31, 1898, Howells wrote Hester that Herne wanted to see him in September. "I do not believe anything will come of it, and I am sure there will not if he expects me to change it radically. The only real chance with him is through the failure of his own play. If that does not succeed he will try ours."[65] Julie Herne confirmed this artistic split between her father and Howells. "We all read and discussed the script and thought it disappointing. I recall that my father told me that Howells said he was 'perfectly satisfied' with Kester's dramatization."[66] Herne suggested changes that Howells would not consent to, and the project was dropped.

That summer Howells moaned to Henry James, "It is strange how the stage can keep on fooling us; what the burnt child does *not* dread is the fire, or least the blue fire of the theatre. I have lately been fool enough to dramatize *Silas Lapham* for an actor who wanted it, and now does *not* want it. What a race! Their obligations are chains of flowers." He also complained to Twain, "I wish I could see some of your plays, in MS, if not on the stage. I have been fool enough to do one (*Silas Lapham*) for an actor who wanted it—and doesn't. I wonder how anyone can be at once so innocent and so sinful, as I am. While I was working at that thing I piled up the riches until I felt as safe from poverty as if I had laid up treasure in heaven."[67]

Howells' *Silas Lapham* still didn't reach the stage, but Howells persisted. On June 30, 1899, he wrote Kester: "I heartily hope you can get it into Mr. Woodward's hands. Of course I am sorry Mr. Herne did not fancy it, but I cannot feel . . . that he has any choice on it, and I do not believe he wants it, or would ever take it. Still he is an old friend, and I think it right, as you do, to notify him of what we intend to do with it."[68]

Another year passed, and in August, 1900, Howells wrote Kester: "I am so glad that there is a chance for poor old Silas that I willingly trust your judgment, in all matters concerning it. Do whatever you think best, and I shall be content."[69]

Howells was content that Kester could do anything to the script, a liberty he had refused Herne. Howells still hungered for a stage success, and hunger inspires compromise, what James Russell Lowell called "a good umbrella, but a poor roof."

The Herne-Howells friendship fractured after *Silas Lapham*. Julie said Howells remained aloof even at Herne's funeral. Yet the break had not been Herne's fault. He had staged Howells' one-act, *Bride Roses*, as a curtain raiser for *Shore Acres* in 1894. This fine-textured work (set in a florist's shop), with its subtle characterizations and symbolic overtones, appealed to Herne.

One other episode probably kindled Howell's resentment. He asked Herne to include a song he wrote in *Shore Acres*. Herne tactfully answered, "The song is an exquisite bit of sentiment— but it doesn't seem to me that it fits *Shore Acres*." He added that a song "would be an interruption" and "break the current of the story."[70] He praised Howells, then asked the novelist to write a play for him and K.C.—an invitation Howells didn't accept.

Howells remains a theatre enigma. He had talent, technique, and energy; he was America's most influential realist and a shrewd businessman. But he was unable to dramatize hard social issues, although he supported the socially conscious Zola, Verga, Tolstoy, and Herne. As one critic wrote in 1883: "Mr. Howells holds himself too far aloof from the real nerve and fiber of our national life—the middle, industrious class. His world is too largely that world of gentlemen and ladies of leisure who can cross and recross the ocean to satisfy refined curiosity, fill sine-cure offices abroad that they may dabble in art, or linger around our summer hotels to study nature and recuperate languid constitutions. While being heartily democratic in his theories, his tastes and sympathies, nevertheless, seem to lead dangerously toward aristocratic exclusiveness."[71]

Howells also hated theatre. Again in his *The Story of a Play*: "Whatever related to the theatre was there, in bizarre solidarity, which was droll enough to Maxwell in one way. But he hated to be mixed up with all that, and he perceived that he must be mixed up with more and more, if he wrote for the theatre. Whether he liked it or not, he was part of the thing which in its entirety meant high-kicking and toe-practice, as well as the expression of the most mystical passions of the heart."[72]

High-kicking and toe-practice. How Howells avoided the "smell of dust . . . mixed with the smell of paint and glue and escaping gas which pervaded the atmosphere of the stage."[73] Herne invited him to rehearsals of *The Country Circus* (1891) in New York, but the novelist sputtered excuses, although he later attended a few rehearsals of *Shore Acres*. Yet Howells wrote in *Harper's* "In our time, as in all times, the dramatic poet should be part of the theatre."[74]

Lillian Sabine finally dramatized Howells' *Silas Lapham* in 1919. The Actors' Guild produced the work, which ran 47 performances. Garland attended its opening. "We were a bit disappointed," he wrote. "The lines lacked the clear strength of Howells' dialogue. The play was a bit confused in outline and the last act an anticlimax; but it put me 'away back there!'—in Boston."[75]

The "away back there" Boston of Herne, Howells—and Henry George.

10 the single tax crank

IF DICKENS MADE me an actor, Henry George made me a thinker,"[1] Herne once told an interviewer. George's single tax based on land values appealed to Herne as a means of erasing want. ("For rent being taken by the State in taxes, would be really common property, and every member of the community would participate in the advantages of its ownership.")[2] He promoted George's *Progress and Poverty* everywhere, reading passages to his company, lecturing in churches, halls, and theatre wings, and giving free copies of the book to converts. In 1896 he wrote George, "My fealty to you and my allegiance to our common cause for now and for all time."[3]

Henry George, whose single-tax treatise *Progress and Poverty* sold millions, attracted other theatricalists besides Herne.

Leo Tolstoy praised it: "People do not argue with the teaching of George; they simply do not know it. He who becomes acquainted with it cannot but agree."[4]

Shaw wrote Garland (who chaired the 25th Progress and Poverty dinner in 1905), "When I was thus swept into the great Socialist revival of 1883, I found that five-sixths of those who were swept in with me had been converted by Henry George."[5]

Francis Neilson (actor, politician, and stage manager under Charles Frohman) wrote: "Here I fell into the company of several men who knew George and loved him. They were James Herne, the actor, George Francis Train, who started the first tramway in England, Mark Twain, Edison, and a man who made hats—Ben Boblin. All of these people were land values men.

Moreover, I became acquainted with many old actors who were students of Henry George's gospel."[6]

And Herne's fellow American dramatist, Henry C. deMille, whose collaborations with David Belasco included *Lord Chumley* and *The Charity Ball*, planned a Georgist play before his death. His son, William deMille, married George's daughter Anne; their daughter was famed choreographer, Agnes deMille. William de-Mille's brother was Hollywood producer Cecil B. deMille.[7]

Howells was skeptical of George's teachings. He wrote Garland, "Understand, I don't argue against you; I don't yet know what is best; but I am reading and thinking about questions that carry me beyond myself and my miserable literary idolatries of the past."[8] He later added: "(George) is *one* of the hopes, but not the only one, it seems to me; and I'm not sure that his truth is the first in order."[9] Garland recalled: "As often as I dared, I tried to win Howells to a belief in the single tax. He gave it his allegiance to the point of saying, 'It is good as far as it goes but reforms should go further.' In other words he was more socialistic than I. We never *argued*—we just stated our theories and convictions."[10]

Although Garland and Herne supported George, neither subscribed to Marxism. Herne opposed the Utopian cant of Edward Bellamy's *Looking Backward*, calling it paternalism. He concluded that free competition wasn't America's problem, just the opposite, a lack of it. That's why George called Karl Marx "a most superficial thinker, entangled in an exact and vicious terminology" and a "prince of muddleheads."[11] Howells seemed to straddle the socialist issue. He accepted Tolstoyan socialism on the surface but, "meantime, I wear a fur-lined overcoat and live in all the luxury my money can buy."[12]

Garland first heard Henry George at Boston's Faneuil Hall, the historic temple where such orators as Wendell Phillips, Ralph Waldo Emerson, Theodore Parker, and William Garrison had spoken. George followed in their footsteps. That night Garland and his brother sat in Faneuil Hall's narrow gallery, peering at the central floor "paved with a closely packed mosaic of derby hats and rough coats of all shades of black and tan," the garb of common humanity. Garland wrote, "We hung over the rail with such intensity of impatience as only Edwin Booth could call from us." Then entered George, "a short red-bearded man of dignified demeanor and keen glance," who spoke powerfully of railroads, interstate commerce and conservation, leading Garland to later exclaim: "I count that speech among the greatest influences of my life."[13]

Garland and his brother attended several Anti-Poverty Society meetings on Sunday evenings in the Horticultural Hall on Tremont Street. When attendance weakened, Garland volunteered his services. "All my speeches," he said, "thereafter helped to dye me deeper than ever with the color of reform."[14]

"The Social Aspect of the Land Tax" was Garland's first venture on the Anti-Poverty Society platform. His speeches echoed Herne's beliefs, as well. Among them:

"... free land is a myth. We have squandered our inheritance. We have given it away in empires, we sell it now in counties. We have prepared the way for our children to be serfs under the control of the land owner."

"Monopolization of land has produced tenement houses, kept vice and drunkenness and ignorance alive, turned millions of young men and women into machines, wearing out their lives in hopeless toil."

"Let us raise taxes from the products of human exertion and tax the land values created by the whole people. Let us free the land. . . ." "Matchless musicians will not waste their lives on lonely farms, nor superb voices be lost in far sierras. Sculptors will not die in dark mines, nor poets be silent for lack of education and encouragement. The reign of justice will have begun."[15]

Other Georgist speeches followed. At the 1890 National Single Tax Conference Garland proclaimed, "I yield to no man in my devotion to the single tax and my admiration to our great leader, Henry George."[16] Garland was elected president of the Boston Single Tax league; he became a Massachusetts delegate to the National Single Tax Conference; he helped in Henry George's 1896 campaign for mayor of New York City; he stirred the Western Farmers' Alliance groups; and he contributed numerous articles to George's single-tax weekly, *The Standard*, incorporating his ideas into short stories, lectures, readings, and novels.

Herne's social consciousness, of course, surfaced long before that second Ashmont meeting when Garland "switched the conversation to the single tax" and "the constitution of matter and Spencer's theories of evolution."[17] The road opened his eyes to all the abuses of the American power structure, to an America in which the poor were growing poorer while the rich grew richer. He could see that just a few people controlled most of the country's wealth.

Working conditions were outrageous, leading President Benjamin Harrison to complain, "American workmen are subjected to peril of life and limb as great as a soldier in time of war."[18] Sweatshop women labored 84 hours a week for five cents an hour. Child labor was rampant. There were the dangers of coal dust and cave-ins in the mines, toxic chemicals in the quarries, and poisonous gases, heat, and generally hazardous conditions in the factories.

Graft and spoilsmanship soiled American politics. The Tweed Ring alone siphoned off $60 million from New York City's coffers, and other cities such as Boston, Chicago, and Philadelphia were also boss-ruled. When George had run for mayor of New York City in 1896, stuffed ballot boxes beat him.

Herne first met George in 1889. The *Standard*'s office was in Union Square, three flights up, three flights well worth climbing to meet the movement's messiah. As Henry George, Jr., recalled: "Mr. Herne was in the happiest mood when he came to the *Standard* office that day to meet my father. That sweet kindness was in his smile and shining light in his eyes which beamed from the face of his *Uncle Dan'l* in 'Shore Acres' soon afterwards. He said that this philosophy explained what before was to him inexplicable, and that he would hereafter do all in his power to preach it."[19]

And he did for years and years.

As late as 1900 the *Brooklyn Eagle* drama critic wrote: "So the afternoon slipped by as the grand old man of the American stage—he is now 63 years old—talked of his art, of his belief in the social future which is to come as surely as the sun shall rise on a new day, of his friendship for Henry George and his share in the advocacy of Henry George's doctrines which he preached every Sunday evening for years after acting every night and two afternoons during the week."[20]

Herne spoke in churches everywhere on such controversial issues as "Religion and the Drama" and "The Drama and Society," usually bringing in the message of the single-tax. Dressed in a Prince Albert coat he became known as "the man in the white tie" to thousands.

While touring the West in *Shore Acres*, for example, he delivered a lecture to the affluent First Congregational Church in Kansas City on "The Theatre as It Is." The *New York Times* concluded that "the audience was probably the largest in numbers that ever gathered in a church edifice in this city." Among Herne's remarks:

"The theatre is a factor of society. Just as much so as is the Church, and in spite of all the stigma that is attached to it, and all the vice and pernicious power, it is charged with, it is still an educator, and its influence is for good, and not for evil. It is not the province of the theatre to preach objectively, but to teach subjectively, and there is no reason why the Church and the theatre should not work together. I claim that they have stood too long apart. That for the good of the race they should join hands at once and aid each other to free mankind."[21]

Herne's straightforward elocution was tough talk. He took theatre's truths to church, its arch enemy through the ages, and people listened.

Another time he spoke to "a large and fashionable assemblage" at St. Paul's Universalist Church in Chicago. "There would be no vicious art if there were no patrons of vicious art; there would be no vicious literature if there were no vicious readers; there would be no vicious plays if there were no vicious audiences. We must not condemn an art nor an institution because a corrupt civilization has somewhat affected it."

Regarding the single tax, Herne said: "I am, as everybody who knows me is aware, what is termed a single tax man, and while I have too much good judgment to infringe on my privileges here by introducing my doctrines here, and talking of single tax, I will ask your permission to say in brief that we believe that in order to elevate men's minds you must free their bodies. In order to bring men to a realization of the benignity of God you must restore to them the right to share God's natural blessings, which right we claim is now withheld from them by men through an unjust system of taxation, which places the relatively heaviest tax upon the poorest member of society, and thus enriches the one and impoverishes the other." Herne concluded that an acceptance of the single tax would "exalt man and dignify labor, and purify the theater, free the church, and bring about the true religious spirit, the brotherhood of man, and the fatherhood of God."[22]

Harsh weather seldom kept Herne from his speaking engagements. One wintery Sunday in February 1890 he and Garland addressed the Edwin Forrest Lodge of the Actors' Order of Friendship, an entertainment provided free by the Manhattan Single Tax Club. Herne wrote in the *Standard* on January 29: "I believe we will be the first speakers, who were not members of the order, ever permitted to address that lodge as a lodge. . . . In it I see the stepping stone to a mass meeting of actors and the general public; from it I see the realization of what the actors have been pleased to term 'Herne's Dream.' "[23]

Herne spoke on "the relation of the player to the wage earner, and the bearing of the single tax on both." He stressed that laws governing men 200 years ago shouldn't govern men today. "The trouble was the struggle for existence on the one side and the fear of possible poverty on the other," he said. "Ensure to all men an opportunity to exercise their industry—let them feel and learn that by industry alone they can command success, and you encourage them to exercise that industry and the conditions of all men are bettered."[24]

Herne invited Henry George to lecture for the Actors' Single Tax League. He wrote: "Well, I'm still in the cause. The more I read, the more I see, the more I investigate other remedies for our social injustices the more I am convinced that the 'single tax' is the one and only absolute cure. At last I got a chance to talk to the actors in New York. I got the use of the Bijou Theatre, managed to get about three hundred and fifty or four hundred actors together and talked to them for about two hours. I gave them the Single Tax, pure and simple, and I believe I've got them thinking. I want, if possible, on my return, to introduce you to them. An hour's talk from you will settle the question. I can now get a theatre without trouble or cost."[25]

George accepted, speaking on "Why Are so Many Actors

Idle?" It was a question that needed answering and commanded attention.

Garland and Herne also did the reading "Under the Lion's Paw" together for several years without charge. As Herne reasoned, "I cannot give money, but I can give my time and my personal effort."[26] Garland felt likewise, charging only carfare wherever Georgists called. "I am ready to read or speak whenever other engagements will allow."[27]

The following are typical Garland-Herne engagements reported in the *Standard*:

December 8, 1889, in Boston. Garland, William Lloyd Garrison, and Herne spoke at Tremont Temple. Herne also read "Under the Lion's Paw" before road performances of *Drifting Apart* in Milford, New Bedford, and Brockton, Massachusetts.[28]

February 6, 1890, in Lynn. Three hundred people gathered to hear Garland and Herne speak. S. C. Bryant remarked in the *Standard*: "At a recent meeting of the common council an order was passed authorizing the mayor to petition the legislature for the right to tax every mile of the horse railroad franchise."[29] Garland and Herne's speech had served as catalyst for the reform.

April 14, 1890, in Dorchester, a suburb of Boston. Garland spoke for fifteen minutes. Herne spoke another fifty-five minutes, then read "Under the Lion's Paw" before Garland answered questions. The 500-seat hall was packed, its doors finally closed. John Lavis called it "one of the most successful single tax meetings ever held in Boston."[30]

"Under the Lion's Paw" attacked American landlordism. Jim Butler, who believes "in land speculation as the surest way of getting rich," shrewdly rents his property to tenant farmers like Haskins. He lets them improve the land and buildings, then doubles the purchase price when tenants can't pay rising rents. The farmer is crushed beneath the lion's paw. The story's climactic scene between Butler and Haskins became a perfect vehicle for Herne and Garland:

> "Fact is, I think I c'n buy the farm this fall, if you'll give me a reasonable show."
> "Um-m! What do you call a reasonable show?"
> "Well, say a quarter down and three years' time."

Butler looked at the huge stack of wheat, which filled the yard, over which the chickens were fluttering and crawling, catching grasshoppers, and out of which the crickets were singing innumerably. He smiled in a peculiar way as he said, "Oh, I won't be hard on yeh. But what did you expect to pay f'r the place?"

"Why, about what you offered it for before, two thousand five hundred, or *possibly* three thousand dollars," he added quickly, as he saw the owner shake his head.

"This farm is worth five thousand and five hundred dollars, said Butler in a careless and decided voice.

"*What!*" almost shrieked the astounded Haskins. "What is that? Five thousand? Why, that's double what you offered it for three years ago."

"Of course, and it's worth it. It was all run down then; now it's in good shape. You've laid out fifteen hundred dollars in improvements, according to your own story."

"But *you* had nothin' t' do about that. It's my work an' my money."

"You bet it was; but it's my land."

"But what's to pay me for all my—"

"Ain't you had the use of 'em?" replied Bulter, smiling calmly into his face.

Haskins was like a man struck on the head with a sandbag; he couldn't think; he stammered as he tried to say: "but—I never'd git the use—You'd rob me! More 'n that: you agreed—you promised that I could buy or rent at the end of three years at—"

"That's all right. But I didn't say I'd let you carry off the improvements, nor that I'd go on renting the farm at two-fifty. The land is doubled in value, it don't matter how; it don't enter into the question; an' now you can pay me five hundred dollars a year rent, or take it on your own terms at fifty-five-hundred, or—git out."

He was turning away when Haskins, the sweat pouring from his face, fronted him, saying again:

"But you've done nothing to make it so. You hain't added a cent. I put it all there myself, expectin' to buy. I worked an' sweat to improve it. I was workin' for myself an' babes—"

"Well, why didn't you buy when I offered to sell? What y' kickin' about?"

"I'm kickin' about payin' you twice f'r my own things,—my own fences, my own kitchen, my own garden."

Butler laughed. "You're too green t' eat, young feller. Your improvements! The law will sing another tune."

"But I trusted your word."

"Never trust anybody, my friend. Besides, I didn't
promise not to do this thing. Why, man don't look at me
like that. Don't take me for a thief. It's the law. The reg'lar
thing. Everybody does it."[31]

The rising cost of theatre sites was influencing managers
to cut total production costs by booking "sure-fire" shows—
farces, musicals, and melodramas—instead of experimental and
literary works. But Garland believed that the single tax would
free theatres from taxes, enabling managers to speculate and
book better plays, thus elevating the American worker's taste.
As Garland put it, "If you would raise the standard of art in
America you must raise the standard of living."

Garland pleaded that "the cause of art is the cause of humanity. . . . There are superb young actors deep in the forests,
singers in the depth of mines, painters toiling on lonely farms.
This waste of human genius would not go on under the new system of things." Herne agreed. "Mr. Herne has indicated in his remarks," Garland wrote, "that there can be no over-production
as long as men have opportunity to satisfy their reasonable
wants. When men have enough to eat, they turn to art and
literature."[32]

Herne's most enduring expression of Georgism was his article, "Art for Truth's Sake in the Drama," published by Benjamin Orange Flower in *The Arena*. Herne's article was the *only*
nineteenth century criticism included in Alan S. Downer's *American Drama and its Critics*. Downer said "it seems to be generally
agreed that the first significant American playwright was James
A. Herne; surprisingly, he is also the author of the first manifesto of an American dramatic theory that bore fruit, not only
in his own work, but in that of other playwrights. And it is a
manifesto that developed out of practical experience as an American and as an actor, rather than from a study of aesthetic
theory."[33]

Barrett H. Clark also applauded Herne's criticism, saying
that nothing like it could "be found in all the writings of all the
native playwrights up to his day."[34] Clark respected Herne's
statement that, "if (the artist) has a truth to manifest and he
can present it without giving offence and still retain its power,
he should so present it, but if he must choose between giving

offence and receding from his position, he should stand by his principle and state his truth fearlessly."[35] Clark said that "the importance of these words, uttered at a time when pleasing the public seemed the sole criterion with playwrights and managers alike, can hardly be overemphasized. The plain fact that he thought as he did, and publicly expressed himself, is remarkable. We shall, I think, find no more courageous or forthright declaration from any playwright until, in the nineteen tewenties... Eugene O'Neill said, 'I intend to use whatever I can make my own, to write about anything under the sun that fits or can be made to fit the subject.... I want to do what gives me pleasure and worth in my own eyes, and don't care to do what doesn't. ...It is just life that interests me as a thing in itself.' "[36]

In his *Arena* essay, Herne first defines his concept of art for truth's sake as opposed to art for art's sake:

> "Art for art's sake" seems to me to concern itself principally with delicacy of touch, with skill. It is aesthetic. It emphasizes beauty. It aims to be attractive. It must always be beautiful. It must contain no distasteful quality. It never offends. It is high-bred, so to speak. It holds that truth is ugly or at least is not always beautiful. The compensation of the artist is the joy of having produced it.
>
> "Art for truth's sake," on the other hand, emphasizes humanity. It is not sufficient that the subject be attractive or beautiful, or that it does not offend. It must first of all express some *large* truth. That is to say, it must always be representative. Truth is not always beautiful, but in art for truth's sake it is indispensible.

Herne reviews his experiences in the old stock company, comparing past and present theatre conditions and conventions. Then he says:

> Art is universal. It can be claimed by no man, creed, race, or time; and all *art* is good. It serves its time and place, and fertilizes the art to come. The artist of to-day is the medium for the expression of the art of to-day, fertilized by race memories of past ages of art—more perfect by reason of the struggles, the failures, the inferiority, and the sublimity of ages of art.

Herne briefly mentions Hamliton Wright Mabie's *Short Studies in Literature* and Goethe's artistic attitude. He concludes:

I stand for art for truth's sake because it perpetuates the everyday life of its time, because it develops the latent beauty of the so-called common places of life, because it dignifies labor and reveals the divinity of the common man.

It is generally held that the province of the drama is to amuse. I claim that it has a higher purpose—that its mission is to interest and to instruct. It should not *preach* objectively, but it should teach subjectively; and so I stand for truth in the drama, because it is elemental, it gets to the bottom of a question. It strikes at unequal standards and unjust systems. It is as unyielding as it is honest. It is as tender as it is inflexible. It has supreme faith in man. It believes that that which was good in the beginning cannot be bad at the end. It sets forth clearly that the concern of one is the concern of all. It stands for the higher development and thus the individual liberty of the human race.[37]

Some critics have linked Herne's statements with Howells' work, *Criticism and Fiction*. Although Edwin H. Cady admits in *The Realist At War* that Herne was "the pioneering realist of American drama" and "a heroic idealist," he also says that "Herne's esthetic, in concepts and especially in vocabulary, derived directly from Howells . . . every word an echo of Howells."[38]

Cady's charge is unjust. *Criticism and Fiction* was published in 1891, after Herne already had written *Drifting Apart, Margaret Fleming,* and *Shore Acres.* (Cady also ignored Herne's experimental work in scene design, lighting techniques, and restrained acting.) Moreover, Herne's aesthetic concepts had congealed long before he met Howells, who helped him gain recognition. Howells himself was influenced by what he had read of writers like Ralph Waldo Emerson, Juan de Valdés and Juan Valera.

It was Valdés who said, "All is equally grand, all is equally just; all is equally beautiful, because all is equally divine," and "things that appear ugliest in reality to the spectator who is not an artist, are transformed into beauty and poetry when the spirit of the artist possesses itself of them." Valera said, "the object of a novel should be to charm through a faithful representation of human actions and human passions, and to create by this fidelity to nature a beautiful work." Long before *Criticism and Fiction*, Emerson had said, "I ask not for the great, the remote, the romantic. . . . I embrace the common; I sit at the feet of the familiar and the low. . . . Man is surprised to find that things near are not less beautiful and wonderous than things remote. . . . The perception of the worth of the vulgar is fruitful in discoveries. . . . The foolish man wonders at the unusual, but the wise man at the usual."[39] Even Garland admitted that *Crumbling Idols* was Emerson restated.

The important point is that Herne had the courage to print publicly his radical views at a time when theatre managers stuffed with romanticism controlled the American stage. His public stand for his beliefs deserves great credit; the phrases and jargon used aren't important. Herne practiced what he preached long before he met Howells. Mark Sullivan later wrote: "He was to the stage what Howells was to fiction, the pioneer American realist. Also, like Howells, he gave encouragement to younger dramatists having the same tastes and convictions, became the idol of a school of them. Much of the realism that had made headway on the American stage by the 1920's had its inspiration in Herne."[40]

Actually Herne was probably swayed less by Howells' Back Bay liberal conservatism than by Flower's "peaceful, progressive, and practical program" of reform, a modified version of Jeffersonian liberalism that became Herne's banner. Flower also supported the populist movement, including William Jennings Bryan, Spencerian individualism, the Single Tax, political cleanups, and women's rights. Helen Gardener became his co-editor for awhile, Herne later adapting her novel, *An Unofficial Patriot*, into his radical Civil War drama, *Griffith Davenport*. Flower rejected "art for art's sake," elevating ethics above aesthetics to reveal moral truths. As he often said, "We must develop the ethical side of man's nature, we must emphasize the idea of moral responsibility."[42]

Herne tried but failed to form "an independent actors' single tax organization."[43] Managers considered his labor views "bad business" and wouldn't rent him their theatres for his Sunday evening lectures. Most actors slid along on tarnished stardust and curtain calls, complaining, "We are artists—not laborers." But Herne kept talking about the single tax.

When he spoke at the first meeting of the Actors' Society of America at the Broadway Theatre, he frankly admitted that his radicalism wasn't very highly revered by the multitude. Scattered remarks from this speech may reveal why:

"Inequality of opportunity is the canker that is eating the heart out of our body politic."

"We cannot elevate our own particular trade, calling, profession, or art unless we are in sympathetic touch with every other trade, profession, calling or art. In short, we cannot elevate the level of the stage until we first elevate the level of humanity."

"I find that one of the evils of labor is incompetence; an unwillingness to think for themselves on the part of the great masses of the workers of the world."

"Under existing social conditions, labor organizations are the only weapons of defense that labor has."

Herne criticized actors who were afraid to become involved in politics. "I tell you fellow actors, the time has come in the life of this republic when I hold it to be criminal for any man having the franchise to absent himself from the polls on election day. Such a man is not a true American citizen."[44]

Although such remarks antagonized many American actors, Herne didn't pull his punches. As Nat Goodwin recalled about Herne's youth, he did everything in the open—from drink to philosophical discussions.

The *Standard* asked Herne to respond to one writer who said, "Actors are cheaper than freaks [because of] jackal managers who value the public as the wild Indian values cattle, for their hide and tallow." The writer suggested a boycott of the dramatic trusts. Herne disagreed, believing that boycotts paved the way for other monopolists. Privileges, not individuals, posed the problem, he said. "Boycotts, dynamite bombs and strikes are effective only so far as they serve to show that great wrongs exist; that the people are oppressed beyond endurance; that they are ready to resort to desperate measures rather than submit to present conditions; but they never have been, are not now, nor ever will be remedies for those wrongs or conditions." He insisted "that the one, only and positive remedy for social injustice . . . lies in the single tax pure and simple, aided only by ballot reform."[45]

Herne's advocacy of women's rights, actors' organizations, and the single-tax contributed to Garland's posthumous appraisal of him: "Herne was a general nonconformist. Some of his theatrical friends considered him a crank, and his managers croaked dismally over the effect of his 'sermons' and his lectures for the single tax; but he kept on in the work."[46] Julie thought the Players Club blackballed her father because he supported George. As one member groaned, "If Herne joins the Club, he will try to convert us all to the single tax."[47] (Herne was invited to join the National Institute of Arts and Letters in 1899, an invitation he valued.)

George's association with Herne, Francis Neilson, and the deMilles seems strange, considering his fundamentalist roots. George seldom attended the theatre, except for a rare voyage into the romantic realm of Shakespeare or the antics of Tony Pastor's Variety Show. Yet the "prophet of San Francisco" watched Herne's plays from the wings and called him a genius. After seeing *Shore Acres,* George wrote Herne: "You have done what you ought to do—made a play pure and noble that people will come to hear. You have taken the strength of realism and added to it the strength that comes from the wider truth that realism fails to see; and in the simple portrayal of homely life, touched a universal chord. . . . In the solemnity of the wonderfully suggestive close, the veil that separates us from heaven seems to grow thin, and things not seen to be felt. . . . I never before saw acting that impressed me so much as yours last night. I did not feel like talking when I left the theater; but I wanted to grasp your hand."[48]

Anna George deMille also called Herne "a finished actor and a brilliant playwright."[49] Henry George, Jr., wrote, "I never knew a man who, displaying so much genius in his profession, at the same time gave so much thought to the great social problems."[50]

The Hernes and Garland visited Annie and Henry George at their brick home on Nineteenth Street. It was "a center for kindred spirits to meet and talk—to ponder, in friendship, the plight and future of mankind." And that's what they did—pondered the plight of humanity while they drank cocoa. Garland recalled: "Of course this home was doctrinaire, but then I liked the flavor, so did the Hernes. Although Katharine's keen sense of humor sometimes made us all seem rather like thorough–going cranks— which we were."[51]

A stroke killed George in 1897 while he was campaigning again for election as New York mayor. Herne was in Buffalo with Julie. After reading the news, he sent telegrams to Mrs. George and K.C., then wandered through the streets for hours. The man Herne had thought would "one day be the *great* man of America"[52] was no more.

Georgism saturated Herne's thought about human life, reaching wherever the monopolists smothered labor and individualism. The Filipino and Boer Wars infuriated him, and he sided with labor during the Homestead Strike of 1892 and the Pullman Strike of 1894. Both aroused Herne's sense of justice.

Herne also backed the 1896 and 1900 Presidential campaigns of William Jennings Bryan, the Protestant evangelist who charged: "Darwin's God was nowhere—he could not find him; Darwin's Bible was nothing—it had lost its inspiration; Darwin's Christ was nobody—he had an ape for an ancestor on both his father's and his mother's side. Such a Christ is impotent to save. Such a Christ cannot meet the world's needs."[53]

Herne, the agnostic, supported Bryan, the fundamentalist, despite their differing religious views. Bryan defended the Populist platform, although he opposed such reforms as unemployment benefits and government ownership. It was at the 1896 Democratic National Convention that he shouted: "You come to us and tell us that the great cities are in favor of the gold standard; we reply that the great cities rest upon our broad and fertile prairies. Burn down your cities and leave our farms, and your cities will spring up again as if by magic; but destroy our farms and the grass will grow in the streets of every city in the country."[54] Then came Bryan's famous blast: "You shall not press down upon the brow of labor this crown of thorns, you shall not crucify mankind upon a cross of gold."[55]

This was Herne's "Boy Orator of the Platte," "The Silver Knight of the West," "The Black Eagle of Nebraska," the dynamic preacher who proclaimed, "I want a dollar that will not be ashamed to look a farmer in the face."[56] But the banks, insurance companies, and manufacturers used their power to marshal votes against Bryan's silver standard. Bryan lost, as Henry George had. Bryan's defeat depressed Herne. He wrote Henry George:

> The battle is evidently against us—but we have made a glorious effort against the combined moneypower—against the partisan press and the dogmatic church in America. To come within reach of a victory is most encouraging.
>
> My faith in the people never left me. From the moment of Mr. Bryan's nomination until mid-night of November 5, I felt sure we would win. The poverty of the people was against us. They had not the courage of their convictions. They let "I dare not—wait upon I would." They feared even while they hoped.
>
> The question now is, "Shall the—or rather *will* the republic live.[57]

Herne wouldn't quit. He rallied again for Bryan in the presidential campaign of 1900. At New York's Lyric Hall he spoke to a predominantly women's audience (single-tax lectures often embraced feminism). Henry George, Jr., introduced Herne, who first recited a Sidney Lanier poem. Then he said:

"Poverty and slavery are not a natural condition. How is it that increasing wealth is accompanied by increasing poverty? Are there too many people in the United States? That cannot be, yet many men find it impossible to get work at any price.

"Is the belief that men are equal before the law a fact, or is it only a sentiment?

"Millions are breathing foul air for the good of the few. The late Henry George frightened the trusts; they are frightened to-day, and would breathe easier to-day if Bryan died. A great truth cannot be buried with the man who uttered it. A single tax is the remedy for our evils. The trusts control labor and dictate terms and conditions to laboring men.

"The single tax will be the paramount issue in the near future. The same issues prevail to-day that prevailed four years ago. If we believe in the Declaration of Independence we must vote for Bryan."

One fellow in the audience hollered: "What you say may be all right, but since McKinley has been President I have had steady employment. I did not have it before."

Angered single taxers cried, "Put him out!" Henry George, Jr., shouted: "Let him alone. Give him a seat." But the anti-Georgist refused the offer and left.[58]

How to satisfy common people theatrically and thrill their senses, yet elevate their aesthetic standard and awaken their social awareness. These ambitions, which confronted Herne throughout the 1890's, remained unfulfilled, except for *Shore Acres*, the play that made a million dollars.

11 a four-legged fortune

MY DEAR FELLOW, just let literary quality and all the rest of that sort of nonsense take care of itself. What is plays written fer, anyhow, I'd like to know! They ain't written ter read; they're written to act!"[1]

This playwright claptrapper made his point loud and clear. The public wanted escapism—a commodity that the managers provided in overdoses. Owen Davis (who wrote about 150 "blood and thunder" melodramas before turning to reputable works like *Detour, The Good Earth, Ethan Frome,* and *Icebound,* his Pulitzer Prize winner), reduced dramaturgy to a formula:

Title: (at least fifty per cent of success.)
Plot: Brief story of the play.
Cast: *Leading Man,* very (even painfully) virtuous.
    Leading Woman, in love with him.
    Comedy Man, always faithful friend of *Hero.*
    Soubrette, very worthy person (poor but honest) and always
        in love with *Comedian.*
    Heavy Man, a villain, not for any special reason, but, like
        "Topsy," "born bad."
    Heavy Woman,—here I had a wider choice, this lady being
        allowed to fasten her affection upon either *Hero* or
        Villain (sometimes both) but never happily.
    Father (or *Mother*), to provide sentiment.
Act I—Start the trouble.
Act II—Here things look bad. The lady having left home, is quite
    at the mercy of *Villain.*
Act III—The lady is saved by the help of the Stage Carpenter,
    (The big scenic and mechanical effects were always in Act
    III.)
Act IV—The lovers are united and the villains are punished.[2]

Davis' success ratio was staggering, except when "he at-

139

tempted to portray the hero as not entirely heroic and the villain as not entirely without redeeming traits."[3]

The *Boston Evening Transcript* complained in 1891, "If a dramatist offers an American manager a play containing a strong but unconventional idea, treated in a strong but unconventional manner, the manager becomes frightened."[4] But the *Evening Transcript* misinterpreted the problem. Like all businessmen, theatre managers feared failure. A few flops meant farewells for both manager and actors. According to the 1890 census, there were 23,200 actors and 4,583 actresses in the country.[5] That's a lot of grease paint.

All managers weren't unimaginative vultures. Some sympathized with serious writers, but empty seats offered actors poor feedback. When Garland sought a *Shore Acres* hearing, one manager admitted: "Herne writes good plays. They are too good to succeed, for the people want rotten plays—not too rotten but just rotten enough."[6]

Herne qualified as one of "those foolhardy souls who attempted to leave the beaten track," as André Antoine, founder of France's Théâtre Libre, called visionaries. Men like Owen Davis left theatre trailblazing to others, waiting for that opportune moment to "cash in" on their efforts. That's why *Margaret Fleming* premiered on July 4, 1890, in Lynn, Massachusetts, instead of in Boston or New York. It violated formula. It wasn't "on the beaten track."

The first advertisement for *Margaret Fleming* appeared in the July 1, 1890, *Lynn Daily Bee*. On July 4 at 8:00 p.m., the Lynn Theatre was to present the:

> First production on any stage of an original American play in five acts, written expressly for Katharine C. Herne, by the popular actor and author, James A. Herne, entitled *Margaret Fleming* (Katharine C. Herne).—as Margaret Fleming, James A. Herne as Philip Fleming, Little Mable Earl, (the Best Child Actress on the Stage) as Little Lucy Fleming, C. P. Flockton as Dr. Larkin, T. H. Bradbury as Joe Fletcher, supported by a carefully selected company. The play will be appropriately staged. This play will, also, be given on the Saturday following (July 5) matinee and evening. Sale of seats now progressing in the theatre box office.[7]

The Lynn Theatre was not the most ideal for Herne's realism nor for furnishing an intimate environment where actors and audience could interact. According to Julie Herne, "The theatre was a great, old-fashioned barn, utterly unsuitable for such an intimate drama, and as Herne could not afford to have special scenery built for the production, he was forced to fall back on the shabby, conventional stock sets belonging to the theatre, and Katharine declared that Margaret's home looked like a ruined baronial castle."[8]

At the opening were a handful of followers, including Garland, author-critic Thomas Sargent, and "a party of news and dramatic writers, from New York and Boston dailies."[9] Curiosity seekers also came. Sargent later wrote Herne: "I was pleased with your play very much indeed. That little point where Fleming spoke of telling his wife when he should have made himself essential to her, was an especially admirable bit. I look upon it as a touch of genius. In general I hate the ordinary play of the period, but yours does not belong to that sort. Your third act was admirable, with its abandonment of the conventional methods, its truthfulness and its pathos. Everyone was moved by it. It is a magnificent task you have set yourself, to paint life and not to copy sundried models. You owe much to your wife's admirable performance of her exhausting part."[10]

The *Lynn Daily Bee* published a long review of *Margaret Fleming* the day after it opened, calling it "the best example of 'Americanism' in the literature of the stage." Their reviewer concluded: "There are no weak points in 'Margaret Fleming,' and it seems beyond question that the drama made a pronounced hit on its initial presentation. This afternoon and evening the play will be given. The Lynn Theatre is finely adapted for the production, and Manager Dexter must be much gratified that this purely American play was first given at his house. The hold that Mr. Herne has obtained on the literati, in his efforts in the direction of national drama, will be augmented by 'Margaret Fleming.' "[11]

Hamlin Garland reviewed *Margaret Fleming* in the July 8, 1890, *Boston Evening Transcript*. This important review outlines the original script, minus later revisions, and relates the dates, character roles, and other production details. Garland wrote:

"Mr. Herne's New Play"

Mr. and Mrs. James A. Herne, on the 4th, at Lynn,
faced the hard conditions of a mid-summer production (necessarily somewhat hurried) with heroic courage, and won
a substantial triumph in face of all. Mr. Herne has hitherto
written of what some people are pleased to call "low-class
persons," mean fisherfolk, backwoodsmen, etc; but in
"Margaret Fleming" he has taken a bolder flight, with intent to enforce a great social lesson by means of a story
of powerful interest, somewhat in the manner of Ibsen.
That he was successful was evident by the attention which
was literally breathless at points, and unbroken from first
to last. The emotion is intellectual, deep and quiet.

The play opens in the private office of Philip Fleming
(Mr. Herne) a silk manufacturer. He is a hail (*sic*) fellow,
coarse and sensual, but a strong thinker and having many
manly qualities. He is married to a fine, strong woman,
Margaret Fleming (Katharine C. Herne.) They have a
tasteful home, a baby several months old and everybody
thinks Fleming one of the luckiest and happiest fellows in
the world. This is the situation as the play begins. But as
he comes in and opens his mail, it develops that he is involved in debt, and after a scene with Joe Fletcher, Dr.
Larkin enters peculiarly grave and reticent. The telephone
bell rings, Fleming goes to it. Margaret is asking when he
will come to dinner, the baby kisses through the telephone.
Fleming, resuming conversation smilingly, is stupefied by
the doctor, who tells with unsurpassed directness and force
that he has just come from the bedside where another child
has been born to Philip Fleming—its mother Lena Schmidt,
a mill girl. Dr. Larkin administers a terrible rebuke, orders
him to go to the dying girl's side, and then stalks out in
anger and disgust too great for words. The telephone rings
again. Fleming goes to it stolidly, speaks to his wife, says
he has business and cannot come home to dinner. As he
drops the receiver and puts on his coat a scene of great
truth and power is ended. The next scene shows Margaret
happy in her motherhood with her baby—a most intimate
and beautiful home picture. She has for nurse Maria, a
German woman of middle age. It is developed that Maria is
the elder sister of the mill girl whom Fleming has ruined,
and that she has come to town in search of her. Maria is a
strong piece of character writing, humorous, but with a sort
of volcanic energy of hate. She loves Margaret very deeply.
Philip returns late, gloomy, ashamed, sullen, but Margaret
drives away his dejection and baby almost makes him forget
his crime.

The second act opens the next morning bright and happy. Fleming has fully recovered his usual careless humor. Dr. Larkin calls; he is treating Margaret for weakness of the eyes. He advises Margaret to get Philip away for awhile, and catching Philip alone, tells him to get Margaret away. She is threatened with blindness, a fatality attended on childbirth in her mother's family. But Margaret has promised Maria to go and see her sister and also to conceal the poor girl's history from her husband. The doctor is very savage with Fleming, tells him his wife's eyesight is periled, cautions him about letting any information of Lena's history reach her—the shock might drive her blind, even insane.

The third act takes place in Mrs. Burton's cottage, where Dr. Larkin is horrified to meet Margaret. He implores her to go home, but she refuses, and inquires about the unfortunate girl and is told she has just died. In an impassioned scene Maria thrusts the terrible truth upon Margaret and threatens Fleming's life. Margaret sends Dr. Larkin away and sends a note to Philip. As she waits in agony too great for tears, the light goes out of her eyes. She hears the wail of the newborn starving baby; its pitiful cries move her motherhood to its depths, she takes the poor little waif to her breast, and as Fleming, too much awed and appalled to speak, stands watching her, the curtain falls.

The intensity of interest finds welcome relief in the next act in the change of scene, four years later, to Boston Common, where Joe Fletcher has a peddler's stand. He has with him Margaret's child Lucy, five years old, whom he believes to be his wife's sister's child. Fleming comes on, broken and dejected, and in conversation with Joe tells the story of his wife's disappearance, of his own failure in business, and of his own remorse and hopelessness. In speaking about the child Joe becomes convinced that she is Margaret's child, and takes Fleming home to let him see for himself. The scene changes to a store on Hanover Street, where Maria is again living with Joe. Here Lucy is waiting on customers. Miss Edwards, a worker in the mission school, comes in to get Lucy for a vacation in the country. After she goes out, Margaret, feeling her way with a cane, enters, inquiring for Miss Edwards. Lucy knows her as a visitor of the mission schools, which Margaret had been in the habit of visiting, hoping to hear of her child. While talking with the child she hears and knows Maria's voice, and the hope that this little waif is her child leads her to demand the name of the mother. Maria sullenly insists it is her sister's child. Margaret is going away in despair, Lucy clinging to her dress, when Maria breaks down, pleads to have Margaret take the child and herself away with her. Margaret consents and takes the child, Maria promising to follow. But when Joe and Fleming return, the hate she feels for Fleming makes her pitiless and she tells him she has sold the child. Fleming goes out, and while Maria is gloating over her subtle revenge the curtain falls.

The last act takes place in the office of inspector of police, a scene which Mr. Herne has studied carefully from the life. Margaret and the child (which she knows is hers), Philip, Joe and Maria are brought in. After a little preliminary examination the inspector leaves them alone "to arrange matters." In this scene the action and thought move on to a height as well as a depth unparalleled in few American plays. The wronged wife faces the shamed and broken man with a patience, kindness and yet firmness that holds the spectator literally enthralled, and Mrs. Herne plays it with such comprehension of its significance, such quiet dignity and intellectual power, that she seems inspired. With her pale face and sightless eyes turned upon her husband, Margaret tells him she cannot go back to him. "The wife-heart has gone out of me. Only the mother-heart remains." He accepts the judgment and they clasp hands. The inspector comes in and seeing them standing thus, rubs his hands jovially. "Ah! you've come to an understanding, I see." "Yes," replies Philip, "we understand each other." "Better than we ever did before," adds the voice of Margaret. The inspector bows them out, returns to his desk, rings a bell. "Send Davis in," and the play is ended; life going on just the same with the inspector and his world.[12]

Why did early reviewers applaud *Margaret Fleming*, while later Bostonians and New Yorkers condemned it? The progressivism of veritists like Garland and Sargent seems logical. Sargent said "everyone was moved" by the play, and Garland wrote that attention "was literally breathless at points." The *Lynn Daily Evening Item* said: "It is bound to be a success ... and it is safe to predict that 'Margaret Fleming' will secure a lasting favor with American play goers."[13] The *Lynn Daily Bee* agreed. Even the *New York Dramatic Mirror* stated: "The play was well received and ran very smooth for a first-night-performance."[14] The *Boston Evening Transcript* mentioned in May 1891 that "on its original production at Lynn the piece made a striking success."[15] Unfortunately, all of *Margaret Fleming*'s later audiences weren't liberals, but approving acceptance marked its first production.

Abraham Lincoln Erlanger (later kingpin of the powerful theatre syndicate in New York) expressed interest in the play. He wrote Herne, "At present, valuable time in New York, is all tied up, and if you will take my advice, you will not produce the play anywhere until you produce it here, it means more money for you and more prestige for the play."[16] That fall Herne revived *Hearts of Oak*, traveling to the Pacific coast, while K.C. stayed home.

Margaret Fleming still received "top priority" with the Hernes that year, but production prospects dimmed as managers refused to budge. Meanwhile, Herne accepted a role in Wilson Barrett's *A Four-Legged Fortune*, a melodrama about the British racetrack. He also directed *A Fair Rebel* by Harry P. Mawson, a Civil War thriller with a tunnel escape from Libby Prison.

Luck then touched Herne. Erlanger asked him: "Jim, how would you like to come in with us as our Stage Manager? We'll fit you up an office here and you can direct all our plays."[17] Herne accepted at $100 a week, a generous salary at that time.

The post with Erlanger forced the Hernes to move from Ashmont to New York City. They took a place at Convent Avenue and 145th Street in Washington Heights, a location Herne disliked because it was an hour's ride from Broadway. K.C. encouraged the move, reasoning that America's main market place for theatre would be New York. She also wanted this house, promising to rent the two maids' rooms in the attic and do the housework with her sister, Mollie, who often stayed with them.

Certain excesses scar everyone, even self-proclaimed saints and culture heroes. Homes were K.C.'s weakness. She later spent a mint on Herne Oaks (their mansion on Long Island) until Herne finally wrote: "Don't make a mistake at Herne Oaks. Don't go too deep and too fast. It's a most beautiful spot, but only beautiful while we can control it and enjoy it. If you make it so complicated and expensive to care for it will enjoy us—not we it. I loved it for its simplicity." K.C. replied, "You are perfectly right in all you say." But she continued spending.[18]

Although audiences and critics acclaimed K.C.'s acting

powers, the domestic urge replaced footlights and curtain calls after her children arrived. Theatre thoughts diminished until she eventually retired during the road tour of Herne's *Griffith Davenport*, not returning to the stage until Herne's last play, *Sag Harbor*.

Julie Herne provided a picture of Washington Heights in the 1890's. "It was still quite rural, with open fields stretching to the Hudson River, heavily wooded vacant lots, and rocky promontories where now and then a goat cropped the woods, or a lonely squatter's shanty made a last stand against the encroaching city. There were shops and tenements on the avenues, and the side streets as well as St. Nicholas Avenue were lined with handsome residences of stone and brick; occasionally a fine old mansion of the pre-brownstone era still stood as a reminder of the time when all this region consisted of country estates."[19]

Chrystal also wrote about number "79" on Convent Avenue, where the Hernes lived for years. "It was the house that witnessed the height of my father's fame and success, the house in which he died. Convent Avenue was a sedate and well-groomed street, at that time, only two blocks in length. The Convent of the Sacret Heart, which gave it its name, still stands at 158th Street. Our new home was one of a short row of five. Five handsome houses, venturing from the proverbial brownstone of this period. Each was of a different design, three of gray stone, two alike, of which one was "79." These were of yellow brick with terra-cotta stone trim.

"But, alas, there were no gardens, just a handkerchief of close cropped grass that ran up to the high, impressive steps mounting to the front door and circled the iron grill, that was the entrance to the basement beneath. There was a small maple tree set in the oval of grass, which garnished the curb in front of each house. I extracted some comfort from the little trees, but my heart was sore and hungry for our dear Ashmont garden. It seemed exceedingly odd to me that the houses had only front and back windows—except the corner one, which was much the grandest.

" '79', I found on entering it, was more pretentious than our old home. Tall mahogany mantelpieces, many mirrors and elaborate chandeliers—gas, of course. The drawing–room—parlor in

Ashmont—was very long and consequently seemed very narrow. The dining room was square and looked out on a dreary yard, sunk to the level of the basement, where the kitchen was. It had a plot of tired grass in the center of its asphalt walk."[20]

Although the Hernes had completed the move to New York, Erlanger's contract left breathing space until fall. So they returned to Boston, still searching for a theatre to present *Margaret Fleming*. John B. Schoeffel, operator of Boston's new Tremont Theatre, expressed interest to K.C., with one condition:

"You'll have to make some changes before I'll consider doing this play at my theatre. That German woman, Maria, for instance—why she takes the name of the Deity in vain!"

This infuriated K.C. who snapped: "Not one line of this play will be changed, Mr. Schoeffel. Good morning." And she stormed out.[21]

12 a monster of morality

BANNED IN BOSTON. The censorship problem haunted American actors during the romantic balmy days. But such was Boston, the city of cultural paradoxes. The venerable William Bradford wrote in *History of Plymouth Plantation 1620–1647* about the revelries at "merie-mounte" where the "schoole of Athisme" drank and danced around the "idoll May-polle."[1] In 1699 the Puritan fathers of Boston passed legislation called "An Act for the Suppressing and Punishing of Rogues, Vagabonds, Common Beggars, and Other Lewd, Idle and Disorderly Persons, And Also for Setting the Poor to Work."[2] Among the undesirables were jugglers, palmsters, common pipers, fiddlers, common night walkers, and players. Their punishment involved fetters or shackles seasoned with "moderate whipping, not exceeding ten strokes at once."[3]

The Puritan purge still shadowed players in 1890. That year the license of Boston's Park Theatre was temporarily revoked when it presented *The Clemenceau Case*, a play by Alexandre Dumas the Younger and Armand d'Artois. In this play an aristocrat murders his wife after she refuses a reconcilement unless he also permits continued meetings with her lover.

The theatre was closed by the Board of Aldermen at the demands of the New England Watch and Ward Society, which had been formed in 1878 as the New England Society for the Suppression of Vice.

The *Boston Evening Transcript* tacitly approved the move to ban *The Clemenceau Case*. "So long as it is objectionable to people who are not prudes and who know where and how to draw the line, a good reason exists for its prohibition." The *Boston Globe* disagreed, making several sarcastic swats: "The Aldermen, in their capacity as saviors of society, visited the Park Theatre, took seats where they could have an uninterrupted view, adjusted their opera-glasses, and for two or three hours gazed upon the undraped model (an actress in tights) in the play as though their salaries and re-elections depended upon their diligence. It is believed that they nearly wore their opera-glasses out, so conscientiously thorough were they in their search for something immoral."[4] The *Globe* concluded that one outcome of the incident would be a more liberal policy regarding alderman passes.

The Park Theatre soon reopened, but *The Clemenceau Case* moved to Lynn for three days. Later that year, the play returned to Boston under a new name; although most critics recognized it, this return engagement made a pretty profit for the Park.

The hassle over *The Clemenceau Case* helps explain why Herne told Garland and Howells, "Every theater in Boston and most of those in New York have refused to consider my new play."[5] One understands Herne's problem, one that Howells solved at a luncheon for Herne at his home on Commonwealth Avenue, reminding him of dramatists like André Antoine, who "brought the public to them by sheer force of their dramatic novelty. Why don't you do as they did—hire a sail-loft or a stable somewhere, and produce your play in simplest fashion? The people will come to see it if it is new and vital."[6]

It was Antoine whose first experiments in naturalism were rehearsed around a billiard table with props borrowed from his mother's dining room and carted to the theatre. "No rooms were available for rental, and even if they were, where would we get the money? As a last resort, I came upon a tiny billiard room in the rear of a barrel-vault in a little tavern which is located in the Rue des Abbesses, next to the Elysée-des-Beaux-Arts. The proprietor has agreed to light it for our rehearsals each evening with a modest gas burner from 8:30 to midnight, on the condition that each of us buy a drink."[7]

Herne resisted at first but finally said, "I'll do it—if I have to mortgage my Ashmont house to get the money."[8]

A theatre search started. Herne looked everywhere, but rentals were expensive. He finally chose Chickering Hall at 152

Tremont Street, between West and Mason Streets. It was an upstairs hall in which recitals and concerts for piano manufacturers were given. It also served as a promotion place for
Chickering's pianos. (Jonas Chickering was America's first piano
manufacturer.) The hall was "the headquarters of the musical
profession and a place for fashionable musicales."[9]

Herne leased Chickering Hall for one week. Chickering allowed alterations, at his expense, as Hamlin had done in Chicago.
Herne studied the auditorium, which looked right and had a seating capacity of about 500, including a small balcony. But the hall
needed reshaping, for Herne wanted an intimate environment, explaining to one interviewer: "There is now a need for a new class
of theatres, small theatres seating only a few hundred, cosey
(sic) and parlor-like places, where the audience is brought into
intimate relations with the stage. . . . In a small theatre the actors can employ the tones of ordinary conversation, and the audience being close at hand, the finest qualities of acting tell."[10]

Herne moved fast, hiring an electrician and a carpenter.
"Chickering Hall was converted for the week into a cosey, parlor-
like theatre; the stage built forward into the auditorium, and
screened by draperies of a quiet and agreeable brown shade. The
stage is an unexpectedly good one, with plenty of room for the
action of a domestic drama, and a dialogue in easy conversational
tones is heard without difficulty throughout the hall."[11]

Margaret Fleming required six sets: Margaret's living-
room, Philip's office, Mrs. Burton's cottage, a painted drop scene
of Boston Common, a grocery shop in the North End, and the
police inspector's office.[12] The budget-conscious Herne, who
spent several thousand dollars on the production, avoided the
usual bunch-lights and other expensive equipment. Draw curtains and proscenium arch were heavy rope and rose velour,
chosen by K.C. who also designed and made her costumes. Like
Antoine, the Hernes either borrowed or bought furniture to dress
the stage. Actors, excited about the possibilities of the experiment, played for minimum salaries. Garland later wrote, "On a
stage of planking, hung with drapery, was produced one of the
most radical plays from a native author ever performed in
America."[13]

Herne hired several musicians, a concession to nineteenth

PALMER'S THEATRE.

Mr. A. M. PALMER .... Sole Lessee and Manager

Wednesday Afternoon, December 9, 1891.

SPECIAL MATINEE

FOR THE PRODUCTION OF

MARGARET FLEMING

A Play of American Life, in five acts, by JAMES HERNE, Esq.

CAST OF CHARACTERS.

PHILLIP FLEMING .... F. M. BELL
DR. LARKIN .... E. M. HOLLAND
JOE FLETCHER .... CHAS. L. HARRIS
INSPECTOR OF POLICE .... WALDEN RAMSAY
DETECTIVE .... E. S. ABELES
OFFICER .... W. H. POPE
BILL HAGGERTY .... REUB. FAX
OFFICE BOY .... BENNIE SINGER
CHARLIE BURTON .... Master HUGHES
JOHNNIE LYNCH .... CAMPBELL MOWAT
MARGARET FLEMING .... Mrs. HERNE
MARIA BINDLY .... MATTIE EARLE
MRS. BURTON }
ELLEN COOK   } .... HELEN GOOLD
MRS. BRADY .... NELLIE LINGARD
OLD LADY .... Mrs. BRITTON
MISS EDWARDS .... ADELAIDE ROWE
THE BABIES .... BY THEMSELVES
LITTLE LUCY .... VIOLA NEILL

SYNOPSIS OF SCENERY.

ACT I.—Scene I.—Phillip Fleming's Office, Canton, Mass.
Curtain 1 minute.
Scene II.—House of Phillip Fleming, Canton, Mass.
ACT II.—Home of Phillip Fleming. Next morning.
ACT III.—Room in Mrs. Burton's Cottage.
Four years elapse.
ACT IV.—Scene I.—Boston Common.
Scene II.—Mrs. Fletcher's Grocery at North End, Boston.
ACT V.—Office of Inspector of Police.

Margaret Fleming's program, Palmer Theatre.
New York Public Library.

Herne and daughter Dorothy in *Margaret Fleming*.
Theatre Collection, Free Library of Philadelphia.

K.C. as Margaret Fleming. New York Public Library.

Hearts of Oak program.

Hearts of Oak poster.
Brooklyn Park Theatre,
Lincoln Center.

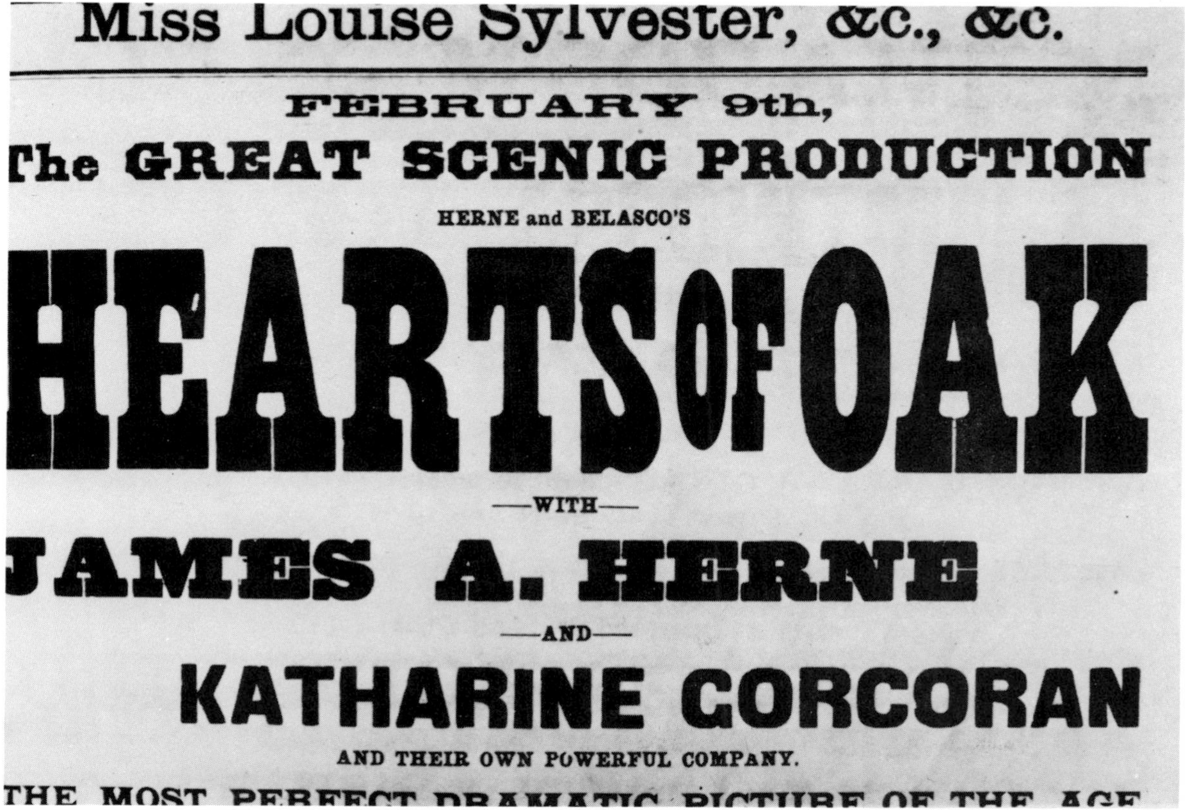

Miss Louise Sylvester, &c., &c.

FEBRUARY 9th,

The GREAT SCENIC PRODUCTION

HERNE and BELASCO'S

HEARTSofOAK

—WITH—

JAMES A. HERNE

—AND—

KATHARINE CORCORAN

AND THEIR OWN POWERFUL COMPANY.

THE MOST PERFECT DRAMATIC PICTURE OF THE AGE

Hearts of Oak play-bill. Walnut Street Theatre, October 27, 1883.
Theatre Collection, Free Library of Philadelphia.

HERALD
SQUARE THEATRE

COMMENCING TUESDAY EVENING, JANUARY 31, 1899

Evenings at 8. Saturday Matinee at 2.

Engagement of the Eminent Character Actor,

JAMES A. HERNE

and production of his Latest American Play, entitled

REV. GRIFFITH DAVENPORT
(CIRCUIT PREACHER),

Founded on HELEN H. GARDENER's novel, "An Unofficial Patriot."

People Represented.

ACT I.

Griffith Davenport..Mr. James A. Herne
Beverly Davenport } his sons, {...........................Mr. Sydney Booth
Roy Davenport... {...Mr. Bert Young
Colonel Armour, a lawyer.....................................Mr. Newton Chisnell
Hamilton Bradley..Mr. F. N. Cornell
Squire Nelson..Mr. Logan Paul
Lengthy Patterson...Mr. Robert Fischer
Uncle Ned } slaves of the Davenports, {......................Mr. Lawrence Merton
Pete....... {...Mr. Joseph H. Hazleton
John, property of Mr. Bradley.................................Mr. John W. Bankson
Free Jim, a free nigger.......................................Mr. H. G. Carleton
Free Jim's boy..Master Kenneth Barnes
Jack, a recent purchase of Mr. Nelson........................Mr. E. P. Sullivan
Katharine Davenport...Mrs. Herne
Emma West, a young Tennessean.................................Miss Julie A. Herne
Sue Hardy, a young Virginian..................................Miss Chrystal Herne
Little Margaret, Davenport's daughter.........................Gertrude Nelson
Sallie, private property of Mrs. Davenport, and married to Mr. Bradley's John
Miss Helen Robertson
Mammy, Margaret's nurse.......................................Miss Mollie Revel
Aunt Judy...Miss Sadie Stringham
Tilly, the cook...Miss Lucy Nelson
Dinah...Miss Dorothy Thornton
Lippy Jane..Miss Rachel Blake
The Twins, children of Pete and Tilly.........................By the Twins
Sallie's Baby...By Herself

ACTS II. and III.

Major Hardy, father of Sue....................................Mr. Thomas M. Hunter
Leader of the Horsemen..Mr. H. G. Carleton
And all of the characters of Act I. excepting Free Jim and his son

ACT IV.

Oliver P. Morton, Governor of Indiana.........................Mr. Warren Conlan
And Griffith Davenport, Roy Davenport, Katherine Davenport, Pete,
Uncle Ned, Mammy, Sallie, Aunt Judy, Tilly and Little Margaret.

Program of *Rev. Griffith Davenport,* Herald Square Theatre, New York.
New York Public Library.

Exterior scene from *Rev. Griffith Davenport.* New York Public Library.

Herne as Griffith Davenport.
Theatre Collection, Free Library of Philadelphia.

century theatre convention, for he disliked both music and opera. Music and theatre were interlocked elements during this period —even the term melodrama means drama with music accompaniment. Charles Hoyt's *A Trip to Chinatown,* for example, introduced two famous songs, "The Bowery" and "After the Ball." Even Herne had used the atmospheric qualities of music to evoke deep emotional responses in *Drifting Apart.*

Meanwhile, Garland played press agent, another *Drifting Apart* replay. He contacted critics, reporters, friends, and prominent Bostonians, including the mayor and governor. Benjamin Orange Flower later recalled Garland's enthusiasm:

" 'Flower,' he exclaimed, 'It is a tremendously fine piece of work, and with Katherine Herne in the title *role* and Herne playing a character part in which he is simply great, I don't see how it can fail; but whether it does or not if we can get it before the Boston public it will introduce Herne to those theatre-goers whom he must win in order to succeed in his work. Now no manager has faith enough in Herne in his new *role* to give him a chance, and a lot of his friends are trying to arrange to have the play produced at Chickering Hall. I want your help.' "[14]

Flower and Garland drafted a circular, mailing it to select Bostonians. It read:

A GENRE DRAMATIC PRODUCTION

Mr. and Mrs. Jas. A. Herne

in

MARGARET FLEMING

"An American Play without a Soliloquy"

at

Chickering Hall, Boston

Week of May 4, 1891.

IN THE INTEREST OF AMERICAN DRAMA

It is generally admitted that the American drama is immeasurably below the work of American painters and novelists, and a despondent tone runs through much that is written upon the subject. We do not share this despondency. We believe with Mr. Howells, Mr. Perry and others of our critics in the comparative school, that literary ideals are relative, and that literature, and especially the drama follows intimately the changes in social life.

Without taking space to detail our reasons, we state

our belief that we are on the eve of a great change in the drama commensurate with that already begun in the novel, that is, the change from the drama of plot and style to the drama of character and purpose.

The American public is large, and we believe there is a growing number of people to whom melodrama no longer appeals, and to whom farce comedy is a weariness, with its heartless as well as thoughtless caricature. This public is ready to welcome serious studies of American life.

We are convinced that this movement toward a higher dramatic art should be made—at least in its inception— along independent lines somewhat as in Paris and Berlin, maintaining, however, the same distinction as to choice of subjects that now exists between the French and American schools of novelists.

As a first modest trial of the independent art theatre we take genuine pleasure in calling attention to Mr. and Mrs. Herne's coming production of their latest play, "Margaret Fleming," at Chickering Hall, beginning May 4th. We do this the more readily because these thorough artists have been working alone and (in a literary way) unrecognized in the attempt to bring the accent of life upon the stage.

"Margaret Fleming" is not a perfect play, it could not reasonably be expected to be, but it has qualities which fit it to stand for the new idea, as Ibsen's "Young Men's Union" stood for the innovation in Norway, in 1869. It is absorbingly interesting, legitimately dramatic, has comedy as well as pathos, and mounts in the last act into an intellectual atmosphere unreached, so far as we know, in any other American play, and Mrs. Herne plays it with that marvelous art which conceals art, leaving the embodied character standing in place of the actress.

We thus publicly endorse Mr. and Mrs. Herne and their purposeful play, because they entirely merit our support, and also because we wish to oppose the pessimistic cry of "the decay of the drama." The drama changes but it never decays. There are scores of plays in America waiting the establishment of a theatre freed from necessity of compromise and whose production would be an honor and an inspiration, as we believe "Margaret Fleming" will prove to our stage.

> B. O. Flower,
> Hamlin Garland.[15]

A letter from William Dean Howells on May 12 strengthened the Flower-Garland block. Any endorsement by Howells was a literary sledgehammer. He wrote Herne:

I am glad there is a prospect of our seeing *Margaret Fleming* on the Boston stage. I told you when you read me the play how highly I thought of it, and I feel it is a great loss not to have been at its production in Lynn. It has qualities which I believe will make a stronger appeal than those of any other American play.

While it is wholly and perfectly true in our conditions, it has the same searching moral vitality as Ibsen's best work, and it is most powerfully dramatic. I have no doubt of its success with a fair chance, and with Mrs. Herne and yourself in it, I predict an epoch-making effect for it. Your fidelity to the ideal of truth, the only ideal worth having, is witnessed in every part of it, and it will be recognized by every one who can feel and think, as a piece of nature and a great work of art.

I do hope you may get it into one of our theatres.[16]

Whether Howells wrote "epoch making" or "epoch marking" has been debated for decades. It was Flower who called *Margaret Fleming* "epoch-marking" in an 1891 *Arena* article.[17] Garland followed suit in another *Arena* article.[18] The *Boston Post,* referring to Howells' original statement, said, "The play has its feeble points as well as its strong ones, and is far from 'epoch-making,' but it is worth intelligent attention."[19]

Howells' "epoch-making" remark pleased Herne who wrote the esteemed novelist in part: "How shall I thank you for that grand letter? I guess by not trying—thanks are so easily expressed, that I'll simply say, 'I'll try to carry out the spirit of your letter in the production of my play,' and trust that you'll never have to say—even to yourself 'I'm sorry I wrote it.' That letter will prove of great value to me."[20]

Promotion continued for *Margaret Fleming.* Garland made a fine press agent. Placards and circulars circulated among Boston's literati (some by daughters Julie and Chrystal), one an open letter to Herne signed by fifty-five notables, including T. S. Perry, Mary E. Wilkins, William Lloyd Garrison, and Mildred Aldrich, which the *Daily Advertiser* called "a sort of printed prommisory (*sic*) note."[21] The letter read: "We have heard of the strength and seriousness of your new play, 'Margaret Fleming,' and earnestly hope it may soon be brought out on the Boston stage. We shall be very glad to attend its representation by yourself and wife." The circular included Herne's reply, "I unhesitatingly seize the chance to state the *truth* in drama without restriction or compromise, so firm is my faith in its ultimate success." And Garland added: "Mr. Herne is thus strengthened, and with reason, in the belief that there is a public ready to support a drama that depicts the life seriously.... Chickering Hall is to be our *théâtre libre* for a week at least. There is a very great general interest in the performance and the radicals in literature are likely to have a play after their most advanced ideas."[22]

The relentless radical Garland also wrote in the *Evening Transcript*: "Boston is to see a trial of a radical play next week in Chickering Hall, and there is considerable interest manifested in Mr. Herne's attempt, because the production of his play in this way involves much more than the mere success or failure of 'Margaret Fleming.' It may involve a departure from hard and fast lines, not only in play writing but in theatre building." Then he elaborated on the need for small "American art theatres" and concluded: "All this talk about 'the laws of the drama' is, in plain terms, nonsense. There is but one law for the drama, and that is, *it must interest the public*—not *the* public but *its* own public."[23]

Opening night of *Margaret Fleming*. May 4, 1891, 8:00 p.m. Chickering Hall, Boston. The birth of modern American drama.

Herne proved false the public's prophecy: "It is folly to expect people to go to a hall to see a play; no one will go."[24] An "exceptionally brilliant audience,"[25] numbering between seventy-five and one hundred,[26] did attend. It consisted mostly of college professors, literary esthetes, and Harvard "hobbledehoys." Flower wrote in *The Arena*: "The character of the audience was as striking as the play was brave and original. It was, indeed, a strange sight to see such well-known and thoughtful men and women as Mr. William Dean Howells, Rev. Minot J. Savage, Rabbi Solomon Schindler, Rev. Edward A. Horton, Mrs. Louise Chandler Moulton, Hamlin Garland, and a score or more of persons almost as well known in literary, religious, and thoughtful circles, assembled on the first night of a dramatic production. Nor was the character of the audience less remarkable during the fortnight it was played. Men and women who are rarely seen at theatres attended two, three, and even four performances."[27] Chrystal Herne also recalled: "All the artistic elite of Boston sat at the feet of my mother and father, coming again and again to watch my mother's supreme acting as Margaret Fleming. Many nights Mr. and Mrs. Thomas Bailey Aldrich would sit in the front row. My mother got to depend on Mrs. Aldrich when the makeshift curtain refused to meet for she would always gently pull it together."[28]

The general theatre public, meanwhile, was patronizing the popular Boston playhouses. *Hands Across the Sea* packed the Boston Museum, and *A Night's Frolic* frolicked at the Park. Francis Wilson (later the first president of Actors Equity) drew audiences to the Globe with the comic opera, *The Merry Monarch*. Boston's biggest bonanza was *The Soudan,* a military thriller. The *Morning Journal* remarked on May 5: "It is said that nothing ever done at the Boston Theatre realized for the managers in 17 weeks what 'The Soudan' did."[29]

Few accounts of that opening of *Margaret Fleming* remain. The *Boston Herald* said, "The audience incessantly rippled with responsive delight all through"[30] Acts I and II. The *Morning Journal* grudgingly admitted that "a small audience attended the performance and applauded with generous warmth," but added that "when 11 o'clock came and the curtain fell, a sense of relief must have risen in the breasts of the few then left in the hall."[31]

Garland said *Margaret Fleming*'s conclusion was "a touch of art which up to that time had never had its equal on our stage." "After having refused reconciliation with her husband, *Philip Fleming, Margaret* was left standing in tragic isolation on the stage, and as the lights were turned out one by one, her figure gradually disappeared in deepening shadow, and when the heavy, soft curtains, dropping together noiselessly, shut in the poignant action of the drama, no one moved or spoke. The return of the actual world in which we lived was made silently."[32]

Garland recorded several audience reactions in the *Evening Transcript* on May 7:

> Mr. Savage said, "A work of immense power, I could wish it included more of life and that the theme dominated rather than absorbed the action; but it is unreasonable, I suppose, to expect an ideal play at the beginning of our dramatic reform. The action of Mr. and Mrs. Herne is simply marvellous."

Mr. Howells said "Magnificently well done; the small theatre gives great gain in reality of utterance. It more than realizes my expectations."

Mrs. Moulton thought the play would have been stronger, though gloomier, by ending at the third act. "Mrs. Herne is a great artist, and Mr. Herne—well, he is simply delicious."

Rabbi Schindler considers the movement very important and endorses it as a powerful protest against the old drama and a potent promise of the new: "It is the first measure taken to lead the stage into new channels here in America. Not only myself but many with whom I have had a chance to discuss the subject, are tired of the old style of stage literature. We need plays with a moral idea for a basis, in which characters and actions are taken from life. When the stage will bring out such plays it will fulfill its mission as an educating element in our society and will certainly help to elevate its moral standard. Mr. Herne's play is a step in the right direction; as such I endorse it."[33]

Some traditionalists voiced their views, too. Among them were writer Thomas Russell Sullivan, who walked out. He criticized *Margaret Fleming* in *The Journal of Thomas Russell Sullivan*:

May 6. To see the new realistic play of "Margaret Fleming," produced by the Hernes at Chickering Hall. This has been brought out at the request of Howells, Tom Perry, Barrett Wendell, and many other distinguished signers of the Articles of Faith. B. W. sent me there, insisting that both play and performers were remarkable. "The best piece of American dramatic work yet given to the world, upon the whole." In spite of this, I thought the play very thin and commonplace, dull beyond description, and badly acted. Henry Rogers, who went with me, was of the same mind, and we came away after the great situation of the third act, when the heroine, in sight of the audience, prepares to suckle her husband's illegitimate child. A small audience of perhaps one hundred souls applauded vigorously the earlier scenes, but received this strong one with depressing coldness. To me it seemed false in sentiment, and my gorge rose at it. Two acts were frittered away with the exposition of household minutiae, the engaging of a new servant, a doctor's visit, a footbath with a real tin tub, etc., etc. If this be art, God help us![34]

Sullivan left—but returned on May 16. This time he wrote:

"Once again to 'Margaret Fleming,' being urged strongly to see and hear it all. Liked the acting somewhat better, but not the play. As before, it bored and depressed me, yet certain of the audience (by the way, chiefly composed of women) were seeing it with joy for the third and fourth time."[35] Sullivan didn't defect to Herne's side. Romanticism remained his refuge. He later saw *Shore Acres* and complained, "With many puerilities and dullnesses, it is, at times, theatrically strong and effective, and is an immense advance over his weak imitation of Zola and Ibsen, which so fluttered the hearts of the 'come-outers' a year ago."[36]

A sadder statement than Sullivan's was written by Henry George, who loved *Shore Acres,* but wrote Herne, "I did not want to see you in that wonderful piece of acting of which they told me, where you reduced man to the mere animal."[37] This was a remarkable statement, since no one understood man's capacity for animalism better than George, who had panhandled on the streets of San Francisco when his wife and child starved. As his daughter told in *Henry George, Citizen of the World*: "Henry was growing desperate when a well-dressed man appeared. The shivering youth walked straight up to the stranger and demanded five dollars.

" 'What for?' the man asked as he studied the gaunt young face with its burning eyes.

" 'My wife has just been confined and I have nothing to give her to eat,' said Henry.

"Whether it was because of pity or fear of bodily assault, the man gave him the money without further question.

" 'If he had not,' said Henry George long afterward, 'I think I was desperate enough to have killed him' "[38]

The reviews of *Margaret Fleming* represented extremes.

The *Boston Morning Journal* was staggered. Its critic cried: "In the case of this play horrors of mental anguish are accumulated on horror's head, and the third commandment is tossed about and aside with a freedom that verges close upon the revolting. In plain and honest truth there is no call for such writing or such presentations as 'Margaret Fleming,' and neither moral stimulus, elevating purpose, nor instructive art is helped by such a work."[39]

The *New York Spirit of the Times* charged that "the dialogue is commonplace, the situations are abortive, and a fair specimen of its realism is Mrs. Herne's unbuttoning the front of her dress to give Lena's baby a lunch. The curtain drops on her display of underclothing." The reviewer also sneered at Herne's women supporters. "Are they not proud to have their names posted as advertisements of a play of seduction, adultery and delerium tremens? Do they really think that nursing a baby on the stage is strongly and seriously dramatic? If so, into what ecstacies they would have fallen had the dramatists made Lena bear twins! When is this Ibsenism nonsense to stop, and how many more otherwise respectable people are to be infected by it?"[40]

Some thought the nursing scene scandalous. They were like the New Yorkers who screamed against Saint-Gaudens' copper Diana, who stood naked to the waist on the roof of the new pleasure palace, Madison Square Garden. Did Margaret really bare her bosom at the end of Act III to nourish the bastard child of her adulterous husband? William Winter, critic of the *New York Tribune,* thought so. Julie Herne, however, wrote Arthur Hobson Quinn, "This was always placed so that the curtain fell just as Margaret started to nurse the child."[41] Thomas Russell Sullivan had used the words "prepared to suckle." The *Lynn Daily Bee*'s reviewer also wrote: "Margaret, with heart torn by anguish sinks on the sofa, where the babe has been laid, and, taking the child in her arms, struggles in the blindness that has overwhelmed her, to a chair, to afford the means that will preserve the babe."[42]

What imaginations those Puritan reporters possessed! Always searching for scum in the sewers of their minds. The onslaught continued:

The *Boston Post* called *Margaret Fleming* "bold beyond the wont of the English-speaking stage," concluding that "Mr. Herne's fourth act is bad art, his fifth act has no place in art at all, and the details in which he is more modern and radical than in anything else—the foot bath and towels and bottles, and what not, to say nothing of bringing into such frequent evidence the functions of maternity and the conditions of the infant stomach —should certainly not have been ventured upon if he was to be as sadly at fault as he has been in the grammar and manners and customs of persons who have 'boudoirs,' and reach the dignity of failing in business."[43]

Although the *Evening Transcript* loved the baby, it called Margaret "a monster of morality." Her lack of forgiveness the paper found unforgivable. The reviewer identified with the "woman who was wronged," and thought she was "endowed with an amiable and whole-hearted superiority which makes the others appear almost despicable by contrast." The critic added: "This is, of course, not what the author intended, and illustrates the deficiency of his literary skill. . . . He has the gift of hewing out bits of character which are really startling in their truth to nature; but when it comes to placing these together, Mr. Herne is by no means a successful architect."[44]

This review infuriated Garland, who wrote the editor, "The moral question at issue seems to be whether 'Margaret Fleming' was right. Of that each must be the judge. As for myself I hold that she was a fine, brave, modern woman who had the courage —I may say the fortitude—to turn her back on a too easy solution of a life problem. That such women exist I know, and that 'Margaret Fleming' finds sympathizers will be still more evident on Wednesday night when the Woman's Press Club learn the whole truth about the play." Garland called Margaret's nursing impulse "a sub-conscious, organic, instinctive maternal action caused by the wailing moan of the child."[45]

A few critics liked *Margaret Fleming*.

The *Daily Globe* wrote: "But were 'Margaret Fleming' far less skilful (*sic*) than it is, the great scenes of the play would save it—the vitalizing humanity of today in America which distinguishes it would give it claim to great consideration, to high praise. The final scene is somewhat too 'long drawn out;' but how consistent, how impressive is the outcome! The man who could go away from 'Margaret Fleming' without feeling something of its power must have a nature which no 'two-edged sword' of conviction could pierce, though wielded by an angel's arm."[46] (The *Daily Globe* had also supported *The Clemenceau Case* in 1890, indicating a liberal policy on theatre that most papers lacked.)

The *Boston Advertiser* also applauded *Margaret Fleming*.

"Margaret Fleming is in the total an exceptionally strong and effective piece, far in advance of the cheap melodrama of our day."[47]

The distinguished *Nation* raved about *Margaret Fleming*, saying the play marked "the beginning of a new epoch in the American stage, the success or failure of which the next generation will know." Their critic also praised Herne's "drift towards realism,"[48] including the telephone conversation, sidewalk vendor, North End store, lady from the "Fresh Air" Committee, and Herne's honest depiction of the doctor.

Herne's greatest tribute came from William Dean Howells, who wrote: "The power of this story, as presented in Mr. Herne's every-day phrase, and in the naked simplicity of Mrs. Herne's acting of the wife's part was terrific. It clutched the heart. It was common; it was pitilessly plain; it was ugly; but it was true, and it was irresistible. At times the wife preached, and that was bad; there were passages of the grossest romanticism in the piece, and yet it was a piece of great realism in its whole effect. This effect in Boston, where it was produced, was most extraordinary. Probably no other new play ever drew such audiences there, in the concert hall where it took refuge after being denied a chance at all the theatres. Literature, fashion, religion, delegated their representatives to see it, and none saw it without profound impression, so that it became the talk of the whole city wherever cultivated people met."[49]

Howells also wrote Mark Twain about *Margaret Fleming*. "Herne's play here was a very strange affair—half bad, but the rest so good that you forgot the bad half. It had the greatest success amongst the intellectuals, but the great money paying populace thought it was the Foregone Conclusion, and stayed away."[50]

Critics unanimously endorsed one element of the *Margaret Fleming* production—K.C.'s powerful portrayal as Margaret. Few actresses in history have received such splendid reviews, especially for a character part most critics resented:

> *Boston Evening Transcript*: "Mrs. Herne plays her part perfectly, both in its sweeter phases and in its later and unwifely manifestations, and it would hardly be possible to speak too highly in her praise."[51] And the following

day: "The character of Margaret is exceptionally beautifully acted."[52]

Boston Post: "Under the transforming influence of Mrs. Herne's exquisite acting it is not only void of offence, but for the moment it is natural and touching."[53]

Boston Herald: "Mrs. Herne, as Margaret Fleming, easily carried off the honors, and well deserved the handsome floral gifts at the end of the third act. 'Great' is hardly too strong a word with which to characterize her performance."[54]

Boston Daily Globe: "Mrs. Herne has given the stage nothing so true, so vivid, so memorable."[55]

Boston Daily Advertiser: "Mrs. Herne led easily, carrying her long and fatiguing part through to the end with splendid naturalness, with fine purity and simplicity of style."[56]

Boston Morning Journal: "Mrs. Herne gave strong effects to all her scenes."[57]

Boston's feminists, of course, embraced K.C., inviting her many places. Mildred Aldrich (Mrs. Thomas Bailey Aldrich) visited her, and Lucy Stone (who refused to use Henry Brown Blackwell's name after their marriage) extended a personal invitation. Others came backstage after performances. A local dinner was also given in K.C.'s honor, guests receiving a souvenir menu with the inscription: "Vernal greetings to Katherine Corcoran Herne. Life is real—Life is earnest."[58] The Hernes, however, rejected most invitations. They didn't belong to Boston's "upper 400" and maintained social distance. Herne's withdrawn manner matched his quiet stage realism (he seldom received anyone at the stagedoors after performances). One Beacon Hill socialite persuaded the celebrated couple to attend a private dinner— which wasn't private. A dozen guests attended, enraging Herne.

Margaret Fleming ran for several weeks at Chickering Hall. "The audiences have not been very large," wrote the *Sunday Herald,* "but they have been of excellent quality."[59] Julie Herne agreed with Howells' comments, recalling that the play was "widely, and often bitterly, discussed. Artistic Boston flocked to see it and it became the talk of the town."[60] As the *Herald* noted, "To admit that you have not seen 'Margaret Fleming' is to acknowledge that you are 'not in the swim.' "[61]

But audiences of excellent quality and controversy didn't

pay bills. Herne had to decide whether or not to close *Margaret Fleming*. Garland pleaded in the *Evening Transcript*, "It only needs a little generous effort on the part of the public and press to put this radical play on a paying basis, and so put new courage into the hearts of realists."[62] This was something the public refused to do.

Herne finally went to New York and staged Klaw and Erlanger's new show, *The Country Circus*, while *Margaret Fleming* folded. He publicly said he was "satisfied in the interest the play had aroused in the literary world of Boston."[63] But he didn't mention the hoped-for mass audience.

The Hernes still held one ace, *My Colleen*, which Herne started writing for Tony Farrell after *Margaret Fleming* closed. He hadn't visited Ireland, but roles in *Handy Andy*, the Boucicault plays, and his adaptation of *Charles O'Malley* helped in the writing. So did K.C.'s Irish roots. Garland recommended research abroad, but Herne settled for three volumes of *Picturesque Ireland*. He also directed *Charles O'Malley* on Broadway for Klaw and Erlanger, which Farrell played for eight years.

Margaret Fleming played a few performances for a few interested people. That's all. It couldn't compete with the likes of Buffalo Bill's Wild West Show of 1884, which attracted more than 40,000 spectators to a single presentation in Chicago.

13 the quintessence of the commonplace

AFRANKNESS ABOUT ADULTERY, alcoholism, delerium tremens, and illegitimacy were all reasons why *Margaret Fleming* shocked starched moralists. Most people clung to traditional stage values, which meant sugar-coated lies. Daniel Frohman said that "unless a love-story shines like a radiating sun through a play, that play will die."[1] Alfred Hennequin warned in an 1890 *Arena* article that "adultery may, indeed, be hinted at in American plays, as it may even form an important element of the plot, but it must not be seriously discussed or even presented as a problem." About the American audience he said, "It will submit to rank and fustian ineffable, to buffoonery and horse-play unspeakable, but it will not listen to the discussion of a serious social problem."[2]

This article must have inspired deep discussion among Boston's veritists, especially regarding *Margaret Fleming*'s proposed production. They attacked the problem head on, like a salmon swimming upstream, fighting a fierce current, unwilling to admit defeat. Other reformist playwrights carried *Margaret Fleming*'s scarf in later years and suffered similar attacks. Shaw's *Mrs. Warren's Profession,* for example, incited the Society for the Suppression of Vice to secure a court injunction, which was later dismissed, and Eugene Walter's *The Easiest Way* was called corrupt because it dealt with a "kept" woman.

Margaret Fleming, the play Howells called "epoch-making," returned to Boston's Chickering Hall (renamed Chickering Hall Theatre)[3] in October under the Klaw and Erlanger banner. This sponsorship worried Herne, who wrote Garland from New York: "They *talk* of *trying* to get time in theatre for it but I know if it *fails* so boldly (*sic*) at the hall—that the theatres will not have it *at all*. Our only hope lies in a *success* at the hall."[4]

Herne returned to Boston in mid-September to direct *Margaret Fleming*'s revival, this time playing the role of Joe Fletcher. Thomas Hunter, a character actor, portrayed Philip, and Garland's brother played Dr. Larkin. K.C., of course, continued as Margaret.[5]

The question of *Margaret Fleming*'s survival now faced Herne. In order to attract a larger audience, he "pulled the plugs," promoting it in the old-fashioned way with ballyhoo. He first issued a circular: "At the expiration of the Chickering Hall engagement, she (Mrs. Herne) will, assisted by the same company of very capable players, make a brief tour of New England prior to her appearance in New York City, where negotiations are pending with a view to her presenting the character there for an *Unlimited Season*."[6]

Herne's rationale for such statements was the cliché, "Nothing succeeds like success." He knew that audiences loved this clattering sound.

The play opened on October 5 to a packed house. By 8:00 p.m., tickets were sold out. K.C. shaped and reshaped her audience's responses, shifting from the playful baby scene to the startling scene of recognition. She created a "deathly stillness"[7] in the makeshift auditorium. Bouquets and recalls followed.

The critics hadn't repented their earlier jeremiads, although the *New York Dramatic Mirror* wrote: "Mrs. Herne's impersonation of Margaret Fleming is even more delightful than it was at the presentation last spring. It charms all and surpasses all the artistic impersonations which this artistic actress has given in the past. It is unquestionably one of the finest bits of strong acting ever seen on the Boston stage."[8]

The *Evening Transcript* admitted that "the audience was as large as the hall could well hold, and followed the play with almost breathless interest." K.C. was applauded. "If this admirable artist could, or would, only rid herself of the besetting vice of modern 'naturalistic' actors, her performance would be flawless. In facial expression, gesture, and inflexion of voice she is perfect: but, like the actors at the Théâtre Libre in Paris, she speaks so low that you lose more than half of what she says." Herne was accused of abusing naturalism. "But what can be more absurd, from a naturalistic point of view, than Philip Fleming's taking a foot-bath in his dining-room? People do not, as a rule, take baths in their dining-rooms."[9]

The *Herald*, however, made an intelligent observation before the play's opening, implying that Herne's link with Boston's high culture had damaged *Margaret Fleming*. In short—audiences were scared.

> It may be that too much stress has been laid upon the literary and artistic quality of this play, and that it has created a little too much discussion of an elaborate and scholarly kind. The question asked and answered in this play is simply and easily comprehended. There is no depth in the work which the average theatre-goer cannot sound. The play is not a sermon of a solemn and repelling kind; its author is not mounted on stilts, nor is he preaching to an audience which demands literature in polysyllables.
>
> 'Margaret Fleming' is simply an interesting, entertaining play, as rich in comedy as in pathos, and an audience of average theatregoers would heartily enjoy it. Realistic, genre, psychologic and a few such terms have been piled upon this play in such a manner as to repel the theatregoer who would under ordinary conditions, go to see Mr. Herne's clever work and thoroughly enjoy the fine acting of Mrs. Herne who has today no superior on the American stage as a representative of emotional, sympathetic, natural woman.[10]

Herne obviously read this review. Perhaps it changed his method of promoting *Margaret Fleming*. He had already altered his selling tactics, offering some tickets for 50 cents.[11] He also resorted to the popular lithographic type of advertising. Statement such as "powerful play, marvellous portrayal,"[12] "25th performance of the stirring sensation, Mrs. Herne as Margaret Fleming,"[13] and "Last 2 performances of the thrilling dramatic sensation Mrs. Herne as Margaret Fleming,"[14] appeared in newspapers.

Herne tried to attract more Harvard students, announcing a *Margaret Fleming* criticism contest, based on "grounds of art, taste, truthfulness, power to interest and moral impressiveness."[15] (Barrett Wendell earlier told his Harvard students in their paper about *Margaret Fleming*, encouraging them to see it.) The prize was a diamond crescent scarf-pin. Charles E. L. Wingate said in *The Critic*: "I was amused when I read the advertisement of 'Margaret Fleming' in the Sunday papers. Evidently Mr. Herne—though he and his associate 'veritists' (to use Mr. Hamlin Garland's coined word) disbelieve in the accepted drama—believes fully in the accepted methods of pushing the drama. What, indeed, could be more significant of the hand of the present-day advance-agent than this pompous declaration:— 'Honorable presentation of Mr. James A. Herne's highly purposeful *genre* play: Mrs. Herne in her masterful impersonation, assisted by an extremely effective company.' And, then, the later advance work of which I have just heard—circular invitation to the students of Harvard College to write the criticism of 'the highly purposeful play, 'Margaret Fleming,' on promise, as a reward to the best critic, of a 'beautiful diamond crescent scarf-pin, now on exhibition—,' etc."[16]

Was Wingate right? One thing is certain—he talked tall on paper, but would he have thrown his reputation and pocketbook on the line for truth?

Public reaction to *Margaret Fleming*'s revival wasn't bad—for a while. Business seemed to boom.

Boston Daily Advertiser: " 'Margaret Fleming' is attracting good audiences to Chickering Hall and is pleasing them."[17]

Boston Evening Transcript: " 'Margaret Fleming' at Chickering Hall had had a welcome hearty enough to justify the managers in continuing on their venture. The drama will be played through next week and probably as much longer as the public shall seem to manifest a desire to see it."[18]

Boston Herald: "The popularity of this play is steadily increasing, and large audiences now attend every performance."[19]

But it wasn't long before *Margaret Fleming* closed—on Saturday, October 17, 1891, following matinee and evening performances[20] Klaw and Erlanger withdrew support after two weeks, considering it a bad investment. But the actors worked without salary, and Benjamin Orange Flower underwrote the production for another week.

Greater Boston failed to mourn when *Margaret Fleming*

folded again. Theatres were potato plentiful. And what peelings:
Buffalo Bill's Wild West comedy with 50 speciality artists, Ker-
nell's High-Class Vaudevilles, Neil Burgess in *The Country Fair,*
Denman Thompson in *The Old Homestead,* and at Austin &
Stone's Museum, the "last week of the fat girls. Ten of the heavi-
est women on earth."

In an ironic epilogue, it was Herne who staged *The Country
Circus,* "one of the greatest productions of the season,"[21] at
Philadelphia's Chestnut Street Theatre in October. It was a potboiler that Herne despised. It forced him to compromise his artistic integrity for a menagerie of dogs, cats, baboons, and monkeys, a weak substitute for *Margaret Fleming.* He wrote Garland: "I look upon the failure of my life.... The author of 'The
Country Circus' read his play to the company to-day. *Oh, God!*
But it'll go, I suppose. Oh, how I'd like to see such rot where it
belongs."[22]

This rot opened on Broadway in late December. Weather
conditions were miserable, but audiences flocked like geese
through the gates. The *New York Times* wrote, "So many ladies
in evening dress have not been seen in the old Academy since Col.
Mapleson gave up the fight for Bellini and Rossini." The play
was "good enough for its purpose, and there is very little of it,
and the circus is good enough to please any one who likes a circus
at all. And who does not?"[23] A major criticism was that *The
Country Circus* didn't have enough horses in the grand entrée.

Herne's staging was highly imaginative, an early example
of environmental theatre, which is the rage today. *The Country
Circus'* big scene unfolded beneath a tent rigged on stage with
ring and sawdust. Its top held brightly colored posters and flags
with the producers' names: Klaw, Erlanger and Jefferson. Another innovation was a mirror hung upstage that reflected the
audience. Performers included everything from acrobats to the
Meers sisters and bareback rider Mlle. Savilla, Queen of the
Arena. One pony wrestled, while another slept before a fireplace.
And everyone adored the fox terrier. Henry George, Jr., sat on
stage during one performance and later wrote:

> In the tent scene we sat around on what seemed to be the
> conventional circus plank seats. The glare of the footlights
> and the roar of laughter that frequently went up from the

real audience in the darkened theater beyond disconcerted
me at first. But this was soon forgotten in the matters that
were occurring on the stage itself. The circus programme
presented several features, one of which was a clown and
a mule. There were several circus attendants who wore caps
and a kind of uniform. Mr. Herne was dressed as one of
these attendants, and he moved about watching and giving
stage directions in an undertone. Another man who wore one
of these uniforms cried out frequently, "Peanuts and red
lemonade." This man soon interested me more than anybody
else, for I found that he was punching tickets presented by
the people in the stage audience.

In this audience were men, women and children—out of
New York's slums I afterwards learned. They were anxious
to have their tickets punched, because upon the number of
these little holes depended the amount of their pay from the
theatrical managers, fifty cents to each man and each
woman for each performance, and twenty-five cents to children. One little tot had forgotten or lost her ticket, and was
in sore grief about it. She tried to stifle her sobs, but they
reached me through all the other hum and noise of the stage.
I motioned to Mr. Herne and drew his attention to the matter. "That's a tragedy to those people," he murmured;
"They come from the tenement regions. We cannot get away
from the social problem. Actors ought to think. They see
these things everywhere.[24]

Months passed. The clowns still clowned, the baboon still
rode the donkey's back and the horses still pranced around the
ring. *The Country Circus* finally closed on March 26, 1892, after
one hundred performances.[25]

One Broadway producer eventually took a chance and accepted *Margaret Fleming*. He was A. M. Palmer, who had attended the play in Boston. He scheduled four matinee performances, telling an interviewer: "I am going to produce Mr.
Herne's play in order to test the sincerity of the demand in certain quarters for perfectly natural plays. I saw *Margaret Fleming* in Boston. If people wish to see a play in which men and
women act and speak exactly as they act and speak in real life,
they will have the opportunity to see such a play when *Margaret
Fleming* is presented here. I found it a very interesting production myself."

The interviewer asked, "Will Mrs. Herne be seen in the same part?"

Palmer answered, "She will act Margaret, supported by a cast selected from my own company."[26]

A. M. Palmer was a Broadway powerhouse classed with Augustin Daly and Charles Frohman, a career maker—or breaker. Among his many productions were: Bartley Campbell's *Peril* and *My Partners*, Twain's *The Gilded Age*, Harte's *Two Men of Sandy Bar*, Bronson Howard's *The Banker's Daughter*, and Augustus Thomas' *Alabama*. He also had founded the Actors' Fund of America in 1882, raising $175,000.[27]

Palmer encouraged plays about American themes, using American language and American settings. He felt that "all the greatest and truest plays in our language are simple and direct, with no straining after effect and no tortuous plots."[28] Starting with *Margaret Fleming*, Palmer offered "authors' *matinees*" (trial runs for native American works). *Marjorie's Lovers* by Brander Matthews, *A Foregone Conclusion* by W. D. Howells, and *Elaine* adapted from Alfred Tennyson's poem by George Parsons Lathrop and Harry Edwards all started as Palmer matinees, which he advertised as "a fair and adequate trial to American works."[29]

Broadway, from the Battery to 159th Street, was a madhouse in 1891. From Tenth Street to Forty-second Street, especially at Union and Madison Squares, were the shopping and theatre districts. Here the streets overflowed with long silver-handled parosols and white gloves, high-topped hats and canes, hansoms, street-cars, and victorias. It was clatter, clatter, clatter until night, and then "all the shop-fronts (were)lighted, and the entrances to the theatres blaze(d) out on the sidewalk like open fireplaces, and when every street-car (went) jumping past loaded down to the railings with well-dressed theatre-goers."[30]

Such was romantic Broadway, but not Herne's Broadway, that Darwinesque world in microcosm of splintered hopes. What tripped through Herne's mind were theatre tickets for *Margaret Fleming* sold to top-hats, white gloves, and pretty parasols.

Margaret Fleming played Palmer's on December 9, 1891, for one matinee performance, advertised as "never before seen on the stage of a theatre."[31] The theatre was "crowded, and almost everybody in the large audience waited patiently for three hours to see the end."[32] But with Palmer's own director in charge, the work had lost its subtle tone. Boston critics had been brazen, but New York's were brutal.

Margaret Fleming was called "monotonous" and talky by the *Herald*. " 'Margaret Fleming' is, indeed, the quintessence of the commonplace. Its language is the colloquial English of the shops and the streets and the kitchen fire-place. Its personages are the every-day nonentities that some folks like to forget when they go to the theatre. It is constructed in defiance of the laws of Aristotle and Horatius Flaccus and Corneille and Hazlitt. It has two 'situations,' and two hours are required to develop the first, while the slow culmination of the second occupies another hour. Its incidental humor is quite as true to nature as the humor of Mr. Harrigan's farces, and of touch the same quality; but it is not emphasized and set off by the lively songs and dances that have secured success to Harrigan. The life it portrays is sordid and mean, and its effect upon a sensitive mind is depressing."[33]

This was praise compared to Edward A. Dithmar's vicious review in the *Times*. Dithmar voiced the same trite criticisms: commonplace, dull and a slender plot. It lacked soliloquies, un-motivated actions, stirring climaxes, and complicated situations. "Yet there is merit to be found in the piece," he sneered, "if we take the playwright's point of view, which is the same point of view we take when we read the morning newspaper and buy meat in the butcher's shop."[34]

The Critic criticized: "It is extremely difficult to imagine what ground there could have been for the notion, widely preva-lent apparently in Boston, that it is a revelation in the direction of true realism, an epoch-making composition, the first-fruits of a new and potent dramatic school and philosophy and a model for the theatre of the future.... (Herne's) views of human nature are abnormal, and his 'realism' when it is not unreal is often ridiculously trivial."[35]

Herne's arch enemy, William Winter of the *Daily Tribune*, slashed unmercifully at *Margaret Fleming*, calling it "the work of a long conversation interrupted from time to time by the fall-ing of the curtain." He ridiculed it: "Several babies are introduced, and at one time the stage is replete with bathtub and sponges, baby pins and diapers, scented soap and powder puff, towels and carminative; and this paraphernalia of the nursery is exploited with abundance of that soft nonsense of prattle which always sounds well beside the cradle and always make people sick in public."[36]

Winter raved for years about Herne, finally writing in *The Life of David Belasco*, "*Margaret Fleming* is mainly the work of Mrs. Herne, and is one of those crude and completely ineffectual pieces of hysterical didacticism which are from time to time produced on the stage with a view to the dismay of libertines by an exhibition of some of the evil consequences of licentious conduct."[37]

Winter symbolized the Victorian theatre. He hated all realists, preferring the romantic roles of Edwin Booth and Henry Irving with their soaring verse, grandiloquent gestures, and two-dimensional drops. Herne wasn't his sole target. Winter called Sarah Bernhardt's *La Tosca* "not only shocking to the nervous system and grossly offensive to persons of true sensibility, but which might, under easily possible circumstances, inflict irreparable injury on persons yet unborn." He considered Shaw's *Candida* a "diseased play" and Edward Sheldon's *Salvation Nell* "one of the most crude and offensive pieces that has ever been intruded on the public attention."[38]

These indictments were mild compared to Winter's attack on Ibsen in his chapter "Ibsen and Ibsenism" in *The Wallet of Time* (1913). "Ibsen, as a writer of a number of variously flaccid, insipid, tainted, obfuscated, and nauseous plays, could be borne, although, even in that aspect, he is an offence to taste and a burden on patience, but Ibsen obtruded as a sound leader of thought is a grotesque absurdity." He also charged that Ibsen's *Hedda Gabler*, *Rosmersholm*, and *Ghosts* filled the mind "with disgust and gloom: they pervert life: they tend to disseminate misinformation, augment ignorance, and mislead weak or ill-educated minds, and therein they are immoral."[39]

Winter's views evoke snickers today, but in 1891 he was Broadway's self-appointed but influential minister of morality. He was puritanism personified. Yet, the *Tribune* denied him an office, forcing him to write reviews standing up. He also remained New York's poorest paid major critic. Critic James Gibbons Huneker called him "Weeping Willie," and Harrison Grey Fiske, publisher of the *Dramatic Mirror* and husband of Minnie Maddern Fiske, said he could "unearth impurity from the quotations of the stock market and wantonness from the Declaration of Independence."[40]

Margaret Fleming's failure at Palmer's didn't destroy Herne's spark, just dampened it. He finally interested Chicago's famous manager, James H. McVicker, then scheduling shows for the 1892 summer season in anticipation of the World's Columbian Exposition. He wrote Herne: "This summer should be extra good as millions are to be spent in preparing for the Fair and the city will be filled with people. . . . Summer audiences do not care for long performances and are fond of heart interest and clean mirth."[41]

McVicker was called the dean of Chicago theatre managers. (His step-daughter, incidentally, married Edwin Booth.) He knew show business inside-out, managing McVicker's Theatre from 1857 to 1896. Even the Great Fire of 1871 and another blaze in 1890, twice destroying his theatre, didn't faze him. Altogether he rebuilt or remodeled his theatre five times.[42] He also fought the combination system (road shows) which "destroys the care and thoroughness which performers would be obliged to bestow were they living in one city. They are in one place today and a long way off tomorrow, and they care little what is thought of them in one town, as they are not relying on its support."[43]

McVicker read *Margaret Fleming* and supported its message but felt public concessions were necessary. "I doubt if the play will ever be a money maker for the reason that it treats of an unpleasant *truth*. It is realistic, purely natural, but the world—or the people in it—lack the courage to adopt the moral it teaches, which all will privately admit, is correct."[44]

McVicker's advice was to avoid childbirth, and let the infant be one or two months old, allow Margaret to accidentally visit Maria's home on a charity mission, then discover the truth, restore her eyesight, and let her regain the child.[45] Their combined effect on *Margaret Fleming*'s script was like removing the spikes from railroad ties. But Herne agreed, and McVicker offered a summer directorship, a post Herne needed badly.

Herne also sent McVicker the manuscript of a second play he had written, called *Shore Acres*. McVicker liked it, providing costs were minimal and the same actors played in both plays. He planned to present *Margaret Fleming* for one week, then *Shore Acres* in relief. Herne liked McVicker's plan.

Margaret Fleming opened in Chicago on July 7, 1892. One blurb blurbed: "What Woman Would Blame Her?... a forcible discussion of the woman question." Tough competition faced McVicker, everything from *The Last Days of Pompeii* to *The Country Circus*.

The Chicago critics were more muted than elsewhere for an obvious reason—Herne had diluted the script. The *Chicago Tribune,* for example, called it "a simple and pathetic play narrow in its scope and affecting in the climax, but not likely to be a reformatory agent in morals or likely to mark a new epoch in playwriting.... Those who reject an Ibsen will not readily be reconciled to the comparative crudities of his American disciple."[46] Likewise, the *Chicago Mail* said: "It is not a play which marks any clear-cut departure from accepted stage traditions."[47]

Margaret Fleming closed on July 16, after twelve performances. McVicker's stock company disbanded (see Chapter XVI) and the Hernes returned home. They were still friends with McVicker, who wrote them: "The very pleasant words contained in yours of yesterday, I assure you are fully reciprocated. The financial results will soon be forgotten by me, while the pleasant thoughts created by yourself and wife will linger 'while memory holds a seat.' We have had a too-brief season of harmony and good feelings and the greatest losers are those we catered to. With kind remembrances to the 'Little mother and three babies' at 79 Convent Avenue, believe me."[48]

Margaret Fleming's next production was by Europeans. Carl and Theodor Rosenfeld, who exhibited German midgets, held the American rights to Gerhart Hauptmann's *Hannele*. They also eyed *Margaret Fleming*, finally producing it at the Fifth Avenue Theatre on April 9, 1894. One critic claimed that the nursing scene "brought the house down,"[49] but the *New York Times* said "It is a well-known work, and has been the subject of much unprofitable discussion which no sound-minded person would care to have revived."[50] George C. D. Odell wrote that "The Dramatic Mirror found the play distressing, and teeming with unhappiness. The Herald thought Philip somewhat deserving of pity—with such a wife!

Although the Rosenfelds offered K.C. a road contract for *Margaret Fleming,* she declined, deciding to spend more time with her children. She never played *Margaret Fleming* again, except for a professional matinee that William Gillette attended. A later 1896 Berlin offer to stage *Margaret Fleming* fell through.[51] The play remained unproduced again until six years after Herne's death, when K.C. directed it at Chicago's New Theatre in 1907.

14 a crucible of civilization

GEORGE BERNARD SHAW once remarked that, "all great truths begin as blasphemies." James Herne and the Boston veritists learned this hard but worthwhile lesson from *Margaret Fleming*. Their blasphemous truth? Women should be liberated from the chains of society. As Hamlin Garland wrote in *The Arena*: "The feudalistic woman has been for centuries either a sovereign or a servant, a heroine or a buffoon. In the ordinary drama she is long-suffering, patient and beautiful, or is pretty and provokes laughter."[1]

Herne's *Margaret Fleming,* of course, didn't provoke laughter. Just the opposite. Benjamin Orange Flower said: "It is the most powerful plea for an equal standard of morals for men and women that I have ever heard.... The theatre is a crucible of civilization. It is a place of human communication. All its phases need to be studied. It is in the theatre that the public soul is formed."[2] These were intelligent words, but the romantics wanted artful lies, half-truths glossed with glamorous heroics, blistering battles, blizzards, burning buildings, and brutality. These the romantics relished. As Garland argued: "The romanticist, notwithstanding his themes of blood and lust and tears, is supposed to be a wholesome and inspiring creature. He can slay men in war, and imprison maidens in donjon keeps, and hound poor peasants to death, and yet be called a joyous and lovely teacher of the splendor and glory of life." He said this was accepted "because the romancer puts his scene afar off and clothes his assassin in scarlet-and-green doublet and in gold-inlaid steel. It is all beautiful and moral and inspiring for our sons and daughters to read."[3]

175

The romantics disagreed. One was Charles L. Dana, in an 1895 *Forum* article, "Are We Degenerating." Referring to the realists, he wrote: "There are among them art and poetry, but it is the stuff that comes from nature's slums. It is the stenching secretion of the diseased growth; it is nature, to be sure, for death and disease are natural; but it has nothing in common with healthful life and the effectiveness of the race.... If the man is really a form of decay, his art will show it in time; like the putrid fish, it may shine but it smells."[4]

It seems that William Shakespeare's mirror reflected many images, some of them contradictions. The war of words between the realists and romantics roared. Henrik Ibsen, the man who became the romancers' target zero, bore the brunt of the attack for years. As late as 1906, *The Theatre* concluded that his characters were "the most pitiless collection of grafters and brutes imaginable. The women of his country are worse than the men of his country."[5]

America's first exposure to Ibsen's "grafters and brutes" was the world premiere of *Ghosts* (1882) at the Aurora Turner Hall in Chicago. Its audience consisted of Scandinavian immigrants. Its star was the Danish actress Helga von Bluhme. A tour followed that included Minneapolis and other midwestern cities where Scandinavian audiences could be gathered.

The first mention of Ibsen in an American magazine dates earlier. Bjørnstjerne Bjørnson visited the United States in 1882, writing a tribute to Ibsen in *Scribner's Monthly Magazine*. "I do not hesitate to say that in my opinion Henrik Ibsen possesses the greatest dramatic power of the age. I am so much the more certain of my judgment from the fact that I do not always like his dramas. It is surprising to me that he is not translated in America. He is one whom him contemporaries should know."[6]

One fellow, however, nearly made American theatre history. William M. Lawrence, a Milwaukee school principal, staged Ibsen's *A Doll's House* in 1882 as *The Child Wife*. "Lawrence set the play in England, introducing an Irish widow to give the play some humour, and of course using the happy ending. In the second act, one of Nora's (or, as Lawrence called her, Eva's) children sang a pretty song, which the audience enjoyed so much that she had to repeat it. 'Love is the theme,' noted one reviewer, 'yet

not a line of the play is impure.' Another critic named Lawrence
as the author, while a third referred to the play as *Henry
Ibsen.*"⁷

Lawrence offered the lead to young Minnie Maddern, who
declined. Years later, as Minnie Maddern Fiske, she became famous for her Ibsen roles, especially Nora.

Lawrence knew theatre. His insight into popular theatre
taste shows in an 1882 letter requesting usable plays from a professor at the University of Wisconsin. "Let me suggest two
points that managers here count as of first importance; first, a
play must have a strong 'leading part,' as for instance 'Nora' in
'Et Dukkehjem.' The 'star' system makes this imperative, and
while I dislike to yield to it, I find that it is better to bend sometimes than break. No one but a genius can afford to be uncom-
promising. Again, the American manager demands more or less
of an undercurrent of comedy in a play, whether light or broad
burlesque, doesn't matter much, as long as people are given an
opportunity—to laugh or smile between the appeals of sentiment.
This, I find, they consider almost an essential, so that one must
almost choose between yielding to this demand and getting no
hearing at all."⁸

But Lawrence, the man Ibsen offered exclusive American
translation rights to all his plays, remained a school principal.

The next production of *A Doll's House* was at Macauley's
Theatre in Louisville, Kentucky, in 1883. It was called *Thora*,
with Helen Modjeska, who had performed the role in St. Peters-
burg and Warsaw, playing the lead. The production survived one
night.

The later American reception of *Ghosts*, which first toured
the land in 1887 under the name *Phantoms or The Sins of his
Father*, was brutal. The play repulsed the critics. In Shaw's *The
Quintessence of Ibsenism*, dozens of quotes appear. Among them:
"an open drain," "a loathsome sore unbandaged," "literary car-
rion," "garbage and offal," and "as foul and filthy a concoction
as has ever been allowed to disgrace the boards of an English
theatre."⁹

The first *notable* American production of an Ibsen play was
on October 30, 1889, at Boston's Globe Theatre, with Beatrice
Cameron, wife of Richard Mansfield, playing the lead.¹⁰ Garland

attended, writing in *The Arena*: "His words come to us at times like thrusts of the naked fist. They shake the hearer with their weight of real passion."[11] Garland bought a copy of Ibsen's *The Pillars of Society and Other Plays,* published in the London Camelot Series in 1888. After reading *The Pillars of Society,* he called it "the most radical departure and the most vital with modern life and thought."[12] Then he scribbled Herne's name next to Dr. Stockmann and K.C.'s next to Mrs. Stockmann in *An Enemy of the People*—an interesting parallel.

Howells also converted to Ibsenism. He read *The Pillars of Society, Enemy of the People,* and *Ghosts,* and then wrote in *Harper's Magazine*: "The action opens so tamely, so flatly, that it seems to you impossible to go on with a thing like that; but at the same moment you find yourself in the grip of a curiosity which intensifies to the most poignant interest, and holds you spell-bound to the end. These dramas are played in Europe. We fancy them offered to the fat optimism that goes to your theatres only to be 'amused.' "[13]

Howells despised American theatre, but he half-endorsed the plays of Edward Harrigan, Charles Hoyt, Neil Burgess, Denman Thompson, and Bronson Howard. "We do not at all pretend that they have produced a great drama, but we do pretend that in such prolongations of sketches as they have given they have made the right beginning of an American drama."[14]

Then came Herne and literary respectability for American drama—native plays with native characters portrayed realistically. He fulfilled Augustin Daly's 1886 prophecy, "Possibly our national drama, from a literary point of view, will reach its best period when native writers vie with each other in illustrating native character and contemporaneous fashions and follies."[15] Brander Matthews also remarked that "one of the chief duties of the theatre is to reflect, as best it can, the life of to-day."[16]

It's difficult to pinpoint the exact influences on Herne's career, seeing that he had experimented with realistic techniques before meeting Garland and Boston's literati. Among his favorite European dramatists, however, were Shaw, Arthur Wing Pinero, Oscar Wilde, Henry Arthur Jones, Gerhart Hauptmann, Ibsen, Sudermann, and Tolstoy, but not the mysticism of Maurice Maeterlinck, which he considered dishonest. This is interesting because both Herne and Maeterlinck attacked the problem of "stage stasis," one realistically and the other abstractly. As Montrose J. Moses remarked in *The American Dramatist,* "Such work, of which Mr. Herne as an actor was capable, is close to Maeterlinck's conception of what *static* drama should be,—the drama of little action and immense interaction of the forces of destiny."[17]

The Hernes' remarks about now-famous plays and players are also interesting. When they saw Shaw's *The Devil's Disciple,* Herne wrote: "I think that play barely escaped being a great piece of work. Mrs. Herne was with me when I saw it. The first two acts were distinctly great, and Mrs. Herne said, 'Now, here is a great play.' We were both delighted; but after the second act it went off into driveling melodrama."[18]

K.C.'s candid remarks about Eleanora Duse and Minnie Maddern Fiske lifted eyebrows. She wrote Herne:

March, 1896: "Duse a heartbreaking failure in *Magda*—that is to me. The house was packed. A failure in all things excepting Duse herself. She was Mrs. Duse in it—high strung, intense—the actress throughout, never the artist, never the intellectual actress even trying to illustrate Sudermann's superb work. Oh, Jim dear, what a lot of pretense there is in this world of ours!"

March 20, 1896: "We saw Minnie Maddern Fiske in *The Doll's House* last night. She gave a straight-forward, business-like performance of our delicate, subtle Nora. Very intelligent, but it all might just as well have been a real-estate transaction as far as atmosphere or suggestion went. She would be a convincing little woman on the platform. She is very precise and decisive in her action and utterance, and gives the impression of a very matter-of-fact and sophisticated Nora indeed. Oh dear! Oh dear! No wonder the music halls are packed!"[19]

Anton Chekhov and August Strindberg had no opportunity to impress Herne, as both were unfamiliar to Americans during the 1890's. In 1904 *The Theatre* published an article called "World Dramatists To-Day," featuring sketches on Ibsen, Pinero, Sudermann, Hauptmann, Paul Hervieu, Clyde Fitch, Augustus Thomas, Edmond Rostand, Maeterlinck, Ambrose Philips, Ludwig Fulda, Victorien Sardou, and Shaw. Strindberg was not mentioned.[20] A year later James Huneker recommended in *The*

Theatre: "There are a half dozen of (Strindberg's) pieces that could be profitably transferred to the English stage, though I fear his gloomy, tragic and fantastic genius would never be very welcome in our theatres." Shaw added, "Of Strindberg I have a high opinion, possibly because I have read very little of him— chiefly a story called 'Memoir of a Madman,' or something like that, but ought to have been called, 'The Truth About my Confounded Wife.' "[21]

One dramatist who really intrigued Herne was Hermann Sudermann. His Spencerian brew of progressive individualism and abandonment of outworn social mores was strongly appealing. Even Howells applauded Sudermann's social stand.

Sudermann's international success stemmed from his thesis play, *Die Ehre* (*Honor*, 1889). Like later works, *Sodoms Ende* (*Destruction of Sodom*, 1891), and *Die Heimat* (*Home*, or *Magda*, 1893), *Die Ehre* was censored. The work dealt honestly with the conflict between German's upper middle class and proletariat. Sudermann called honor a conventional lie and demanded a higher sense of justice. As his spokesman in *Die Ehre* preached: "What we commonly call honor is nothing more than the shadow we throw in the sunlight of publicity. But the worst part of it is that we have as many kinds of honor as we have business circles and strata. How can one find his way among them?"[22] James Huneker said in *Iconoclasts* that *Die Ehre* shot "a bolt toward Nietzsche's land where good and evil blend in one hazy hue." He also defined Sudermann's central theme: "The moral law must submit to the variations of time and place, even though its infraction spells sin, even though the individual in his thirst for self-seeking smashes the slate of morality and perishes in the attempt."[23]

William Dean Howells saw *Die Ehre* in Europe and commented: "We cannot indeed truly say that the average of acting we saw at the American theatres was so high as that we found one night at the German theatre, where we went to hear a play that made all our American plays seem playthings. This was *Die Ehre*, a piece by the young dramatist Sudermann, who has dared to put more truth into it than has been put into any other modern play except, perhaps *La Morte Civile*."[24]

Sudermann's second drama, *Sodoms Ende*, appeared in 1891,

the same year as *Margaret Fleming*, and received similar abusive treatment. Sudermann savagely attacked Germany's feeble bourgeoisie in *Sodoms Ende*, a naturalistic specimen study of decadence in modern Berlin that "laid bare the cancer of modern German civilization."[25] The plot concerned a gifted painter seduced by a rich woman.

Magda, which K.C. called "Sudermann's superb work," remains his best-known play in the English-speaking world. It is a play that Allardyce Nicoll regarded as "the *Dame Aux Camélias* of the nineties."[26] Sarah Bernhardt, Eleanora Duse, Mrs. Patrick Campbell, and Minnie Maddern Fiske all tackled it with varying degrees of success. "Not since (August) Kotzebue has a German drama been so widely translated and produced as *Die Heimat*,"[27] wrote Marvin Carlson.

Magda, or *Die Heimat*, deals with the same thematic values as *Die Ehre*: a conflict between the old and new orders. But *Magda*'s hero is a woman, an actress who defies the social code that forces a woman to marry her child's father. Her despotic father demands that she abandon the stage, marry her lover, and surrender the child. She refuses. He tries to shoot her but suffers a stroke and dies. *Magda*'s social plea is "Gag us, stupefy us, shut us up in harems or in cloisters—and that perhaps would be best. But if you give us our freedom, do not wonder if we take advantage of it."[28]

Sudermann, however, doesn't answer the *big* question: Did Herne imitate Ibsen, or did his radicalism evolve independently of European influences. The answer is very complex.

Herne greatly admired Ibsen. He also greatly admired Tolstoy, Sudermann, and other European realists. This he admitted. As his friend J. J. Enneking wrote, "The realism of Ibsen, Tolstoi, and Sudermann served to blaze the way for Mr. Herne." Another friend, Benjamin Orange Flower, wrote that Herne "came under the influence of the threefold revolution that marked the closing half of the nineteenth century—the evolutionary theory as expounded by Herbert Spencer, the revolt against artificiality in literature and art as led by Tolstoi, Ibsen, Sudermann, and Mr. Howells, and the social gospel as proclaimed by Henry George."[29]

Did Herne's realistic theory and practice emerge *before* or *after* his introduction to the scowling Norwegian's genius? Garland answered that "epoch-marking as it was, it (*Margaret Fleming*) was only a logical, latest, outcome of the work the Hernes have been doing for the last ten years."[30]

Julie Herne wrote that "my father would be the first person to acknowledge his indebtedness to Ibsen and to the other modern European dramatists and novelists. The point that I think should be made clear, however is, that my father's 'originality,' the qualities that entitle him to be considered a pioneer in the field of American realistic drama, are present in his earliest melodramas, though possibly they are not as evident there as in his later plays. As far back as *Hearts of Oak* audiences were commenting that seeing it was not like watching a play. It was what happened every day in their own homes. This play and *Drifting Apart* were written before my father came under Ibsen's influence. It must also not be forgotten that he himself owed allegiance to Dickens. I have heard him say repeatedly that Dickens taught him to act."[31]

The pre-Ibsen realism in Herne's works can be seen in his portrayals of Bill Sykes and Rip Van Winkle, both acclaimed. Dorothy Foxglove in *The Minute Men of 1774–1775* and later the villainess of *Hearts of Oak* represented early threads in Herne's search for "fidelity to truth." Garland first introduced Herne to Boston's literati because *Drifting Apart* was a work far advanced. Garland wrote that the "play is far from perfect, but it has moments when it rises above any other American play," and Howells added, "Upon the whole he has produced a play fresh in motive, pure in tone, high in purpose and very simple and honest in method."

Julie also said Herne started *Margaret Fleming* before meeting Garland, an important remark because Herne supposedly completed the first draft of *Shore Acres* before starting *Margaret Fleming*. (*Shore Acres* was the phenomenal success that supported the social gospel of Henry George, feminism, agnosticism, and evolution.) Garland reinforced Julie's statement. Regarding the *Drifting Apart* days, he said that Herne "was at this time working on two plays which were to bring lasting fame and a considerable fortune. One of these was a picture of New England coast life and the other was a study of factory life. One became *Shore Acres* and the other *Margaret Fleming*.[32]

Radicalism was Herne's trademark in playwriting, acting, directing, scene design, and social reform until the day he died. As Barrett Clark and George Freedley comment in *A History of Modern Drama*, "To realize the novelty introduced by Herne it is necessary only to read any other play produced at the same time."[33] Many critics, however, weren't interested in Herne's "novelty" ideas. They wanted packaged plays easily chewed and digested. So many pasted Ibsen labels on *Margaret Fleming*, not to draw parallels but because Ibsen's name symbolized everything despised about realism. Others accused Herne of imitating Bjørnson's *The Gauntlet* and a stack of novels, including Howells' *A Modern Instance*. William Winter even said Herne plagiarized sections of Wilkie Collins, *Hide and Seek*.

Herne, of course, never said *Margaret Fleming* was perfect. He admitted, "The play was faulty, didactic in places, but there has been nothing *just* like it given to the stage, before nor since."[34] Garland and Howells felt the same. *This is the central issue.* Nothing like *Margaret Fleming* had appeared on the American stage before. Other playwrights lacked the courage and conviction to mount such a radical work, fearing the backlash by critics and commercial managers.

Montrose J. Moses makes a thoughtful statement in *The American Dramatist* regarding Herne influences. "Some would say that the influences which bore upon him at the time he wrote 'Margaret Fleming' and 'Griffith Davenport' were imported from such men as Ibsen and Tolstoy. If this were true, I would rather relate the Herne dramas, as Norman Hapgood suggested, to some of the German dramas of the time, if only Mr. Herne had known these German dramas. But his range of reading was limited. He saw the inward light of this realism which was claiming letters. He may be said to have been endowed with that luminosity of spiritual vision which, even at an advanced age, kept him thoroughly attuned to progressive movements in art and politics."[35]

Herne seemed to intuitively sense the time's changing temper, later admitting that he "had been unconsciously working along the lines of thought held by some of the great modern masters of art."[36] He even wrote Howells on June 1, 1890, one month before the premiere of *Margaret Fleming* at Lynn: "The time is coming for a truly great play. That's certain. I'd like to have a hand in the writing or production of it, or at least play a part in it."[37] It was the remark of a visionary who fulfilled his own prediction. As Julie later said about the realist movement, "It seems to have been a subconscious impulse rather than a deliberate mental attitude, that arose almost simultaneously in several countries, and that awoke varying responses as it swept across the world."[38]

Julie's remark may be a simplification, but consider the parallel research of Charles Darwin and Alfred Russell Wallace. Ibsen admitted, "I don't read books. I leave them to my wife and [son] Sigurd."[39] John Fiske wrote about Herbert Spencer: "Of historical and literary knowledge, such as one usually gets from books, Spencer had a great deal, and of an accurate and well-digested sort; he had some incomprehensible way of absorbing it through the pores of his skin—at least he never seemed to read books."[40] One fact must be faced—historical events often ignore the logician's reliance on such terms as probability and predictability.

The realists never accused Herne of imitating Ibsen, but the romantics, some of the popular critics, and a few current scholars find convenient parallels between *Margaret Fleming* and Ibsen's *A Doll's House* and *Ghosts* without analyzing Herne's career in depth. But this story is old. Ibsen once protested that "critics were eager to find a double meaning, a hidden symbol, in every word or action," and that they looked "for obscurities in his work where none existed."[41] Howells wrote Herne that *Margaret Fleming* had "the same searching moral vitality as Ibsen's best work," and Garland said that "we are not to imitate Ibsen. We must accept his theory; but do our own work in our own color."[42] Another key difference between the work of Herne and Ibsen was tonal coloration. Arthur Hobson Quinn, who attended a rare revival of *Margaret Fleming* by Philadelphia's "Plays and Players," observed, "It never occurred to me that there was any imitation of Ibsen in either this play or any others by Herne. The whole atmosphere was different."[43]

Critics unfamiliar with Herne's career neglect the fact that *Margaret Fleming* was only *one* expression of Herne's radicalism.

Herne's *Margaret Fleming* was also "the first of all the 'Little Theatres' in America,"[44] according to Garland. In 1893

Herne told a reporter from the *Boston Journal*, "A quiet play is lost in a big theatre; one cannot produce the best effects there unless his subject is broad, or unless he has grand scenic effects to fall back upon."[45] It was a statement based on experience, one made two years after he had produced *Margaret Fleming*.

Herne's dramatic criticism, "Art for Truth's Sake in the Drama," has been called "a significant document in the history of the American drama"[46] by historian Arthur M. Schlesinger, Sr.—perhaps the most significant single dramatic criticism by an American in the nineteenth century. Herne was an American pragmatist, not an impractical theorist.

Herne independently practiced realistic acting techniques long before the European schools gained acceptance. Helen Ormsbee wrote in *Backstage with Actors*: "At rehearsals he had a great knack in directing, and could draw abilities out of players that they scarcely knew they had. He used to urge them to regard their parts as real people—to know what those people had been doing before the play begun. The whole life of the character was what the performer must have in mind. In Russia, Stanislavsky had not yet started the Moscow Art Theatre, yet here was Herne using Stanislavsky's philosophy."[47] Julie Herne wrote: "He constantly told his actors: '*Think* what your lines mean first. When you have their meaning clearly in your mind, you can't help but express it in your voice, your face and your action."[48] Garland remarked that Herne "profoundly influenced the art of acting."[49]

Chrystal Herne said her father was a "pathfinder, and his ideas were as modern as those of any of our present producers. ... If he were in the theatre today he would not need to change. He was ahead of his time. When I played 'Craig's Wife' in 1925, I had a long silent scene at the end: it summed up the whole story. The author, George Kelly, had planned it to do that very thing. It was considered so new. But I often thought of Father's last scene in 'Shore Acres' so many years before."[50] In this scene, Herne mimed nearly ten minutes of detailed stage business, making him the talk of theatre circles everywhere.

It took critics thirty-five years to accept Herne's restrained method. In 1900 Charles Frohman didn't hire him for the lead in *David Harum* because "his method was too casual and slow."[51]

Herne once told a *New York Times* reporter: "I was always a natural actor. Critics said that I was cold. I always tried to make a personage on the stage seem real. There are critics of realism who have said to me, 'If you wish to put on the stage a real hodcarrier, why do you not go among the laborers and select one?' The reason is that a real hodcarrier will not seem real on the stage. He will not have the art to give protection to his naturalness. I was told that Antoine selected for the Théâtre Libre in Paris a company of players who were not actors. They were not professional, but they were actors. I am sure I could form a similar company anywhere."[52]

Herne's vocal range was limited. (He jokingly said nature endowed him with two notes.) For years a hoarseness hounded him, causing a noticeable rasp. During the early 90's he consulted a famous New York throat specialist, who removed a bony growth from his nose, relieving the condition. Considering the rave reviews Herne received from modernist critics, he must have honed his technique to a fine edge, turning a liability into an artistic asset.

Herne also was considered America's leading realistic director and lighting experimentalist.

Herne was an outspoken leader among American actors opposing the encroachment of the theatre syndicate. He proposed an actor's union decades before Actor's Equity was formed.

Herne was also America's earliest playwright to recognize blacks as three-dimensional stage figures—in *The New South*, *Coon Hollow* (unproduced), and *Griffith Davenport*. He early recognized Paul Dunbar, America's first widely known black poet.

And he didn't quit. In 1899, when past sixty, he staged *Griffith Davenport*, the play William Archer acclaimed "the cornerstone of a national drama."[53] It was another radical work that audiences ignored.

Herne wrote *Margaret Fleming* for three reasons:

One. He believed that theatre should teach subjectively, that it should be more than amusement, that it should reflect truth and be morally uplifting. He rejected Zola's scientific determinism. *Margaret Fleming* was a hybrid between humanism and science, an example of evolutionary idealism. Unlike the wretched beings of European naturalism, Margaret resists resignation. She asserts the rights of equality; she symbolized to Herne the Spencerian concepts of individuality and progress. Ibsen loathed Zola, saying, "Zola descends into the sewer to bathe in it; I, to cleanse it."[54]

Two. He sensed the shifting literary trends toward realism. His association with Garland, Howells, and other Boston veritists strengthened this view.

Three. He wanted to make K.C. America's leading actress and believed *Margaret Fleming* was the vehicle. As Herne told one reporter: "Take the way I wrote 'Margaret Fleming' for instance. I had long wanted to find something that would give the world a knowledge of the really marvelous talents of Mrs. Herne. One day the situation on which 'Margaret Fleming' turns came into my mind, and I saw at once that that was what I wanted. I therefore made a play that would give play to her powers."[55] K.C. starred in *all* the Herne dramas except *Sag Harbor*. Herne wrote his works for her: Dorothy Foxglove in *The Minute Men of 1774–1775*, Mary Miller in *Drifting Apart*, Margaret Fleming in *Margaret Fleming*, Ann Berry in *Shore Acres*, and Katharine Davenport in *Griffith Davenport*.

If Herne hadn't married Katharine Corcoran would he have become America's answer to Ibsen, or just another second-class actor-playwright? Flower called K.C. "a woman of superior ability, both as an artist and thinker," and Enneking wrote that "from no one did Mr. Herne receive so much inspiration, sympathy, and help as from his devoted and accomplished wife, Katharine Herne, who ever understood and encouraged him."[56] Garland, who knew the Hernes personally, also commented that "Mrs. Herne is a woman of extraordinary powers, both of acquired knowledge and natural insight, and her suggestions and criticism have been of the greatest value to her husband in his writing, and she had large part in the inception as well as in the production of *Margaret Fleming*. Her knowledge of life and books, like that of her husband, is self-acquired, but I have met few people on any walk of life with the same wide and thorough range of thought."[57]

K.C. obviously was a powerful influence on James A. Herne.

She was the woman who helped mold the man who raised American drama to a position of social and intellectual significance.

Margaret Fleming's central premise was the influence of environment. As *The Arena* stated in 1891, "The greatest factor in the development or debasement of a race is the environment to which its component parts are subjected."[58] These are words squeezed through the Darwin-Spencer wringer, words Herne explored in *Drifting Apart, Margaret Fleming, Shore Acres,* and *Griffith Davenport.* But most of all in *Margaret Fleming.*

When Dr. Larkin condemns Philip's liaison with Lena Schmidt, he doesn't blame the girl. "She's a product of her environment," he says. "Under present social conditions, she'd probably have gone wrong anyhow." But Philip's behavior he finds repulsive. "If we can't look for decency in men like you—representative men,—where in God's name are we to look for it, I'd like to know."[59] (The word representative helped separate Herne and Boston's veritists from the French naturalistic school that dealt with abnormalities, including sexual perversion.)

Margaret Fleming's supreme irony was that Philip's infidelity didn't create intellectual chaos behind Boston drawing-room doors and critic's closets. If was the double standard—Margaret's refusal to forgive and forget—that did. Imagine the traditionalist's reaction to the play's original shocking conclusion:

> *Philip.*   Suppose I could come to you some day and say, Margaret, I'm *now* an honest man. Would you live with me again?
> *Margaret.*   The wife-heart has gone out of me, Philip.
> *Philip.*   I'll wait, Margaret. Perhaps it may come back again. Who knows?... Is it degrading to forgive?
> *Margaret.*   No, but it is to condone. Suppose I had broken faith with you?
> *Philip.*   Ah, Margaret!
> *Margaret.*   I know! But suppose I had? Why should a wife bear the whole stigma of infidelity? Isn't it just-as revolting in a husband?... Then can't you see that it is simply impossible for me to live with you again?
> *Philip.*   That's my sentence.... We'll be friends?
> *Margaret.*   Yes, friends. We'll respect each other as friends. We never could as man and wife. *As they clasp hands, something latent, organic rushes over her. She masters it, puts his hand aside:* "Ring the bell!"[60]

The power of this moment is that Margaret still feels for

Philip but cannot forgive his infidelity. He has abused marriage's sacred trust, something she has honored. Philip, a weaker person who inherits his father's large mill, lacks his father's managerial skill. Although dependent on Margaret, he becomes involved with a common girl who gets pregnant. Philip pressures her to have an abortion; when she refuses, he abandons her, substituting cash for conscience. It was chance that Margaret's nursemaid, Maria Bindley, was also the girl's older sister. Otherwise, Margaret wouldn't have learned of Philip's adultery. The irony, of course, is that Philip has reformed, telling Joe Fletcher: "I've got through with all that foolishness. I've sowed my wild oats."[61] But fate intervenes. Philip loses Margaret, and both lives are wrecked.

Moralists either ignored or missed these sensitive issues. They thought Margaret's rejection of Philip was an immoral act, that she had taken a ridiculous and irresponsible stand. Fast and furious flew facts and fancies about Margaret Fleming, that "monster of morality." *The Woman's Journal* fumed: "Let anyone imagine the case reversed. Suppose a woman who had led a dissolute life should marry, leaving her husband in ignorance of her past (for it is not to be supposed that a woman like Margaret would have had him if she had known it); suppose she were afterwards unfaithful to him, and led a double life with much gaiety and complacency until she was in danger of being found out; and then, after the discovery, drowned her remorse in a course of hard drinking, resulting in delirium tremens, and finally came back much humbled and begged forgiveness. Would anyone blame the husband if, while forgiving her and consenting to be friends with her, he declined to sleep with her again."[62]

But women's rights weren't right for all. *Nineteenth Century* published an article, "The Wild Women as Social Insurgents" in 1891. Among their verbal assaults: "Mistress of herself, the Wild Woman as a social insurgent preaches the 'lesson of liberty' broadened into lawlessness and license. Unconsciously she exemplifies how beauty can degenerate into ugliness, and shows how the once fragrant flower, run to seed, is good for neither food nor ornament." The essayist added: "She appears on the public stage and executes dances which one would not like one's daughter to see, still less perform. She herself knows no shame in showing her skill—and her legs."[63] *The Arena* differed with the last remark, saying, "Women cannot have brains till they have ankles."[64]

Margaret Fleming almost showed her breasts. Yet Herne avoided one social issue: divorce, a generally unspeakable topic during the nineteenth century. Before the Civil War divorced women lost custody of their children, whether they were in the right or wrong. Prior to Howells' *A Modern Instance* in 1881, the only novels about divorce were T. S. Arthur's *The Hand but Not the Heart* (1858) and *Out in the World* (1865).[65] The theme didn't exist in American drama until 1871, the year Augustin Daly presented *Divorce*. The following dialogue from this play mirrors society's narrowness then:

> *Mrs. Kemp.*   You have not implicitly obeyed his wishes.
> *Fanny.*   Don't use that word to me, I can't bear it.
> *Mrs. Kemp.*   Why, my dear, it's the duty of a true wife.
> *Fanny.*   Right or wrong?
> *Mrs. Kemp.*   Right or wrong.
> *Fanny.*   This is your doctrine?
> *Mrs. Kemp.*   I have lived by it forty years.[66]

But 1881 was a feminist year. Besides Howells' *A Modern Instance,* the New England Reform League was established and Congress authorized funds to collect statistics on marriage and divorce. These were enlightened events. Several other divorce plays followed: *Young Mrs. Winthrop* (1882) and *The Lottery of Love* (1888). Each was satirical. Even in Herne's *Sag Harbor* (1900), Martha chides: "Divorce? Ben, you talk like a child. Do you suppose I'm going to allow you to disgrace yourself and me?"[67]

The outspoken Robert R. Ingersoll, whose reformist views both Garland and Herne embraced, boldly asked in the *North American Review,* "Is Divorce Wrong?" His answer made traditionalists' teeth chatter:

Is it possible to conceive of anything more immoral than for a husband to insist on living with a wife who has no love for him? Is not this a perpetual crime? Is the wife to lose her personality? Has she no right of choice? Is her modesty the property of another? Is the man she hates the lord of her desire? Has she no right to guard the jewels of her soul? Is there a depth be-

low this? And is this the foundation of morality? this the cornerstone of society? this the arch that supports the dome of civilization? Is this pathetic sacrifice on the one hand, this sacrilege
on the other, pleasing in the sight of heaven?[68]

These were words of savage honesty that describe Herne's
original *Margaret Fleming*. Philip became an alcoholic, Margaret
remained blind, and they separated. Several revisions between
1890 and 1929, however, diluted the work's original strength. In
the present text in Arthur Hobson Quinn's *Representative American Dramas*, Margaret encourages Philip to resume both mill
and domestic duties, offering the hope of a distant reconciliation.
She also accepts his illegitimate son:

> *Margaret.*   The past is dead. We must face the living future.
> Now, Philip, there are big things ahead for you, if you will
> only look for them. They certainly will not come to *you.* I will
> help you—we will fight this together.[69]

This version was a far cry from Herne's first searing resolution. K.C. and Garland rewrote *Margaret Fleming* in 1914. Garland recollected: "We spent the evening at this work, she reading
and I making suggestions from time to time. Happily, my memory retained most of Herne's exact intonations, as well as many
of his phrases, and together we got the first act pretty nearly
exact. There was a melancholy pleasure in this, for it brought
back to us both those wonderful days, more than twenty-five
years ago."[70] Arthur Hobson Quinn recalled that when K.C. revised the script she said "that unhappiness is not necessarily
artistic, unless it is inevitable, and that, given the character of
Margaret and the personality of Philip, they would probably be
reconciled."[71]

This was the same K.C. who told a Boston manager she
wouldn't alter a line of *Margaret Fleming*. But then Katharine
Corcoran Herne was past sixty in 1914, a mellow age far removed
from her younger dreams of fire. The difference between K.C.
and James A. Herne is that he still led the charge against theatre's old order at sixty, remaining a generation ahead of others.

When Quinn decided to include *Margaret Fleming* in *Representative American Plays*, he contacted K.C., who made minor
revisions, including dialect changes at Quinn's request because
he felt dialect "always made a play hard reading." Julie later

wrote Quinn: "I believe that my mother, when reconstructing the play, formalized the dialogue deliberately. Philip and Margaret were always played as educated people of the upper middle class, so I suppose she decided to write them that way."[72] Julie traced the play's history in another letter to Quinn:

> In the production at Lynn, July 4, 1890 (first performance) and in Boston in May and October, 1891, and at Palmer's Theatre in New York, December 9, 1891, the original fourth act was used. That is, there was a lapse of years between Acts III and IV and the action proceeded as described in the article, ending in the police court scene. My father was never completely satisfied with this act and before the play was produced at McVicker's Theatre, Chicago in the summer of '92, he re-wrote it, substituting the present fourth act. Incidentally, there was never at any time any idea that Margaret's blindness was the result of syphilis. (Some critics suggested this.)
>
> The new fourth act was used at McVicker's and also at Miner's Fifth Avenue Theatre when the play was produced there May 4, 1894 and at the New Theatre, Chicago, during the winter of 1906–07, when my sister Chrystal appeared as Margaret.
>
> All manuscripts of the play were burned in the fire that destroyed Herne Oaks in December, 1909. My mother reconstructed the play from memory in the spring of 1914. I played in this reconstructed version when it was given at the Keith-Bronx Theatre in the summer of 1915. She re-wrote the opening scenes of Act I between Philip, Bobby, Foster and William. From then on the play is substantially as written by my father, though possibly some lines may be altered or missing, due to faults of memory and length of time that had elapsed since my mother acted in the play. I saw the play many times in both versions and remember it clearly, and I cannot find any vital changes. Neither can my sister, who played in it in 1907, before the original scripts were destroyed.[73]

Julie's chronology, however, includes the vague remarks, "substantially as written by my father" and "I cannot find any vital changes." Herne reshaped all his works over long periods. It's not likely that *Margaret Fleming* was the exception, especially with numerous social groups pressuring change. The *Boston Daily Globe* remarked on October 6, 1891: "The play has been closer knit since its last season here, and is now in much better dramatic form."[74] This isn't proof, however, that the play was rewritten. Yet Herne had already written Howells on July 13 that he planned to "cut out a word here and there and put another in its place."[75] Several years passed before *Margaret Fleming* resurfaced in 1894 and audiences witnessed a more conventional work. The *New York Times* detailed its major changes:

> "Margaret Fleming" has a new fourth act. The superfluous infant does not die, the properly-accredited infant is not stolen by Maria Bindley, there is no lapse of seven years, and the scenes on Boston Common and in the grocery shop are dispensed with. The action new proceeds in Fleming's house, where Margaret shelters the illegitimate child and its deplorable aunt. The act begins with a conversation between the doctor and Maria about charity and forgiveness, and continues with a thrilling dialogue on the subject of glaucoma and its cure—Margaret being threatened with total blindness—between Margaret and that upright, high-minded, but irritating, physician, for whom she says earlier in the play, she has a "strange feeling," because he "brought her child into the world." Presently Philip Fleming returns to his home, and then follows the unsatisfactory conversation between husband and wife, which ended the play in its original form. Before he departs, Philip asks Margaret to shake hands with him. As he touches her, she utters a loud exclamation, and lifts her hand to her eyes. The stage suddenly grows dark, and we hear Philip speaking his mournful goodbye, but cannot see him. This is probably intended as a pictorial symbol of Margaret's blindness and the desolation of her life.[76]

Even this account isn't the "watered down" version K.C. later approved for inclusion in *Representative American Plays*. Herne's use of darkness to symbolize Margaret's emptiness and inner suffering still vibrates with dramatic energy. The Quinn conclusion is in these romanticized stage directions. "Philip *goes quickly to the door opening upon the garden and gazes out eagerly.* Margaret, *at the table, pauses in her work; gives a long sigh of relief and contentment. Her eyes look into the darkness and a serene joy illuminates her face. The picture slowly fades out as* Philip *steps buoyantly into the garden.*[77]

The original *Margaret Fleming,* in Howells' words, was an "epoch-making" drama. It forced critics to revise archaic standards of criticism, brought realism to the American stage, inspired playwrights to write more intelligent native works, and proved that "little" theatres worked in practice. Finally, it created interest in an independent American theatre association.

Margaret Fleming's epitaph is one shared by few plays in history.

15 art for truth's sake

SERIOUS TALK ABOUT a free theatre movement similar to those in Europe started with Beatrice Cameron's historic Boston production of *Ghosts* in 1889. There was the Théâtre Libre in Paris, the Freie Bühne in Berlin, and London's Independent Theatre. Why not a free theatre in Boston, America's cultural mecca, too?

William Archer helped launch the project. He met with Howells, who suggested a subscription theatre with membership fees between $300 and $400 and yearly dues of $25. "If the experiment were tried in ten or twenty places, we should have at once a free theatre, where good work could make that appeal to the public which it can now do only on almost impossible terms."[1]

Garland agreed. In an editorial in the *Boston Evening Transcript* he called for the formation of an Ibsen Club or a Radical Dramatic Club. He lamented, "So mainly we find our managers importing the most nauseating English, French or German melodrama, because they are assured of successes, and disposing of the really literary plays of men like Ibsen and Howells as 'too talky, won't draw.' "[2] His recommendation was a club offering both Ibsen and native American plays at matinee performances, or even better, a permanent theatre.

What really triggered the movement was Herne's *Margaret Fleming*. When Bostonians realized that realism worked, they grew interested. Thomas Bailey Aldrich, Garland, Flower, Ralph A. Cram, Herne, and others scheduled a meeting at Pierce Hall on May 21, 1891. Sympathetic realists soon received notices inviting them "to consider plays for the establishment of a distinc-

tively American theatre. . . . It is designed to forward the building of a theatre on the co-operative plan, and to open a stage
whereon the Drama shall be considered a Work of Art, and produced as such—independent of cheap popularity, and where
Americanism and modernity shall be the prime requisites. We in-
vite your co-operation at the meeting named above, believing
that a Theatre of this general scope must have a great influence
upon our literature and especially upon the development of Dramatic Art."[3]

Julie frankly admitted that Herne lacked interest in the In-
depent Theatre movement but supported it on principle. Even
before *Margaret Fleming* opened, the *Boston Herald* stated, "In
Mr. Herne, some of our lovers of the dramatic art believe that
they have found an André Antoine for a Boston Théâtre Libre."[4] (Antoine now replaced Ibsen as a Herne connective. The
slightest chance to draw parallels was a critic's delight.) *The
Critic* guessed that Herne would "be called to the management
of the house if it is built."[5] But Herne didn't like art theatres.
He knew about their inherent snob appeal, irreconcilable artistic
views, and impractical philosophies.

Garland guided the movement. The publication of *Main-
Travelled Roads* in 1891 provided literary leverage, especially
when associates started calling him the "Kipling of the West."
Charles E. L. Wingate wrote, "I have spoken of this theatre as
Mr. Garland's scheme, because I regard him as the leading
spirit."[6] Garland became secretary of the First Independent Theatre Association, also drafting its prospectus, which read:

"TRUTH FOR ART'S SAKE"

A Prospectus of the First Independent Theatre Association.
Issued by the committee of organization, Boston, Mass.

THE OBJECTS OF THE ASSOCIATION

Are first and in general to encourage truth and progress in American Dramatic Art. Second, and specifically,
to secure and maintain a stage whereon the best and most
unconventional studies of modern life and distinctively
American life, may get a proper hearing. We believe the
present poverty of Dramatic Art in America is due to un-
favorable conditions, rather than to a lack of playwriting
talent, and it is the purpose of the Association to remove as
far as possible, the commercial consideration and give the
Dramatist the artistic atmosphere for his work, and bring

to his production the most intelligent and sympathetic acting in America.

THE SCOPE OF THE THEATRE

It is designed to be distinctively but not exclusively
modern and American, and it will encourage the use of the
wealth of native material lying at your hand. Its scope may
be indicated thus:
I.   Studies of American Society.
     (a)   Social Dramas.
     (b)   Comedies of Life.
II. Studies in American History.
     (a)   Dramas of Colonial Times.
     (b)   Dramas of the Revolution.
     (c)   Dramas of Border History.
     (d)   Dramas of the Civil War.
III. Famous Modern Plays by
     the Best Dramatists of Europe.

We believe that the above plan is sufficiently exten-
sive to claim the support of all lovers of the Drama, while
at the same time it maintains its distinctive character. We
believe that with the encouragement of a fair trial for their
plays, a part of the confessedly great talent of our novelists
could be directed to the production of plays as modern and
as American in flavor as our famous short stories.

METHODS OF WORK

The Association while it has in mind the great work
done by a few unknown men in the Freie Buehne of Berlin,
the Théâtre Libre of Paris, and the Independent Theatre of
London, does not propose to model itself upon either of
these organizations, but to make all helpful hints and use
them in its own way.

It is designed to have all enterprises conducted upon
the co-operative principle as far as possible. A corporation
will be formed to build within the coming year a small
theatre, and to sell season tickets by subscription, very much
as in the Freie Buehne. The season will last thirty weeks
and will include the production of ten or twelve new plays.
Tickets to admit subscribers three nights in the week and
to be transferable. The unsold seats on subscribers' nights
and the entire house on alternate performances will be open
to the general public.

PLAYS

A Reading Committee will have entire charge of the
selection of plays. To place all plays on equal footing, the
MSS, must be submitted to the Secretary, in typewriting,

unsigned, accompanied by the name of the author in a sealed envelope. If the play is accepted the envelope will remain unbroken till the last performance of the first week's trial. If the play is returned no one but the Secretary will know the name of its author.

It is designed also to extend the co-operative principle to the plays, the Association to retain an interest in the plays it produces.

A PLEA FOR ART

It seems to us that the most fitting city in America to begin the great work is Boston. Boston is at once the most conservative and the most progressive of cities. She has an autonomy that is lacking in most of our towns, and her influence on art is greater than any other American city. The establishment here of a theatre with "Truth for Art's Sake" as a motto would unquestionably result in the formation of similar enterprises in other places. We appeal to the art-loving population of Boston to assist us in the carrying out of this plan which we believe will result in the birth of a genuine, truthful, buoyant American drama. . . .[7]

The *Boston Herald* helped, mailing questionnaires to selected Bostonians, writers, critics, and clergy. The questionnaire asked:

1. Are you in favor of the establishment of an independent theatre in Boston, on general principles?
2. If not, why not?
3. If so, what, in your mind, should be the prime object for which it should exist?
4. What should be some of its other objects?
5. Do you believe that such a theatre should confine itself entirely to the production of American plays, or should it give room as well for translations of foreign authors never before played in this country?
6. Would you favor the following of any particular "school" of the drama?
7. What do you understand by the use of the words "realism" and "realist" as applied to the drama?

Sample replies appeared in the July 10, 1891, issue of the *Herald*. Some approved the venture and some didn't.

Rabbi Solomon Schindler: "I believe that the stage, as it has been and is at present, is misleading, and corrupts the thoughts of people by representing men and things, not as they are, but as it would suit people to believe they are."

Sigmund B. Alexander: "There is little doubt, in my mind, that a large proportion of the theatre going public would patronize the proposed offering of dramatic sense in preference to the present overabundant feast of nonsense as offered them in the puerile farce-comedies of the hour; works many of which do not deserve the dignity of the title farce, not to speak of comedy."

F. E. Chase: "What is to be feared for it is that it will become a mere receptacle for the bizarre, the eccentric, the risky, or other products of a deformed originality, which have been rightly enough refused admission elsewhere. In this probability lies its chance of shipwreck."

T. Russell Sullivan (who left *Margaret Fleming* after the nursing scene) : "I can only say that I am not in sympathy with the present movement which seems as I understand it, too much in the spirit of what is known in Paris as the 'Théâtre Libre.' "

Edward Fuller: "The ideal which is realized in 'Margaret Fleming' is not to my mind, a healthy one."

James Henry Wiggin, chairman of the May 21 meeting in the Pierce Building, commented that an independent theatre "should have one director only. . . . Ten directors would have a hundredfold more prejudices than one." He felt also that there would be "too much reliance on Back Bay." He recalled that "during a performance of the Herne drama, at Chickering Hall, in May, I chanced to mingle in the conversation of a trio of silver gray aristocrats. They liked the play, and praised the acting as better than Bernhardt's; but their conversation showed them to be strangely ignorant of both plays and players; nor did they even follow that simple plot intelligently. Give us a theatre so located and so democratic as to reach all classes of people. This alone will test the real efficacy of the enterprise."[8]

Boston theatre managers also were asked for opinions about an Independent Theatre. Their thoughts were negative. "I consider the whole idea chimerical and unpractical to the last degree," declared John B. Schoeffel of the Tremont Theatre, whose stage manager added that "the 'everyday' existence does not appeal to people." Isaac B. Rich of the Hollis Street Theatre agreed: "What is the necessity of such a theatre? Any play can get a chance for production by guaranteeing the expenses to the management in any theatre in Boston." The Globe Theatre's John Stetson added that such a theatre "would be merely a dramatic school and an institution for producing worthless plays."[9]

Thus spoke Boston's aesthetic philosophers of commercial claptrap—its theatre managers.

Meanwhile, a ways and means committee appointed Cram and Wentworth of Boston to design an intimate theatre patterned after the private playhouses of French palaces during the age of Louis XIV such as Fontainebleau and Versailles. It would be an intimate theatre with about 600 seats, a 50' x 20' stagehouse, a balcony, and an orchestra hidden beneath the stage. There would be a row of fourteen private boxes for subscribers in place of the usual orchestra circle. Three public and two private performances per week within a repertory season of thirty weeks was planned. Another innovation would be a 50' x 20' foyer for audience discussion between acts. The general interior color scheme was to be ivory white and gold, with a damask curtain and exterior of yellow brick and white terracotta. The structure's cost was estimated at $100,000, which didn't include production expenses.[10]

The Independent Theatre Association bubbled like champagne for a while but then fizzled. The *New York Times* asked: "Independent of what? It is likely that the experiment will not induce the sordid manager to repent him of his suppression of native genius, and that he will go on stealing his society drama from Paris, remaining strictly dependent on the box-office and glorying in his shame."[11]

The ambitious Garland also stormed Chicago, where he persuaded Dr. Emil Blum, an associate of Sudermann, to sign the prospectus. By January 1892 Garland was promoting a similar independent theatre in Chicago, but funds for it fell short, as it had in Boston. Garland was to become president of the Chicago Theatre Society in 1911.

Herne and Howells moved to New York, Garland soon following for a while. But discussion of an independent theatre in Boston grew louder and louder.

Edward Fuller, in *Lippincott's Magazine,* remarked that Boston's Ibsenists "offer their restorative waters to everyone that thirsteth; but here the trouble is that few persons have acquired a taste for the draught." (He meant plays like *Margaret Fleming.*) "To unaccustomed nostrils the moral stench of the play is intolerable, whether foot-baths or the state of the infant stomach, adultery or insanity, are under discussion. . . . It is not by Ibsen or by Mr. Herne that the English stage is to be redeemed. . . . We are more concerned in applauding the talent of Mr. Clyde Fitch or Mr. Augustus Thomas than in making a Golden Calf out of Mr. Herne."[12]

It seems that Herne had also inspired the Independent or Free Theatre of New York: According to another *Lippincott's* article, "A decided impetus was given to the project early in December last, when A. M. Palmer gave New Yorkers an opportunity to see James A. Herne's 'Margaret Fleming.' " Among the New York group's founders were Bronson Howard, W. D. Howells, Frank R. Stockton, Mrs. Mary Mapes Dodge, Laurence Hutton, Edward Harrigan, Brander Matthews, and George W. Cable—an impressive list.[13]

Helene Modjeska voiced her views on America's decadent theatre in *Forum.* She was appalled, especially about its public pandering. "Huge posters, lithographs, quotations from the press on the bills, pictures of Shakespeare standing side by side with advertisements of patent medicines and dog-shows were placed in such a way as to catch the eye of every passerby and disfigure the walls." The worst Shakespearean put-down was an advertisement for trained monkeys below a *Julius Caesar* notice. She also complained about dingy dressing rooms, lack of stock companies, and theatres squeezed between buildings, some with entrances through drug stores. Where were Europe's majestic edifices, she asked.

Madame Modjeska's solution was an endowed theatre supported by the super rich, the same super rich who supported museums, symphonies, and other cultural institutions. It would be an endowed theatre freed from managerial speculation and commercialism and with a stock company committed to reputable drama, both past and present. She added, "I have heard two of the most eminent divines of this age declare that next to the pulpit the stage can have the greatest influence for good."[14] It seems likely that one of these 'divines' was Herne.

Some listened to Madame Modjeska's remarks, shaking their heads, both pro and con, but nothing happened. In 1896 an American traveling through Europe called his country's lack of a subsidized national theatre "one of the most distressing and humiliating defects in our civilization."[15] There was nothing except for a few little-theatre rustlings until 1906 and Chicago's New Theatre, five years after Herne's death.

The New Theatre of Chicago blossomed when a group of culturally-minded citizens spearheaded a drive that raised $30,000 and sold $25,000 worth of season tickets. It was an encouraging start. A thirty-week season of repertory involving fifteen plays rotating every two weeks was proposed.[16] Victor Mapes, first director of this non-profit organization, later stated its policies in *The Theatre*:

1. The elimination of the "star" system. There was to be no "star" in the cast and no "featured" players. The company was to be formed of as capable actors as could be procured, who were all to be on a basis of equality and ready to accept any part that might be assigned them.
2. There were to be no "long runs." Whatever the success of any play the number of its performances was to be strictly limited, so that new productions might follow one another at stated intervals.
3. As to the selection of plays the guiding principle was summed up succinctly in the words "plays worth while." No one cult or school was to dominate. The general effort would be to offer as wide a variety as possible of plays, new or old, that should interest intelligent people, without making them feel that they were wasting their time.
4. No pretensions were to be made in the way of elaborate scenery, costumes or accessories, the aim being merely to give each play an adequate, if modest, presentation as nearly correct as possible.[17]

The New Theatre opened with three short plays: *Sainera* by Ernest d'Hervilly, *Engaged* by W. S. Gilbert, and *Marse Covington* by George Ade. José Echegaray's *The Great Galeoto* and a one-act play, *Shades of Night*, by Robert Marshall followed. Then came James MacArthur's adaptation of Rex Beach's novel, *The Spoilers,* a brawling melodrama that grossed more than all the previous five plays. Mixed reviews greeted the next double bill, Emile Augier's *The Son-in-Law* and Henry Arthur Jones' *The Goal.*

Mapes started worrying about salvaging the project. He hired Chrystal Herne, who had been contracted by Charles Dillingham for the following season, but her appearance in the double bill of Gerhart Hauptmann's *Elga* and Dion Boucicault's one-act *Kerry* didn't boost receipts. They collected only $376 at the box office in two weeks. Chrystal then starred in Arthur Wing Pinero's *Sweet Lavender.*

Mapes resigned as director after the opening of Sardou's *Diplomacy,* staged as *Dora.* "Never did a mountain's labor bring forth a more ridiculous mouse," roared *The Dial,* which traced the theatre's downfall to its coterie audience. "Its sponsors were largely of a class better known for the possession of worldly goods than for other qualities, and their names were advertised much more extensively than the names of the performers."[18]

Mapes' replacement at the New Theatre was Katharine Corcoran Herne, who had assisted in *Dora*'s rehearsals. She immediately disputed Mapes' statement that the project failed because Chicago didn't want better plays, saying that not all Chicagoans liked light plays. An audience existed for different kinds of works, too. Besides, the moods of theatre patrons shifted from day to day, ranging from musical comedies to light and heavy dramas. Satisfying these shifting moods could save the New Theatre, she believed.

But K.C.'s tenure was brief, for another producer had already leased the theatre for musicals. Nevertheless, she managed to stage Ludwig Fulda's *Masquerade* and a revival of *Margaret Fleming* for five performances. Both productions received praise.

Amy Leslie wrote about *Masquerade*: "Mrs. Herne and her daughter are both responsible in a measure for the signs of life in that deceased and tedious routine of wretched work continued for months at the endowed theatre. Mrs. Herne by her practical, energetic and sane understanding of the mission of the stage, where she is so at home, and whose husband was the master-builder and craftsman who taught them all. And Miss Chrystal

Herne by her easy flow of magnetic genuineness, her vivid talent and by no means least of all her beauty."[19]

The New Theatre's production of *Margaret Fleming*, in January 1907, was the play's first revival since 1894. K.C. changed the time to 1905 and used Herne's original shocking ending. What was the critical assessment in 1907 of the play William Dean Howells called "epoch-making" in 1891? Were its style, structure, and premise dated?

Chicago Evening Post: "As presented by the stock company of the New Theater last evening [*Margaret Fleming*] inspired the first serious appreciation of that institution and lifted the curse of mediocrity that has hung over the enterprise since its inception."[20]

Chicago Record Herald: "The play will hold the boards only a week. The New Theater ought to be crowded to the doors for that period, for not a peep show, but a hymn to womanhood is there, and Madonna is walking along the byways of the here and now."[21]

Chicago Tribune: "It is entirely reasonable to expect that now this greatest of Herne dramas will find wide recognition at the American public's hands, and that it will be accepted for what it is—one of the strongest, best plays yet written by any American ... for none of the modern dramatists of Norway, Russia, Germany, Spain, France, Belgium, or Italy have produced a better."[22]

Chicago Daily News: "Herne was always years ahead of his day. He lived too soon and not long enough. ... Out of the violent crusade urged against James A. Herne that eventful year (meaning 1891), when 'Margaret Fleming' brought the blush of prim defiance to the wrinkled cheek of Boston, came the first cry for a national and an endowed theater."[23]

And Burns Mantle stated in the *Chicago Interocean:* "Herne was the first of American realists in the drama. He was the first man to grasp that great common essential of reflected life, the simplicity of human motives. 'What a play I could write, Mr. Herne, if I only had a plot,' a young man once said to him. 'There **are** plots all around you, my son,' was his reply."[24]

President Arthur T. Aldis of Chicago's New Theatre gave **three** basic reasons for the theatre's failure:

1. The sale of the leasehold interest in the New Theatre has made it expedient for the trustees to close their enterprise in that theatre sooner than we expected.
2. The receipts through the box office from the general public have been much smaller than was originally estimated.
3. Owing to this, the guarantee fund originally subscribed and then deemed sufficient together with a further guarantee fund added to the first one by some of the trustees most interested, will have been used up and the resources of the association therefore exhausted, and it has not been thought expedient to make any further call for this season upon those of the guarantors who have made this opening experiment possible.[25]

No one can say if the New Theatre failed because of snob appeal, if a more perceptive administration might have attracted more audiences, or if K.C. would have been a better original director than Mapes. K.C. soon retired from theatre life, leaving Chrystal and Julie to make their marks on the art, which both did.

In her unpublished autobiography, *I Remember Me* (which tells too little about her father's life), Chrystal romanticizes about her youth, recalling her first stage role in *Griffith Davenport*:

"I know that Julie, who had already toured with my father in *Shore Acres*, was to play one of the ingenue parts. My father went over the cast of characters, stopping at each name, to jot down that of the actor he thought would be right for it. ' "Sue Hardy," he said looking so solemnly, his pencil poised. 'For " 'Sue,' " he said at last, 'I have a young girl in mind. Of course, it's a chance, she's had no experience.' I hung on his words. 'Sue' was a lovely part. I wondered who this lucky young actress would be. He pondered for a long moment.

" 'Kacy,'—that was his name for my mother—'Kacy, I am thinking of giving 'Sue' to a young girl named Chrystal Herne. What do you think? After all she was always in my mind when I was writing those scenes.' "[26]

Was Chrystal really truthful? Actually, Herne opposed theatre as a career for his children. He wanted Julie to write, reasoning: "The stage is all very fine if you are lucky enough to be successful as I have been. It's quite another story if you are in the position of Mrs. . . . and he mentioned an actress in his company who, after a lifetime on the stage, had never risen above character parts."

K.C. told Chrystal: "I will 'let' you be anything you wish to be. But if you want to act, you must study and perfect yourself—and be ready for your opportunity when it comes. Remember, everything you study—music, dancing, singing, languages—will help you to become a better actress. It is an art that demands everything you have to give."[27]

The Hernes understood failure. They understood the heartaches, the loneliness, the struggles, and the separations of theatre life. While Herne was on the road, he and K.C. frequently exchanged letters. Among K.C.'s remarks: "How I look forward to those promised times when we shall be together, *never, never,* to be parted again. Will it ever be?" During one of Herne's illnesses, she wrote: "Dear Heart, A great weight has been taken from my mind now that you are yourself once more, yet I cannot help marveling at the good fortune that you have had in your recovery. Good night, God bless you and make you happy. Love and kisses from all."[28] But Julie and Chrystal were young hopefuls. They had to learn through experience; so Herne finally started both girls in show business.

Minor parts in Herne's *The Reverend Griffith Davenport* and *Sag Harbor* sharpened Chrystal's talents. She later played opposite E. H. Sothern, Nat Goodwin, Arthur Byron, and Arnold Daly in Shaw's *Candida, You Never Can Tell, John Bull's Other Island,* and *Mrs. Warren's Profession.* By 1909 her credits included over fifty characters. Many more plays followed, including Israel Zangwill's *The Melting Pot,* Augustus Thomas' *As A Man Thinks,* and Rachel Crothers, *Expressing Willie.* But stardom eluded her until 1925, when she portrayed Mrs. Craig in George Kelly's Pulitzer Prize winner, *Craig's Wife.*

Chrystal's private life was very private, although she was considered one of America's best-dressed women. She married Harold Stanley Pollard, *New York World-Telegram and Sun* chief editorial writer, and lived until 1950.[29] Edmund M. Gagey writes in *Notable American Women:* "As an actress Chrystal Herne made no pretense of being a glamour girl or an emotional star, and she specialized in sophisticated and often in unsympathetic roles, but her interpretations were always competent and intelligent. She took her art seriously, and worthily carried on a high family tradition."[30]

Julie distinguished herself as Herne's leading lady in *The Reverend Griffith Davenport, Shore Acres,* and *Sag Harbor.* Among her later credits was *Ben Hur,* the staggering spectacle produced by Abraham Lincoln Erlanger. In 1906 her own play, *Richter's Wife,* made Broadway.

Richter's Wife opened at the Manhattan Theatre on February 27, 1906, running until March 3 as a matinee piece. Both Julie and Chrystal played in this forgotten domestic drama about a young wife whose husband, a conductor of the Beethoven Orchestra, loves his wife's cousin who lives with them. Audiences were chilled by the climax, in which the wife drinks a glass of poison.

The Theatre thought Julie gave "promise of a brilliant career as a dramatist" and added: "Her father, James A. Herne, was, in simplicity, episode, naturalism and remoteness from conventionlism, the greatest dramatist the American stage has ever had. To say that Julie Herne learned nothing from such a man, and inherited everything from him, is foolish. 'Richter's Wife' has, by far, more of James A. Herne in it than it has of Ibsen. There is more of mature force in it than there is of immaturity."[31]

Fifteen years earlier, when *Margaret Fleming* opened in 1891 at Chickering Hall to an audience of 100, such praise of Herne would have been startling.

16 make culture hum!

J IM HERNE! YOU'RE just the man we want to see. We want you for the part of a Negro in our new play, and we'll pay you a hundred and fifty dollars a week."[1]

That's how it happened. Broadway theatre manager William A. Brady, also manager of heavyweight boxing champion James J. Corbett, hired Herne on a New York street. The 150-a-week offer was for a fifteen-minute supporting role in *The New South*, a post-Civil War drama by Clay M. Greene and Joseph R. Grismer. Most Broadway matinee idols with inflated star complexes would have rejected the role, but the Hernes were living on advances from *My Colleen* and *The Volunteers* while trying to place *Shore Acres* minus strings. So Herne accepted.

The play dealt with two social issues: the practice of leasing convicts and the use of federal troops at elections. Squeezed between these splinter ideas lodged an 1875 Georgia tale of murder and poetic justice. Promoted as "a play of today,"[2] *The New South* later competed against Herne's *Shore Acres* in Boston.

The *New York Times* probably pinpointed *The New South*'s worth when it reported that "except in one or two short scenes, [it] is painfully unnatural, extravagant and unimaginative."[3] The *Herald* commented, "It is all wrong, but it is all interesting."[4] They were typical critical contradictions.

Although *The New South* ran for ten weeks, it failed financially and closed January 30, 1893. Brady later admitted, "The only profit I ever derived from 'The New South' was my first lesson in what not to do about dramatic criticism."[5] Nearly all the critics—Nym Crinkle, William Winter, Alan Dale, and Acton Davies—panned the play. This infuriated Brady, who ran ads quoting the worst reviews, offering a money-back guarantee, but audiences didn't bite. Receipts seldom topped $100 a night. Considering the theatre's rent ran $3,000 a week, Brady had a problem. After dropping $30,000, he dropped the curtain for good.

What bothered Brady most was that nobody cared, especially the critics.

The New South deserves mention because of Herne's realistic portrayal of Samson, the black politician-turned-murderer. His artistic method involved detailed studies of blacks on streets and elevated trains—their complexions, mannerisms, and voices. Always searching for fidelity to the truth, Herne used grease paint instead of burnt cork and commissioned a famous wig maker to create a special hair piece.

Word soon reached Chicago. McVicker wrote Herne: "The New South has been spoken of here in the papers as a success—it is said that you have elevated the negro by giving him a character he was not supposed to possess—I believe the stage is a proper place to present great problems—when they can be done judiciously—the drama did more to stomp out slavery—whether doing so was right or wrong—than all the sermons and strong speeches written with the same view."[6]

Trouble brewed backstage during *The New South*'s run. The star, Joseph R. Grismer, decided to edit some lines, most of them in Herne's big scene. A professional matinee neared, so Herne waved his contract, threatening legal action, and the management listened. That weekend recall after recall followed Herne's performance, and some called Samson a black Bill Sykes.

Audience response confirmed Herne's belief in a role's quality rather than size. He once said, "Give me one moment of real acting in any part and I'll hold my own with any star on earth."[7] Stanislavsky later made a similar statement, that there are no small roles, only small actors.

A black actor wasn't hired to play Samson in *The New South* because whites traditionally played black roles in the 1890's. Black characters in plays were few and far between. Jim Crow Rice popularized Ethiopian minstrelsy, and a few other parts existed for whites willing to play blacks: Zeke in *Fashion,* Pete in *The*

Octoroon, and both Uncle Tom and Topsy, whom Charles Reade called "idiopathic,"[8] in *Uncle Tom's Cabin.* But there were no serious roles, just clowns and morons. Black tragedian Ira Aldridge, "The American Roscius," fled the United States, later gaining fame on European soil.

Black entertainer George W. Walker recalled that "Black-faced white comedians used to make themselves look as ridiculous as they could when portraying 'darky' characters. In their 'makeup' they always had tremendously big red lips and their costumes were frightfully exaggerated."[9] This exaggeration gave Walker an idea, and he and Bert Williams organized a successful act called the "Two Real Coons." They also devised the later faddish "cakewalk."

Herne tried to change the black idiotic tradition in *The New South,* in *Coon Hollow* (an unproduced work), and in *Griffith Davenport.* It was another uphill struggle against theatre tradition. He also discovered Paul Dunbar, a former Toledo elevator operator who became America's first notable black poet. Dunbar sent Herne a book of his poems called *Majors and Minors,* and Herne mailed it to Howells, who praised the work in *Harper's Magazine.* Dunbar later wrote Howells: "I have written to thank Mr. Herne for putting the book in your hands. I have only seen the man on the stage but have laughed and cried with him until I love him."[10]

Dunbar also wrote lyrics for George W. Walker and Bert Williams. Among his musicals with Marion Cook were *Clorindy; or, the Origin of the Cakewalk* (1898) and a one-acter, *Uncle Eph's Christmas* (1900).

Herne had been drawn to the sea since his boyhood along the banks of the Erie Canal in Troy. He vacationed on the coasts of Maine, Massachusetts, and Long Island, a fleeting chance to smell the odors and hear the pulse of life's ancient source. His sea plays reflect such longings. *Hearts of Oak* is set on the coast of Marblehead, Massachusetts (both Terry and Ned in the play are mariners). *Drifting Apart*'s setting is near the fishing village of Gloucester, Massachusetts (Jack escapes his sense of guilt through the sea). Herne's last play, *Sag Harbor,* sets its sails at Islip, Long Island, and portrays "Capt'n" Dan Marble, owner of the sloop Kacy (Herne's nickname for K.C.). *Shore Acres* has lighthouses, boat skippers, and fishing folk galore. Its inspiration was Herne's stay at Lamoine, Maine.

During the summer of 1888, K.C. and the girls vacationed at Lamoine, on Frenchman's Bay, a setting K.C. soon realized could help Herne's completion of *The Hawthornes*. But he couldn't join her until the following summer, a trip also prompted by Hamlin Garland, who wrote: "I tell you, Herne," (he frequently prefaced his statements to Herne with this phrase), "that's the country for you. There's where you should finish your play. You should see those people, the old fishermen with beards under their chins, looking as though they had sprouted from their chests."[11]

Lamoine's people fascinated Herne. For several months he studied their dress, dialect, and lifestyle, admitting that *The Hawthornes* "sloughed off its old skin and took on new form and color. Its stage people began by degrees to assume the character and affect the speech of the typical men and women of Maine, imbued with all the spirituality and intensity of co-existent life. . . . I did not set myself the task of writing 'Shore Acres' as it now stands; it grew, and I grew with it."[12]

Lamoine's land boom also influenced Herne's embyronic script. The place crawled with speculators. Poor Henry George. They threw his single-tax theories in Frenchman's Bay. As Josiah Blake tells Martin in *Shore Acres*:

> This shore front makes your land val'able. Not to plant potatoes in—but to build summer cottages on. I tell yeh, the boom's a-comin' here jes' as sure as you're born. Bar Harbor's got s' high, yeh can't touch a foot of it—not by coverin' it with gold dollars. This has got to be the next p'int. . . . You pool your land with mine—We'll lay out quarter-acre lots, cut avenoos, plant trees, build a driveway to the shore, hang on to all the shore front an' corner lots— sell every one o' the others, see!!! They'll build on 'em an' that'll double the value of ours—see!—they'll have to pay the heft o' the taxes 'cause they've built; we'll be taxed light 'cause we didn't—see?[13]

Even K.C. bought "a beautiful rolling meadow overlooking the Bay, with a cranberry bog, and, of course, the indispensable shore front."[14] She paid an exorbitant price. Then the boom busted, leaving Herne a worthless deed and mortgage, similar to the situation he protested in *Shore Acres* through the harsh conflict between brothers Uncle Nat and Martin Berry.

Herne wrote Garland on August 5, 1889, "I've finished 'The Hawthornes'—'rough finished'—and you'll like some of it."[15] Meanwhile, he continued studying "Down-East" folk, working the land boom and other localisms into the script. A trip on the boat Minnehaha across Frenchman's Bay helped. Herne saw a lighthouse that became *Shore Acres'* lighthouse. A newspaper article on the trip called the Hernes "very entertaining, pleasant people."[16]

Shore Acres crystallized by mid-August and Herne gave an informal reading for guests at the Hotel Gault. One reporter wrote: "It is after the Joshua Whitcomb style, but entirely original, with some very pathetic and touching situations. The setting will be unique, and the whole play will appeal to the hearts of all lovers of Home spelled with a large H. Mr. Herne read it very effectively, and his hearers were extremely grateful to him for his kindness."[17]

Shore Acres' main thread involves friction between two ideologies: religious fundamentalism and scientific agnosticism. Martin Berry, owner of Shore Acres and keeper of Berry light, labels free-thinkers heretics. His daughter, Helen, however, upsets the applecart. She loves Sam Warren (Herne's spokesman), a young doctor whose Darwinesque views alienate him from the town's provincial thinking. Martin, of course, forbids Helen to see Sam, an ultimatum that ruptures their relationship. The lovers eventually head West, where Sam succeeds and Helen becomes a mother. A last-act Christmas eve reconciliation scene follows.

On the surface, *Shore Acres* appears to be just another melodrama, but beneath the gloss Herne knitted themes more socially provocative than those in *Margaret Fleming*. The work's structure offered radical elements that are detailed in later chapters of this book.

Finding a playhouse to produce *Shore Acres* was inevitably a problem for Herne. Managers highly respected him and many envied his convictions. Yet, all refused *Shore Acres* because of the earlier experiences with *Drifting Apart* and *Margaret Flem-*

ing. His name spelled risk, an unspeakable word among managers.

Then Abraham Lincoln Erlanger, who still employed Herne, decided to stage *Shore Acres*—but on one condition. He wanted Joseph Jefferson III to play Nat Berry. Herne resented this because he had created Uncle Nat for himself. An explosive scene followed and Erlanger fired Herne, calling him an anarchist.

Erlanger's name may be little known today, but during the 1890's he helped rule America's feared theatre syndicate with Bismarckian power. Under his managerial thumb crouched thousands of actors, directors, playwrights, and managers from Hoboken to Honolulu. His word was law.

The theatre syndicate was a vicious trust controlled by six commercialists: Erlanger, Marc Klaw, Samuel F. Nixon, J. Frederick Zimmerman, Al Hayman, and Charles Frohman. Frohman was called by his antagonists the "Napoleon of the Drama," the "Little Giant," and the "Master Mind Upstairs."[18] Frohman was considered by some to be the syndicate's backstage Mr. Big.

Through the years, Frohman's acting stalls at the Empire Theatre in New York bulged with stars such as Maude Adams, Ethel Barrymore, Annie Russell, Elsie Ferguson, Billie Burke, William Gillette, John Drew, and William Faversham, all bigname draws. It was what *The Theatre* called the "Faversham brand of canned actors, manufacturing direct from the raw material a kind of Thespian food."[19]

Money was Frohman's manifesto. Art was all right, too, if it sold seats. He often said, "Great successes are those that take hold of the masses, not the classes."[20] He imported European plays instead of encouraging native American dramatists, even though it had been Bronson Howard's *Shenandoah* that launched his empire in 1889. (Among Frohman's blunders were rejections of Augustus Thomas' *Arizona*, Eugene Walter's *Paid in Full*, and Winchell Smith's *The Fortune Hunter*. He was nevertheless a great power in New York theatre until his death in the sinking of the *Lusitania* in 1915.)

The syndicate made big promises, which the American theatre bought because of its chaotic conditions. Contracts were often worthless, road companies played against each other in towns unable to support one town hall, and booking agents lacked contacts to organize an entire season for managers. The syndicate offered a package deal that guaranteed actors a full season on the road with advance promotion, managers a full season show-case, and producers lots of revenue. The catch was that every-one lost their independence and the syndicate enforced grudges, punishing dissenters ruthlessly. Take David Belasco's *The Dar-ling of the Gods.* Although he routed it through Klaw and Er-langer, they studied his schedule, then presented in advance *The Japanese Nightingale,* an inferior work that cut Belasco's profits. The syndicate also demanded bloated kickbacks on the road. Belasco recalled, "When I brought forward David Warfield as a star, I was forced to relinquish a full fifty percent of all profits that might accrue from 'The Auctioneer.' "[21]

Marc Klaw replied to Belasco's allegations in *Cosmopolitan,* denying that theatre's primary function was educational. "The theater is governed by the rules and observances of all other commercial enterprises. It is not out to dictate to public taste. It is out to satisfy the public demand."[22]

The inevitable happened. A handful of super stars defied Broadway's robber barons. Among them were Joseph Jefferson, Richard Mansfield, Francis Wilson, James A. Herne, and Minnie Maddern Fiske. Their public soundingboard was the *Dramatic Mirror,* which printed a series of articles that led to a $100,000 lawsuit by the incensed syndicate.

Joseph Jefferson said, "When the Trust was formed, I gave my opinion as against it, considering it inimical to the theatrical profession. I think so still."[23] But Jefferson's opinions were hushed because his son, Joseph Jefferson IV, belonged to the Klaw and Erlanger syndicate.

Richard Mansfield said "It is not conceivable that any artist, who respects himself and his profession, can be forced to submit to these speculators; unless the actor is wilfully (*sic*) blind he must know the method the Trust employs. Every actor who puts a dollar into the pocket of the Trust is supplying a new link for his own fetters. Every actor who works for the Trust is working against his fellow artists."[24] Mansfield, however, could not hold out, and eventually he joined the syndicate's ranks, too.

Francis Wilson said, "There are few of us nobler spirits, and I think I may justly say that we are nobler spirits, who will not submit to the dictation of the Trust. Some of those who do not wear the yoke of this combination are Richard Mansfield, James A. Herne, Mrs. Fiske and three or four others, and we hope that we may be permitted to follow our art without paying tribute to the Trust."[25] But the Trust soon "bought" Wilson as well, with a $50,000 half interest in his business.

Herne wrote several articles for the *Dramatic Mirror*, the first a reprint from *The World*:

> Art is a corner stone of progress and liberty.
> Literature humanizes civilization.
> A trust is an "enemy" of society.
> It matters not what a trust proposes to deal with, or what it assumes to stand for. It is an enemy of society—its real purpose being to grow rich and fat upon the labor and the needs of the community at large.
> A trust in art like a trust in the daily sustenances of the human family aims a blow at the life of the nation, and it should be fearlessly opposed. The underlying principle of a theatrical trust is to subjugate the playwright and the actor. Its effect will be to degrade the art of acting, to lower the standard of the drama and to nullify the influences of the theatre.
> The dissolution of all trusts should be a common cause. This is a truth which my fellow actors may be speedily brought to realize.
> Following a natural law, a trust being a common enemy, can hold but a brief place in society at best. Natural unconscious opposition will kill it.[26]

Herne linked the syndicate with other monopolies and private ownership of land, both anti-Georgist principles. In the *Dramatic Mirror* of January 29, 1898, he scorched the syndicate, accusing it of "greed, cunning and human selfishness." He compared it to "a wolf which will devour its fellow wolf when he falls by the way." This article was called "Words of Wisdom from Mr. Herne." It continued:

> Every actor in America should at once join the Actors' Society of America.
> Stars heading successful organizations should learn this truth: Self interest is best secured through the ability of the many to gratify their reasonable wants, not through the ability of the few to dictate terms and conditions.

Privates in the great army of actors may exert a powerful influence through silent opposition. Psychic force is more potent than it is generally understood to be.

Few actors struggling for acknowledgment and position, as is the truly great artist, Wilton Lackaye, dare be as outspoken as he, but all may think untrammelled. Thought cannot be coerced. Therefore, fellow actors, one and all, be at least mentally free and oppose this trust and all trusts in thought with heart and soul. And remember capital does not create labor, but labor created the first capital and all the capital there is in the world to-day.

The few leading actors who are standing for the independence of the American actor and for the liberty of the stage will not desert you: They cannot be cajoled, intimidated or bribed. You may trust them. They may be beaten, but not subjugated.

I regret that Mr. Jefferson has taken no action. He was cradled in the theatre. The theatre made him famous. The actors loved and honored him. I can well wish he had espoused their cause.

I hope that Mr. Goodwin, who does stand for the highest art he sees, will speedily learn that the trust which grants him personal immunity will withdraw that concession the instant it is strong enough to do without him. He is an artist and his place is among the independent stars.

As for me, I was an actor when the members of the trust were in swaddling clothes. It is conceded that I have contributed something to the literature of the stage and to dramatic art, and I, therefore, refuse to be driven from the stage of my country by the gentlemen who have the lessees and owners of a number of playhouses by the throat.[27]

Julie Herne said that her father fought the syndicate throughout the '90's; yet they granted him amnesty, like Augustin Daly, who ignored their threats. Perhaps Erlanger still admired Herne. He once admitted that Herne taught him all the ropes of show business.

Two actresses also stood strong against the syndicate: Minnie Maddern Fiske and Sarah Bernhardt.

Mrs. Fiske charged: "The incompetent men who have seized upon the affairs of the stage in this country have all but killed art, worthly ambition and decency."[28] The syndicate retaliated. Mrs. Fiske played—in churches, meeting halls, and third-rate theatres—but she played. Her husband, Harrison Grey Fiske, influential editor of the *Dramatic Mirror,* defended her, even knocking down A. L. Erlanger on the street. Along with Henrietta Crossman and James K. Hackett, Mrs. Fiske established an "Independent Booking Agency."[29] And the fight continued.

In 1905 Sarah Bernhardt arrived in New York with a peg-leg and a coffin to complete her "Farewell American Tour." When the syndicate tried to bar her from theatres, she played in skating rinks. The Shubert brothers, who managed Madame Sarah, eventually uprooted the trust, becoming theatre czars themselves. Eventually, in 1919, American actors unionized as Herne had advocated decades before.

Shortly after Herne's break with Erlanger, he received a telegram. Chrystal recalled his waving the yellow paper. " 'Listen to this,' he cried. 'Can you find sixteen weeks at my theatre with a repertoire of your plays. Signed J. H. McVicker.' "[30]

McVicker's contract included a *Shore Acres* production, but with changes. These included elimination of dialogue during the storm scene, toning down Blake's harsh character, avoiding the "front scene" rig ride to the silver wedding dinner, and a faster resolution. Herne agreed.

McVicker made several other production suggestions, including a Revolutionary War drama called *Ye Early Trouble*. Herne tried to substitute a revival of *The Minute Men*. McVicker also thought actors should be hired for one play at a time, and he opposed starring K.C. in *Margaret Fleming*.[31]

Then came a curious letter from McVicker. "Are you familiar with Ibsen's plays?" he wrote. "I have just read *The Pillars of Society*, which, properly cut, would be strong and in the line of human plays. If you have not read it, do so. You can buy a volume for 60 cents of Lovell's Series of foreign literature which contains *Doll's House*, *Ghosts*, *Rosmersholm*, and *The Pillars of Society*. With a slight alteration, and a woman capable of grasping and acting the part in *The Doll's House*, it's a fortune to the woman—but where is she?" He added: "I have not read *Ghosts* but will. We shall have plenty of plays and if we get good intelligent people who can weigh words, I see nothing to fear."[32]

The general critical contention is that when Herne produced *Margaret Fleming* in 1890, the American theatre buzzed with Ibsen talk. McVicker, with connections everywhere, reigned as Chicago's foremost manager. Yet he didn't read Ibsen until 1892, a reading that didn't include *Ghosts*.

Contrary to McVicker's hopes, *Shore Acres* presented technical problems, which meant money, time, and energy—elements commercial managers avoided.

First McVicker opposed the title, preferring something general like *Booming* or *Our Town Lots* with national appeal. He finally settled for *Shore Acres Subdivision*, which became *Uncle Nat* when attendance slumped.

Second came a set problem. McVicker liked simplicity, but Herne's plans included a large movable staircase, a lighthouse, and a boat that floundered in a fierce storm. Nevertheless, McVicker allowed the carpenters to keep hammering.

The third problem involved the final curtain. McVicker chose a humorous ending (an old army gun discharge) instead of Herne's radical silent stage business. When Herne protested, he said: "Oh, no, my dear Mr. Herne. I fear you have made a mistake. The public would not wait for that. It is too unconventional. Your story is told when the young couple have returned from the West and 'made up' with the father of Helen Berry. Let the curtain fall as soon as possible after that climax is reached."[33]

Herne liked McVicker and didn't later resent his decision to change the final scene. He told an interviewer from the *Boston Journal*: "McVicker personally was in full sympathy with me as he is to-day. It was the audience he feared. He is one of the grandest men on earth, a noble soul, one of the few managers who manage a theatre for love of it as a theatre and not as a temple of Mammon. He was the first to open his doors to my new thought. He produced my plays, 'Shore Acres' and 'Margaret Fleming' at his own expense and at his own risk, giving me carte blanche to engage whom I chose, demanding only that the performances be worthy of the plays and of his theatre."[34]

Shore Acres opened on May 23, 1892. The *Chicago Tribune* thought it showed original thought, had well-written dialogue, and ranked "with that of the best of the dialect stories." Another critic called Herne "a sort of Thoreau among play-makers," concluding that the work had "all the elements of popularity that gave *The Old Homestead* a place in the affections of the public, and is a more vital, purposeful drama."[35]

In spite of good reviews, it closed in three weeks.

Following *Shore Acres* was *My Colleen* and then *Margaret Fleming*'s revival, both short-lived productions. McVicker's object lesson was that the American repertory system belonged to the balmy days of the past. New audiences wanted new plays and new faces.

McVicker and Herne tried to salvage the summer with *The Volunteers*. Their bait was "a grand, novel, and extremely realistic balloon acension. . . . The balloon is inflated on the stage and to save the hero and heroine from the danger of a pitched battle, they are placed in the basket . . . and the mammoth airship with its precious burden soars into the clouds, it encounters a severe storm; finally it descends; down, down, till a bird's eye view of our Nation's capital bursts into view."[36]

The press and public ignored hero, heroine, and inflated balloon. *The Volunteers* was another flop, which ended the hoped-for security of Herne's summer.

The balloon ascension, however, intrigued two small-time Chicago "wheeler-dealers," Shunk and Davis, who offered Herne a road contract. But his terms had stiffened: $2500 to rewrite *The Volunteers*, $100 a week, and a guaranteed 10 percent of the season's net take. Silence followed. Davis withdrew. Shunk sent a contract, but reneged when someone offered to purchase the scenery and props. More silence followed. Shunk then wrote a letter to Herne, promising $10,000, but the funds never materialized.

Herne wasn't America's only dramatist who suffered a blow during the Chicago World's Fair. More tragic was Steele Mac-Kaye, inventor of the elevator stage, fireproof scenery, folding chairs, air-cooling and purifying mechanisms, and illumination devices. He also wrote *Hazel Kirke* (1880), a melodrama without the conventional stage villain, and *Paul Kauver* (1887), America's first ensemble play, five years before Gerhart Hauptmann's historic *The Weavers* (1892). Subtitled *Anarchy*, this work protested the unfair trial of the anarchists who were involved in the 1886 Chicago Haymarket Riot.

Both Herne and MacKaye were too advanced for the times. Wilkie Collins asked about MacKaye in the *New York Tribune*, April, 1885: "Have these novelties, and many more, all directly contributing to public health, public comfort and public pleasure, helped to draw audiences on their own merits? Little or nothing. Pure air, the comforts of spaciousness, have not, it seems, sufficiently interested the audience to make it talk about them. The friends of [MacKaye] urge him to increase the number of his advertisements, and to mention particularly that he is the author of 'Hazel Kirke'; in short, to seek notoriety just as much as if he were proprietor of the hottest and dirtiest theatre on the face of the earth.

"What is the moral of this?

"The truth is: in the theatre we offer no encouragement to reform."[37]

MacKaye kept reforming. "In dramatic art, there is work to be done in this country, of extraordinary importance," he said. "The influence of the art is so powerful that the use made of it is a question of great significance to the community."[38]

MacKaye's biggest dream probably was his Spectatorium at the Chicago World's Fair. It included a luxauleator (curtain of light), nebulator (cloud creator), proscenium adjustor, wave maker, sliding stage, telescopic stage, floating stage, and new illuminating techniques. Later he wrote a spectacle called *The World Finder* for this grand edifice, hiring Anton Dvorak, Victor Herbert, and Anton Seidl as musical associates.

This historic drama dealt with Columbus' voyage to America, involving full-scale reproductions of the Pinta, Santa Maria, and Nina, all manned by real sailors. In a *New York Times* interview MacKaye said that his long-range goals were to "make an alliance between nature and art such as has never before been effected, and to utilize this alliance for the most impressive illustrations of the grandest stories of human struggle and achievement in history."[39]

The financial panic of 1893 turned MacKaye's drama into trauma. An $850,000 investment eventually sold for $2,250 as junk. The *Pittsburgh Dispatch* wrote, "Probably never in the history of the world was so vast an amount of money expended on a structure which brought so little on a forced sale."[40]

MacKaye died six months later—broken.

The Chicago World's Fair, of course, made history, attracting more than 27,000,000 under its motto: "Make Culture Hum!" Seventy-two foreign nations exhibited at the Fair. There were many firsts: America's first massive use of electric lights, the first ferris wheel (250 feet tall), the first electric iron, the nation's first commemorative stamps, and endless innovative ideas.

Theatre attractions at the fair included Lillian Russell singing "La Cigale" on the Midway Plaisance, Buffalo Bill's Wild West Show with Annie Oakley, and the gyrations of Little Egypt. Tourists with higher tastes could attend David Belasco's production of *The Girl I Left Behind Me*, which included howling Indians and a besieged fort.

American culture really hummed its message—much of it mediocre, but loud and clear for all to hear.

17 the ruralist

STUFFED ANIMALS, DIORAMAS, wax figures, and other curiosities were exhibited at the Boston Museum and Gallery of Fine Arts. It was founded on June 14, 1841, by Moses Kimball, a friend of Phineas Taylor Barnum, who also opened the American Museum and Garden and Gallery of Fine Arts in New York that same year. These two entrepreneurs exchanged exhibits, schemes, and theatre talk. Barnum's "lecture room" (a theatre in disguise) prospered within his museum's framework. So did Kimball's "music saloon" over his museum. Its prosperity allowed a move in 1846 to Tremont Street near Court Street, which became the museum's permanent home.

William W. Clapp, Jr., wrote about the Boston Museum's audience in *A Record of the Boston Stage* (1853). "The Museum was then and is now patronized by a large class who do not frequent theatres, but who have a nice perception of the difference between tweedle-*dum* and tweedle-*dee*.[1] It seems that Kimball catered to the culturalists, not the later "ten-twent-thirt" crowd.

Many luminaries left stardust in the cracks of the Museum's stage, including famed comedian William Warren, the theatre's principal player. (In the old days, actors often made their reputations in a single city, remaining there for years.) Edwin Booth debuted here at sixteen years of age in 1849, supporting his father, Junius Brutus Booth, as Tressel in *Richard III*.[2] And James A. Herne smashed all Museum records in 1893 with *Shore Acres*.

During *The New South* rehearsals, R. M. Field, manager of

the Museum, had contacted Herne about *Shore Acres*, although he'd earlier rebuffed the work. An English import had failed on the road, and Field needed a two-week "filler" for February. This was another major stroke of luck for Herne, like Garland's attending *Drifting Apart*, McVicker's Chicago premiere of *Shore Acres*, and *The New South* part. Field's stage manager, Edward E. Rose, met Herne in New York to make detailed arrangements. He approved *Shore Acres*, and Field scheduled it, a move that was to reap riches.

Herne later said: "To Mr. Rose, then, I am indebted for its production, just as I owed much of the success of the play to my wife for sending me down to Frenchman's Bay after my atmosphere. Still, you can't blame managers for fighting shy of homemade work. The cost of running a modern theatre in a big city is enormous, and a failure means a dead loss of $20,000 or $40,000."[3]

Elisabeth Marbury, who encouraged Herne's "fidelity to truth" dramas, wrote: "I remember how 'Shore Acres' by Herne was hawked about in New York, refused by everyone, until we succeeded in persuading Mr. Field of its merits. The theatre was called after the Museum and retained the glass cases lining the lobby and entrance hall in which were a varied collection of stuffed birds and animals with an occasional exhibit of insects and butterflies. Here and there a dilapidated plaster cast covered with the dust of ages shared the honor."[4]

If it meant a home for his production at last, Herne was delighted to share honors with stuffed birds, butterflies, and dilapidated plaster casts.

Shore Acres opened at the Boston Museum on February 20, 1893, the season's coldest night, to "a large and very attentive audience."[5] At the opening were Herne's old friends, the Flowers, Ennekings, Chamberlain of the *Transcript*, Mildred Aldrich, Mary E. Wilkins, and Garland, who stood talking together before the performance, recalling the *Drifting Apart* and *Margaret Fleming* days.

Herne didn't fail again. A thrilled audience demanded curtain call after curtain call. Following the third act, Herne appeared, thanking the Museum staff and his audience.[6] A life's ambition was fulfilled. "I used to walk past the old Boston Museum," Herne once recalled, "and looking up at the long rows of gas lamps as they shine out a warm welcome to the public, I mentally expressed the hope that some day I might bring out one of my plays in the cosey, (sic) comfortable, compact theatre."[7]

Shore Acres' advance sale became the largest in the Museum's history. Newspaper reviewers helped.

Boston Post: "As a picture of Down East farm life, 'Shore Acres' is well-nigh perfect."[8]

Boston Evening Transcript: "Should it meet its deserts—and this the cordial, universal and sustained enthusiasm of Monday night's spectators seems to promise—it will rank with the conspicuous successes not alone of the season, but of the dramatic generation."[9]

Boston Journal: "It was the most charming bit of dramatic realism witnessed in a long period. . . . The piece is capitally staged and is deserving of a long and prosperous run. It will undoubtedly attract larger crowds to the Museum than have been seen there for years."[10]

The tables had finally turned. After forty years, Herne was now able to dictate stiff terms. Field listened because he knew other managers would grab *Shore Acres* if he didn't. Herne demanded $250 a week for playing Nat Berry, a pittance compared with his authorial terms: 50 percent of the net profits up to $25,000, 60 percent to $35,000, 70 percent to $45,000 and 75 percent above this.[11] All cast members had to receive his approval, and promotion had to headline him, not mentioning the Museum's company. All promotion attached K.C.'s name to Herne's, wherever possible.

Herne frankly told Field: "I have artistic as well as financial ambition. My desire was in the beginning and is now, not only that *Shore Acres* should be a success, but that James A. Herne should be a success in Nathaniel Berry, so that your audience might say, 'Go and see Mr. Herne as Nathaniel Berry,' not merely 'Go and see *Shore Acres*.' I have, as you know, achieved that result. I now desire to retain and if possible increase the personal hold I have as an actor. I have proved my right to stand among the great character actors of the day by my work in *The New South* in New York, and have established that fact beyond question here. I have been doing fine work all my life but have been careless of the fruits of it, both artistically and financially." He also said K.C. was "as great an actress as Eleanora Duse."[12]

Herne still wanted to make K.C. America's foremost actress. She was his "silent collaborator" on *Shore Acres, Margaret Fleming,* and other earlier works. "She is my critic, my counselor, my incentive to nobler effort," he told one interviewer. "Sometimes, when I think I have written something that is clever, I read it to my wife, and she honestly, fearlessly shows me that it is rubbish. And sometimes, when my work appears to be of little value, my wife will discern in it beauty and force, and by her intuitive sense of the fitness of things will point out its strength and its weakness."[13]

K.C. suggested the child Mandy in *Shore Acres* and also influenced Herne's subtle interpretation of Uncle Nat. "I was turning on the tear taps at rehearsal and working the pumps pretty hard," Herne told Otis Skinner, "when Mrs. Herne, who was watching from out in front, said 'why are you working so, why do you cry? Aren't you going to leave some of that for the audience to do?' If I had played Uncle Nat the way I had played similar parts as a young man, I should have sobbed and suffered and had a terrible time. No, I tell the story quietly, recalling the memories with a little smile. It's wonderful how you can pick an audience up into your arms that way."[14]

Although most reviewers praised *Shore Acres,* attendance still dipped after a few nights. Other plays were siphoning off the profits: Charles Hoyt's *A Temperance Town,* Nat C. Goodwin in *A Gilded Fool,* and even a recital by Ignace Paderewski at the Music Hall. The most ironic note was that Klaw and Erlanger's *The Country Circus* was packing the Boston Theatre.

Shore Acres limped along for three weeks before the house once again began filling. At season's end, Herne wrote Garland: "Everything looks well for me in the future. We closed here last Saturday night, 113 performances to a tremendous house. We've not had a bad house during the run. Field has cleared over $50,000.[15]

Things continued to look well for the Hernes, after fifteen years of difficulties and struggles. As Chrystal recalled, "From then on all was on the up and up with us—the goose hung high."[16]

Shore Acres' closing marked an historic event at the Museum. After fifty years, this distinguished showplace disbanded its stock company, becoming a "combination house," showcasing a different road show every week. Kate Ryan later reminisced in *Old Boston Museum Days*: "There was indeed a sickening feeling of pain when we realized the passing of the old Museum days.... When the final curtain fell that last night, we of the Old Guard passed out of the theater with eyes bedimmed with tears, our hearts flooded with memories, pleasant and unpleasant."[17]

A week before *Shore Acres* closed at the Boston Museum, a local paper wrote, "This play and its able and natural acting have been talked of far from Boston, so that the next season other cities will have an opportunity to learn the quaint New England story and to become acquainted with Mr. Herne's double creation of the touching character of Nathaniel Berry."[18]

How right they were. Herne had already signed a contract to reopen *Shore Acres* at Miner's Fifth Avenue Theatre in New York on October 30.

Miner had seen *Shore Acres* at the Boston Museum and tried to persuade Herne to change houses. He wrote, "If you want to do business with me, why just write or telephone and I will come on and meet you anywhere you say."[19] But Herne wanted the Museum's prestigious name associated with *Shore Acres*, for a while at least.

Conservatism, however, crowded Field's mind. He didn't speculate, and he didn't act intuitively. Miner did. That's why Herne eventually severed ties with Field (they hadn't signed a legal contract) and made Miner his manager. Miner already owned four theatres: the People's, the Bowery, the Eighth Avenue, and the Newark in New Jersey. He also had road-show interests, a drug business, a lithographing company, and an eventual Congressional seat. It was Miner who had staged *The Minute Men* years before.

Shore Acres opened at Miner's Fifth Avenue Theatre on October 30, 1893. First nighters flocked to see it. Among them were Gertrude Atherton, Mrs. Frank (Miriam Follin) Leslie, and "Diamond Jim" Brady. Again reviewers raved:

New York Mercury: "Mr. Herne's play marks an epoch in the drama of the American stage."

New York Journal: "Last night there was seen one of those pieces of theatrical work that comes but a few times in a century—those outbursts of genius that sweep aside old ideas, traditions, remembrances of all that our fathers held dear. One of those plays that mark an epoch as did *Hernani*. Last night's play was *Shore Acres*. James A. Herne wrote it, and it is the best American play that we have had."

New York Evening World: "In *Shore Acres* he [Herne] has written a play so absolutely satisfying to truth that one marvels at the directness of the touches that are apparently aimed carelessly. I would take criminals in a body to see it, and rely more upon its effect than on all the sermons that coldly innundate those unfortunate."[20]

Garland later called *Shore Acres* "by far the best play Herne had ever done,"[21] a statement that included *Drifting Apart, Margaret Fleming,* and *Griffith Davenport.* His brother, still with Herne's company, told Garland: "I'm going to get some sort of headquarters in New York. If you'll come on we'll hire a little apartment up town and 'bach' it. I'm sick of theatrical boardinghouses." Garland liked the idea. "Very well. Get your fiat. I'd like to spend a winter in the old town anyway."[22] That winter he often dined with the Hernes on Sundays at their Convent Avenue home, and again acted "up front." It was like the old days in Boston.

Herne cautiously worded his contract with Miner, one clause covering *Shore Acres'* run, at least four weeks, regardless of attendance. "A most important proviso," he told Garland, "for 'Shore Acres' must have time for our kind of people to find out what sort of a play it is."[23] Miner agreed to Herne's terms. He was convinced a Boston smash hit would become a hit on Broadway overnight.

Garland told what happened in *Roadside Meetings*:

"The first night [Miner] was jubilant. He posed in the lobby, glorious in evening dress, a shining figure. 'We've got 'em coming, Jimmy, my boy,' he said to Herne after the first act. But James A., whose face remained an impenetrable mask while Miner was looking at him, winked at me with full understanding of the situation.

" 'Watch him to-morrow night,' he said after Miner left the dressing room.

"Tuesday's house was light and Wednesday's still lighter, and on Thursday Miner fell into the dumps. 'We've got to take it off, Jim,' he mournfully announced.

" 'You'll do nothing of the kind,' retorted Herne. 'You'll keep it on four weeks according to contract, if it doesn't bring in a cent.'

"Miner was furious. He stormed about, declaring himself on the verge of ruin—all to no effect. Herne's face was stern as a New England granite boulder.

" 'You'll keep your contract,' he calmly repeated.

"Miner's attitude during the second week was comical. He became morose and was seen no more in the lobby. He brooded over the contract as though Herne had done him a grievous wrong, and all the employees came ultimately to share his resentful attitude. The house acquired a dank, depressing, tragic atmosphere and then, magically, came a change. The people began to come—our kind of people. At the end of the second week the house was filled. Miner ordered the lobby lighted up and reappeared in evening dress. He strutted once more in dazzling, confident splendor. He expanded. He appeared taller, larger. He clapped Herne on the back. 'They're coming back, Jimmy, my boy!' he shouted, forgetting all his resentment, all his hard words, all his tragical gloom. 'We'll be turning them into the street next week,' he exultingly ended. 'Your fortune is made.' "[24]

Herne's son, John, later wrote: "It was *Shore Acres* that made [his father] a millionaire and while $1,000,000 ain't exactly hay even now, in 1900 it bought an awful lot of groceries."[25] In 1896, Miner refused $100,000 for his interest in *Shore Acres*.[26]

Herne relished playing Uncle Nat, remarking once: "It's a great way to go. I've often thought I would like to die some night when I reach the top of the stairs in the last act."[27]

Herne nearly got his wish. Each performance he climbed the lighthouse stairs, where an offstage platform lowered him to the ground. One night in November, 1893, he tumbled off. The crew carried him backstage and called a doctor. Although he suffered two broken ribs and a sprained ankle, Herne insisted the doctor "strap him up," so he could continue the show—bolstered with adhesive and a shot of whiskey.

Charles Craig (who played Martin) took Herne's place as Uncle Nat, but attendance slipped. Herne soon realized that audiences still paid to see stars, not shows. This included *Shore Acres'* audiences. Miraculously, Herne recovered and was able to resume the role within ten days, and tickets sold again.

Shore Acres played Miner's until late December. The final week Herne gave a professional matinee that contained a moving moment. The past month's strain, coupled with a fantastic ovation, overpowered the actor-playwright. He broke down and couldn't continue during a curtain call. His audience wept.

After its profitable run at Miner's, *Shore Acres* moved to Daly's, where the 1893–94 season attendance had sagged while Daly managed a new London theatre. But prosperity soon returned and *Shore Acres* set a 180-consecutive-performance record. George C. D. Odell wrote that "on December 25th, it began that splendid career at Daly's which is still part of theatrical history and about the only thing in Herne's career known to the man in the street or in the club window."[28]

Several days after the Daly opening, Henry Irving, Ellen Terry, and the entire London Lyceum Theatre Company and members of the American Dramatists' Club attended a performance. (Irving was playing Tennyson's *Becket* and *King Henry VIII* at the Knickerbocker.) After the third act, Irving went backstage and told Herne, "I don't know anything of New England Mr. Herne, but I feel the sincerity of your play."[29]

That evening Herne delivered a curtain speech, in which he said that William Winter had erroneously traced *Shore Acres'* lineage to James E. Murdock's *Lighthouse Cliffs*, an earlier melodrama by the writer of *Davy Crockett*. Herne then threatened legal action.[30]

Henry Irving, incidentally, asked Herne to stage *Shore Acres* at the Lyceum Theatre in London, but plans collapsed. So did Miner's later negotiations with English actor-manager William Terriss. Contracts were forwarded in 1897 for Terriss' signature, but a deranged actor murdered him at the Adelphi Theatre, which ended Herne's English stage hopes, as well, for the time being.

Shore Acres eventually played in London, with a mediocre

company. William Archer wrote in the May 22, 1906, issue of
The London *Tribune*: "To say that (*Shore Acres*) loses nothing
by transference from New England to Cornwall would be to do
injustice to Herne's peculiar art. With him each figure was a
study from the life, and every intonation of the dialect was re-
produced with a nicety worthy of a professor of phonetics. In
the English version we have, so far as the minor characters are
concerned, little more than the conventional rustic types of the
melodramatic stage."[31]

Shore Acres played its 150th performance at Daly's on May
1, 1894. "The season will close when 'Shore Acres' fails to draw
a certain amount of money weekly, but there is nothing as yet
to indicate when that time will come," said a journalist in the
New York Times. "Mr. Herne himself is almost as much of a dis-
ciplinarian as Mr. Daly. Whenever he sees the least sign of flag-
ging in the work of his company, he calls a rehearsal, and 'Shore
Acres' is played through to the empty benches of a darkened
house, the players being as thoroughly drilled for their work as
though they were rehearsing a new play."[32]

Herne played *Shore Acres* on the road for five years. He
knew the parks, playhouses, boardinghouses, and restaurants in
scores of towns and cities. Each with its own pulse, and each a
unique experience for the road-weary performer. There also
were friends like James Whitcomb Riley, who loved children as
Herne did. Sometimes when Herne's company passed through
Indianapolis, he and Riley would spend half the night in talk,
one time in a park until daybreak.

Packed audiences greeted *Shore Acres* almost everywhere.
Most reviews were glowing. The Cincinnati *Commercial Tribune*'s critic, for example, called Herne "first among the masters
of stagecraft of this day," and *Shore Acres* "a masterpiece of
dramatic fiction."[33] When Herne returned to Boston in 1896,
the *Boston Sunday Post* predicted, "When the history of the
past decade in the drama is written the performance of James
A. Herne as Nathaniel Berry will receive the most attention."[34]

All Herne's memorable experiences on the road, however,
weren't of theatrical success. During *Shore Acres'* last tour, the
company played Fort Worth during a cattlemen's convention.
The rough and tumble cowboys wanted more action in the love

scene between Sam and Helen and started a ruckus. Herne finally appeared on stage in makeup, announcing: "Ladies and gentlemen, we are giving the same performance tonight we have given in all the big cities of the country. Those of you who are dissatisfied may have your money refunded at the box office, but we cannot allow those who wish to hear the play to be disturbed. We must have quiet."

"At this point, someone in the audience shouted, 'We don't mean any harm, old man! We want Sam to kiss the gal—jes' once—that's all.'

"From all over the house came the cry, 'Yes, go ahead, Sam! Kiss her! Kiss her!' Herne smiled, but ignored the plea, and said, 'If there is any further noise, I must order the curtain rung down.' The audience suddenly became silent. 'Now,' Herne said, 'We will go on with the performance.' "[35]

Herne's cowpoke audience remained quiet for the rest of the play, including the lighthouse scene that usually received several curtain calls.

Shore Acres was still playing town halls and opera houses in 1899. (Miner's second company continued several years after Herne's death, making a second fortune for its shrewd manager.) That year the *New York Dramatic Mirror* praised the play in a poem called "The Ruralist":

> He has somehow caught the gladness
>   Of the sunny fields of May;
> And he's dramatized the sadness
>   Of the Winter's bleakest day.
> And the romance of the humble
>   He has placed upon the stage,
> As a contrast to the vileness
>   Of this mercenary age.
>
> Can it be he's undecided
>   As to whether he will go?
> Are there other paths that lure him
>   From the fields we used to know?
> "Never!" Say the keen first-nighters,
>   "Never must he turn away
> From the realistic romance
>   Of the rugged, rural play!"[36]

18 frogs
an' bugs
an' things

HERNE WROTE *SHORE Acres* as a starring vehicle for himself. He also wanted to depict truthfully the lifestyle of rural New England and expose the greed, hypocrisy, and injustice within America's fabric. These themes were strengthened through his association with Boston's literati, Henry George's "single tax," and Spencerian individualism.

A surface glance at *Shore Acres* doesn't reveal its unconventional framework, blistering social statement, and poetic language, but *Shore Acres* was not simply another "Down-East" sentimental farce. Norman Hapgood called it "first among American rural dramas"[1] and Benjamin Orange Flower thought it was "a victory of far-reaching significance for the drama."[2] Ima Honaker Herron wrote, "*Shore Acres,* unusual for its time, connects the hazards of young love with serious social problems affecting even village life: the land boom and speculation in the lighthouse village of Berry, near Bar Harbor; the rebellion of youth asserting its rights to work out its own destiny unobstructed: religious narrowness; and liberal thinking about evolution."[3]

Frederick Morton, who calls *Shore Acres* "a milestone in dramas of the American scene," traces the social realism of Clifford Odets and Sidney Howard to Herne's early efforts. "There is little actual difference between Herne's lowly folk and those of Odets except a few labels. Herne's men fight with the storms of nature on their farms and their ships, and Odets' fight with the machine." Morton also considers Howard's *Ned McCobb's*

Daughter a lineal descendent of *Shore Acres* and *Sag Harbor*, concluding, "The essential elements of human relationship and much of the action in *Sag Harbor* are duplicated in *They Knew What They Wanted.*"[4]

Herne slammed conventionalism in *Shore Acres*, even though the *New York Times* labeled it "a simple play of farm life,"[5] and the *Boston Post* "wholesome entertainment."[6] William Dean Howells called it a "sweet and gentle play."[7] The *Boston Budget* remarked: "One cannot but wonder that the author of *Shore Acres* is the same James A. Herne who wrote *Margaret Fleming*. The latter play, Zolaesque in motive and Ibsenesque in treatment is realistic and repellent; the former is realistic and attractive. The same man wrote both; but where in the first, he carried his hearers into the depths, in the second we see him struggling to reach the heights."[8]

Herne's religious attitude was given voice in *Shore Acres*. When Josiah Blake, the postmaster, tells Martin about the lovers' secret meetings, he ridicules Sam's liberalism, a statement really ridiculing his own ignorance. "First he reads Emmanuel Swedenborg, 'an a lot o' them kind o' lunatics an' began to study frogs an' bugs an' things. Why sir! One mornin,' a spell ago, as I was goin' to Ellsworth, I seed him a-settin' on his hunkers in the middle of the rud, watchin' a lot of ants runnin' in an' out a hole."[9]

A counterpoint scene follows between Helen and Sam. Sam says, "A fellow that knows some things his great-great-grandfather didn't know is an object of suspicion here."[10] Helen continues:

> *Helen.* (*still amused.*) Why, the other day I was trying to tell Father something about evolution and "The Descent of Man," but he got mad and wouldn't listen.
> *Sam.* (*laughing.*) Family pride! You know, Nell, there are lots of people who wouldn't be happy in this world if they couldn't look forward to a burning lake in the next. (*Takes a book out of his pocket and carelessly flips over the pages, looking at her as he talks.*)
> *Helen.* Kind of sad, isn't it?
> *Sam.* Oh! I don't know! They take a heap of comfort preparing to keep out of it, I suppose.
> *Helen.* (*Seeing the book in* Sam's *hand, rises and goes toward*

him.) What book's that? (*Trying to read the title on the cover.*)
Sam.   (*Rising.*) "A Hazard of New Fortunes."[11]

A Hazard of New Fortunes, of course, was Howells' new novel. Its mention in the script was Herne's way of thanking Howells, whom he wrote: "It's a tremendous book—the greatest picture of New York life that I ever read. It will be of great historic value in the future,"[12] and again: "The allusion to your book . . . is simply a bit of truth. In the face of your public endorsement here it might have been perhaps as well omitted. Still it is a forceful truth—and displays the minds of Helen and women."[13]

Several reviewers thought this tribute superfluous. As the *Boston Evening Transcript* chided: "The introduction of Mr. Howells' name and fame in the first act could, considering that gentleman's much advertised endorsement of the play, be spared, with conspicuous gain to good taste." This reviewer, of course, also thought "the elaborate attention to the toilet of the infant's nose in the second act," and "the enormity of young Warren's apostasies [could] be made quite clear, with much less dissertation on Darwin."[14]

Herne occasionally referred to writers such as Sidney Lanier in his speeches, and in *Drifting Apart,* Mary says to Jack, "Do you remember Bella and John in *Our Mutual Friend*—that I read to you?"[15] In *Sag Harbor,* Martha says to Cap'n Dan: "No, you're a great, big, splendid man. (*With deep feeling.*) Do you remember Whitcomb Riley's poem 'Jim?'" Then she recites the verse: "When God made Jim, I'll bet you/He didn't do anything else that day/But just set around and feel good."[16]

The critical references to Howells were made because of his influence on Herne's career and his eminent position among Boston's Brahmins. It also gave the critics something to write about.

Herne appreciated the feminist overtones of *A Hazard of New Fortunes,* which, as he said, showed "the minds of Helen and women." Helens were rare during the 1890's, especially in rural America, where most homespun girls settled for homespun lives. But Helen is another Margaret Fleming, a woman who asserts her Spencerian individuality and right to live independently of social mores. Yet she's only seventeen. When Blake boasts,

"Your father's set his mind on you an' me gettin' married y'know," she answers: "My father had better mind his own business."[17] Later she nearly attacks her father when he threatens to kill Sam, but Uncle Nat interferes.

Helen's father, Martin Berry, typifies the traditional New England patriarch, a stiff-necked Puritan who argues with Sam:

> *Martin.* (*Goaded by* Sam's *manner, fiercely.*) I don't want to know nothin"! An' I don't want *her* to know nothin' thet I don't want her to know! (*Indicating* Helen *with a nod of his head.*)
>
> *Sam.* (*Making another effort to conciliate him.*) Why you see, Mr. Berry—you can't help—
>
> *Martin.* (*Breaking in and shouting at him.*) I'm a-bringin' up my family! An' I don't want no interference from you—nor Darwin—nor any o' the rest o' the breed! (*With a passionate sweep of his arm. He half turns as if to go.*)
>
> *Sam.* (*Smiling.*) Darwin's dead, Mr. Berry—
>
> *Martin.* (*Turning and interrupting, resentfully.*) Them *books* ain't dead.
>
> *Sam.* (*Very positive and very much satisfied with his statement.*) No! "Them books" are going to be pretty hard to kill."[18]

Martin is Uncle Nat's opposite, almost a villain like Dyke Hampton in *The Minute Men.* Was this Herne's intention? Perhaps Martin was a cathartic release or possibly Herne's father transported into fiction. Herne wrote Howells: "The character of Martin is not represented as written. Mr. Harris who plays the part accentuates the melodramatic in him—projects the brute force and entirely loses sight of the subtleties of Martin's nature. Properly presented, Martin would never be called a murderer. (Herne here refers to the lighthouse scene.) At all events, no such term was applied to him in Chicago. Nor did I see that in him when I wrote him."[19]

Henry George indirectly influenced Martin's character through his single-tax theories. One writer declared: "The real inspiration of 'Shore Acres' was 'Progress and Poverty.' If the latter had never been written the former could not have been."[20]

Imagine Herne's reaction to K.C.'s land speculation rip-off at Lamoine, Maine, after all his Georgist speeches. Thus Martin becomes a pawn to heighten Herne's opposition to American land grabs. Besides "selling out" Shore Acres, Martin even is willing to exhume his mother's grave, all for hard cash, although he preaches "holy writ" and traditionalism.

Herne made a questionable but understandable concession in *Shore Acres*, after *Drifting Apart* and *Margaret Fleming* had drained his resources. He allowed Uncle Nat's last-minute pension to save the day, a sophisticated treatment of a threadbare resolution. He later apologized to Howells: "The pension episode I was forced to introduce to appease the public and get a hearing from the managers. I hope to be strong enough to walk alone some day."[21] Herne originally had planned another *Margaret Fleming* ending, brutally honest and true to life.

Sam's agnosticism in *Shore Acres* is Herne's agnosticism, the kind Spencer supported in *First Principles*. "May we not without hesitation affirm that a sincere recognition of the truth that our own and all other existence is a mystery absolutely . . . beyond our comprehension, contains more of true religion than all the dogmatic theology ever written."[22]

Herne reaffirmed such transcendentalism about Maine in "Art for Truth's Sake in the Drama." He wrote: "What an exalted idea of God one gets down in that old pine state! One must recognize the sublimity which constantly manifests itself there. It is worth something to live for two summer months at Lamoine on Frenchman's Bay—that beautiful inconstant bay, one minute white with rage, the next all smiles, and gently lapping the foothills of old Mount Desert, with the purple mist on the Blue Hills in the distance, on the one hand, the Schoodic range on the other, the perfume of the pine trees in every breath you inhale, the roar of the ocean eight miles away, and the bluest of blue skies overarching all. In such a spot a man must realize, if he never has realized it before, that he and this planet are one, a part of the universal whole."[23]

The reception of *Shore Acres* by audiences and critics alike is amazing. (It played to packed houses during the 1893 depression.) Both groups identified with Sam, the agnostic, and Helen, the liberated girl. This was because Uncle Nat's homespun dialogue and the universal appeal of young love muted Herne's message. He admitted: "I think it is doubtful whether there is any larger proportion of the 'Shore Acres' audience which understands the psychology and sociology of that play."[24] It was a good assessment since few read Darwin or Spencer in the 1890's. As Martin Berry boasts: "I read *The Bangor Whig,* an' *The Agriculturist,* an' the *Bible,* an' thet's enough. There ain't no lies in *them.*"[25]

Shore Acres' literary values received divided analysis, depending on the critics' school of thought, although all applauded Herne's portrayal of Uncle Nat. Howells wrote Field that the work had "a strain of fine poetry in it,"[26] but the *New York Times* condemned Herne's use of hell, saying it didn't "ennoble his drama or make it more satisfying to intelligent persons."[27] Several reviewers mentioned Dickens' influence. The *Sunday Post* said, "Mr. Herne has much of the Englishman's power of observing the humorous side of everyday life in lowly places and the power to draw the finest pathos from the simplest happenings."[28] But the *Daily Advertiser* called Martin's conversion "so Dickensy that we should think it would have turned Mr. Howells' realistic stomach, so to speak."[29] The *New York Times* also compared *Shore Acres* to Dickens' *The Cricket on the Hearth,*[30] while the *Boston Daily Advertiser* complained that "a series of more or less dramatic dialogues do not necessarily make a play any more than a series of clauses makes a sentence."[31] One critic even questioned the silver wedding dinner clash, saying it opposed New England custom. "The people among whom such a breach of manners would be possible would be of a social station even lower than the Berrys."[32]

Shore Acres' most important structural contribution, of course, was Herne's realistic study of the American stage Yankee.

The stage Yankee had thrived on American platforms since Royall Tyler's Jonathan in *The Contrast* (1787). He was a clownish character with red wig, bell-shaped hat, and striped coat and trousers, a "Yankee Doodle" whistling country cracker who found city life and city people enigmatic. As the original Jonathan exclaims: "Gor! She's gone off in a swinging passion, before I had time to think of consequences. If this is the way with your city ladies, give me the twenty acres of rock, the bible, the cow, and Tabitha, and a little peaceable bundling."[33]

Generations of these patchwork pieces followed, each with its cardboard Jonathan: Jonathan Ploughboy in *The Forest*

Rose, Jedidiah Homebred in *The Green Mountain Boy*, Deuteronomy Dutiful in *Vermont Wool Dealer*, Lot Sap Sago in *Yankee Land*, Hiram Dodge in *Yankee Peddler*, Solomon Swap in *Jonathan in England*, and Solon Shingle in *The People's Lawyer*.[34]

Shore Acres humanized the stage Yankee. Character replaced caricature, truth replaced artifice, and purpose replaced plot. Uncle Nat didn't wear a wig or broad striped vest, and he wasn't brash or boastful, just a simple soul seeking peace and love. Herne wrote and portrayed him as a man whose sense of reality seemed to transcend staginess. To thousands Herne *was* Uncle Nat. People stopped him on the streets, asking questions:

"You're Mr. Herne ain't you? Well, how did you know anything about Si Leach?" [a character in *Shore Acres*]

Herne replied he'd made his acquaintance while writing the play.

"Well, he weren't lost in no storm, Mr. Herne. He was drowned on a sunshiny day out-a-trolleying."

Another fellow said, "I was born right on that very knoll you speak of in the play, Mr. Herne," and a Scotchman said, "All I have to do is to shut my e'en and I fancy myself back in the Hielands." One playgoer shook Herne's hand, saying, "I was darned glad that you showed up that dirty scoundrel who wanted to turn his mother's graveyard into building lots."[35]

During one *Shore Acres'* performance, Benjamin Orange Flower overheard someone mutter that he couldn't recall Berry Lighthouse along the shore. "To each of them, as apparently to the vast audience," wrote Flower, "it was history rather than fiction which was being unfolded."[36]

Shore Acres provided Herne his greatest stage triumph. The finale was cited by writers for years, and theatre historians still mention it in texts.

Mary E. Wilkins told Field, "how delighted" she was with *Shore Acres*. "Of course, it appeals to me very strongly since it deals with my own New England characters and scenes, but it is not that feature alone which pleases me. It seems to me that Nathan'l Berry is a great dramatic creation, and the last scene is simply extraordinary in its originality and simplicity."[37]

The scene that impressed Miss Wilkins was the scene that

managers wouldn't touch. The same scene McVicker cut during the summer of '92, and Field tried to eliminate in Boston, the same scene the *New York Telegram* later called "Herne's greatest contribution to drama."[38] This was the silent ending.

Field's stage manager, Rose, who recommended *Shore Acres,* also secretly agreed to try the radical experiment, even though Field insisted, "The curtain must come down when the ancient musket is fired, accidentally, and the stage is in excited turmoil."[39]

Instead of McVicker's "slambang" ending, Uncle Nat puttered around for nearly ten minutes on stage, alone and without dialogue. Just mime: He scratched frost off the kitchen window, peering into the mysteries of night, then tried the door lock, readjusted the mat, closed the stove's damper, bolted the woodhouse door, hung the stockings, and finally lighted a candle. A whispered monologue punctuated these many minute details. Then Uncle Nat climbed a few steps and paused. Herne, who wrote detailed stage directions like Shaw and Galsworthy, finished the scene with these remarks:

> *For a moment he is lost in thought; his right arm slowly relaxes. Then he turns and starts to climb slowly up the stairs, his heavy footfalls echoing through the empty room. The wind howls outside; the sharp snow tinkles rhythmically upon the window-pane. The stage darkens slightly. He reaches the top of the stairs and goes off, closing the door after him. The stage is left in darkness except for the firelight flickering through the chinks of the stove. The cuckoo clock strikes twelve and the curtain slowly descends.*[40]

Herne's audience sat silent. Then wild applause. Many returned five and six times to see this scene. Flower wrote: "During the four times I saw 'Shore Acres' performed, the audience seemed rapt until Uncle Nat disappeared. It was one of the most remarkable illustrations of the unconscious tribute paid by the people to the genius of the artist and his fidelity to truth that I have ever seen."[41]

One night while Herne climbed the creaky stairs, someone in the audience cried, "Good night, old man—God bless you."[42] Herne staggered inwardly. Would the audience laugh, breaking the illusion? It didn't. Deafening applause followed Uncle Nat's exit, as always.

Ten years later the Moscow Art Theatre produced Chekhov's *The Cherry Orchard*. In the last scene, Firs (the old servant) stands alone, the last vestige of a passing order. The faint sound of workers chopping cherry trees floats across stage. Firs lies prostrate on the floor as the curtain falls. Critics soon parallelled Firs and Uncle Nat. Again Herne had pioneered. As Channing Pollock wrote during the 1940's: "The notion that today's actors discovered the virtues of repose and repression is of a piece with the theory that today's authors discovered sex. William Gillette displayed these virtues in *Held by the Enemy*, James A. Herne in *Shore Acres* and Edwin Booth in *Hamlet* as conspicuously as any player of our own time."[43]

Herne mastered the art of expressing man's inner self in *Shore Acres*. His brilliant performance, now lost in time, astonished audiences and critics:

Boston Daily Advertiser: "A finer illustration of the beauty and power of dramatic impersonation where the movement of the will and intelligence seems to be from the inside out, not from the outside in has been seldom given on our stages.... And the monologue in the first act in which he told the story of his father's shipwreck and his mother's mental alienation would not have discredited the finest artist of the house of Molière."[44]

Boston Post: "Mr. Herne's impersonation of the leading role needs no words of comment. It has long since taken its place among the classics of the American stage."[45]

Boston Evening Transcript: "Mr. Herne's Uncle Nat is a portrait worthy to hang forever in the Museum gallery of great traditions."[46]

This review moved Herne to write this last critic: "How should I express my feelings in regard to it? It seemed to come from one who had sat beside me during the writing of the play so forcefully does it set forth all my thoughts and hopes.... You have looked into my very soul, it seems—taken what of good you have found there and published it to the world."[47]

It's difficult now to appreciate Herne's portrayal of Uncle Nat, a portrayal that ranked "with the best character interpre-

tations known to the American stage."[48] Historic in its significance, the lost performance is like the roles of Booth, Jefferson, and Warren. Reading *Shore Acres* is like reading a blueprint
without experiencing the building's dimensionality, or analyzing
a musical score without full orchestration. They are weak substi-
tutes. Again, there is the endless conflict between drama and
theatre. The *Boston Daily Advertiser* estimated in 1893 that
Shore Acres spent "nearly one half of its time with stage
business."[49]

Walter Prichard Eaton, who saw *Shore Acres,* wrote: "It
was pantomime raised to poetry, it was the realism of fact doing
the work of language, and doing it for once quite as well. The
play is still presented every season, though it was written fifteen years ago. How much deeper or more poetically, you ask,
have our playwrights wrought since? How far has the prose
drama of contemporary life advanced beyond the point where
Herne left it? How much nearer is it to the ideal goal of literature? For surely a domestic pantomime, depending for its effect
absolutely on a stage and actors, cannot be considered as literature, for it cannot be printed."[50]

Thus, the problem. The "fleshy" part of Uncle Nat has been
reduced to italicized stage directions, leaving words without vocal subtlety or emotional coloration, just symbolic scratchings.
The *Boston Journal,* for example, commented on the first act's
powerful sense of honest pathos, "The sincere sorrow depicted
by Mr. Herne as he stands picking the frayed-out fragment of
his jacket, unable to find words to express his pain on account
of his brother's . . . conduct, and his words of quiet rebuke, were
perhaps the most telling and artistic moments in the play."[51]

Herne's hands, the slightest twist or finger flick, intrigued
playgoers. As Chrystal recalled: "Father had wonderfully expressive and sensitive hands and fingers. (Amy Leslie also had
remarked about Herne's expressive hands.) He could tell an entire story by their movements. I can see him now (*in Drifting
Apart*), standing on the stage, after my mother had left him, his
head bowed, a little gray cap in his hands, and his fingers
clutching it, rolling it up and unrolling it, passing restlessly over
it. They told far more graphically, convincingly, and dramati-

cally, than words could have done, his grief and sorrow and heartbreak."[52]

Herne had earned a reputation for versatility. Starting with such romantic figures as the Benedicts, Petruchios, and Claude Melnottes, he progressed through Bill Sykes and Rip Van Winkle to both Philip Fleming and Joe Fletcher in *Margaret Fleming*, to the Rev. Griffith Davenport, and to his memorable "Down-East" roles as Terry Dennison, Jack Hepburne, Uncle Nat, and Cap't Dan Marble in *Sag Harbor*. Herne was a stage chameleon. Some playgoers failed to recognize him as Samson in *The New South*, acclaiming a new Black talent. During the professional matinee, Herne's actor-audience rose as he exited, forcing his return, while the stars were ignored. He accomplished this in a fifteen-minute supporting role.

Herne rightly was called "The Apostle of Realism on the American Stage."[53] Uncle Nat's characterization was *one* extension of his search for "fidelity to truth." *Shore Acres'* stage settings also mirrored this aesthetic philosophy. Whetstones, scythes, milk pails, and clam shells all helped to create an exacting picture of external reality. (A horse upstaged actors in one scene.) Imagine the following first-act scene at Shore Acres Farm near Bar Harbor. It's a sensory appetizer:

> To the left of the stage is an old barn, its doors open, its littered yard enclosed by a rail fence. A dove cote is built into the peak of its gabled roof, and doves come and go leisurely.
>
> Outside the fence, at the upper end, is a pump, beneath which is a trough filled with water. Against the lower end of the fence lies a plough. Trees overhang the roof of the barn, and join those overhanging the house from the other side. At right centre is a gnarled old tree, and beneath it is a bench. Down left, below the fence, is a wheelbarrow.
>
> At the rise of the curtain, and until the act is well in progress, the wind gently sways the foliage with a slight rustling sound. Birds sing, and flit to and fro. The sound of multitudinous insects is the one distinct note of the scene. The bay is calm, quiet, and in the distance a catboat is occassionally seen sailing lazily, appearing and disappearing among the islands. A tiny steam launch appears once, about the middle of the act, and is seen no more. A mowing machine is heard at work in the distance off left. It stops, turns, goes on again,

while the voice of the driver is heard guiding his horses, with
"Whoa! Stiddy! Get up! Whoa Bill! (All this must be very
distant.) [54]

These details were starters. A fully-furnished kitchen filled
the stage for Herne's famous second-act turkey dinner. Stage
business included everything from preparing cranberry sauce
and gravy on a real range with a real fire to turkey turning, the
delicious aromas drifting into the audience. A local restaurant
supplied the food, and one actress peeled and mashed eighteen
potatoes at each performance. The *Boston Post* was full of
praise. "The spectator actually lives in the home of Nathaniel
and Martin Berry on the rugged Maine coast."[55] But the *New
York Times* complained that the turkey's "giblets [were]
missing."[56]

Other turkey rumors were spread by gobbling critics. One
story asserted that the turkey repulsed Herne's stage children.
Munsey's printed an article called, "The 'Shore Acres' Turkey
Victims," which asked the Society for the Prevention of Cruelty
to Children to investigate, charging that the girl who played
Mandy "is stuffed with turkey and cranberry sauce till her very
soul revolts at sight of the thanksgiving bird. . . . It is positively
shocking to see this flagrant atrocity perpetuated with
impunity."[57]

The Society for the Prevention of Cruelty to Children eventually investigated Herne's turkey abuses, under the New York
Penal Code, section 292: "A person who employs or causes to be
employed, or who exhibits, uses or has in custody or trains for
the purpose of exhibition, use, or employment, any child apparently or actually under the age of sixteen years—Or who
neglects or refuses to restrain such a child from such training
or from engaging or acting either in peddling, singing, or playing upon a musical instrument or *in a theatrical exhibition*—is
guilty of a misdemeanor."[58]

This section of the New York ordinance meant that any
theatre could be fined for employing child actors. Herne's company at Daly's, "where the moral atmosphere of play and playhouse was unimpeachable,"[59] received a dispensation, which
pleased all, especially the cast children, who loved turkey and

always wanted more. They'd cling to Florence Enneking's skirt (J. J. Enneking's oldest daughter), pleading: "O Perley, just a wing or a little weeny, teeny bit of breast. Can't I have a leg? Just one little, little leg?"[60] The food that *Shore Acres'* children didn't devour, the stagehands did.

Incidentally, Herne's stage children received applause, as always, from reviewers. The *Boston Budget* wrote, "A word of high praise should be given the children, especially little Florence Lynott, who, though she spoke not a word, did more acting than five-sixths of her older associates."[61] The Boston *Evening Transcript* concluded its review with, "The stage management was excellent, the settings fit and beautiful and the swarm of pretty babies would immortalize the play all by themselves."[62]

Shore Acres offered something for all, including those who enjoyed controversial issues. It offered a turkey dinner, Darwinistic overtones, and a radical silent ending. It also offered this realistic lighthouse sequence:

After Sam and Helen flee on the Liddy Ann, with Uncle Nat's help, a fierce storm arises, and the tower's light fails, increasing the danger of a crash on the breakers. The enraged Martin tries to stop Uncle Nat from relighting the beacon. A frenzied fight follows between brothers. Uncle Nat finally flings Martin across the room with a burst of superhuman energy. He then grabs a lantern and painfully climbs the tower stairs, falling as the curtain falls.

The next scene is an exterior of Berry Lighthouse. The ship's gun echoes as the boat tosses helplessly against the splashing waves. The storm intensifies. Herne's directions read: "*Then a tiny light appears in the lowest window of the lighthouse. For a second it wavers, then slowly it rises from window to window, as* Uncle Nat *climbs the stairs to the tower. In another moment the light in the tower blazes forth, showing the 'Liddy Ann' her course.*"[63]

The *Boston Daily Globe* said the lighthouse scenes were "borrowed from the workshop of the melodramatist. It may be suspected that they were introduced as a concession to the box office. The play would be more artistic if the temptation to indulge the taste for sensation had been resisted, but it would perhaps have appealed to a smaller clientage."[64] Herne's great admirer, William Archer, agreed. "Thus the late James A. Herne inserted into a charming idyllic picture of rural life, entitled *Shore Acres*, a melodramatic scene in a lighthouse, which was hopelessly out of key with the rest of the play."[65]

Benjamin Orange Flower, however, attached a more symbolic meaning to the lighthouse. "The scene in the lighthouse is as true as any which precede or follow it. It pictures a supreme and terrible moment in life, and we catch a vivid glimpse of the incarnate god grappling with the aroused savagery of the animal —unselfish love battling with a nature rendered insanely blind through passion—*a scene which typifies the struggle of the ages*. The student of present-day events sees in it a miniature representation of the conflict now raging, upon whose issue hangs the civilization of the morrow. That no such idea as this entered the brain of the dramatist, is highly probable; for a genius continually reflects colossal thought upon his canvas, and deals with types without knowing the deeper significance of his own creation."[66]

Modern behavioral scientists would probably applaud Flower's implied reference to the subconscious. Herne needed an audience, even when he ingeniously criticized its most cherished values, which he considered outmoded, like most theatre conventions.

19 an unofficial patriot

ELAXING IN HIS Fifth Avenue Theatre dressing room, James A. Herne fanned himself with Uncle Nat Berry's straw hat as a *Dramatic Mirror* reporter entered. A chat followed. "I have just finished my new play, and it is being considered by the new syndicate of managers," Herne said. "The locale of the play is Virginia, quite a departure for me, as every play that I have hitherto written has had its scene of action in New England. I shan't be satisfied with it, however, till I have spent eight or ten months in Virginia. At present I feel that the play lacks local color and atmosphere. The story is all right, and so is the dialogue. But I want to be in perfect sympathy with my characters, and the only way to gain that is to go down to Virginia and absorb some of its rural life."[1]

Herne never reached Virginia because *Shore Acres* toured until December, 1898, when it finally closed at the Boston Theatre.[2] His new play, *The Reverend Griffith Davenport* (based on Helen M. Gardener's best-selling Civil War novel, *An Unofficial Patriot*), incubated until early 1899. (The play's name was later shortened to *Griffith Davenport*.)

Henry C. Miner, who had staged *Shore Acres,* was interested in producing the new play, but he withdrew, even though Herne had already contracted for models of the stage sets. Miner thought the Civil War was a dead issue. Besides, Herne's play dealt with an individual's crisis rather than external events as in Bronson Howard's *Shenandoah* or William Gillette's *Held by the Enemy* and *Secret Service.* This meant that Herne's play had more talk and less action.

During this time, the Hernes had attended Richard Mansfield's production of *Cyrano de Bergerac* at the Garden Theatre. A. M. Palmer, whose crumpled career had forced him to take a position as Mansfield's business manager, said: "We would not have dared to risk doing a play like this a few years ago. There would have been no audience for it. We owe a great deal to you, Mr. Herne."[3] But Herne, the man who had revolutionized American drama, couldn't find a producer for *Griffith Davenport*.

Evans and Mann finally agreed that autumn to stage *The Reverend Griffith Davenport* at the Herald Square Theatre, but at Herne's expense. It was the old routine but he accepted their terms, since it was a lot easier than peddling the work for years and then settling for a mediocre production. The Boston profits from *Shore Acres* helped influence his decision.

Herne wrote two versions of this military drama, the first at Sayville on Great South Bay in 1894, the second four years later at Herne Oaks, his sprawling neo-classical retreat on Long Island's Peconic Bay. The play was K.C.'s idea. Helen M. Gardener was one of her closest friends. After reading *An Unofficial Patriot*, K.C. told Herne, "There's a great play in it, Jim, and Helen wants you to dramatize it."[4] He listened.

But about Herne Oaks. Miner wrote Herne in June 1895: "Hoping that you and Mrs. H—and the family are enjoying good health, that you are eating your own butter, drinking your own milk, driving your own horses, raising your own poultry and raising H—in general."[5] Herne wanted to become a part-time gentleman farmer at their summer home, Herne Oaks, purchasing a Jersey cow, poultry, and horses from Miner, who also farmed on the side. The idea was programmed by K.C. who also named Herne Oaks. "Mamma built the place," Herne told friends, "and I and the girls came down to board with her."[6]

When K.C. had first visited Peconic Bay, she found thirty acres of woodland between Southampton and Sag Harbor. She liked the land and bought it, following Herne's advice: "Have plenty of money with you in small bills, and when you find a place you like, spread them on the table before the owner when you start negotiations. These country people never have much cash, and they can't resist the sight of it."[7]

Construction dragged at Herne Oaks. When Herne arrived

in May, the house stood unfinished. Lumber, shingles, paint pots, and tar paper littered the grounds as workers drained the swamp and chopped trees. The Hernes' first mid-day dinner was beneath trees surrounded with groceries and furniture crates. It was very romantic and also very depressing.

There were three separate houses at Herne Oaks. All charmed visitors with their Queen Anne gables, Greek columns, and sprawling verandas. The grounds included stables, croquet lawns, and a dock for Herne's small yacht, *The Gretchen*. Inside, portraits of William Dean Howells, John J. Enneking, Hamlin Garland, and Henry George dignified the hall, along with seamen canvasses on the bookcases. Herne wrote in the second floor "tower-room" (a semi-circular workshop with six windows overlooking the woods and bay.)

Here fond memories were replayed each summer: K.C. interpreting the works of Shakespeare, Sheridan, and Sudermann for Julie and Chrystal in her "Grove of the Muses," banquet meals, and leisure evenings on the veranda. Herne's schedule, however, regimented all except K.C., who demanded a sense of freedom. Herne's schedule in brief:

6:30 a.m. Bicycle ride.
8:00 a.m. Breakfast.
9:00 a.m. Writing, Correspondence, until 1:00 p.m.
1:00 p.m. Dinner.
2:00 p.m. Nap.
3:00 p.m. Tennis.
4:00 p.m. Rowing and swimming.
6:00 p.m. Supper.
7:00 p.m. Reading, playing cards, etc.
9:00 p.m. Bed.[8]

At Herne Oaks, too, John Temple Herne (named after Herne's brother and mother) was born on October 11, 1894. Herne excitedly wrote Garland about his newborn son: "This past summer has been one of great joy to us. We lived every moment of it, and now comes another soul to bless the memory of it."[9]

Herne (nearing sixty) treated the baby John royally. The first Christmas, K.C. recalled, he "brought home the most remarkable collection of presents that, I verily believe, were ever offered to a child but a few weeks old. There were sleds, skates, boxing-gloves, and every other thing that a lusty eighteen year-old boy could wish for, including, I think, a razor. Mr. Herne denies the razor, however."[10]

Herne nicknamed John "Commodore," and they spent long summer hours together, sometimes sailing on *The Gretchen* along Long Island's coast. Herne loved the sea and now had a son to share his mystic awe. (Later, as an adult, John became an officer in the United States Navy. His wife, Carolyn Thomson, was a singer who played in *Maytime* with John Charles Thomas and *The Vagabond King* and then pursued a career on the road.)

The Hernes' first summer at Herne Oaks, however, nearly ended disastrously when Herne rented a small sloop and went sailing with Julie, Dorothy, Chrystal, and Uncle Rodolph. As Chrystal recalled: "When we were out, far from land, a sudden black squall engulfed us. The old oysterman (the boat's skipper) had tied his mainsail and in his panic, could not release it. He screamed for a knife; Uncle Rodolph, who took one out of his pocket, promptly threw it overboard in his excitement. The little sloop capsized, her mainsail flat on the water, the heavy seas churning over her. It was a real shipwreck, and not a boat in sight. Above the roar of the wind, and the water and our voices crying out, my father's rose, calm and steady. I was clinging to the gunwale, my chilled fingers gradually losing their hold. 'I'm going, I can't hold on,' I cried. My father grabbed and held me, just as Dorothy was swept under the weight of the submerged sail. With superhuman strength, never letting go of me, he, in some miraculous way, pulled her to safety. Never for an instant did he lose his presence of mind, his assured and controlled calm. By the very timbre of his voice he averted panic."[11]

Herne died in 1901, and in 1909 a blaze destroyed Herne Oaks, including Herne's valued papers, souvenirs, and the manuscripts of *Margaret Fleming* and *The Reverend Griffith Davenport*. (Act IV of *Griffith Davenport* later materialized in William Archer's papers and was given to Brander Matthews who allowed Arthur Hobson Quinn to publish it in *America's Lost Plays*.) The fire started sometime in mid-afternoon on December 11, while K.C. and John prepared to spend the Christmas holidays with Chrystal and Dorothy in New York (Julie was touring in Canada). K.C. smelled smoke and rushed downstairs. She was too late. The fire raged uncontrollably. She and John used a garden hose and some buckets, but within an hour only ashes remained. Flames had spread to nearby trees, nearly causing a forest fire.

Herne Oaks suffered $65,000 damage, and there wasn't enough insurance to cover the loss. "Outside of my clothes and those of my sister Dorothy, which are kept in our apartment at 57 West Fifth Street," Chrystal wrote at the time, "we have nothing in the world."[12]

K.C. first believed a defective furnace rod caused the blaze. But as the basement door was found open, suspicion was directed toward a recently fired coachman who had threatened, "I'm never discharged from any place but what I leave my mark." For lack of evidence, however, charges were not pressed. (The Hernes had discharged another domestic who hid a butcher knife under her bed, forcing them to call the police.)

In recalling the fire, Chrystal said that "we all felt so badly over the fire that we didn't realize what had happened until it was too late. Mother said that she had several things in her hands to save, and when she looked at them, she wondered why she was carrying them, then unconsciously dropped them."[13]

It was at Herne Oaks that Herne completed the second version of *Griffith Davenport*. The play portrayed a former Virginia Methodist circuit rider and slaveholder who rejects the Southern system and frees his slaves. He also votes for Abraham Lincoln, an act his neighbors resent. When questioned, he replies: "Ah haven't considered personal interests in this mattah at all—mah own no' anybody's else. Ah tell you, Colonel, the day when personal interest comes to be used to place a man in the White Ho'se is going to be a vehy serious one fo' ouah republic." He later adds: "Ah voted fo' Mistah Lincoln, gentlemen, but ah love mah native state, and ah will not lift mah voice against heh."[14] When neighbors threaten to fire the mansion, the Davenports move to Washington, D.C.

When the Civil War erupts, Davenport's two sons choose opposite camps, a split "symbolic of the whole country,"[15] as

Katharine says in Act III. Then President Lincoln asks Davenport to guide Northern forces through the Shenandoah Valley, an offensive planned to shorten the war, avoiding further bloodshed. A difficult decision confronts Davenport, who seizes the moral issue involved: should human worth be sacrificed for politics? His answer is rational, not stemming from a naive trust in the virtues of Christian duty but motivated by fidelity to truth. He agrees to be a guide.

Herne textured Davenport's character, creating "an entirely new figure in the drama" as the *New York Times* reviewer later noted, adding that "no play dealing with the romance of the war has hitherto presented so elaborate and complex a study of traits and moods, sentiment and prejudice as are compounded in the character of Griffith Davenport."[16] The majority of critics, even the traditionalists who rejected the play's structure, felt likewise.

Davenport exemplified the ancient Greek concept, "character is destiny," defending honor above personal interest and ignoring fearful consequences. He loves the South but frees his slaves. He votes for Lincoln but supports Virginia. When the Governor of Indiana offers him a Professor of Theology post at Asbury Institute, he refuses because slaves are forbidden in the state. Even while guiding Union soldiers into Southern territory, his sense of duty compels him to serve with a colonel's commission gratis. Such convictions, of course, nearly destory him.

Civil War plays flourished on American stages during the nineteenth century's last two decades. Among them were Dion Boucicault's *Belle Lamar* (1882), David Belasco's *May Blossom* (1884) and *The Heart of Maryland* (1895), Bronson Howard's *Shenandoah* (1888), William Gillette's *Held by the Enemy* (1886) and *Secret Service* (1895), Clyde Fitch's *Barbara Frietchie* (1899)—and Herne's *Griffith Davenport* (1899).

"With one exception, *The Reverend Griffith Davenport*, the plays are almost devoid of any serious content,"[17] wrote Herbert Bergman. The usual emphasis was on romantic melodrama sprinkled with comic relief, cascading action, stock types, and plenty of poetic justice, everything the "unthinking multitudes" rushed to see on stage.

Griffith Davenport, however, provided more than pablum

for the "unthinking multitudes." It provided a serious theme, the absurdity of war, especially a war pitting state against state, neighbor against neighbor, and brother against brother. When Beverly and Roy divide on the sectional issue, they clash:

> "Roy, if this thing ever comes to a war between the North and the South, which side are you going to fight on?"
> "On my side," replies Roy, laughing.
> Beverly looks at him thoughtfully. "Roy, if I ever met you in a battle, I believe I'd kill you quicker than I would a real Yankee."
> Roy takes a deep breath, and then, "I'm sorry, Bev," he says, "but I'm afraid I'll have to give you the chance!"[18]

This was dialogue far removed from conventional heroic cliches and feminine squeals of devotion. In *Belle Lamar,* when the heroine chooses death, she emotes: "This willful, proud, but living heart has never wandered from you as I have done: never had any cause but one—its faithful love. Let me stay and die—if die you must—by your side." Likewise, Belasco's *May Blossom* declares: "War is not for women—we may feel—reason—and sacrifice like soldiers in our patriotism—but a glimpse of a loved one in peril—and we women again—straight our hand goes out to save, no matter what the consequences." Bronson Howard wrote in *Shenandoah*: "Every woman's heart, the world over, belongs not to any country or any flag, but to her husband—and her lover. Pray for the man you love, sister—It would be treason not to."[19]

In *Griffith Davenport* Katharine also loves her husband, but on a higher plane than poetic phrases and tears. She supports slavery but accepts Davenport's decision to free their slaves. She publicly defends his vote for Lincoln and moves to Washington, D.C., a city whose culture seems crude compared to Virginia's aristocratic traditions. But when he accepts Lincoln's charge to lead Northern troops through the Shenandoah Valley, she cries: "Griffith, this is a *brutal* war. You have said so yourself a hundred times. It isn't a war against oppression; it hasn't the righteousness of 1776 to sanctify it. It's a *factional fight*—it's a *political war!* Patriotism! Think of our two brave boys with guns in their hands, ready to murder each other in the name of patriotism, and now you want to kill me (*Weeps*) under the same delusion."[20] Katharine returns to Virginia, where she opens a field hospital in their former mansion, while Davenport becomes "an unofficial patriot" who is captured by his own son Beverly and is sent to Libby Prison.

Griffith Davenport's final scene, however, received jaundiced scowls from the serious critics. Davenport and Katharine are reconciled on the steps of their former home, Griffith singing a verse from "Jeanette and Jeannot," one of Herne's favorite songs:

Oh, if I were King of France,
Or still better Pope of Rome,
I'd have no fighting men abroad,
Or weeping maids at home.
All the world should be at peace,
And if men must show their might,
I'd have those who make the quarrels be
The only ones to fight;
I'd have those who make the quarrels be
The only ones to fight!"[21]

This wasn't the original ending of *Griffith Davenport*. Herne softened the brutal conclusion in which a deranged girl tries to shoot Griffith. Hateful cries from the crowd pierce the night air, and the stage is silent as the curtain falls. The romanticized new ending was a forced concession, one the critics recognized.

Like Herne's other dramas, *Griffith Davenport* mirrored his truthful treatment credo. K.C. searched antique shops, finding Chippendale and Sheraton pieces for the Georgian study in Acts II and III. These later filled the Herne Oaks dining room just as the soft rose velour stage curtains in *Margaret Fleming* also became Herne furnishings. The Act IV Washington house had "real glass in the windowpanes." Throughout the act "rain and sleet beat on the panes at intervals," and "there is heard at intervals drum corps, bands, and the noise and movement of marching men—very distant—to suggest war times in Washington in '62."[22] K.C. also supervised the authentic period costumes, patterned from *Godey's Ladies Book,* and helped direct the ensemble scenes. (Exhausted, she caught the grippe and couldn't attend opening rehearsals.) Other Herne details included light on the hillside, real dust, and even a parrot.

Garland, who attended a rehearsal of *Griffith Davenport*, said he "was less interested in this play than in any of [Herne's] others, mainly for the reason that it was based on a book by another writer." The rehearsal fatigued Garland who always promoted "up front" and on paper. The blocking, stage business, and endless repetition of lines bored him. "I marveled at his patience and endurance and in the end came away limp as a rag. My brain echoes for hours with his hammering drill. For me it was all a waste of time."[23] When Garland later attended the play in New York with Israel Zangwill and the Guggenheims, he wrote in his diary, "It cannot succeed and I feel sorry for the man."[24]

They were prophetic words.

Griffith Davenport opened at the Lafayette Square Theatre in Washington, D.C., on January 16, 1899. Attending were many senators and representatives as well as the Army Quartermaster General and the Secretary of the Navy, who sent Herne a congratulatory note. The *Washington Post* reported: "The actor-author made an impressive figure as the patriot preacher, and his Southern accent sounds as natural from his life as did his 'down-east' drawl. Mrs. Herne, as the representative of the suffering womanhood of that day and generation, achieved a splendid piece of characterization, while their two daughters, Julia and Chrystal, were entirely acceptable in quaint ingenue roles."[25] Both girls at the time were still teenagers.

Following a short run in Washington, D.C., *Griffith Davenport* opened at the Herald Square Theatre in New York on January 31, 1899, where it played twenty performances.[26]

William Dean Howells called *Griffith Davenport* "the only new thing of importance,"[27] elevating it above *Cyrano de Bergerac* and *Trelawny of the Wells*. But he caught its failing: the chattel slavery issue lacked immediacy, as did the Civil War. Older people wanted to forget while younger people didn't remember. Only romanticized history remained. K.C. wanted a scene for Emma in Act III because the play lacked youth appeal. Herne finally wrote in the scene shortly before rehearsals in 1898.

Perhaps the Lincoln issue also damaged the play. Herne originally had included President Lincoln as a character, but K.C. persuaded him to substitute Governor Morton, reasoning that Lincoln's presence would overshadow Griffith Davenport. (Lincoln's interview with Griffith was a highlight of the novel.) Although Herne agreed, Lincoln's spirit still pervades the play. All acts relate to his career and two include his name: Act II, "The Nomination of Abraham Lincoln," and Act III, "The Election of Abraham Lincoln." Characters also discuss Lincoln throughout the play. Such subtle devices strengthened Lincoln through suggestion, a technique Herne often used. William Archer noted, "In James Herne's sadly underrated play, *Griffith Davenport,* we were always conscious of "Mr. Lincoln" in the background; and the act in which Governor Morton of Indiana brought the President's instructions to Davenport might fairly be called an obligatory scene, inasmuch as it gave us the requisite sense of personal nearness to the master-spirit, without involving any risk of belittlement through imperfections of representation."[28]

Arthur Hobson Quinn offered another possible reason for the play's failure. "Perhaps the failure of that play to win popular success may have been due to a subconscious feeling that a man should remain true to his own people, as the universal hero worship of Robert E. Lee has indicated."[29]

Herne's realism disturbed John Corbin, who admitted, "If any one were to say to [Herne] that the piece lacks dramatic unity, dramatic situations and development, and dramatic climaxes, he would doubtless answer that he knew it well enough, and had never tried for any of these things."[30] Still Corbin wouldn't accept *Griffith Davenport* on its own terms, clinging to traditional guidelines. Howells said, "But it is no new thing in the history of literature: whatever is established is sacred with those who do not think." He added, "The misfortune rather than the fault of our individual critic is that he is the heir of the false theory and bad manners of the English school."[31] Corbin refused to accept Herne's truthful premise. "The value of the world of paint and footlights lies in the fact that it is not real, and that the people who move in it cannot by any possibility be regarded as real."[32]

Yet Corbin admired Herne's method, which intrigued him.

"Mr. Herne appears never to have an emotion of the kind that speaks. Mrs. Herne's utterance is less hampered, and therefore more appealing, though still far from being positively expressive." But he called Herne's technique "marvellous," the first-act movement "subtle magic," and the features "transparent to his soul." Corbin concluded, "In its best moments his art has a richness of humor and a truth of feeling impossible except to the highest order of creative power."[33]

It was a high compliment from a severe critic.

A reviewer in *Players Weekly* also couldn't "see what many of the passages were about, if indeed they were about anything." He also complained, "To object that it lacked climaxes would be to confess an appreciation of the author's attention, but one is forced to admit that the play was monotonous to a degree."[34]

Apparently the reviewer wanted action-packed claptrap that Howells called literary "fungus-growth" and "the shoreless lakes of ditchwater."[35] Herne offered movement, more than enough to satisfy the intelligent theatre-goer. Take the attempted house-burning scene in Act III when Davenport, who has freed his slaves, is confronted by his slaveowning neighbors:

> *Bradley.* Will yo' fight with heh if she secedes?
> *Griffith.* No—no' will ah fight against heh.
> *Nelson.* Theah is no neutral ground now. If yo' awe not with us, yo' awe against us.
> *Bradley.* Then, Squiah, will yo' leave Virginia?
> *Griffith.* (*With calm determination*) No.
> *Bradley.* (*With quiet, dignified determination*) Yo' *must.*
> *Griffith.* (*Determined*) Nevah! Ah'll not stir one step until ah get good and ready. All the secessionists this side of hell awe not going to drive me.
> *Nelson.* (*Livid with rage*) Set fiah to the ho'se! We'll buhn the damn Abolition nest ovah his haid! (*The cry is taken up*)
> *All the Horsemen.* Yes—Set fiah to the ho'se. (*A general movement. The Negroes wail and wring their hands.*)
> *Roy.* (*At the top of his voice, drawing a revolver.* Lengthy seconds him with his rifle) Ah'll shoot the fi'st man—
> *Beverly.* (*Springing between the crowd and* Roy, *knocks the pistol from* Roy's *hand and fairly shrieks.*) Stop! Gentlemen! This is mah mothah's home! (*They stop out of respect for the woman; take off hats*)
> *Katharine.* (*With great dignity*) Yo' need not bu'n the ho'se, gentlemen—we will go.[36]

Herne's mob-scene sources remain vague. In *An Unofficial Patriot*, Beverly, editor of an Abolitionist newspaper, flees when his plant is burned. But Herne also read an earlier novel, Judge Tourgee's *A Fool's Errand*, which had such a scene. His choice probably was a composite of both mingled with a creative imagination. (Herne also had read Stephen Crane's *The Red Badge of Courage* before completing *Griffith Davenport*.)

There is more action in *Griffith Davenport*, such as the runaway slave sequence in Act II. Sampson, one of Nelson's slaves, breaks his chains and storms into Davenport's Georgian home, a pruning knife clutched in his hands. When Nelson enters, the slave cries: "Ef you come neah me I'll cut mah throat."

Davenport then offers. "I'll buy him from you, Nelson!"

But Nelson declines. "I won't sell him!"

As Nelson lunges for Sampson, the slave plunges a knife into his throat, falling at their feet. "There goes fifteen hundred dollars!" growls Nelson, who yells at Davenport, "This is what your damn anti-slavery theories have come to!"[37] Melodramatic? *The Literary World* called it "a ghastly and deeply moving situation."[38]

Herne apparently constructed this harrowing scene from two sources: a brief incident in Helen Gardener's novel and a story actor-friend F. F. MacKay had told him. Once while playing in Memphis, Tennessee, MacKay saw some whites seize an escaped slave. The slave then slit his throat and fell at MacKay's feet. It was an experience he long remembered.

Herne treated the slavery issue objectively in *Griffith Davenport*, without the usual rhetoric of latter-day abolitionists. "Its exposition of the slavery question is the clearest, frankest that has been written, giving fair, open treatment to both sides of the case, utterly without prejudice"[39] commended the *Dramatic Mirror*.

Earlier Civil War dramas either ignored the black slaves or painted them as Uncle Toms. Herne's blacks looked real, even fooling some critics. (Many recalled Herne's startling performance in *The New South*.) When Davenport releases his slaves, they're confused. "You're free—you don't belong to us any more," says Katharine. But they stand dumbfounded. Earlier they had abused Free Jim's boy, who lives with his father in a

shack 'thout no fam'ly nor nothin." Suddenly, they're "free nig-
gahs!" who "not belong to nobody!"[40] Katharine tells Davenport, "I'm afraid it's all a failure, Griffith." He replies: "I fear
it is."[41]

Griffith Davenport became another celebrated Herne failure
like *Margaret Fleming,* only more expensive. The Hernes spent
$9,000 producing it, a terrific investment in 1899.[42] Lewis S.
Strang called it "not only the strongest and most artistic drama
written by an American playwright during the past decade, but
I would even go a step further, and declare that up to the last act
it is the greatest American play ever written."[43] James O. G.
Duffy regarded it as "the best American play that ever was
written."[44] Norman Hapgood also praised it. "The fourth act is
wholly made up of one scene, unsurpassed, as far as my experience goes, for high dramatic elements, in any American drama."[45]

Herne's greatest compliments, however, came from William
Archer, who saw *Griffith Davenport* with Brander Matthews at
the Harlem Opera House, where it was playing to "half-empty
benches."[46] Archer raved about the work, calling it "the cornerstone of a national drama."[47] "Never did I see a play better
acted than 'Griffith Davenport,'" he said. "The individual actors, with the exception of Mrs. Herne, were not specially distinguished; but Mr. Herne has a genius for instructing his company, which enabled them, in this case, to achieve the perfection
of naturalness. 'Griffith Davenport' is a piece of really national
dramatic literature."[48] Archer added: "The third act, which
passed in a sitting room in Washington, was placed on the stage
with a perfection that would have done credit to the Comédie
Française, and acted with a quiet naturalness from which the
Comédie Française might have learnt a lesson. I felt throughout
that here I was in the presence of what I had come to seek, and
had not found elsewhere—original American art. And America,
to its indelible discredit, failed to recognize it."[49]

The cast of *Griffith Davenport* included K.C. as Katharine,
Julie as Emma West, and Chrystal as Sue Hardy. Sidney Booth
(son of Junius Brutus Booth and nephew of Edwin Booth) was
cast as Beverly and Bert Young as his brother Roy. Herne also
hired Thomas Hunter, who had played Joe Fletcher in *Margaret
Fleming,* as Major Hardy and Robert Fischer, *Shore Acres'* Mar-

tin Berry, as Lengthy Patterson, Griffith's mountaineer friend. And little Tommy Ince, who played the boy in *Shore Acres*, was the Southern deserter, Bill Harper, whom the Northern soldiers freed because of his ill mother. Tommy Ince later became one of Hollywood's most famous film directors.

Archer touched the nerve center of Herne's problem when he called *Griffith Davenport* "dramatic literature," something usually shunned on American stages. Herne considered plays with complex plots, "dead as a doornail"[50] and tried to simplify structure, a decision that slammed stagedoors everywhere. His basic rules were suggested by K.C.: A drama should be true to life, artistic, and forceful. Artistic freedom for self-expression lay within this aesthetic framework.

The Literary World commented on Herne's radical structure in *Griffith Davenport*. "It reveals the phenomenon of an actor who, in spite of many years of service behind the footlights, has worked away from the conventions of the theater to the simple truth of realistic literature. So indifferent to stage conventions has Mr. Herne become, that he has in several instances apparently avoided making his situations strong, and has allowed them to talk themselves out."[51]

Herne admitted this technique, telling one *Dramatic Mirror* reporter: "In my new play I have a little love scene between a young boy and girl. He tells her the story of his parent's courtship as he learned it from his mother. Then he says, 'Let's follow suit.' But the girl says 'Not now. Some time when we're older you can come and talk to me that way. But not now.' And there it ends. Through the rest of the play they figure in the story, but never come together again. That is what I mean by letting a play develop itself. Only in that way is a logical, natural story attained."[52]

He also told the *Boston Journal*:

"Some people sweepingly allege that my plays leave little or nothing for the imagination. As 'Shore Acres' is the one that is likely soon to be best known in this part of the world, allow me to call your attention to instances where imagination is not superseded by realism. Let us take, for instance, the character of Joel Gates, of which Mr. Wilson has made so much by his true interpretation of the little part and by his remarkable makeup. Do you recall the few words which

I utter when I open to the audience a whole volume of sorrow and unhappiness in one brief sentence?

"Joel Gates in the first act comes in, accompanied by
his shy little daughter, and, referring to the child, I remark:

" 'She's growin' isn't she? She's growin' just like a
weed. My, my, my! How like her mother she do look!'

"Joel—'Yep; gets to look more and more like her every
day in the week.'

"Nathan-l—'I' spose you never heard nuthin' of her
since have ye?'

"Joel—'No, nuthin.'

"Now, Joel is a grass widower. His wife ran away with
another man; but nothing appears in the dialogue concerning her except the above. Does not that leave something
for the imagination?"[53]

Audiences, of course, failed to appreciate Herne's radical departure from simple types with simple motivations and simple
values. As Richard Moody says: "... it was not until *The Reverend Griffith Davenport*, by James A. Herne, was produced on
January 16, 1899, that a Civil War play received an almost completely realistic treatment. The problem of slavery had hardly
been mentioned in previous Civil War dramas, whereas in
Herne's play it was the starting point."[54] Audiences still
wanted what Howells called "a great, whirling splendor of peril
and achievement, a wild scene of heroic adventure and of emotional ground and lofty tumbling, with a stage 'picture' at the
fall of the curtain, and all the good characters in a row, their left
hands pressed upon their hearts, and kissing their right hands
to the audience, in the good old way that has always charmed and
always will charm."[55]

Herne's Herald Square Theatre contract for *Griffith Davenport* included a four-week guarantee, but his audience kept
shrinking. A snowstorm forced the theatre's closing one night.
Then came a bitter cold spell, and people stayed at home. One of
Herne's few consolations during the play's slimly-attended run
was a guest of honor supper given by the American Dramatists'
Club at the Manhattan Hotel. Included among the forty guests
were Bronson Howard, William Faversham, and Wilton Lackaye,
who cheered Herne with their tributes.

Griffith Davenport closed on February 25, 1899, a four-week
failure for Herne's favorite work, with its four sets, forty-two

characters, and radical structure. "I wouldn't mind, he said, "if they came to see my play and said it was bad. But they won't come."[56]

Herne wondered: Where were the thousands who flocked to see *Shore Acres?* A fraction of them could have saved this historically-important play. But its only supporters were the handful of faithful who were interested in promoting the literary potential of American theatre. Maybe he should have stayed with *Shore Acres* instead of exploring radical ideas again. When Joseph Jefferson heard about Herne's decision to leave *Shore Acres* for *Griffith Davenport,* he asked, "He's got a success—why doesn't he stick to it?"[57]

After *Griffith Davenport* closed, Herne managed to secure an eleven-week road tour from Erlanger, including two weeks each in Philadelphia and Boston at first-rate houses. This was miraculous considering Herne's brutal attacks on the syndicate, but Erlanger respected America's Ibsen.

When *Griffith Davenport* played the Boston Theatre, *The Arena*'s Mario Tiempo interviewed Herne. Tiempo realized the work wasn't "calculated to catch the ears of the groundlings at once," but he predicted, "It will hold the boards long after most of the 'war dramas,' that now make meretricious appeal to the morbid militarism of the moment, are forgotten."[58]

Although Herne had removed Davenport's gray wig, he still wore the dust-covered long clerical black coat. When Tiempo asked for a comparison between *Shore Acres* and *Griffith Davenport*, Herne replied in detail:

> From the artistic point of view, 'Griffith Davenport' is a distinct advance over 'Shore Acres.' It is complex where 'Shore Acres' is simple, picturing human conditions rather than human nature. Of course, at bottom it is human nature that is mirrored in both plays. What I mean is, that in 'Griffith Davenport' the workings of this wonderful human nature are displayed as modified by certain distinct and peculiar social conditions, of intense interest, perhaps, yet requiring to be understood before the resulting emotions, ideals, struggles, sacrifices, and conquests are appreciated and enjoyed. The social conditions pictured in 'Shore Acres,' while, of course, having sufficient local color to give them concrete verity, closely resemble the conditions with which we are all fairly familiar from actual personal contact in

our own day. In 'Griffith Davenport,' on the contrary, the conditions are peculiar to a time and place now unfamiliar, and these in themselves so largely affect the psychological development of the characters, that a clear grasp of them is essential. This, I fear, is against the present popularity of the play. The average theatregoer comes to a play to be entertained, and is too weary to cooperate in the process. He refuses to think. Hasn't he paid for his seat at the box-office, and so paid other people to think for him? He is like the Shah of Persia who, when invited at the court ball in London to dance, replied that he was rich enough to hire girls to dance for him. People who really want to enjoy such a play as 'Griffith Davenport' must bring their brains as well as their pocketbooks to the theatre. So, while I have been more than gratified by the congratulations that have poured in on me from genuine critics and lovers of the drama, I hardly look for a popular success for the play in the present state of the public taste in things theatrical."[59]

Griffith Davenport finally closed in Stamford, Connecticut, on May 13, 1899, at the Grand Opera House. Its final review was another affirmation of Archer's indictment that "America, to its indelible discredit, failed to recognize it." The *Daily Advocate*'s critic expressed surprise at Stamford's indifference. "For a dramatic production of such merit and so eminent an actor as James A. Herne in the cast the house was a very light one."[60]

20 a descendant
of aaron

ISRAEL ZANGWILL SAW *Griffith Davenport*
while adapting his novel, *Children of the Ghetto,*
for the Broadway stage. He was impressed and
chose Herne as director of his play. George C. Tyler, producer for
Liebler & Company, wanted to please Zangwill and offered
Herne $500 a week, an exorbitant fee. But Tyler considered
Herne "the best director alive," later adding that "anything written by and produced by and acted in by James A. Herne was the
best of good judgment."[1]

Without connections Tyler had crashed Broadway's impossible barrier and made millions. A former tramp-printer and advance agent for James O'Neill's *The Count of Monte Cristo,* he
persuaded a lithographer named Liebler to sink his last $3,000
in *The Royal Box* starring Charles Coghlan. Then the brassy Tyler—with only six dollars in assets—hired Viola Allen to star in
Hall Caine's best-seller, *The Christian,* which was another
Charles Frohman reject. The rest is history, including the
$500,000 profit. Millions more poured into Tyler's pockets with
later successes like Booth Tarkington and Harry Leon Wilson's
The Man from Home, E. M. Boyle's *The Squaw Man,* and *Mrs.
Wiggs of the Cabbage Patch* by Mrs. Rice and Mrs. Flexner.
Tyler also showcased Synge's *The Playboy of the Western World*
with the Irish Players and George Arliss' starring vehicle *Disraeli.*

Tyler's offer enticed Herne, who respected Zangwill, a
former London teacher turned author who first wrote short
stories, then gained fame and fortune as a novelist and playwright. A Zionist leader, Zangwill had founded the International

Jewish Territorial Organization. Garland called him "a gentle, weary, wise and deep-thinking Jew. Quite simple, genuine and profound. . . . A queer, stumbling, rapt, swift-thoughted creature with immense powers of absorption."[2]

Herne, who invited Zangwill to Herne Oaks, became his friend while tightening the script and discussing interpretative problems. (Herne's contribution to *Children of the Ghetto* is conjectural.) The Southampton dunes and windmills intrigued Zangwill, along with its fresh air. He enjoyed croquet, fencing, tennis, and Herne's children, especially Chrystal, who became Allegra in Zangwill's novel, *The Mantle of Elijah*, part of which Zangwill wrote at Herne Oaks.

August rehearsals at the Herald Square Theatre forced Herne and Zangwill to brave the New York summer. Herne always hated the sweltering summer heat, preferring the cool seashore breezes of New England. (During the 1890's, air conditioners didn't exist, one reason why the Broadway theatres closed for the summer.)

Herne's and Zangwill's artistic views harmonized. Whenever Herne suggested a revision or cut, Zangwill asked: "Is it for the good of the play? . . . I will consent to any change that is for the good of the play, but I will not take out *one line* for the sake of getting the curtain down at eleven o'clock."[3]

The theatre's technical elements baffled Zangwill, as they did Howells and James. Herne supervised the production, which involved four sets (sitting room, lounging room of People's Club, Reb Shemuel's home, and the ghetto Market), and thirty-six characters. Meanwhile, though suffering from failing health, Herne planned *Sag Harbor*'s opening and a *Hearts of Oak* revival. He even roamed the slums of Washington for Jewish children to capture the *Children of the Ghetto*'s subtle tones. One youth named Asa Yoelson played three performances, earning 75 cents before his cantor father removed him. Asa Yoelson later became Al Jolson.[4]

An old problem pinched Herne's nerves during rehearsals for *Children of the Ghetto*—the "staritis" problem. Tyler grabbed ten overpaid stars, including Blanche Bates, Frank Worthing, and Wilton Lackaye, the famed Svengali of *Trilby*, without consulting Herne. Overspending remained Tyler's major weakness. He admitted being "crazy about big names and famous people and such," recalling about *Children of the Ghetto*: "We were doing things in style at last and damn the expense. Why, if Shakespeare and Mrs. Siddons had still been alive, I'd have cabled them to come over on the next boat and talk over a play I had in mind for them."[5]

Herne was just the opposite. He practiced ensemble acting, opposing the star system because everyone tried to upstage everyone else. He once said the ideal theatre would ban applause until the final curtain. Herne especially disliked "matinee idols," those lithographic creations whom "matinee girls" swarmed and swooned to see on leisure afternoons. Those paper idols whose dream-world dilemmas charmed and chagrined: Chauncey Olcott, James J. Hackett, William Faversham, Henry Miller, Robert Mantell, and the inimitable John Drew, lauded as "the first gentleman of the stage." They all reigned as heart-throbbing myth makers.

Staritis almost ruined *Children of the Ghetto*.

Lackaye, who played the Rabbi Samuel Jacobs (called Reb Shemuel), resented Herne's direction. Rehearsal air rippled with tension because Lackaye "fluffed" lines, then improvised. Herne finally confronted the cast. According to Willard Holcombe:

> Herne called him [Lackaye] to book several times, whereat the actor, who was accustomed to dictate rather than be disciplined, waxed wroth and replied sharply, "The words are synonymous, and one is just as expressive as the other."
>
> "If the author had wanted to use that word he would have so written it," rejoined Herne calmly, but firmly. "It is his right to have his words delivered exactly as he wrote them, for he is held responsible for them by the critics and the public. A generation ago, when we used to change the bill every night, it was permissible to "fake" and paraphrase, since no memory could hold all the lines exactly; but nowadays, when plays are classed as literature, and we devote months of study and rehearsal to them, there is no excuse."
>
> Whereat the actor aforesaid became sulky and whiled away his time 'upstage' by growling sullen asides to the scenery, or whomever was near enough to hear him. The air was electric with foreboding . . . and the company was on the *qui vive*, expecting a clash of authority. Herne ap-

parently paid no attention to the irate player's asides, but at the close of the scene he arose from his seat in the orchestra, and began in that deliberate down East drawl which characterized his Uncle Nat in *Shore Acres*.

"Ladies and gentlemen of the company," said he, "I want to explain my position. I am here on a salary, just as you are, and my sole interest in this play is to give it the best possible production. There is this difference, however; while my interest in the play ends with the first performance, yours does not. You remain, and will be held responsible by the public for your individual and collective performances. Therefore, it is even more to your interest than to mine to get this thing right. And what I tell you to do is right"—this with a shade more of firmness in his voice. "I have spent more years of study and hard work on the stage than any of you, and I know. I have consulted with the author, and am endeavoring to help you interpret his ideas to the public through this play. Whatever comes of it, whether it proves a failure or a success, it deserves our best endeavors."

Then, relapsing into his accustomed drawl, 'Now, I don't want to have trouble with anybody—and what's more, I won't. I have the reputation of being the most even-tempered stage manager in America, and whether it is true or not, I'm not going to lose it now. But I know that I am right, and I am not here to be bulldozed. Call the next act!"

This little speech was like oil on troubled waters. Everybody drew a breath of relief. Even the belligerent actor, calmed by words which embodied the acme of common sense, without a sign of irritation or personal animus, came down to make his peace with the suave old stage manager, and everything went smoothly after that. This is only one example of Herne's quiet mastery over the most nervous and emotional of artists.[6]

Actors seldom ruffled Herne, who rarely swore. "He is the only stage director that I have ever seen at work who never swore at rehearsals,"[7] remarked Israel Zangwill, and K.C. could recall only one swearing incident during a rehearsal of *Hearts of Oak*.

Children of the Ghetto opened at the National Theatre in Washington, D.C., on September 18, 1899. Both audience and critics cheered, one reviewer noting the applause "had a ready-money sound about it."[8] The *Dramatic Mirror* concluded that Herne had "done his work well."[9]

Children of the Ghetto was another *Margaret Fleming*, a serious work that attacked religious tradition, this time Jewish tradition. An uproar followed. "The storm of discussion which the production of this play has raised is one of the literary events of the year," wrote the *Forum*'s critic. "Few works of art have awakened so much acrimony, on the one hand, and so much enthusiastic praise, on the other."[10]

The literary tantrums erupted because Herne-Zangwill questioned sacred Talmudic law found in the Pentateuch (*Leviticus*, Chapter 21, verse 7). This involved the issue of divorce, or *Gelt*.

> *Reb Shemuel.* My daughter cannot marry you; you are a Cohen.
> *David.* Not marry a priest? Why, I thought they were Israel's aristocracy?
> *Reb Shemuel.* That is why. A descendant of Aaron cannot marry a divorced woman. A woman who has had *Gelt* cannot marry a Cohen.[11]

In the play, Sam Levine, a practical joker, took the right hand of Hannah Jacobs, Reb Shemuel's daughter, and put a ring on her forefinger, saying: " . . . thou are consecrated unto me by this ring, according to the Law of Moses and Israel." Joke or not, his act constituted a genuine marriage. Hannah, of course, gets a divorce, and Reb Shemuel later admonishes her: "If you play with fire, you must expect to be scorched."[12]

Children of the Ghetto didn't follow the conventional "boy wins girl" formula, with a last-minute reversal saving the day. Although Hannah deeply loves David, she succumbs to tradition, closing the shutters on him while Reb Shemuel chants in another room. Imagine the following confrontation between David and Reb Shemuel, one reason *Forum* called this "the first drama of real Jewish life ever put on a Gentile stage."[13]

> "The law knows no exception, the Law is perfect," moans Reb Shemuel. "You are a Cohen—a priest."
> "A priest! Ha! Ha!" David laughs bitterly. "A Jewish priest in the nineteenth century, when the Temple has been destroyed these two thousand years!"
> "It will be rebuilt, please God. We must be ready for it."

"Oh yes, I'll be ready! Ha! Ha! Ha! Holy unto the
Lord! I a priest! Ha! Ha! Do you know what my holiness
consists in? In eating *trepha* meat and going to synagogue
a few times a year.... So the first sacrifice the priest is
called up to make is your daughter ... and this is the end
of the nineteenth century.

God lives in all centuries."[14]

Children of the Ghetto wasn't all serious, however. Zangwill, one of the ghetto's children, understood the tragic evocation
that underscores such lives. He also understood its comic inter-
ludes, the peculiar fermentation of opposites called humanism.
He inserted in each program a prologue called "The Author to
the Audience." It read: "But do not deem the Ghetto is all
gloom/The Comic Spirit mocks the age's doom/And weaves
athwart the woof of tragic drama/The humors of the human
panorama."[15]

The Herne-Zangwill "fidelity to truth" credo brought bar-
rages of protests. Sacrilege, some shouted. It was another case
that brought to mind one of *Margaret Fleming*'s custodians of
morality who wanted candy-coated characters and wanted to preserve past traditions. Critics especially resented the Jewish boy
who lit a cigarette with religious ceremonial candles, and they resented the cantor and his choir singing behind stage. *Forum* consulted Rabbi Jacob Vidrovitz, the rabbi of the Exile of Moscow,
who said:

"A very pretty tale. It is all correct, too; for once the maiden
has accepted the ring in the presence of two witnesses who don't
break the Sabbath and are honest men, she is consecrated to the
man who put it on her finger. Such is the law! Such is the law!"

Regarding the sacrilege question, he said: "If they don't utter the Name (of God), and the whole play is not calculated to
make fun of our religion or our people, there can be no objection.
There is no Name in *Kaddish*, and if the cantor does not pro-
nounce the Name in *Yigdal* and *Borchu* there is no offence."[16]

The sacrilege issue was just another strike against Herne
and Zangwill. Critical abuse spread among reviewers who still
fumed over Zangwill's boiling lecture, "The Drama as a Fine
Art," in which he had knocked their claptrap ideas and said that
the only great plays since Shakespeare were *She Stoops to Con-*

quer and *The School for Scandal.* Herne's radicalism made other enemies, too. This was evident in John Corbin's biased review in *Harper's Weekly*: "The peculiar fidelity and the skill in stage realism with which these scenes of Jewish life are presented would suggest Mr. James A. Herne and 'Shore Acres,' even if the programme did not tell one that Mr. Herne staged the play." Corbin charged that Herne's work expressed "the very pedantry of realism, and a plot that harks back to the guileless melodrama of 'Hearts of Oak,' " while Zangwill's play developed "a true and inevitable dramatic motive and develop(ed) it with a simplicity of scenic construction as an inevitability of form worthy of comparison with the best plays of Ibsen."[17] The defect in Corbin's logic lies in the fact that Herne helped Zangwill rewrite *Children of the Ghetto.*

Other critics stressed the play's radical structure, its plotless linear design, and its truthful characterizations. *The Critic* commented, "The entire absence of anything resembling a plot was, indeed, the most obvious difficulty in his way, and it cannot be said that he has overcome it triumphantly."[18] *The Athenaeum* said: "Concerning the fidelity of Mr. Zangwill's types we have nothing to say. His Jews, shabby or comic, are not, however, an attractive people, and bring to one's mind Heine's witty and profane satires on his race." They referred to individual portraits as "repulsive," "giddy," and "too unpleasing in appearance."[19] William Winter later called the play "redundant with needless incidents, prolix in language, and unmercifully tedious in the exposition of the commonplace of actual and very stupid life."[20]

Zangwill made the mistake of challenging the critics as Henry Miner had done with *The New South.* "Mr. Zangwill in public treated everybody badly," wrote Norman Hapgood. "He repeated on opening night his frequent assertion that literary men did not write for the stage in England and America as they do in other countries." But Hapgood added that "the dialogue was exquisite."[21]

Zangwill's outspoken ideas and the realistic portrayals contributed to the failure of *Children of the Ghetto.* In addition, there was a competitive Jewish play called *The Ghetto,* which had opened three days earlier. Billing and advance notices for

Children of the Ghetto, therefore, read *The Zangwill Play*, to avoid confusion. Both plays failed.

Herne and Zangwill had humanized the stage Jew, usually characterized in gentile plays by caricature. It was another American first. As Shylock asked: "If you prick us, do we not bleed? If you tickle us, do we not laugh? If you poison us, do we not die?" Meanwhile, the New York reviewers waited with sharpened claws.

In discussing the problems of *Children of the Ghetto*, Tyler said, "Its history is the complete and truthful story of the awful things that can happen in the theatre, and, I repeat, the fact that we had to fight for it like wild Indians and take our licking in the end endeared it to us as nothing else on earth could have."[22]

When *Children of the Ghetto* reached Broadway on October 16, Tyler had expected a success. But *Children of the Ghetto* wasn't a smash. "After four weeks of watching the poor thing starving to death," wrote Tyler," I dug farther down into our well-filled pockets and shipped the whole company, barring the supers, over to London." His London director, however, was unconcerned about "fidelity to truth," and contracted Cockneys who "looked like Weber and Fields with a dash of Fagin."[23] This staggered Tyler who trotted down to Petticoat Lane, London's ghetto, searching for real Jews.

The London show clicked—until fate struck again. The British defeat by the Boers at Spion Kop dampened theatre attendance. A London fog halted traffic for two days. Tyler called it quits, returning home to organize a road show. That season Tyler lost $75,000. The apologetic Zangwill refused royalties on *Children of the Ghetto*, later writing two smashes for Tyler, *Merely Mary Ann* and *The Melting Pot*, which starred Chrystal Herne.

M. J. Landa later wrote in *The Jew in Drama* that *Children of the Ghetto* "was an extraordinary achievement, a veritable *tour de force*, for Zangwill had compressed into it a goodly portion of his novel." But Landa also was critical. "Zangwill's skill and cunning were patent throughout, but the accentuation of the curious and the ungainly made for incongruity rather than unity, and the atmosphere was not too pleasant. The ghetto was not shown at its best; its denizens seemed motived by a note of forced humor."[24] Landa's book, however, was written in 1968, and the author couldn't have seen the original production, which weakens his remarks somewhat.

Dramatized novels saturated American stages during the 1890's: Paul M. Potter's *Trilby*, Langdon Mitchell's *Becky Sharp*, William Gillette's *Sherlock Holmes*, *The Christian*, and Minnie Maddern Fiske's famous production of Thackeray's *Vanity Fair*. All were topped by *Ben Hur*, Lew Wallace's historical novel that inspired Sears and Roebuck to order one million copies in 1913.[25]

The sudden flow of plays based on novels can be explained by the 1891 International Copyright Act, which encouraged dramatists to adapt American novels for the stage instead of pirating foreign ones. Producers presented "best sellers" and split the profits with both novelist and dramatist. Some novelists decided to rework their own novels for the stage. Herne opposed the practice, although he dramatized *Griffith Davenport* and *Children of the Ghetto*. Both were commercial failures. His advice to hopefuls: "First read the book, then throw it away and write your own play."[26]

When George C. Tyler purchased rights to F. Marion Crawford's *In the Palace of the King*, a historical romance adapted by Lorimer Stoddard for Viola Allen, she refused it. Tyler asked Herne to play script doctor. Herne hated "cloak and dagger" melodramas but agreed to meet with Tyler and Allen at Herne Oaks, a decision that thrilled the Herne girls. But Viola Allen's icy personality appalled the Hernes. Her arrogance had been fostered through roles opposite John McCullough, Tommaso Salvini, and Joseph Jefferson, besides credits in Bronson Howard's *Shenandoah* and *The Christian*, and an illustrious former membership in Frohman's Empire Stock Company.

The script of *In the Palace of the King* was ridiculous. "Good God, Julie!" Herne gasped. "What horrible stuff! Tyler must be mad to produce this thing! (Tyler was mad—about Viola Allen—once nearly jumping out of a window because of her.) What can I say? What can I tell him?"

They thought for a while. Julie suggested a rewrite.

"What's the use of re-writing such trash? It's hopeless," replied Herne.[27]

Tyler finally persuaded Viola Allen to star in the play. It became a Broadway smash.

Herne expressed his views about stage adaptations in an interview shortly before his death. His views still make sense:

> "Why the large proportion of failures?" he was asked.
>
> "Too many dramatizations, which means bad plays," was his answer.
>
> "Good novels," he continued, "do not of necessity turn out good plays—that has been clearly demonstrated. Next season I think we will see a wide departure from the prevailing fashion of book plays. The fashion indeed, has been going out since the early fall, when so many plays of that sort came to grief. Producing managers are already returning to their senses.
>
> "The public in attending the theatre wants primarily to see a good play—to be entertained to the full cost of the sittings. All the advantages of advance notoriety is woefully discounted after the first performance in each city if the merchandise is not delivered generously.
>
> "The season's avalanche of book plays has not done any particular harm, but it has not profited the managers at all, and I doubt if the sorry dramatizations have greatly edified theatregoers or encouraged theatre going. On the whole, I think the reverse is true and that it were better for both producers and public to have fewer plays and better ones.
>
> "I do not decry novels as a source of inspiration for dramatists, but I think the experiences of the year may be molded into aphorisms, perhaps axioms, for further guidance, as follows:
>
> "First—Novelists are rarely dramatists.
>
> "Second—Novelists should turn their characters and dramatic material over to a competent (sympathetic, if possible) dramatist, then leave him absolutely free to turn out the play.
>
> "Third—The dramatist needs no less a practical producer or stage director, who should, if possible, be actor as well.
>
> "With this arrangement the distinctly dramatic works of current fiction might be tapped for plays, with good results. The novelist's method is so diffuse, and so elaborate in character, that he rarely acquires the dramatist's faculty for elimination, condensation, and concentration.

"The book play of the day, hacked out bodily with scissors and the fragments pasted together, is a mistake, if not an impudent affront to an intelligent public. Play-making—whatever the source—is a resolving process, and a difficult and delicate one, indeed."[28]

21 the poet of the poor

THE EXHAUSTED HERNE returned to Convent Avenue in New York after *Children of the Ghetto* closed. Less than two years remained of his life, *Sag Harbor* (originally a rewrite of *Hearts of Oak*) needed revision for a Boston premiere in October.

Like his other plays, Herne molded and reshaped *Sag Harbor* for several years, finishing the first draft in September 1898, when he wrote Julie: "I've published the first draft of *Hearts of Oak*. Of course, I've got to go over and over it—but it's penned and written—full of faults and full of beauties whose last I can see better than I can see the first of them."[1] Herne originally called this work *Sag Harbor Folks*, then shortened it to *Sag Harbor*.[2]

The old whaling village Sag Harbor seeped with history. During the War of 1812 the British tried to burn it, but citizens loaded cannon with spikes, driving them off. James Fenimore Cooper wrote in *The Sea Lions*, "As a whaling town, Sag Harbor is the third or fourth port in the country, and maintains something like that rank in importance."[3]

Herne conceived *Sag Harbor* at Herne Oaks. The folkways on the sound between Sag Harbor and Southampton helped define this work like the folkways of Bar Harbor helped define *Shore Acres* years before. "*Sag Harbor* is the very essence of our life at Herne Oaks," wrote Chrystal. "The sum and distillation of long, golden afternoons sailed over Great Peconic Bay; of merry mornings when we visited the little shore towns and shopped and joked; of the squalls 'becalms' and storms, the wind and rain and summer sunshine; and last of all, of the good brown captain, our staunch friend. My father's great love for the sea was satisfied there, but strangely enough he never sailed after 'Sag Harbor' was finished."[4]

The Herne's "staunch friend" was Captain Petersen, who supervised Herne's yacht, *The Gretchen,* and provided Herne with local-color material for *Sag Harbor.* "Much has been written concerning the origins of my characters in this play," wrote Herne. "There were no originals, strictly speaking. I copied no one who lived at Sag Harbor, but there were little peculiarities of speech of Captain Petersen's of which I made use, and certainly I owed him much for information conveyed to me in his ordinary conversation, which nearly always had reference to the life of the people in this vicinity."[5]

The *Sag Harbor* production excited Herne. Liebler & Company shouldered the finances, giving him *carte blanche* backstage. Flawless casting resulted, one reason for the play's Boston success: Forrest Robinson and Sidney Booth as the brothers Ben and Frank Turner, Marion Abbott as Elizabeth, and veteran actress Mrs. Sol Smith as Mrs. Russell. Julie played Martha Reese and Chrystal, Jane Cauldwell. Herne hired Will Hodge, a lanky redhead with a hilarious voice, to play Freeman Whitmarsh. His performance prompted the *New York Times* to comment: "Mr. Hodge may not turn out to be a versatile comedian, and Whitmarsh may be his best part, but it will give him wide fame while it lasts."[6] Whitmarsh wasn't Hodge's best part. He later starred as Daniel Voorhees Pike in Booth Tarkington's *The Man from Home* and Mr. Stubbins in *Mrs. Wiggs of the Cabbage Patch.* Both were George C. Tyler shows.

When *Sag Harbor* later moved to Broadway, Herne "hired but fired" another novice actor, twenty-two year old Lionel Barrymore, whose performance as Frank annoyed the *Times*: "He plays the boyish and selfish young sailor in too saturnine and brutal a way. He gains not a bit of sympathy, even in his scene of self-sacrifice. Yet there is promise in his acting."[7] Barrymore's later promise included Milt Shanks in Augustus Thomas' *The Copperhead,* Neri in Benelli's *The Jest,* and his famous *Macbeth.* Hollywood later reduced him to Doctor Gillespie in the Doctor Kildare film series.

In *We Barrymores*, Lionel recounts his *Sag Harbor* experience with Herne:

> " 'Lionel,' he said to me, 'This is a disaster for which only I can be blamed. I have done you a dis-service for which I hope you can forgive me. Due to my own ineptness, and for no other reason at all, you have been cast in an impossible part.
>
> " 'Oh, you have created a brilliant role out of it, but it is of course not for you and gives you no scope whatsoever for your talents. I should be ruining your career, which is going to be brilliant, if I did not urge you at once to drop this very poor role and take a vacation.
>
> " 'Yes, that's it, what you need is a vacation, my boy, you just take a vacation. Do not, I beg of you, hold this lapse against me.' "

Barrymore also wrote: "Mr. Herne was one of the greatest actors that ever lived, a great man in his own right quite aside from acting, and he was a kind man.... I have never received such wonderful treatment as I received from James A. Herne. I should like to repeat the experience and get fired by that man all over again. Not even my grandmother was kinder."[8]

Sag Harbor was rehearsed at the Herald Square Theatre in New York, Herne shelving the Boston opening because of last-minute snags. This allowed a preview for theatre and company managers and a handful of friends. A reporter asked Herne if he was tense. Herne replied: "Personally, I have about as few nerves as a fish, but I realize the fact that it is not so with all actors, especially the inexperienced ones. Why, in the old stock days, when we used to change the bill nightly, one actor was expected to go on after practically one rehearsal, and fill in the scene with his own lines if he could not remember the words of the book. But nowadays we have changed all that."

Herne also noted changes in acting styles. "We are gradually getting around to the point where we realize that Shakespeare spoke the everlasting truth when he said that the aim of acting is and ever will be to hold, as 'twere the mirror up to nature.' That's what our younger players and a few of us older ones are trying to do."[9]

Sag Harbor opened at Boston's Comedy Theatre, the Park, on October 24, 1899. It became an overnight smash, running 107 performances and establishing a record for the Park. Most reviews glowed:

Boston Evening Traveler: "Mr. Herne is the foremost American representative of realism in dramatic art."[10]

Boston Globe: "His Captain Marble is a characterization which will surely live long in the memory of Mr. Herne's admirers and will take rank among the best that this finished actor and gifted author has ever given to the stage."[11]

Boston Herald: "He is a wonder as a stage manager. America has not his equal in producing perfect illusion in scenes of simple country life. His opening act, the scene in the second act, where carpenters and painters are at work, and his dinner scene, could not have been handled with such skill by any other producer in this country or in Europe. These scenes were simply perfect in detail."[12]

Boston Sunday Journal: "It is genius to be able to amuse and to instruct at the same time without preaching... with the possible exception of Ibsen, we can think of no modern writer for the stage who delivers in his plays both pleasure and profit with an almost equal hand."[13]

Boston Sunday Post: "A success of very large proportions is now assured for this popular actor-author, who may in many ways be fairly considered as the saving grace or perhaps the bulwark par excellence of the native American drama."[14]

All critics, however, didn't throw roses. The *Boston Advertiser* wrote: "*Sag Harbor* will detract from Mr. Herne's reputation as a literateur. As a work of art and a product of thought it is not to be named in the same day with 'Griffith Davenport.'"[15] A few reviewers also sneered at certain "vulgar and coarse"[16] speeches, among them Cap'n Marble's humorous references to all the "begats" in *The Book of Genesis* and his remark to Whitmarsh: "You've raised hell here." But people still packed the house.

Although Julie claimed that *Sag Harbor* wasn't a revision of *Hearts of Oak*, but "a totally new play,"[17] the two plays share kinship. Herne even subtitled *Sag Harbor* "An Old Story" and during his curtain speech defended it as "an old story (with) a new treatment."[18] The threadbare plot of two fellows after the same girl weakens both plays. *Sag Harbor* also suffers from such contrivances as exposition through newspaper reading, Ben over-hearing talk between Frank and Martha, and the absurd ending when Frank suddenly tumbles for Jane Cauldwell, who always wanted him.

What salvages *Sag Harbor* are Herne's detailed portrait of simple country people and the performances of the cast. The *Dramatic Mirror* claimed: "There is not a character nor a line in the play that is not true to life, and at once recognized by any one acquainted with the scene of the play."[19] John Bouve Clapp and Edwin Francis Edgett wrote: "In 'Sag Harbor,' the basis of his plot—one woman loved by two brothers—is as old as the melo-dramatic hills, and in the treatment of neither incident nor char-acter does Mr. Herne show any originality. But he does create original effects by means of his inborn dramatic sense, and it is in these subtle effects, sometimes of atmosphere, sometimes of eloquent pauses in the action, sometimes of a clever turn in the dialogue, which make his 'Shore Acres' and 'Sag Harbor' dis-tinctive among the thousand other plays of the modern stage."[20]

Perhaps the most gratifying part of *Sag Harbor*'s success was the recognition it brought Chrystal and Julie. Before the opening-night performance, the girls received this note: "That our two noble daughters may tonight establish themselves firmly in the difficult calling they have chosen—is the uppermost with in the hearts of their Father and Mother."[21]

Sag Harbor, of course, carried Herne's "fidelity to truth" trademark with its rustic shipyard on Gardiner's Bay littered with pine shavings, sawhorses, shipbuilder's tools, and rope, and the stern of a forty-foot sloop stage center. Painters painted with real paint, and two boat builders from Lawley's yard in south Boston planed their spars each performance.

Another Herne dinner rivaled *Shore Acres*' giblets and gravy in Act III. Each night the Adams House Restaurant pro-vided a steaming clam pie for $2.00. There also was champagne. When Ben Turner and Martha Reese announce their marriage plans everyone celebrates. But Herne didn't violate Sag Harbor ways. He noted in the script, "George should not bring on cham-pagne goblets, but very coarse, cheap, drinking goblets," and in Act III, "The tablecloth and napkins are of a good material, snow-white, and must be laundered for every performance." Dur-

K.C. as Mary Miller in *Drifting Apart*. The University of Maine.

Walnut St. Theatre

Messrs. AL. HAYMAN, KLAW & ERLANGER, - Directors
MR. FRANK HOWE, JR., - - - Manager

Week Beginning Monday. February 4th. 1901.
Regular Matinees Wednesdays and Saturdays.

MR. JAMES A. HERNE

(LIEBLER & CO , Managers), In Nis New Play

SAG HARBOR,

"AN OLD STORY"

NOTE —The story of "Sag Harbor" begins with the first line of the play; therefore it is advisable that the audience be seated when the curtain rises.

CAST OF CHARACTERS:

WILLIAM TURNER . . . . FRANK MONROE
Formerly of Islip, Long Island, now of Sag Harbor, agent for
seamer 'Antelope."
BEN TURNER, his son, a boat builder . . FORREST ROBINSON
FRANK TURNER . . . . J. WOOSTER DEAN
Ben's youngest brother, seam n in U S. N
CAPT. DAN MARBLE . . . . JAMES A. HERNE
Owns the sloop "Kacy"; scallops in her winters; sails
company in her summers.
PREEMAN WHITMARSH . . . . W. T. HODGE
House, sign and ornamental painter and glazer, lead- the choir.
GEO. SALTER, Ben's right-hand man . . . . W. F. WHITMAN
HOSEA STEVENS, barkeeper at "Nassau" . JOHN D. GARRICK
JIM ADAMS, } Baymen { . . . . . . T. H. BURKE
ED. MILLS, } { . . . . . ROBERT GILLIG
MRS. JOHN RUSSELL, a widow . . . . . . MRS SOL. SMITH
ELIZABETH ANN TURNER . . . . MARION ABBOTT
William's maiden sister.
MARTHA REESE, an orphan . . . . JULIE A. HERNE
JANE CALDWELL . . . . CHRYSTAL HERNE
Of Bridgehamton, music teacher.
FRANCES TOWD, of Water-Mill . . . . . MOLLIE REVEL
MISS BAILY, of Gloversville, N. Y. . . . FLORENCE HORSFALL
SUSAN MURPHY, the hired girl . . . . EDYTHE SKERRETT
Ship Carpenters, Man-o'-war's men, etc

SYNOPSIS OF SCENES:

ACT I.—May, 1895. A little old country ship-yard. (Ernest Albert.)
ACT II.—The next afternoon. Work shop of ship-yard. (Gates & Morange.)
ACT III.—April, 1807. A regular Saturday night at home. (Gates & Morange.)
(But two minutes intermission between Acts III and IV.)
ACT IV.—The next day. Easter Sunday. (Gates & Morange)

EXECUTIVE STAFF FOR LIEB ER & Co.

Geo. C. Tyler . . . . General Manager
Harry Askin . . . . Acting Manager
Robert Hunter . . . . Business Manager
Frank Monroe . . . . Stage Director
Max Stewart . . . . Advertising Agent

NEXT WEEK
JAMES A. HERNE in "Sag Harbor"

Sag Harbor program. Theatre Collection,
Free Library of Philadelphia.

Exterior scene from *Sag Harbor*. New York Public Library.

Herne as Cap'n Dan Marble in *Sag Harbor*.
New York Public Library.

Chrystal Herne in *Sag Harbor*. New York Public Library.

Shore Acres' program at the Boston Museum.
New York Public Library.

Reconciliation scene from *Shore Acres*. Theatre Collection, Free Library of Philadelphia.

Herne as Nat Berry in *Shore Acres*.
The University of Maine.

ing this scene "a light snowstorm (could) be seen falling outside."[22]

In the champagne scene the corkscrew didn't work one night, which threw Herne's lines because the dialogue was related to stage business. But Herne quickly improvised: "B'Gosh! I thought I could pull the durn thing with my fingers, Hoses, but I guess I jest fooled myself a little this time."[23] The audience roared and loud applause followed.

Sag Harbor awed Sag Harborites who attended the show. Everything was so real: sawdust on the stage floor and a clampie dinner. One old fellow, however, informed a reporter: "I am seventy-five years old, but I am hale and hearty still, and I shall carry with me a certain heavy cane which years ago I carved out of the jawbone of a sperm whale that was killed in the South Seas. I shall be constrained to use it if I find that Herne has allowed his pen too much freedom with the characteristics and personalities of certain estimable young and old ladies of Sag Harbor, Bridgehampton and East Side."[24]

An eight-week tour followed *Sag Harbor's* Boston closing. They were eight weeks of torture for Herne. The constant shifting from town to town, coupled with New England's harsh winter, plagued his rheumatism. Each performance became a miracle of endurance. Julie later wrote that "he bore it uncomplainingly, but he rarely joked, ate little, and slept less, and his face was often drawn with pain. More than ten years previously, Herne, then in the fullness of his power, had played that same territory in *Drifting Apart*, but no one would come to see him. Now he was old. . . and they were crowding into the theatre."[25] Garland, who saw *Sag Harbor* with his wife, later remarked in *A Daughter of the Middle Border*: "Herne was growing old, and in failing health but he showed no decline of power that night."[26]

The company finally reached Chicago, playing at the Grand Opera House on March 19, 1900, to overwhelming applause. Yet Herne's health continued to deteriorate. An ulcerated foot agonized him, on and off stage, forcing sleepless nights in a chair. A specialist recommended a toe amputation to avoid blood poisoning. The operation succeeded, but *Sag Harbor* closed without Herne.

A trip to the baths in Hot Springs, Arkansas, followed in April, a six-week trip that baffled K.C. and the girls because Herne went alone, which was unusual for him. While there he mapped out the next season. Besides retaining *Sag Harbor*, he re-purchased *Shore Acres* from the Miner estate and planned a revival of *Hearts of Oak*, that perennial favorite. (Herne had intuitively distrusted Miner, but couldn't explain why. His judgement proved true. Miner resented Herne's managerial choice for *Sag Harbor* and planned a London production of *Shore Acres* with a second star shortly before his death.)

Herne's inner thoughts at Hot Springs were expressed in a letter to K.C. that reveals more about him than reams of critical reviews:

> Dear Heart:
>   No, I do not brace up to write home—I simply commune with myself now that I have no one to *harp* at—and I have been reading Ruskin—*Sesame and Lilies,* and Mabie,—*Nature and Culture,* and I find what an ignorant, selfish boor I've been all my life, particularly during the last year and a half. Pity such books could not have come to one beginning life, instead of to one ending it. I know now that I was sent into the world to do good—to make the world better for my having lived in it. What have I done? Why, just to the contrary.
>   True, I've given some audiences an evening's pleasure; given them perhaps, food for thought here and there. But in the main, I've wasted my life, and my life's plan. Ah well! Perhaps I'm wrong, and that I was just sent here with a suggestion of good in me to be dominated and snowed under by the indolent and vicious in me. As you have said many a time, "you preach humanity, but never practice it!"
>   ...I'm well all but my confounded rheumatism....I walk without a cane, and if I could only get some sun and hot weather, I feel I would get well....Yesterday was the first summer day since I've been here, and a glory it was. ...I spent most of it under the trees. At 6 last evening I got an old horse and an older buggy—advertised as "Thoroughbred Kentucky Horses and Up-to-date Rigs"—and I drove up on top of the mountain. Ah! The pines up there and the perfume....Of course, it lacks the variety of Herne Oaks; it's always the same. It lacks the everchanging beauty of the bay....
>   I did not go to see *Sapho.* Nay, nay, Pauline! I would

not go to see it in the city, why here?—with a bum company. One of the posters they put out was a New York
policeman chasing Sapho through the Tenderloin. And
Traubel says it's all good, all art. Perhaps it is.

... I'm glad, oh, so glad, to get the cheerful letters
from you all. It is certainly a glorious and inspiring spot
down there. I did some good work there. I don't blame you
for loving it. May you have me and it always.... Tell Jack
that I miss him (most) of all.... Happiness and health and
love to you all.[27]

Chrystal and Julie aggravated Herne's weakened condition.
Both decided to strike out on their own at this critical time.
George Tyler offered Chrystal a role in the road-show revival of
The Christian, and Julie begged Herne to secure an interview
with Charles Frohman. "You girls had better not be in such a
hurry to desert the old man," he said. "I'm going to write a lot
of good plays yet."[28] But he arranged the Frohman interview
for Julie.

Following its record-breaking Boston run and road tour, *Sag
Harbor* docked on Broadway, with Herne still starring. New York
was a port seldom receptive to his dramas, and things hadn't
changed.

George C. Tyler planned a Labor Day opening at Oscar Hammerstein's new Republic Theatre on West 42nd Street but postponed it because Hammerstein hadn't finished the building. Klaw
and Erlanger offered financial help, but Hammerstein backed
off. He knew they would dictate terms. Meanwhile, Herne arrived in New York to rehearse the new road shows of *Shore
Acres* and *Hearts of Oak.*

Herne admired Hammerstein, that Broadway character with
the Prince Albert coat, top hat, and dangling cigar who built the
Harlem Opera House, Columbus Theatre, Manhattan Opera
House, and Olympia Music Hall and then went broke and was arrested for entering his own theatre. Yet, he assured the *New
York Herald,* "Fortunately I have an iron constitution and in
spite of all I have been through I have just as much energy and
pluck as ever, and still expect to fight my way up again to the
top of the heap. I want to get back that million and add to it."[29]

Hammerstein kept his word. He invented cigar-making machines, suspenders, and inkwells. He wrote operas, his first love. He invested in real estate. He first staged Ibsen's *The Pillars of Society* in America (unsuccessfully) and later Tolstoy's *Resurrection* (a curious success that made $100,000.) At each performance he sat in the wings on a kitchen chair, always in command, as befitted the man who made Times Square. (His namesake grandson later contributed *Oklahoma, South Pacific,* and *The King and I* to American musicals.)

Hammerstein's miraculous recovery started with the Victoria Theatre, at Forty-second Street and Seventh Avenue, which he built in three months from used materials for $80,000. Here Hammerstein presented everything from Marie Dressler to Don, the Talking Dog, and after the shows audiences retired to the theatre's spacious roof garden. The roof garden helped business at the adjoining Theatre Republic, too, as their roofs connected, and patrons of both theatres could enjoy the garden.

For Hammerstein it was always another theatre. As his son Arthur once said, "If Father could buy enough plush to make a theater curtain, there would be a theater built around it!"[30]

A smaller theatre than its sprawling sister the Victoria, the Republic's Venetian exterior of brown stone, dark gray Powhattan brick, and Doric columns was impressive. Beyond a low-ceilinged vestibule the theatre's interior featured greens, reds, and gilding, allegorical figures of Harmony and Melody supporting a golden lyre that adorned the thirty-five foot proscenium arch. These masked the musician's gallery with its organ electrically connected to an antiphonal behind the first balcony. (Twelve musicians played each performance, except for opera presentations that featured twenty-one.) The Republic offered excellent acoustics, advanced ventilation including hot and cold circulating air through the floor ducts (which faulted on opening night), spacious seating, and fireproof materials, except for upholstery and the plank sheathing on the floors. The *Dramatic Mirror* praised: "There are no sheaves, pulleys and counterweights, as in the ordinary stage. All the scenery, as well as the curtain, being operated by an electric motor controlled by one man from a switchboard on the stage."[31]

Carpenters finished the Republic on opening night, while actors made up backstage. (A *Dramatic Mirror* photo on September 29, 1900, shows the Republic's unfinished exterior. Boards surround a huge poster of Herne, his name in large print.)

During the third-act entre-acte, Herne appeared on stage and praised Hammerstein, calling the Republic the "finest building in New York"[32] (a slight exaggeration). He also admired the magnificent dome, patterned after Washington's capitol. Then he questioned *Sag Harbor's* chances for success in New York, an unusual remark for a curtain speech, but a prophetic one.

Hammerstein also spoke, expressing hopes that the Theatre Republic would become another Comédie Française or Imperial Opera House. "I have designed the Theatre Republic to be a drawing room of the drama, dedicated to all that is best in dramatic and lyric art. The policy of the house is best illustrated by its bookings. For its opening attraction I have secured James A. Herne, whom I consider the representative American actor-author, if not the founder of our National drama, in his latest successful play, 'Sag Harbor,' which ran nearly four months in Boston and a month in Chicago, besides scoring a remarkable record on the road last season. This will be followed in due season by Miss Viola Allen in her new play, 'In the Palace of the King,' and other attractions of the same class."[33]

But the syndicate squelched Hammerstein's grand goals. Unable to secure stars, he arranged to lease the Republic to David Belasco for $30,000 a year plus 10 percent of the house's gross receipts. "That lease," Belasco told William Winter, "was a great thing for Hammerstein—but it was a greater thing for me, and I did not forget that afterwards, when I was paying him from $60,000 to $72,000 a year for his theatre. When some of my friends used to say to me, 'Don't you realize that you are paying Hammerstein an *unheard-of* rent for his house?' I used to answer, 'And don't *you* realize how very lucky I am *to be in a position* to pay him an unheard of rent?' "[34]

Sag Harbor's reception at the Republic was lukewarm, nothing like in Boston. Audiences laughed at Hodge's Freeman Whitmarsh, applauded Chrystal's last-act scene, and whispered about the realistic details. But that's all. Herne, who "was strangely apathetic, his bubbling Irish humor muted" after returning from Hot Springs, received "a devastatingly bad press" in New York.

Chrystal later said, "I have always thought the failure of *Griffith Davenport* broke my father's heart—but the abuse poured over *Sag Harbor* left him unmoved."[35]

The *New York Times* still waxed about *Margaret Fleming,* that dramatic desecration. "The famous nursery episode of Mr. Herne's 'Margaret Fleming' is here quite outdone. Miss Evelyn Millard, the London actress, whose refusal to speak on the stage a line alluding to a babe unborn was recently cabled to this country, might find Mr. Herne's play very distasteful."[36] *The Commercial Advertiser* also found *Sag Harbor* distasteful. "Mr. Herne is a critic of life; there are few writers in America, dramatists or not, who rival him in immediateness, delicacy and individuality; but he apparently wrote his latest comedy without inspiration. It looks as if he had set about the construction of a popular drama with a certain local atmosphere, without having a story to tell, a character to present, or one strong mood to create; in short, without having anything to say."[37]

Tyler wanted to close *Sag Harbor,* but Herne remembered *Shore Acres'* uphill fight. So he compromised again, working free for the entire run. Tyler agreed to return his $5,000 salary after the play surfaced on the road, a promise unfulfilled. K.C. later sued, but Tyler pressured witnesses, including Will Hodge, whom Herne had discovered, to successfully defend him. Shoestring schemes filled Tyler's early career. In *Whatever Goes Up,* he details the "kiting" check system, saying "with the proper juggling you could make it go a long way."[38] (Kiting is cashing checks, each larger than the previous one, without funds, and then covering them fast.)

Sag Harbor closed on December 1, after a nine-week run. Poor reviews, a late start, Herne's illness, and feeble audiences crushed it. The work became another Broadway flop soon forgotten, like hundreds of others.

Broadway marquees blazed with stars during the 1900 season: Maude Adams in *L'Aiglon, David Harum* with William H. Crane, Richard Mansfield's revival of *Henry V,* E. H. Sothern's portrayal of *Hamlet,* the antics of Weber and Field's *Fiddle-Dee-Dee,* the memorable performance of Otis Skinner in *Prince Otto,* David Belasco's *Zaza* with Mrs. Leslie Carter, Clyde Fitch's *The Climbers,* and Augustus Thomas' *Arizona.* Sarah Bernhardt also

played in repertory at the Garden Theatre, and the Floradora
Girls danced on and on.

Sag Harbor's problems continued. The road production attracted customers but returned slim profits. More friction followed Herne's death. George C. Tyler, who assumed managership
of Liebler & Co., informed K.C. he'd let the play to stock companies. She objected, seeking a restraining order on *Sag Harbor*.
Sparks flew during the case's disposition, but because the original five-year contract between Herne and Liebler & Co. hadn't
expired, the New York Supreme Court denied the injunction."[39]

Herne's health worsened throughout 1900 and the following
spring. While playing *Sag Harbor* in Cleveland, he left the cast
for one week with a harsh cough. In Baltimore a doctor remained
backstage to give oxygen treatments. One-night stands in Pennsylvania forced another temporary withdrawal, and before Chicago's opening Herne spent ten days at West Badin, Indiana.

The inevitable finally happened, and Herne could not maintain a good performance in Chicago. High attendance, however,
continued, despite ruthless reviews. But Herne caught cold, finally collapsing in a hotel room after fluffing lines during a
third-week performance. When Tyler learned he couldn't continue, he rushed to Chicago, enraged. One glance at the ailing
actor, however, mellowed his greedy anger.

In the old days a star's name remained on the marquee, even
after he left the show. Herne realized this, insisting he play a
minor role in *Sag Harbor*. "So, hardly able to speak, almost too
weak to stand, my father made his last appearance on the stage,"
wrote Chrystal. "There was still the unquenchable Irish twinkle
in his gray eyes, still the perfect reading, the perfect timing in
these last words that he spoke in the theatre."[40] The next day,
someone told Forrest Robinson: "What a fine-looking man Mr.
Herne is! We enjoyed his performance as Cap'n Dan. But we did
feel sorry for that poor old man who played a small part. He
looked so very ill!"[41]

When Garland learned about Herne's illness he wrote in his
diary: "Late mail today brought report that Herne was dying in
Chicago. I at once got off a wire of sympathy to Mrs. Herne. I
fear the worst. The old man had felt the effects of his hard

drinking each time more keenly and his superb constitution was undermined and laid open to the grippe. He seemingly could not come to Chicago without falling into the hands of some one who could and did destroy him. Who they were I do not know but they belonged to the underworld. He was his own worst enemy. A man of great powers and of great charm even when in liquor, which he used too frequently. He was, after all is said and done, the most original of our dramatists."[42]

Garland wrote these notes on May 13, 1901, at West Salem, almost three weeks before Herne's death. Garland speaks in past tense, and his comments are vague, implying that drink was becoming a chronic problem for Herne and that someone in Chicago had taken advantage of or exploited him. Evidence doesn't exist to support either assumption.

When Herne finally returned home to Herne Oaks, he was accompanied by a nurse and his loyal servant Julius. The girls fought farewell tears, remaining in *Sag Harbor*'s Chicago cast. When Herne arrived in New York, his condition shocked K.C., who bitterly wrote the girls: "Your father has been in a most frightful condition in Chicago, and they would not tell you nor me. It is shameful. Mr. Liebler came here Sunday while I was away and blurted out the whole thing to Dorothy. Your father did not know it either. He would not have persisted in going about and trying to play if the doctors had told him the truth. . . . Please say nothing to Mr. Askin of what Mr. Liebler told Dorothy. What's the use? They are a lot of money grubbers—not one of them to be trusted. If you were dangerously sick tomorrow neither he nor anyone else in the company would take the trouble to let me know."[43]

Herne's health improved for a while, but there was a relapse in May. Both girls finally returned home after K.C.'s appeal— first Julie from Denver, then Chrystal from San Francisco. Pleuro-pneumonia spread, weakening Herne's heart. Two doctors and a nurse remained on constant duty, but his condition was hopeless. On June 2, 1901, he suffered a painful seizure. Only opiates offered relief. Death arrived at 5 o'clock, in the morning, following a deep coma.

Herne's death caused a national stir, hundreds of newspapers and magazines printing eulogies. Some were very extravagant:

Julie Marlowe: "He was the most unusual and striking figure in the American theatre. He was one of the few connected with the American drama who may be said to have equally possessed foresight—that is—prophecy—and courage."[44]

Henry Starr Richardson: "He was the only force in the professional theatrical world tending toward real art in the theater. He was a genius. He was one of the few men who, dying, leave behind them actually a void which cannot be filled."[45]

The Star: "In the death of James A. Herne the American stage has lost its most brilliant light."[46]

New York Post: "The sad part of it all is that there is no one in the profession who can fill Mr. Herne's place satisfactorily."[47]

Gloucester Daily News: "(Along with Joseph Jefferson) he was the representative of the whole dramatic profession in the United States."[48]

New York Dramatic Mirror: "As an actor Mr. Herne was unique in *genre* parts of his own creation; as a stage-manager he was unsurpassed in the school of drama of which he was the foremost exponent in this country.... His plays led in this country the advance of a realism that has come strongly to influence the drama of the world, and they have a literary quality that has won the admiration of the foremost womens-authors and critics—in the field of books."[49] (The paper printed a large center picture of Herne.)

K.C. collapsed after Herne's death, retreating to an upper room. She wept uncontrollably. Decisions waited. Single-taxers wanted a public funeral and memorial meeting, but K.C. declined. She favored a simple home service that would honor Herne's own wishes: no mourning clothes, no clergymen, no religious rituals—just family and friends.

Tuesday, June 4, 1901. A plain oaken coffin, banked with flowers from Julia Marlowe, Mrs. Sol Smith Russell, Grace Filkins, the Actors' Order of Friendship, the American Dramatists Club, and others, held Herne's remains. Speakers included single-taxer John S. Crosby, actor Milton Nobles, J. J. Spikes, representing the Actor's Order of Friendship, and playwright Augustus Thomas, who eulogized in part: "James A. Herne was a poet of the poor.... For useless convention of any kind he had that disregard which is a mark of genius.... His fidelity in every work was compelling and he added a gentle ideality hopeful and uplifting as the breath of morn."[50]

Ruth Draper sang "All Through the Night," and as Herne's body was carried from his home three musicians played his favorite song, "Do They Think of Me at Home?" A twelve-carriage cortege removed him to Fresh Pond, where a cremation followed.[51]

Herne's will testified to his generosity. Instead of several hundred thousand, he left only $29,500. "My old man was never the Great Star," recalled John. "Any old actor could walk in the stage door and even catch him in the wings before he went on, and get a fast buck."[52] (The last entries in Herne's checkbook, incidentally, were to needy old friends.) K.C. received the entire estate, including trusteeship of $15,000 to educate the children, the principal to be equally divided among them at twenty-five years of age. She also became executrix over Herne's plays and copyrights.[53]

K.C.'s grief was intense. As Helen H. Gardener wrote in *An Unofficial Patriot*: "It was night ... to Katharine is seemed that the darkness must be eternal. Yet the sun rose on the morrow, and life took up its threads and wove on another loom."[54]

Katharine Corcoran Herne died many years later, on February 8, 1943, at the River Crest Sanitarium, in New York City, following a long illness. She was 86.[55] She was also the true "first lady" of America's modern theatre, the original *Margaret Fleming*.

The career of James A. Herne took place during an era of stars and managers in the American theatre, yet he never became the self-centered figure of most stars, and he remained the most developmental and generous of managers.

The contributions of his wisdom, skill and foresight in the management of actors and companies affected the careers of hundreds, and influenced thousands in the time when a national theatre art was coming of age. As an author, actor and director, his contribution of realism in theatre was perhaps the most significant of any American dramatist. He pioneered what was to become the thrust of the future in dramatic literature and dramatic art in America.

He was a man active socially, politically, philosophically and artistically throughout his lifetime, leaving a legacy of humanism in all the areas of life that he touched—a legacy still felt today in countless subtle effects upon the development of the American theatre tradition.

notes

1 The Dog of Montargis

1. James A. Herne, "Old Stock Days in the Theatre," *The Arena*, 6 (September, 1892), 402.

2. Meade Minnigerode, *The Fabulous Forties* (New York: G. P. Putnam's Sons, 1924), p. 52.

3. E. Douglas Branch, *The Sentimental Years* (New York: Hill and Wang, 1965), p. 109.

4. Minnigerode, *Fabulous Forties*, p. 74.

5. Julie Herne, "James A. Herne, Actor and Dramatist" (unpublished biography, Herbert J. Edwards Collection, University of Maine Library), p. 6.

6. Mrs. James A. Herne, ed., *Shore Acres and Other Plays* (New York: Samuel French, 1928), p. ix.

7. Julie Herne, "James A. Herne," p. 13.

8. *Ibid.*, pp. 13B–14.

9. James A. Herne, "The Present Outlook for the American Drama," *The Coming Age*, 1 (March, 1899), p. 250.

10. Mrs. James A. Herne, *Shore Acres*, p. ix.

11. *Ibid.*, p. x.

12. James A. Herne, "Old Stock Days," p. 402.

13. James A. Herne, "Forty Years Before the Foot-Lights," *The Coming Age*, (August, 1899), p. 122.

14. *Ibid.*

15. James A. Herne, "Old Stock Days," pp. 404–05.

16. James A. Herne, "Forty Years," p. 126.

17. *Ibid.*, p. 123.

18. Henry Dickinson Stone, *Theatrical Reminiscences* (New York: Benjamin Blom, 1969), p. 69.

19. H. P. Phelps, *Players of a Century* (New York: Benjamin Blom, 1972), p. 325.

20. James A. Herne, "Old Stock Days," pp. 406–07.

21. Edwin Duerr, *The Length and Depth of Acting* (New York: Holt, Rinehart and Winston, 1963), p. 363.

22. James A. Herne, "Forty Years," p. 251.

23. Julie Herne, "James A. Herne," p. 46.

24. James A. Herne, "Old Stock Days," p. 416.

25. Nat C. Goodwin, *Nat Goodwin's Book* (Boston: Richard G. Badger, 1914), p. 277.

26. Theatre Collection, New York Public Library at Lincoln Center, (undated clipping).

2   Lay On Macduff!

1. Richard Moody, *Edwin Forrest, First Star of the American Stage* (New York: Alfred A. Knopf, 1960), pp. 76–77.

2. James A. Herne, *op. cit.*, "Forty Years," p. 125.

3. James A. Herne, *op. cit.*, "Old Stock Days," p. 364.

4. *Ibid.*, p. 416.

5 W. B. Wood, *Personal Recollections of the Stage* (Philadelphia: Henry Carey Baird, 1855), p. 393.

6. *Ibid.*, p. 440.

7. Mary Anderson, *A Few Memories* (New York: Harper & Brothers Publishers, 1896), p. 88.

8. *Ibid.*, p. 87.

9. Julie Herne, "James A. Herne," p. 48.

10. Robert L. Sherman, *Chicago Stage, Its Record and Achievements* (Chicago: Robert L. Sherman, 1947), p. 401.

11. Herbert J. Edwards and Julie A. Herne, *James A. Herne: Rise of Realism in the American Drama* (Orono: University of Maine, 1964), p. 13.

12. T. Allison Brown, *History of the American Stage* (New York: Dick & Fitzgerald, 1879), p. 171.

13. George C. D. Odell, *Annals of the New York Stage,* III (New York: Columbia University Press, 1949), pp. 36, 532.

14. *Chicago Daily News,* January 23, 1908, p. 7.

15. *Ibid.*

16. Moody, *Edwin Forrest,* p. 75.

17. Joseph Jefferson, *The Autobiography of Joseph Jefferson* (New York: The Century Co., 1889), p. 18.

18. M. R. Werner, *Brigham Young* (New York: Harcourt Brace and Company, 1925), p. 443.

19. M. B. Leavitt, *Fifty Years in Theatrical Management* (New York: Broadway Publishing Co., 1912), p. 57.

20. *New York Times,* June 20, 1869, p. 5.

21. George D. Pyper, *The Romance of an Old Playhouse* (Salt Lake City: George D. Pyper, 1928), p. 170.

22. *Anaconda Standard,* April 24, 1898, p. 20.

23. James A. Herne, "Art for Truth's Sake in the Drama," *The Arena,* 17 (February, 1897), p. 365.

24. Julie Herne, "James A. Herne," p. 46.

25. James A. Herne, "Old Stock Days," pp. 365–66.

26. *Boston Sunday Post,* May 3, 1896, p. 11.

27. Townsend Walsh Collection, New York Public Library at Lincoln Center (undated clipping).

28. Brown, *History of the American Stage,* p. 599.

29. Odell, *New York Stage,* VIII, p. 457.

30. *New York Times,* June 21, 1869, p. 5.

31. Townsend Walsh Collection, New York Public Library at Lincoln Center (undated clipping).

32. *New York Spirit of the Times,* September 18, 1869.

33. Robert H. Fuller, *Jubilee Jim* (New York: The Macmillan Company, 1928), p. 433.

34. W. A. Swanberg, *Jim Fiske, The Career of an Improbable Rascal* (New York: Charles Scribner's Sons, 1959), p. 182.

35. Theatre Collection, New York Public Library at Lincoln Center (undated clipping).

36. Olive Logan, *Before the Footlights and Behind the Scenes* (Philadelphia: Parmelee & Co., 1870), p. 93.

37. Clara Morris, *Stage Confidences* (Boston: Lothrop Publishing Company, 1902), p. 149.

38. James A. Herne, "Forty Years," p. 254.

39. *Pittsburgh Post,* October 15, 1870, p. 2.

40. Howard Mumford Jones, *The Age of Energy* (New York: The Viking Press, 1971), p. 104.

3   The City of Canvas

1. Steward Edward White, *The Forty Niners* (New Haven: Yale University Press, 1918), p. 120.

2. Walter M. Leman, *Memories of an Old Actor* (New York: Benjamin Blom, 1886), p. 238.

3. W. Eugene Hollon, *Frontier Violence* (New York: Oxford University Press, 1974), p. 72.

4. *Ibid.,* p. 74.

5. *Ibid.,* p. 75.

6. Dixon Wecter, "Instruments of Culture on the Frontier," *The Yale Review,* (fall, 1947), pp. 255–56.

7. Ronald L. Davis, "They Played for Gold: Theater on the Mining Frontier," *Southwest Review*, 51 (1966), 179.

8. Leman, *Memories of an Old Actor*, pp. 232–33.

9. Edmund M. Gagey, *The San Francisco Stage, A History* (New York: Columbia University Press, 1950), p. 142.

10. *San Francisco Sunday Chronicle*, August 24, 1879, p. 4.

11. Amy Leslie, *Some Players*, pp. 381–82.

12. *San Francisco Sunday Chronicle*, May 3, 1874, p. 1.

13. *San Francisco Chronicle*, October 18, 1894, p. 2.

14. William Winter, *The Life of David Belasco* (New York: Moffat Yard & Company, 1918), p. 168.

15. *San Francisco Chronicle*, October 21, 1874, p. 4.

16. *San Francisco Chronicle*, November 9, 1874, p. 4, and *San Francisco Sunday Chronicle*, November 15, 1874, p. 2.

17. *San Francisco Chronicle*, December 2, 1874, p. 3.

18. Mrs. Thomas Whiffen, *Keeping off the Shelf* (New York: E. P. Dutton & Co., Inc., 1928), p. 106.

19. *Ibid.*, pp. 106–07.

20. *The Oregonian*, March 25, 1875, p. 3.

21. *The Oregonian*, March 26, 1875, p. 3.

22. *Ibid.*

23. Alice Henson Ernst, *Trouping in the Oregon Country* (Portland: Oregon Historical Society, 1961), p. 109.

24. Ishbel Ross, *The Uncrowned Queen* (New York: Harper & Row, Publishers, 1972), p. 232.

25. Leman, *Memories of an Old Actor*, pp. 276–77.

26. Charles Warren Stoddard, "Behind the Scenes," *Atlantic Monthly*, 34 (1874), p. 527.

27. George R. MacMinn, *The Theater of the Golden Age in California* (Caldwell, Idaho: The Caxton Printers, Ltd., 1941), pp. 58–59. See also: William G. B. Carson, *The Theatre on the Frontier* (New York: Benjamin Blom, 1932).

4   Monstrosity in Art

1. *San Francisco Daily Evening Bulletin*, March 6, 1876, p. 3.

2. Jefferson Williamson, *The American Hotel, An Anecdotal History* (New York: Alfred A. Knopf, 1930), pp. 95–96.

3. Julia Cooley Altrocchi, *The Spectacular San Franciscans* (New York: E. P. Dutton and Company, Inc., 1949), pp. 175, 216.

4. *San Francisco Daily Alta California*, March 6, 1876, p. 1.

5. *San Francisco Daily Evening Bulletin*, March 7, 1876, p. 3.

6. *San Francisco Daily Alta California*, March 4, 1876, p. 1.

7. *San Francisco Daily Alta California,* March 7, 1876, p. 1.

8. *San Francisco Daily Alta California,* March 5, 1876, p. 1.

9. William H. Crane, *Footprints and Echoes* (New York: E. P. Dutton and Company, 1925), pp. 73–74.

10. Robert M. Sillard, *Barry Sullivan and his Contemporaries* (London: T. Fisher Unwin, 1901), pp. 173–74.

11. *San Francisco Chronicle,* March 6, 1876, p. 3.

12. *San Francisco Chronicle,* March 7, 1876, p. 3.

13. *San Francisco Daily Evening Bulletin,* March 7, 1876, p. 3.

14. Lewis C. Strang, *Famous Actors in America* (Boston: L. C. Page and Company, 1900), pp. 138–39.

15. Crane, *Footprints and Echoes,* pp. 73–74.

16. William Davidge, *Footlight Flashes* (New York: The American News Company, 1866), pp. 171–72.

17. Dion Boucicault, "Theatres, Halls, and Audiences," *North American Review,* 149 (July–December, 1889), pp. 434.

18. Chrystal Herne, "Some Memories of My Father," *Green Book* (April, 1909), pp. 746.

19. Winter, *David Belasco,* p. 181.

20. Letter from John T. Herne to Richard Moody, August 21, 1960, Richard Moody Collection, Indiana University.

21. Herbert J. Edwards and Julie A. Herne, *James A. Herne, Rise of Realism in the American Drama* (Orono: University of Maine, 1964), pp. 20–22.

22. W. C. Cawley Collection, New York Public Library at Lincoln Center (undated clipping).

23. *San Francisco Sunday Chronicle,* August 24, 1879, p. 4.

24. Winter, *David Belasco,* p. 181.

25. *San Francisco Daily Alta California,* March 12, 1876, p. 1.

26. David Belasco, "Why I Believe in the Little Things," *Ladies Home Journal,* September, 1911, p. 65.

27. Winter, *David Belasco,* p. 110.

28. *San Francisco Chronicle,* February 15, 1879, p. 4.

29. *San Francisco Sunday Chronicle,* February 16, 1879, p. 2.

30. Winter, *David Belasco,* p. 113.

31. Letter from Julie Herne to Arthur Hobson Quinn, July 21, 1925, Arthur Hobson Quinn Collection, University of Pennsylvania Library.

32. Craig Timberlake, *The Life & Work of David Belasco, the Bishop of Broadway* (New York: Library Publishers, 1954), p. 85.

33. *Ibid.,* p. 86.

34. *Ibid.,* p. 70.

35. Winter, *David Belasco,* p. 124.

36. Louis Sheaffer, *O'Neill, Son and Playwright* (Boston: Little, Brown and Company, 1968), p. 33.

37. Timberlake, *op. cit.*, pp. 77–78.

38. *Ibid.*, pp. 78–79.

39. *Ibid.*, p. 80.

40. Arthur and Barbara Gelb, *O'Neill* (New York: Harper & Brothers, 1962), p. 46.

41. Winter, *David Belasco*, p. 125.

42. *Chicago Interocean*, May 17, 1897, p. 3.

43. Altrocchi, *Spectacular San Franciscans*, pp. 206–07.

44. *San Francisco Chronicle*, March 24, 1879, p. 4.

45. *San Francisco Chronicle*, April 8, 1879, p. 5.

46. *San Francisco Chronicle*, May 25, 1879, p. 2.

47. Winter, *David Belasco*, p. 128.

48. *Ibid.*, p. 183.

49. *San Francisco Chronicle*, August 19, 1879, p. 2.

50. *San Francisco Chronicle*, September 3, 1879, p. 4.

5   Babies, Beans, and Buckwheat Cakes

1. *San Francisco Sunday Chronicle*, September 14, 1879, p. 2.

2. Mrs. James A. Herne, *Shore Acres*, pp. 303–04.

3. *San Francisco Sunday Chronicle*, September 14, 1879, p. 2.

4. Belasco, "Little Things," pp. 15, 73.

5. Mordecai Gorelik, *New Theatres for Old* (New York: E. P. Dutton and Company, 1940), p. 165.

6. Belasco, "Little Things," p. 65.

7. Letter from James A. Herne to William Dean Howells, February 9, 189?, Houghton Library, Harvard University.

8. Mrs. James A. Herne, *Shore Acres*, p. 291.

9. *San Francisco Sunday Chronicle*, September 14, 1879, p. 4.

10. The Players Collection, New York Public Library, (undated clipping).

11. Forrest Izard, *Heroines of the Modern Stage* (New York: Sturgis & Walton Company, 1915), p. 328.

12. Acton Davies, *Maude Adams* (New York: Frederick A. Stokes Company, 1901), pp. 21–22.

13. Laurence Hutton, *Curiosities of the American Stage* (New York: Harper & Brothers, 1891), p. 222.

14. *Ibid.*, pp. 229–30.

15. Arthur Hobson Quinn Collection, University of Pennsylvania Library, clipping, June 27, 1901.

16. James A. Herne, "Forty Years," p. 129.

17. *San Francisco Chronicle*, September 25, 1879, p. 3.

18. Winter, *David Belasco*, p. 191.

19. Lester Wallack, *Memories of Fifty Years* (New York: Charles Scribner's Sons, 1889), pp. 54–55.

20. Winter, *David Belasco*, p. 192.

21. *Ibid.*, pp. 192–93.

22. James A. Herne, "Forty Years," p. 128.

23. Winter, *David Belasco*, p. 193.

24. *Chicago Tribune*, November 18, 1879, p. 5.

25. Winter, *David Belasco*, p. 195.

26. Frederick Warde, *Fifty Years of Make-Believe* (Los Angeles: Times-Mirror Press, 1923), pp. 203–04.

27. *New York Times*, March 30, 1880, p. 5.

28. *New York Daily Tribune*, March 30, 1880, p. 5.

29. *New York Spirit of the Times*, April 3, 1880.

30. *New York Spirit of the Times*, April 10, 1880.

31. Belasco, "Little Things," p. 73.

32. W. C. Cawley Collection, New York Public Library at Lincoln Center (undated clipping).

33. Arthur Hobson Quinn, *A History of the American Drama From the Civil War to the Present Day* (New York: Appleton-Century-Crofts, 1936), p. 135.

34. Mrs. James A. Herne, *Shore Acres*, p. 316.

35. James A. Herne, "Forty Years," p. 254.

36. Winter, *David Belasco*, pp. 198, 200.

37. *Ibid.*, pp. 206–07.

38. Timberlake, *David Belasco*, pp. 90–91.

39. Winter, *David Belasco*, p. 189.

40. *Ibid.*, p. 199.

41. *Ibid.*, pp. 201–02.

42. Julie Herne, "James A. Herne," p. 141.

43. Timberlake, *David Belasco*, p. 93.

44. The Merriman Scrapbook Collection, University of Pittsburgh Library, March 21, 1881.

45. *Daily Memphis Avalanche*, January 1, 1881, p. 4.

46. *Pittsburgh Post*, March 22, 1881, p. 4.

47. Arthur Hobson Quinn Collection, University of Pennsylvania Library, (clipping), February 12, 1881.

48. Arthur Hobson Quinn Collection, University of Pennsylvania Library, (undated clipping).

49. Mary Anderson, *A Few Memories* (New York: Harper & Brothers Publishers, 1896), p. 208.

6   The Dramatic Junoration of the Age

1. Glenn Hughes, *A History of the American Theatre 1700–1950* (New York: Samuel French, 1951), p. 70.

2. Julie Herne, "James A. Herne," p. 182.

3. *New York Dramatic Mirror*, January 4, 1896, p. 2.

4. *Philadelphia Public Ledger*, April 6, 1886, p. 4.

5. *Philadelphia Inquirer*, April 7, 1886, p. 4.

6. *Philadelphia Public Ledger*, April 7, 1886, p. 4.

7. James A. Herne, "Forty Years," p. 252.

8. Albert Keiser, *The Indian in American Literature* (New York: Oxford University Press, 1933), p. 102.

9. James Grossman, *James Fenimore Cooper* (Stanford: Stanford University Press, 1967), p. 46.

10. James Russell Lowell, *A Fable for Critics* (New York: G. F. Putnam, 1848), p. 49.

11. James Fenimore Cooper, A Re-Appraisal (Cooperstown, New York: New York State Historical Association, 1954), pp. 451–52.

12. Lowell, *Fable for Critics*, p. 49.

13. Keiser, *Indian in American Literature*, p. 142.

14. James L. Ford, *Forty-Odd Years in the Literary Shop* (New York: E. P. Dutton & Company, 1921), p. 91.

15. Theodora R. Henness, "New York Theatre," *Atlantic Monthly*, XLIII (1879), p. 44.

16. Arthur Hobson Quinn, ed., *The Early Plays of James A. Herne*, VII (Bloomington: Indiana University Press, 1964), p. 81.

17. Henry Collins Brown, *In the Golden Nineties* (Hastings-on-Hudson: Valentine's Manual, Inc., 1928), p. 178.

18. Quinn, *Early Plays*, p. 45.

19. *Ibid.*, p. 82.

20. *Ibid.*, p. 45.

21. *Ibid.*, p. 96.

22. *Ibid.*, p. 68.

23. Henry Nash Smith, *Virgin Land* (Cambridge: Harvard University Press, 1970), p. 119.

24. Keiser, *Indian in American Literature*, p. 85.

25. Quinn, *Early Plays*, p. 48.

26. *Ibid.*

27. *Ibid.*, p. 49.

28. *Ibid.*, p. 48.

29. *Ibid.*, p. 51.

30. James A. Herne, "Old Stock Days," p. 366.

31. Bloomfield-Moore, *Sensible Etiquette* (Philadelphia: Porter & Coates, 1878), pp. 334–35.

32. Mary Elizabeth Sherwood, *Manners and Social Uses* (New York: Harper & Brothers Publishers, 1907), p. 147.

33. Allan Nevins, ed., *America Through British Eyes* (New York: Oxford University Press, 1948), p. 222.

34. Quinn, *Early Plays*, p. 77.

35. *Ibid.*, p. 53.

36. *Philadelphia Inquirer*, April 7, 1886, p. 4.

37. Quinn, *Early Plays*, p. 137.

38. Julian Ralph, "The Bowery," *The Century*, 43 (November, 1891–April, 1892), pp. 234–35.

39. Alvin F. Harlow, *Old Bowery Days* (New York: D. Appleton and Company, 1931), p. 454.

40. Harlow, *Old Bowery Days*, pp. 383–84.

41. Frances Trollope, *Domestic Manners of the Americans* (New York: Alfred A. Knopf, 1949), p. 339.

42. *Ibid.*, p. 340.

43. Theatre Collection, New York Public Library at Lincoln Center, clipping, September 14, 1886.

44. Theatre Collection, New York Public Library at Lincoln Center, clipping, September 14, 1886.

45. Julie Herne, "James A. Herne," p. 194.

46. Richard A. Willis, "The Hazards of Nineteenth Century Theatres," *Players Magazine*, 46 (October–September, 1970–71), p. 127.

7   Turn Your Glasses Upside Down

1. Arthur Hobson Quinn, *The Literature of the American People* (New York: Appleton-Century-Crofts, 1951), p. 805.

2. *Boston Evening Transcript*, May 22, 1920, part III, p. 5.

3. Lilian Whiting, "Literary Boston," *Cosmopolitan*, 10 (November-April, 1890–91), p. 206.

4. Walter Blackburn Harte, "The Back Bay: Boston's Throne of Wealth," *The Arena*, 10 (1894), p. 18.

5. Hamlin Garland, *Roadside Meetings*, (New York: The Macmillan Company, 1930), p. 7.

6. B. O. Flower, *Civilization's Inferno* (Boston: Arena Publishing Company, 1893), pp. 13–14.

7. "Destitution in Boston with Striking Illustrations and Practical Suggestions," *The Arena*, 7 (1890), pp. 748, 738, 747.

8. George P. Lathrop, "Literary and Social Boston," *Harper's Monthly*, LXII (December-May, 1880–81), p. 381.

9. Garland, *Roadside Meetings*, p. 8.

10. Hamlin Garland, *A Son of the Middle Border* (New York: The Macmillan Company, 1922), p. 332.

11. Lars Ahnebrink, *The Beginnings of Naturalism in American Fiction* (Cambridge, Mass: Harvard University Press, 1950), p. 66.

12. Herbert Spencer, *First Principles* (New York: D. Appleton and Company, 1885), p. 396.

13. Donald Pizer, *Hamlin Garland's Early Work and Career* (Berkeley and Los Angeles: University of California Press, 1960), p. 12.

14. Donald Pizer, "Herbert Spencer and the Genesis of Hamlin Garland's Critical System," *Tulane Studies in English* (1957), pp. 157–58.

15. Richard Hofstadter, *Social Darwinism in American Thought* (Boston: Beacon Press, 1955), p. 46.

16. Garland, *Son of the Middle Border*, p. 324.

17. Ahnebrink, *American Fiction*, p. 140.

18. David H. Dickason, "Benjamin Orange Flower, Patron of the Realists," *American Literature*, 14 (1942–43), p. 148.

19. H. F. Cline, "Benjamin Orange Flower and the Arena, 1889–1909," *Journalism Quarterly*, 17 (1940), p. 141.

20. Garland, *Son of the Middle Border*, p. 323.

21. Hamlin Garland, "Some of my Youthful Enthusiasms," *English Journal*, 20 (May, 1931), p. 360–61.

22. Pizer, "Herbert Spencer," p. 165.

23. Garland, *Son of the Middle Border*, p. 391.

24. *Ibid.*

25. Hamlin Garland, "Truth in the Drama," *The Literary World*, p. 20 (1889), 307–08.

26. Garland, *Roadside Meetings*, p. 67.

27. *Boston Evening Transcript*, April 29, 1891, p. 6.

28. Hamlin Garland, J. J. Enneking and B. O. Flower, "James A. Herne: Actor, Dramatist and Man," *The Arena*, 26 (September, 1901), p. 288.

29. Quinn, *Literature of the American People*, p. 103.

30. *Ibid.*, p. 131.

31. *Ibid.*, p. 134.

32. *Ibid.*, p. 138.

33. Hamlin Garland, "Mr. and Mrs. Herne," *The Arena*, 4 (October, 1891), p. 545.

34. Hamlin Garland, "On the Road with James A. Herne," *The Century Magazine*, August, 1914, p. 575.

35. Mrs. James A. Herne, *Shore Acres*, pp. 109–10.

36. *Ibid.*, p. 119.

37. Brown, *Golden Nineties*, p. 177.

38. Julie Herne, "James A. Herne," pp. 209–11.

39. Edwards and Herne, *James A. Herne*, p. 41.

40. Julie Herne, "James A. Herne," p. 222.

41. Garland, "Truth in Drama," p. 307.

42. Quinn, *Literature of the American People*, p. 115.

43. Hamlin Garland, *Crumbling Idols* (Cambridge: The Belknap Press of Harvard University Press, 1960), p. 72.

44. Garland, *Roadside Meetings*, p. 68.

45. Letter from James A. Herne to Hamlin Garland, January 19, 1889, Hamlin Garland Collection, University of Southern California Library.

46. Garland, *Son of the Middle Border*, p. 392.

47. William Dean Howells, "Mr. Garland's Books," *The North American Review*, 196 (July-December, 1912), p. 525.

48. *Boston Evening Transcript*, January 12, 1889, p. 10.

49. Garland, "Truth in Drama," p. 308.

50. William Dean Howells, "Editor's Study," *Harper's*, 81 (June-November, 1890), p. 154.

8   Those Ashmont Days

1. Julie Herne, "James A. Herne," p. 148.

2. Montrose J. Moses, *The American Dramatist* (New York: Benjamin Blom, Inc., 1939), pp. 226, 211.

3. Julie Herne, "James A. Herne," p. 160.

4. Garland, "On the Road," p. 581.

5. Garland, *Roadside Meetings*, p. 69.

6. Garland, "On the Road," p. 580.

7. Chrystal Herne, *I Remember Me* (unpublished autobiography, Queens College Library), p. 17.

8. *Boston Herald*, June 7, 1901, p. 10.

9. Garland, *Roadside Meetings*, p. 83.

10. *Ibid.*, pp. 69, 70.

11. Garland, "Mr. and Mrs. Herne," p. 553.

12. *Ibid.*, p. 551.

13. Ahnebrink, *American Fiction*, p. 68.

14. Van Wyck Brooks, *Howells, His Life and World* (New York: E. P. Dutton & Co., Inc., 1959), p. 110.

15. William Dean Howells, *My Literary Passions* (New York: Greenwood Press, Publishers, 1969), p. 99.

16. Garland, "Mr. and Mrs. Herne," p. 552.

17. Julie Herne, "James A. Herne," p. 247.

18. *Ibid.*, p. 157.

19. *Ibid.*, p. 333.

20. Garland, *Son of the Middle Border*, p. 192.

21. Hamlin Garland, *Main-Travelled Roads* (New York: Harper & Brothers, 1891), p. 209.

22. Garland, *Son of the Middle Border*, p. 393.

23. Garland, *Roadside Meetings*, p. 71.

24. F. O. Mattheson and Kenneth B. Murdock, eds., *The Notebooks of Henry James* (New York: Oxford University Press, 1947), p. 100.

25. Garland, "On the Road," p. 575.

26. *Ibid.*

27. Julie Herne, "James A. Herne," p. 214.

28. William G. B. Carson, "Bumping Over the Road in the 70's," *Educational Theatre Journal*, 10 (1958), p. 205.

29. *Ibid.*, pp. 207–08.

30. Letter from James A. Herne to Hamlin Garland, June 4, 1889, Hamlin Garland Collection, University of Southern California Library.

31. Letter from James A. Herne to Hamlin Garland, August 5, 1889, Hamlin Garland Collection, University of Southern California Library.

32. Garland, *A Son of the Middle Border*, p. 383.

33. Letter from James A. Herne to Hamlin Garland, April 29, 1889, Hamlin Garland Collection, University of Southern California Library.

34. Garland, *Roadside Meetings*, p. 73.

35. Garland, "On the Road," p. 580.

36. Chrystal Herne, *I Remember Me*, p. 17.

37. "The New Taste in Theatricals," *Atlantic Monthly*, 23 (January-June, 1869), p. 636.

38. Julie Herne, "James A. Herne," p. 245.

39. "New Figures in Literature and Art," *Atlantic Monthly*, 76 (July-December, 1895), p. 841.

40. Ahnebrink, *American Fiction*, p. 71.

41. Bernard I. Duffey, "Hamlin Garland's 'Decline' from Realism," *American Literature*, 25 (1953–54), p. 72. See also: *Hamlin Garland and the Critics, an Annotated Bibliography*, compiled by Jackson R. Bryer and Eugene Harding with the assistance of Robert A. Rees. (Troy: The Whitston Publishing Company, 1973).

42. Hamlin Garland, *Afternoon Neighbors* (New York: The Macmillan Company, 1934), p. 233.

43. *Ibid.*, p. 235.

44. *Ibid.*, p. 250.

45. Lewis O. Saum, "Hamlin Garland and Reform" *South Dakota Review*, 10 (1972–73), p. 36.

46. Duffey, "Decline from Realism," p. 71.

47. Hamlin Garland, "Ibsen as a Dramatist," *The Arena*, 11 (June, 1890), p. 72.

48. C. Hartley Grattan, "Ex-Literary Radical," *The Nation*, 131 (July-December, 1930), p. 351.

49. Bernard I. Duffey, "Mr. Koerner's Reply Considered," *American Literature*, 26 (1954–55), p. 433.

50. Garland, Enneking, and Flower, "James A. Herne," p. 283.

51. B. O. Flower, *Progressive Men, Women, and Movements of the Past Twenty-Five Years* (Boston: The New Arena, 1914), p. 76.

52. Duffey, "Mr. Koerner's," p. 73.

53. Saum, "Hamlin Garland," p. 38.

54. Hamlin Garland, "The Future of Fiction," *The Arena*, VII (April, 1893), p. 522.

55. Garland, *Son of the Middle Border*, p. 395.

9   A Miserable Lot of Twaddle

1. Garland, *Roadside Meetings*, p. 48.

2. Drew B. Pallette, "Garland and the Prince of Players," *Western Speech*, 21 (1957), p. 161.

3. Garland, *Roadside Meetings*, pp. 48–49.

4. Pizer, "Herbert Spencer," p. 78.

5. Letter from Hamlin Garland to Gilder, January 10, 1890, Gilder Collection, New York Public Library.

6. Letter from Hamlin Garland to Gilder, (last week of January, 1890), Gilder Collection, New York Public Library.

7. Ahnebrink, *American Fiction*, pp. 75–76.

8. *Standard*, August 27, 1890, p. 6.

9. Pizer, "Herbert Spencer," p. 82.

10. Hamlin Garland, "Under the Wheel," *The Arena*, II (July, 1890), p. 195.

11. *Ibid.*, p. 209.

12. *Ibid.*, p. 227.

13. Julie Herne, "James A. Herne," p. 248.

14. Hamlin Garland, "The Future of Fiction," *The Arena*, VII (April, 1893), p. 516.

15. Letter from B. O. Flower to Hamlin Garland, September 3, 1890, Hamlin Garland Collection, University of Southern California.

16. Letter from Hamlin Garland to William Dean Howells, October

29, 1890, Houghton Library, Harvard University.

17. Ahnebrink, *American Fiction*, pp. 457–58.

18. Walter Fuller Taylor, *The Economic Novel in America* (New York: Octagon Books, Inc., 1964), p. 164.

19. Casper H. Nannes, *Politics in the American Drama* (Washington, D.C.: The Catholic University of America Press, 1960), pp. 7, 24.

20. Letter from James A. Herne to William Dean Howells, May 19, 1890, Houghton Library, Harvard University.

21. Lloyd A. Arvidson, ed., *Hamlin Garland* (Los Angeles: University of Southern California, 1962), pp. 46–47.

22. Edwards and Herne, *James A. Herne*, p. 163.

23. Julie Herne, "James A. Herne," p. 249.

24. *New York Times*, November 20, 1966, p. D3.

25. Mark Twain, *Mark Twain in Eruption* (New York: Harper & Brothers Publishers, 1922), p. 255.

26. Rodman Gilder, "Mark Twain Detested the Theatre," *Theatre Arts*, 28 (1944), p. 109.

27. Brander Matthews, *Playwrights on Playmaking* (New York: Charles Scribner's Sons, 1923), pp. 169–70.

28. Van Wyck Brooks, *Howells, His Life and World* (New York: E. P. Dutton & Co., Inc., 1959), p. 97.

29. *The Theatre*, III, October 11, 1887, p. 267.

30. *New York Tribune*, September 24, 1887, p. 4.

31. Walter J. Meserve, "Colonel Sellers as a Scientist," *Modern Drama*, I (1958–59), p. 154.

32. Henry Nash Smith and William M. Gibson, eds., *Mark Twain-Howells Letters* (Cambridge: The Belknap Press of Harvard University Press, 1960). p. 628.

33. *Ibid.*, p. 630.

34. *Ibid.*

35. Letter from James A. Herne to William Dean Howells, February 9, 1890, Houghton Library, Harvard University.

36. Letter from James A. Herne to William Dean Howells, June 1, 1890, Houghton Library, Harvard University.

37. Letter from James A. Herne to William Dean Howells, February 9, 1890, Houghton Library, Harvard University.

38. Joseph Francis Daly, *The Life of Augustin Daly* (New York: The Macmillan Company, 1917), p. 234.

39. *New York Times*, August 29, 1876, p. 5.

40. Richard O'Connor, *Bret Harte, A Biography* (Boston: Little, Brown and Company, 1966), p. 177.

41. Matthews, *Playwrights on Playmaking*, p. 175.

42. Margaret Duckett, *Mark Twain & Bret Harte* (Norman: University of Oklahoma Press, 1964), p. 122.

43. O'Connor, *Bret Harte*, p. 180.

44. Daly, *Augustin Daly*, p. 234.

45. Delancey Ferguson, "Mark Twain's Lost Curtain Speeches," *South Atlantic Quarterly*, 42 (1943), pp. 267–68.

46. Edgar Pemberton, *The Life of Bret Harte* (London: C. Arthur Pearson, Limited, 1903), p. 270.

47. Edna Kenton, "The Plays of Henry James," *Theatre Arts*, 12 (1928), p. 347.

48. Henry James, *A Small Boy and Others* (New York: Charles Scribner's Sons, 1913), pp. 155–56, 165, 169.

49. Leon Edel, ed., *Henry James' Guy Domville* (Philadelphia: J. B. Lippincott Company, 1960), pp. 76–77.

50. Howard Taubman, *The Making of the American Theatre* (New York: Coward McCann, Inc., 1965), p. 108.

51. Leon Edel, ed., *The Complete Plays of Henry James* (Philadelphia: J. B. Lippincott Company, 1949), p. 117.

52. *Ibid.*, p. 205.

53. *Ibid.*, p. 62.

54. *Ibid.*, p. 188.

55. *Ibid.*, pp. 96, 101.

56. Percy Lubbock, ed., *The Letters of Henry James*, I (New York: Charles Scribner's Sons, 1920), pp. 232–33.

57. William Dean Howells, *The Story of a Play* (New York: Harper & Brothers Publishers, 1898), p. 78.

58. Edwin H. Cady, *The Realist at War* (Syracuse: Syracuse University Press, 1958), p. 230.

59. Marbin Felheim, *The Theater of Augustin Daly* (Cambridge: Harvard University Press, 1956), p. 303.

60. Moses, *American Dramatist*, p. 181.

61. Letter from James A. Herne to Hamlin Garland, "date probably 1889," Hamlin Garland Collection, University of Southern California.

62. Mildred Howells, ed., *Life in Letters of William Dean Howells*, II (Garden City: Doubleday, Doran & Company, Inc., 1928), p. 91.

63. Letter from James A. Herne to William Dean Howells, June 8, 1898, Paul Kester Collection, New York Public Library.

64. Letter from William Dean Howells to Paul Kester, June 10, 1898, Paul Kester Collection, New York Public Library.

65. Letter from William Dean Howells to Paul Kester, July 31, 1898, Paul Kester Collection, New York Public Library.

66. Herbert Edwards, "Howells and Herne," *American Literature*,

22 (1950–51), 440.

67. Mildred Howells, *William Dean Howells*, II, pp. 94, 96.

68. Letter from William Dean Howells to Paul Kester, June 30, 1895, Paul Kester Collection, New York Public Library.

69. Letter from William Dean Howells to Paul Kester, August 6, 1900, Paul Kester Collection, New York Public Library.

70. Letter from James A. Herne to William Dean Howells, April 1, 189?, Houghton Library, Harvard University.

71. G. H. Badger, "Howells as an Interpreter of American Life," *International Review*, 14 (January-June, 1883), p. 383.

72. Howells, *Story of a Play*, p. 216.

73. *Ibid.*, p. 291.

74. William Dean Howells, "Editor's Study," *Harper's*, 79 (June-November, 1889), p. 319.

75. Hamlin Garland, *My Friendly Contemporaries* (New York: The Macmillan Company, 1932, p. 269.

10   The Single Tax Crank

1. Julie Herne, "James A. Herne," p. 260.

2. *Significant Paragraphs from Henry George's Progress and Poverty* (New York: Robert Schalkenbach Foundation, 1935), pp. 30, 33.

3. Herbert Edwards, "Herne, Garland, and Henry George," *American Literature*, 28 (1956–57), p. 365.

4. Anna George deMille, *Henry George, Citizen of the World* (Chapel Hill: The University of North Carolina Press, 1950), pp. 3–4.

5. Archibald Henderson, *Bernard Shaw, Playboy and Prophet* (New York: D. Appleton and Company, 1932), p. 150.

6. Francis Neilson, *My Life in Two Worlds*, I (Appleton, Wisconsin: C. C. Nelson Publishing Co., 1952), p. 241.

7. Letter from V. G. Peterson to John Perry, October 6, 1975, Robert Schalkenbach Foundation.

8. Howells, "Editor's Study," p. 408.

9. Letter from W. D. Howells to Hamlin Garland, October 21, 1888, Hamlin Garland Collection, University of Southern California Library.

10. Howells, "Editor's Study," p. 407.

11. deMille, *Henry George*, p. 127.

12. Kenneth S. Lynn, *William Dean Howells, An American Life* (New York: Harcourt Brace, Jovanovich, Inc., 1971), p. 8.

13. Hamlin Garland, "Memories of Henry George," *The Libertarian*, 28 (November, 1925), pp. 280, 281, 281–82.

14. Garland, *A Son of the Middle Border*, p. 381.

15. *Standard*, December 10, 1887, p. 5.

16. Donald Pizer, "Hamlin Garland in the *Standard*," *American Literature*, 6 (1954–55), p. 411.

17. Garland, "On the Road," pp. 574–75.

18. Otto L. Bettman, *The Good Old Days—They were Terrible!* (Random House: New York, 1974), p. 70.

19. Henry George, Jr., "James A. Herne," *Single Tax Review*, I (July 15, 1901), p. 1.

20. *Brooklyn Eagle*, July 29, 1900, p. 15.

21. *New York Times*, February 2, 1897, p. 7.

22. *Chicago Interocean*, May 17, 1897, p. 3.

23. *Standard*, January 29, 1890, p. 11.

24. *New York Dramatic Mirror*, February 8, 1890, p. 6.

25. Letter from James A. Herne to Henry George, September 29, 1890, Arthur Hobson Quinn Collection, University of Pennsylvania Library.

26. Julie Herne, "James A. Herne," p. 263.

27. *Standard*, September 28, 1889, p. 3.

28. *Standard*, November 16, 1889, p. 10.

29. *Standard*, February 12, 1890, p. 12.

30. *Standard*, April 23, 1890, p. 13.

31. Garland, *Main-Travelled Roads*, pp. 208, 214–15.

32. Hamlin Garland, "The Land Question, and its Relation to Art and Literature," *The Arena*, 9 (January, 1894), pp. 166, 174, 173.

33. Alan S. Downer, ed., *American Drama and its Critics* (Chicago: The University of Chicago Press, 1965), p. xiii.

34. Barrett H. Clark, "The United States," in *A History of Modern Drama*, ed by Barrett H. Clark and George Freedley (New York: Appleton-Century-Crofts, Inc., 1947), p. 650.

35. James A. Herne, "Old Stock Days," p. 363.

36. Clark, "United States," p. 650.

37. James A. Herne, "Art for Truth's Sake in the Drama," *The Area*, 17 (1896–97), pp. 362, 369–70.

38. Edwin H. Cady, *The Realist at War* (Syracuse: Syracuse University Press, 1958), pp. 144, 232, 144–45.

39. William Dean Howells, *Criticism and Fiction* (New York: New York University Press, 1959), pp. 34, 37, 41, 40.

40. Mark Sullivan, *Our Times: The Turn of the Century* (New York: Charles Scribner's Sons, 1928), pp. 222–23.

41. Larzer Ziff, *The American 1890's: Life and Times of a Lost Generation* (New York: The Viking Press, 1973), pp. 323–24.

42. H. F. Cline, "Benjamin Orange Flower and the Arena, 1889–1909," *Journalism Quarterly*, 17 (1940), pp. 146, 142.

43. *Standard*, October 8, 1890, p. 5.

44. *New York Dramatic Mirror*, November, 1896, p. 3.

45. *Standard*, December 14, 1889, p. 13.

46. "James A. Herne," *The Conservator*, 12 (June, 1901), p. 54.

47. Julie Herne, "James A. Herne," p. 261.

48. Henry George, Jr., *The Life of Henry George* (Toronto: The Poole Publishing Company, 1900), p. 550.

49. deMille, *Henry George*, p. 187.

50. Henry George, Jr., *Henry George*, p. 1.

51. Charles Albro Barker, *Henry George* (New York: Oxford University Press, 1955), pp. 590, 592.

52. Letter from John Herne to Julie A. Herne, January 8, 1950, Arthur Hobson Quinn Collection, University of Pennsylvania Library.

53. M. R. Werner, *Bryan* (New York: Harcourt, Brace and Company, 1929), p. 294.

54. *Ibid.*, p. 74.

55. *Ibid.*, p. 75.

56. J. C. Long, *Bryan, The Great Commoner* (New York: D. Appleton & Company, 1928), p. 94.

57. Letter from James A. Herne to Henry George, November 5, 1896, Henry George Collection, New York Public Library.

58. *New York Times*, October 15, 1900, p. 2.

11   A Four-Legged Fortune

1. Lewis Goff, "The Owen Davis–Al Woods Melodrama Factory," *Educational Theatre Journal*, 11 (1959), p. 200.

2. Owen Davis, "Why I Quit Writing Melodrama," *American Magazine*, 78 (September, 1914), p. 29.

3. Walter Prichard Eaton, "Why Do You Fear Me, Nellie?" *Harper's Magazine*, 183 (June-November, 1941), p. 165.

4. *Boston Evening Transcript*, May 15, 1891, p. 5.

5. *This Fabulous Century*, 1870–1900 (New York: Time-Life Books, 1974), p. 125.

6. B. O. Flower, *Progressive Men, Women, and Movements of the Past Twenty-Five Years* (Boston: The New Arena, 1914), p. 286.

7. *Lynn Daily Bee*, July 1, 1890, p. 8.

8. Julie Herne, "James A. Herne," p. 288.

9. *Lynn Daily Evening Item*, July 5, 1890, p. 3.

10. Julie Herne, "James A. Herne," p. 289.

11. *Lynn Daily Bee,* July 5, 1890, p. 8.

12. *Boston Evening Transcript,* July 8, 1890, p. 6. See also: Donald Pizer, "An 1890 Account of Margaret Fleming," *American Literature,* 27 (1955–56), pp. 264–67.

13. *Lynn Daily Evening Item,* July 5, 1890, p. 3.

14. W. C. Cawley Collection, New York Public Library, (undated clipping).

15. *Boston Evening Transcript,* May 2, 1891, p. 7.

16. Julie Herne, "James A. Herne," p. 290.

17. *Ibid.,* pp. 298–99.

18. *Ibid.,* p. 589.

19. *Ibid.,* pp. 341–42.

20. Chrystal Herne, *I Remember Me,* pp. 28–29.

21. Julie Herne, "James A. Herne," p. 303.

22. *Ibid.,* p. 304.

12   A Monster of Morality

1. William Robert Reardon, "Banned in Boston: A Study of Theatrical Censorship in Boston from 1630 to 1950," (unpublished Ph.D. dissertation, Stanford University, 1952), p. 7.

2. *Ibid.,* p. 10.

3. *Ibid.,* p. 11.

4. Garland, "On the Road," p. 576.

5. Reardon, "Banned in Boston," pp. 63–64.

6. Garland, "On the Road," p. 576.

7. H. D. Albright, ed., *Andre Antoine's Memories of the Theatre-Libre* (Coral Gables: University of Miami Press, 1964), p. 14.

8. *Boston Evening Transcript,* May 22, 1930, p. 5.

9. Letter from Florence Connolly to John Perry, Boston Public Library, March 26, 1975.

10. Alice M. Robinson, "James A. Herne and his Theatre Libre," *Players Magazine,* 47–48 (1971/72–1972/73), p. 206.

11. *Boston Herald,* May 5, 1891, p. 6.

12. *Boston Evening Transcript,* May 2, 1891, p. 7.

13. Garland, "Future of Fiction," p. 543.

14. Flower, *Civilization's Inferno,* pp. 285–86.

15. Ahnebrink, *American Fiction,* pp. 454–55.

16. Julie Herne, "James A. Herne," p. 313.

17. B. O. Flower, "An Epoch-Making Drama," *The Arena, 4* (1891), p. 247.

18. Garland, "Mr. and Mrs. Herne," p. 543.

19. *Boston Post*, May 12, 1891, p. 4.

20. Letter from James A. Herne to William Dean Howells, Houghton Library, Harvard University, (undated).

21. *Boston Daily Advertiser*, May 5, 1891, p. 8.

22. Edwards and Herne, *James A. Herne*, p. 66.

23. *Boston Evening Transcript*, April 29, 1891, p. 6.

24. *Boston Evening Transcript*, May 9, 1891, p. 12.

25. *Boston Herald*, May 5, 1891, p. 6.

26. *Boston Evening Transcript*, May 5, 1891, p. 4.

27. Flower, *Civilization's Inferno*, p. 247.

28. Chrystal Herne, *I Remember Me*, p. 21.

29. *Boston Morning Journal*, May 5, 1891, p. 4.

30. *Boston Herald*, May 5, 1891, p. 6.

31. *Boston Morning Journal*, May 5, 1891, p. 4.

32. Garland, *Roadside Meetings*, p. 77.

33. *Boston Evening Transcript*, May 7, 1891, p. 12.

34. Thomas Russell Sullivan, *The Journal of Thomas Russell Sullivan* (Boston: Houghton Mifflin Company, 1917), pp. 12–13.

35. *Ibid.*, p. 15.

36. *Ibid.*, p. 96.

37. Henry George, Jr., *Henry George*, p. 550.

38. deMille, *Henry George*, p. 42.

39. *Boston Morning Journal*, May 5, 1891, p. 4.

40. *New York Spirit of the Times*, May 9, 1891.

41. Arthur Hobson Quinn, "Ibsen and Herne—Theory and Facts," *American Literature*, 19 (1947–48), p. 174.

42. Lynn *Daily Bee*, July 5, 1890, p. 8.

43. *Boston Post*, May 5, 1891, p. 4.

44. *Boston Evening Transcript*, May 5, 1891, p. 4.

45. *Boston Evening Transcript*, May 9, 1891, p. 6.

46. *Boston Daily Globe*, May 5, 1891, p. 2.

47. *Boston Daily Advertiser*, May 5, 1891, p. 8.

48. "Herne's Margaret Fleming" *The Nation*, 52 (May 14, 1891), p. 400.

49. William Dean Howells, "Editor's Study," *Harper's*, 83 (June-November, 1891), p. 478.

50. Smith and Gibson, *Mark Twain-Howell Letters*, p. 644.

51. *Boston Evening Transcript*, May 5, 1891, p. 4.

52. *Boston Evening Transcript*, May 6, 1891, p. 4.

53. *Boston Post*, May 5, 1891, p. 4.

54. *Boston Herald*, May 5, 1891, p. 6.

55. *Boston Daily Globe*, May 5, 1891, p. 8.

56. *Boston Daily Advertiser*, May 5, 1891, p. 8.

57. *Boston Morning Journal*, May 5, 1891, p. 4.

58. *Boston Daily Globe*, May 8, 1891, p. 4.

59. *Boston Sunday Herald*, May 10, 1891, p. 10.

60. Mrs. James A. Herne, *Shore Acres*, p. xxi.

61. *Boston Herald*, May 12, 1891, p. 7.

62. *Boston Evening Transcript*, May 9, 1891, p. 12.

63. Charles E. L. Wingate, "Boston Letter," *The Critic*, 18 (May 23, 1891), p. 277.

13   The Quintessence of the Commonplace

1. Daniel Frohman, "The Tendencies of the American Stage," *Cosmopolitan*, 38 (November-April, 1904–05), p. 19.

2. Alfred Hennequin, "Characteristics of the American Drama," *The Arena*, 1 (December-May, 1889–1890), p. 708.

3. *Boston Evening Transcript*, October 5, 1891, p. 5.

4. *Boston Journal*, October 1, 1891, p. 8.

5. Letter from James A. Herne to Hamlin Garland, October 8, 1891, Hamlin Garland Collection, University of Southern California Library.

6. Julie Herne, "James A. Herne," p. 334.

7. *Boston Herald*, October 6, 1891, p. 3.

8. *New York Dramatic Mirror*, October 17, 1891, p. 12.

9. *Boston Evening Transcript*, October 6, 1891, p. 5.

10. *Boston Sunday Herald*, October 4, 1891, p. 10.

11. *Boston Sunday Globe*, October 4, 1891, p. 10.

12. *Boston Herald*, October 8, 1891, p. 7.

13. *Boston Herald*, October 10, 1891, p. 7.

14. *Boston Herald*, October 17, 1891, p. 3.

15. *Boston Evening Transcript*, October 1, 1891, p. 4.

16. Charles E. L. Wingate, "Boston Letter," *The Critic*, 19 (October 10, 1891), p. 184.

17. *Boston Daily Advertiser*, October 8, 1891, p. 5.

18. *Boston Evening Transcript*, October 10, 1891, p. 7.

19. *Boston Herald*, October 13, 1891, p. 6.

20. *Boston Herald*, October 17, 1891, p. 3.

21. *Boston Sunday Herald*, October 18, 1891, pp. 10–11.

22. Garland, *Roadside Meetings*, p. 78.

23. *New York Times*, December 31, 1891, p. 4.

24. Henry George, Jr., *Henry George*, p. 2.

25. *New York Daily Tribune*, December 10, 1891, p. 7.

26. *New York Dramatic Mirror*, October 31, 1891, p. 8.

27. A. E. Lancaster, "A. M. Palmer and the Union Square Theatre," *The Theatre*, III (March, 1903), p. 65.

28. A. M. Palmer, "Why Theatrical Managers Reject Plays," *The Forum*, 15 (March-August, 1893), p. 619.

29. Odell, *New York Stage*, XV, p. 9.

30. Richard Harding Davis, "Broadway," *Scribner's Magazine*, 9 (1891), p. 598.

31. Odell, *New York Stage*, XV, p. 9.

32. *New York Times*, December 13, 1891, p. 13.

33. Odell, *New York Stage*, XV, p. 9.

34. *New York Times*, December 10, 1891, p. 5.

35. "Margaret Fleming," *The Critic*, 19 (December 19, 1891), p. 353.

36. *New York Daily Tribune*, December 10, 1891, p. 7.

37. Winter, *David Belasco*, p. 199.

38. Charles J. McGaw, "William Winter As a Dramatic Critic," *Educational Theatre Journal*, 4 (1952), pp. 117, 19, 20.

39. William Winter, *The Wallet of Time* (New York: Moffat, Yard & Company, 1913), pp. 600–01.

40. Brooks Atkinson, *Broadway* (New York: The Macmillan Company, 1970), pp. 91, 93.

41. Julie Herne, "James A. Herne," p. 378.

42. Harry B. Smith, "The Reopening of McVicker's," *America*, 6 (April 2–September 24, 1891), p. 28.

43. Jay F. Ludwig, "James H. McVicker and his Theatre," *Quarterly Journal of Speech*, 46 (February, 1960), p. 21.

44. Julie Herne, "James A. Herne," p. 370.

45. Letter from James McVicker to James A. Herne, Arthur Hobson Quinn Collection, University of Pennsylvania Library, (undated clipping).

46. *Chicago Tribune*, July 8, 1892, p. 4.

47. *Chicago Mail*, July 8, 1892, p. 5.

48. Letter from James H. McVicker to James A. Herne, July 29, 1892, Arthur Hobson Quinn Collection, University of Pennsylvania Library.

49. Hamlin Garland Collection, University of Southern California Library, (undated clipping).

50. *New York Times*, April 11, 1894, p. 4.

51. Robinson, "James A. Herne," p. 209.

14   A Crucible of Civilization

1. Garland, "Future of Fiction," p. 79.

2. Flower, *Civilization's Inferno*, p. 248.

3. Hamlin Garland, "Productive Conditions of American Literature," *The Forum*, 17 (March-August, 1894), pp. 694-95.

4. Charles L. Dana, "Are We Degenerating?" *The Forum*, 19 (March-August, 1895), pp. 462-63.

5. Henrik Ibsen—His Plays and His Philosophy," *The Theatre*, VI (January-December, 1906), 177.

6. Michael Meyer, *Ibsen, A Biography* (Garden City: Doubleday & Company, Inc., 1971), p. 474.

7. *Ibid.*, pp. 496-97.

8. Einar I. Haugen, "Ibsen in America: A Forgotten Performance and an Unpublished Letter," *Journal of English and Germanic Philology*, 33 (1934), p. 413.

9. George Bernard Shaw, *The Quintessence of Ibsenism* (New York: Brentano's MCMIV), pp. 93-94.

10. Rorber Harndon Fife and Ansten Andstensen, "Henrik Ibsen on the American Stage," *The American Scandinavian Review*, 16 (April, 1928), pp. 218-28.

11. Hamlin Garland, "Ibsen as a Dramatist," *The Arena*, 11 (June, 1890), p. 74.

12. Pizer, "Hamlin Garland," p. 185.

13. William Dean Howells, "Editor's Study," *Harper's Magazine*, 78 (December, 1888–May, 1889), p. 985.

14. William Dean Howells, "Editor's Study," *Harper's Magazine*, 79 (June–November, 1889), p. 319.

15. Augustin Daly, "The American Dramatist," *North American Review*, 142 (January–June, 1886), p. 488.

16. Brander Matthews, "The Dramatic Outlook in America," *Harper's Magazine*, 78 (December, 1888 to May, 1889), p. 925.

17. Moses, *American Dramatist*, p. 215.

18. James A. Herne, *The Coming Age*, p. 254.

19. Julie Herne, "James A. Herne," p. 586.

20. Henry Tyrrell, "World-Dramatists of To-Day," *The Theatre*, 4 (1904), pp. 299-301.

21. James Huneker, "August Strindberg and His Plays," *The Theatre*, 5 (January, 1905–December, 1905), p. 91.

22. Hermann Sudermann, *Honor* (New York: Samuel French, 1915), p. 55.

23. James Huneker, *Iconoclasts* (New York: Greenwood Press, Publishers, 1969), p. 288.

24. William Dean Howells, "Editor's Study," *Harper's Magazine*, 81 (June–November, 1890), p. 156.

25. William F. Mainland, "Hermann Sudermann," in *German Men*

of Letters, edited by Alex Natan (London: Oswald Wolff Publishers, Limited, 1963), p. 44.

26. Allardyce Nicoll, *World Drama: From Aeschylus to Anouilh* (London: George G. Harrap & Company, Ltd., 1964), p. 567.

27. Marvin Carlson, *The German Stage in the Nineteenth Century* (Metuchen, New Jersey: The Scarecrow Press, Inc., 1972), p. 218.

28. E. Bradlee Watson and Benfield Pressey, eds., *Contemporary Drama* (Chicago: Charles Scribner's Sons, 1941), p. 209.

29. Garland, Enneking, and Flower, "James A. Herne," pp. 285, 287.

30. Garland, "Future of Fiction," *The Arena,* p. 543.

31. Arthur Hobson Quinn, "Ibsen and Herne—Theory and Facts," *American Literature,* 19 (1947–48), pp. 171–72.

32. Garland, *Son of the Middle Border,* p. 394.

33. Clark, "United States," p. 650.

34. James A. Herne, "Old Stock Days," p. 367.

35. Moses, *American Dramatist,* p. 212.

36. James A. Herne, "Old Stock Days," *The Arena,* p. 367.

37. Letter from James A. Herne to William Dean Howells, June 1, 1890, Houghton Library, Harvard University.

38. Julie Herne, "James A. Herne," p. 286.

39. Meyer, *Ibsen,* p. 475.

40. J. D. Y. Peel, Herbert Spencer, *The Evolution of a Specialist* (New York: Basic Books, Inc., Publishers, 1971), p. 29.

41. Meyer, *Ibsen,* p. 476.

42. Garland, *Roadside Meetings,* p. 67.

43. Quinn, "Ibsen and Herne," p. 176.

44. Garland, *Son of the Middle Border,* p. 394.

45. *Boston Journal,* February 25, 1893, p. 10.

46. Arthure M. Schlesinger and Dixon Ryan Fox, eds., *A History of American Life* (New York: Macmillan Company, 1933), p. 295.

47. Helen Ormsbee, *Backstage with Actors* (New York: Benjamin Blom, 1969), p. 172.

48. Julie Herne, "James A. Herne," p. 639.

49. Garland, *Roadside Meetings,* p. 82.

50. Ormsbee, *Backstage with Actors,* p. 172.

51. Crane, *Footprints and Echoes,* p. 183.

52. *New York Times,* June 3, 1901, p. 7.

53. William Archer, *Pall Mall Magazine,* January, 1900, p. 37.

54. Meyer, *Ibsen,* p. 489.

55. Hamlin Garland Collection, University of Southern California Library, (undated clipping).

56. Garland, Enneking and Flower, "James A. Herne," pp. 287, 285–86.

57. Garland, "Future of Fiction," pp. 550–51.

58. Arthür Dudley Vinton, "Morality and Environment," *The Arena*, 3 (December–May, 1890–91), p. 567.

59. Arthur Hobson Quinn, ed., *Representative American Plays* (New York: Appleton-Century-Crofts, Inc., 1953), p. 525.

60. Garland, "Future of Fiction," pp. 557–58.

61. Quinn, "Ibsen and Herne," p. 523.

62. *The Woman's Journal*, 21–22 (May 16, 1891), p. 153.

63. Lynn Linton, "The Wild Women as Social Insurgents," *Nineteenth Century*, 30 (1891), pp. 596, 600.

64. H. F. Cline, "Flower and the Arena: Purpose and Content," *Journalism Quarterly*, 17 (1940), p. 250.

65. See: Donald Nelson Koster, "The Theme of Divorce in American Drama 1871–1939," in *Pennsylvania Dissertations* (Philadelphia: University of Pennsylvania, 1942), p. 39.

66. John Geoffrey Hartman, *The Development of American Social Comedy from 1789 to 1936* (New York: Octagon Books, 1971), p. 95.

67. Mrs. James A. Herne, "Shore Acres," p. 233.

68. Robert G. Ingersoll, "Is Divorce Wrong?" *North American Review*, 149 (July–December, 1889), p. 538.

69. Quinn, "Ibsen and Herne," p. 544.

70. Garland, *My Friendly Contemporaries*, p. 49.

71. Quinn, "Ibsen and Herne," p. 516.

72. Quinn, *op. cit.*, p. 174. See also: Dorothy S. Bucks and Arthur H. Nethercot, "Ibsen and Herne's Margaret Fleming: A Study of the Early Ibsen Movement in America," *American Literature*, 17 (1945–46), pp. 311–33.

73. *Ibid.*, p. 173.

74. *Boston Daily Globe,* October 6, 1891, p. 2.

75. Letter from James A. Herne to William Dean Howells, July 13, 1891, Houghton Library, Harvard University.

76. *New York Times*, April 15, 1894, p. 12.

77. Quinn, "Ibsen and Herne," p. 544.

15 Art for Truth's Sake

1. William Dean Howells, "A Subscription Theatre," *Literature*, 1 (April 14, 1889), p. 314.

2. *Boston Evening Transcript*, November 9, 1889, p. 5.

3. Quinn, "Ibsen and Herne," p. 141.

4. Robinson, "James A. Herne," p. 206.

5. Charles E. L. Wingate, "Boston Letter," *The Critic*, 18 (May 30, 1891), p. 289.

6. Charles E. L. Wingate, "Boston Letter," *The Critic*, 19 (July 18, 1891), p. 32.

7. Ahnebrink, *American Fiction*, pp. 451-53.

8. *Boston Herald*, July 10, 1891, p. 10.

9. Robinson, "James A. Herne," p. 208.

10. J. H. Wilson, "The Independent Theatre in Boston," *Harper's Weekly*, 35 (November 7, 1891), pp. 874-75.

11. *New York Times*, December 13, 1891, p. 4.

12. Edward Fuller, "An Independent Theatre," *Lippincott's Magazine*, 49 (1892), pp. 371, 373, 374.

13. James L. Ford, "The Independent or Free Theatre of New York," *Lippincott's Magazine*, 49 (1892), p. 376.

14. Helena Modjeska, "Endowed Theatres and the American Stage," *The Forum*, 14 (1892-93), pp. 338, 341.

15. Frederic Ives Carpenter, "An American Endowed Theatre," *The Dial*, 21 (1896), p. 182.

16. James H. Highlander, "America's First Art Theatre: The New Theatre of Chicago," *Educational Theatre Journal*, 11 (December, 1959), p. 285.

17. Victor Mapes, "An Art Theatre in Operation," *The Theatre*, 7 (January, 1907-December, 1907), p. 203.

18. "A Theatrical Autopsy," *The Dial*, 42 (1907), p. 130.

19. *Chicago Daily News*, January 15, 1907, p. 12.

20. *Chicago Evening Post*, January 30, 1907, p. 5.

21. *Chicago Record Herald*, January 31, 1907, p. 8.

22. *Chicago Tribune*, January 30, 1907, p. 8.

23. *Chicago Daily News*, January 30, 1907, p. 14.

24. *Chicago Interocean*, January 31, 1907, p. 6.

25. *Chicago Tribune*, January 19, 1907, p. 3.

26. Chrystal Herne, *I Remember Me*, pp. 50-51.

27. Julie Herne, "James A. Herne," pp. 420-21.

28. Edwards and Herne, "James A. Herne," p. 38.

29. See: *New York Times*, September 20, 1950, p. 31.

30. Edmund M. Gagey, "Chrystal Katharine Herne," in *Notable American Women* (Cambridge: Harvard University Press, 1971), p. 187.

31. "The Current Plays," *The Theatre*, 5 (January, 1905-December, 1905), p. 80.

16 Make Culture Hum!

1. Edwards and Herne, "James A. Herne," p. 99.
2. *Boston Budget,* February 26, 1893, p. 9.
3. *New York Times,* January 3, 1893, p. 4.
4. Odell, *New York Stage,* XV, p. 316.
5. William A. Brady, *Showman* (New York: E. P. Dutton & Company, Inc., 1937), p. 152.
6. Letter from James M. McVicker to James A. Herne, January 22, 1893, Arthur Hobson Quinn Collection, University of Pennsylvania Library.
7. Edwards and Herne, "James A. Herne," p. 99.
8. Laurence Hutton, "The Negro on the Stage," *Harper's Magazine,* 79 (1889), p. 133.
9. George W. Walker, "The Real 'Coon' on the American Stage." *The Theatre,* 6 (January, 1906–December, 1906), p. ii.
10. Mildred Howells, *William Dean Howells,* p. 67.
11. Edwards and Herne, "James A. Herne," p. 87.
12. James A. Herne, "Old Stock Days," p. 368.
13. Mrs. James A. Herne, "Shore Acres," pp. 17–18.
14. Julie Herne, "James A. Herne," pp. 227–27.
15. Garland, *Roadside Meetings,* p. 72.
16. Richard S. Tallman, "James A. Herne and Lamoine, Maine," *New England Quarterly,* 46 (1973), p. 102.
17. *Ibid.*
18. Ignotus, "Charles Frohman—Manager," *The Theatre,* 22 (Christmas Number, 1902), p. 29.
19. "Charles and Daniel Frohman," *The Theatre,* 16 (June, 1902), p. 30.
20. Allen Churchill, *The Great White Way* (New York: E. P. Dutton & Co., Inc., 1962), p. 68.
21. David Belasco, "The Theatrical Syndicate, One Side," *Cosmopolitan,* 38 (November–April, 1904–05), p. 196.
22. Marc Klaw, "The Theatrical Syndicate, The Other Side," *Cosmopolitan,* 38 (November–April, 1904–05), p. 200.
23. Norman Hapgood, "The Theatrical Syndicate," *The International Monthly,* 1 (1900), p. 107.
24. *Ibid.,* p. 108.
25. *Ibid.,* p. 109.
26. *New York Dramatic Mirror,* December 11, 1897, p. 1.
27. *New York Dramatic Mirror,* January 29, 1898, p. 2.
28. Hapgood, "Theatrical Syndicate," p. 107.

29. Charles Hawtrey, "Theatrical Business in America," *The Fortnightly Review*, 79 (June, 1903), p. 1016.

30. Chrystal Herne, *I Remember Me*, p. 34.

31. Letter from James McVicker to James A. Herne, March 23, 1892, Arthur Hobson Quinn Collection, University of Pennsylvania Library.

32. Letter from James McVicker to James A. Herne, Arthur Hobson Quinn Collection, University of Pennsylvania Library, (undated).

33. *Boston Journal*, February 25, 1893, p. 10.

34. *Ibid.*

35. Julie Herne, "James A. Herne," p. 399.

36. *Ibid.*, p .408.

37. Percy MacKaye, "Steele MacKaye," *Drama*, 2 (1912), p. 161.

36. *Ibid.*, p. 408.

37. Percy MacKaye, "Steele MacKaye," *Drama*, 2 (1912), p. 161.

40 Percy MacKaye, *Epoch* (New York: Boni & Liveright, 1927), pp. 413–14.

17   The Ruralist

1. William W. Clapp, Jr., *A Record of the Boston Stage* (New York: Benjamin Blom, 1968), p. 471.

2. See: Oliver B. Stebbins, "The Oldest Theatre Now in Boston," *The Bostonian*, I (November, 1894), p. 113–30.

3. *New York Dramatic Mirror*, January 4, 1896, p. 2.

4. Elisabeth Marbury, *My Crystal Ball* (New York: Boni and Liveright, 1923), p. 73.

5. *Boston Daily Advertiser*, February 21, 1893, p. 5.

6. *Boston Journal*, February 21, 1893, p. 7.

7. *Boston Journal*, February 25, 1893, p. 10.

8. *Boston Post*, February 21, 1893, p. 5.

9. *Boston Evening Transcript*, February 21, 1893, p. 4.

10. *Boston Journal*, February 21, 1893, p. 7.

11. Edwards and Herne, "James A. Herne," p. 105.

12. Julie Herne, "James A. Herne," pp. 447–48.

13. *Boston Journal*, February 25, 1893, p. 10.

14. Otis Skinner, *Footlights and Spotlights* (New York: Blue Ribbon Books, 1923), p. 126.

15. Letter from James A. Herne to Hamlin Garland, May 29, 1893, Hamlin Garland Collection, University of Southern California Library.

16. Chrystal Herne, *I Remember Me*, p. 36.

17. Kate Ryan, *Old Boston Museum Days* (Boston: Little, Brown, and Company, 1915), pp. 237–38.

18. *Boston* Public Library, (undated clipping).

19. Letter from Henry C. Miner to James A. Herne, April 15, 1893, Hamlin Garland Collection, University of Southern California Library.

20. Julie Herne, "James A. Herne," p. 470.

21. Garland, *Roadside Meetings*, p. 79.

22. Garland, *Son of the Middle Border*, p. 429.

23. Garland, *Roadside Meetings*, p. 80.

24. *Ibid.*, pp. 80–81.

25. Richard Moody, ed., *Dramas from the American Theatre 1762–1909* (New York: The World Publishing Company, 1966), p. 671.

26. *Boston Globe*, May 3, 1896, p. 18.

27. Julie Herne, "James A. Herne," p. 488.

28. Odell, *New York Stage*, XV, p. 557.

29. *New York Dramatic Mirror*, January 4, 1896, p. 2.

30. *New York Times*, May 1, 1894, p. 5.

31. *London Tribune*, May 22, 1906, p. 7.

32. *New York Times*, May 1, 1894, p. 5.

33. *Cincinnati Commercial Tribune*, (undated clipping), Merriman Scrapbooks, University of Pittsburgh Library.

34. *Boston Sunday Post*, May 3, 1896, p. 11.

35. Edwards and Herne, "James A. Herne," p. 167.

36. *New York Dramatic Mirror*, March 4, 1899, p. 2.

18 Frogs an' Bugs an' Things

1. Norman Hapgood, *The Stage in America, 1897–1900* (New York: The Macmillan Company, 1901), p. 63.

2. B. O. Flower, "Mask or Mirror," *The Arena*, 8 (1893), p. 306.

3. Ima Honaker Herron, *The Small Town in American Drama* (Dallas: Southern Methodist University Press, 1969), p. 79.

4. Frederick Morton, "James A. Herne," *Theatre Arts*, 24 (December, 1940), pp. 899, 900.

5. *New York Times*, May 13, 1894, p. 12.

6. *Boston Post*, May 5, 1896, p. 5.

7. Edwards and Herne, "James A. Herne," p. 83.

8. *Boston Budget*, February 26, 1893, p. 9.

9. Mrs. James A. Herne, "Shore Acres," p. 21.

10. *Ibid.*, p. 24.

11. *Ibid.*, pp. 24–25.

12. Letter from James A. Herne to William Dean Howells, February 9, 189?, Houghton Library, Harvard University.

13. Letter from James A. Herne to William Dean Howells, June 1, 189?, Houghton Library, Harvard University.

14. *Boston Evening Transcript*, February 21, 1893, p. 4.

15. Quinn, "Ibsen and Herne," p. 117.

16. Mrs. James A. Herne, "Shore Acres," p. 177.

17. *Ibid.*, p. 60.

18. *Ibid.*, pp. 29–30.

19. Letter from James A. Herne to William Dean Howells, February 22, 1893, Houghton Library, Harvard University.

20. Tallman, "James A. Herne," p. 98.

21. Letter from James A. Herne to William Dean Howells, February 22, 1893, Houghton Library, Harvard University.

22. Herbert Spencer, *First Principles* (New York: 1865), p. 112.

23. James A. Herne, "Old Stock Days," *The Arena*, pp. 367–68.

24. James A. Herne, *The Coming Age*, p. 129.

25. Mrs. James A. Herne, "Shore Acres," p. 30.

26. Letter from William Dean Howells to R. M. Field, March 1, 1893, Hamlin Garland Collection, University of Southern California Library.

27. *New York Times*, November 5, 1893, p. 10.

28. *Boston Sunday Post*, May 3, 1896, p. 11.

29. *Boston Daily Advertiser*, February 21, 1893, p. 5.

30. *New York Times*, November 5, 1893, p. 10.

31. *Boston Daily Advertiser*, February 21, 1893, p. 5.

32. *Boston Globe*, February 21, 1893, p. 3.

33. Moody, *American Theatre*, p. 49.

34. See: Richard M. Dorson, "The Yankee on the Stage—A Folk Hero of American Drama," *New England Quarterly*, 13 (1940), pp. 467–93.

35. *New York Dramatic Mirror*, January 4, 1896, p. 2.

36. Flower, "Mask or Mirror," p. 308.

37. Letter from Mary E. Wilkins to E. M. Field, March 1, 1893, Hamlin Garland Collection, University of Southern California Library.

38. *New York Telegram*, January 18, 1920, Theatre Collection, New York Public Library.

39. Chrystal Herne, *I Remember Me*, p. 36.

40. Mrs. James A. Herne, "Shore Acres," p. 121.

41. Flower, "Mask or Mirror," p. 311.

42. Ward Morehouse, *Matinee Tomorrow* (New York: McGraw Hill Book Company, Inc., 1949), p. 12.

43. Channing Pollock, *Harvest of My Years, An Autobiography* (New York: The Bobbs-Merrill Company, 1943), pp. 88–89.

44. *Boston Daily Advertiser*, February 21, 1893, p. 5.

45. *Boston Post*, May 5, 1896, p. 5.

46. *Boston Evening Transcript,* February 21, 1893, p. 4.

47. Letter from James A. Herne to Miss Sutherland, February 21, 1893, Rare Book Collection, Boston Public Library.

48. *Boston Globe,* May 3, 1896, p. 18.

49. *Boston Daily Advertiser,* February 21, 1893, p. 5.

50. Walter Prichard Eaton, *The American Stage of To-Day* (Boston: Small, Maynard and Company, 1908), p. 12.

51. *Boston Journal,* February 21, 1893, p. 7.

52. Chrystal Herne, *I Remember Me,* p. 745.

53. *Boston Journal,* February 25, 1893, p. 10.

54. Mrs. James A. Herne, "Shore Acres," pp. 5–6.

55. *Boston Post,* May 5, 1896, p. 5.

56. *New York Times,* May 13, 1894, p. 12.

57. "The 'Shore Acres' Turkey Victims," *Munsey's,* 14 (January, 1896), p. 491.

58. Arthur Hornblow, "The Children of the Stage," *Munsey's,* 12 (October, 1894), p. 33.

59. *Ibid.,* p. 39.

60. Hamlin Garland Collection, University of Southern California Library, (undated clipping).

61. *Boston Budget,* February 26, 1893, p. 9.

62. *Boston Evening Transcript,* February 21, 1893, p. 4.

63. Mrs. James A. Herne, "Shore Acres," p. 88.

64. *Boston Daily Globe,* February 21, 1893, p. 3.

65. William Archer, *Play-Making* (Boston: Small, Maynard and Company, 1912), p. 20.

66. Flower, "Mask or Mirror," p. 310.

19   An Unofficial Patriot

1. *New York Dramatic Mirror,* January 4, 1896, p. 2.

2. *New York Dramatic Mirror,* December 10, 1898, p. 12.

3. Julie Herne, "James A. Herne," p. 696.

4. Edwards and Herne, "James A. Herne," p. 113.

5. Letter from H. C. Miner to James A. Herne, June 8, 1895, Arthur Hobson Quinn Collection, University of Pennsylvania Library.

6. Arthur Hobson Quinn Collection, University of Pennsylvania Library, (undated clipping).

7. Julie Herne, "James A. Herne," p. 551.

8. *Ibid.,* p. 536.

9. Letter from James A. Herne to Hamlin Garland, October 11, 1894, Hamlin Garland Collection, University of Southern California Library.

10. W. C. Cawley Collection, New York Public Library, (undated clipping).

11. Chrystal Herne, *I Remember Me*, pp. 41–42.

12. *New York Telegram*, December 10, 1909, Theatre Collection, New York Public Library.

13. Theatre Collection, New York Public Library, (undated clipping).

14. Arthur Hobson Quinn, "Act III of James A. Herne's *Griffith Davenport*," *American Literature*, 24 (1952–53), pp. 336, 345.

15. *Ibid.*, p. 338.

16. *New York Times*, February 1, 1899, p. 7.

17. Herbert Bergman, "Major Civil War Plays 1882–1899," *Southern Speech Journal*, 9 (193–54), p. 224.

18. Act IV of *Griffith Davenport* in *The Early Plays of James A. Herne*, edited by Arthur Hobson Quinn (Bloomington: Indiana University Press, 1960), pp. 142–43.

19. Bergman, "Civil War Plays," pp. 224–25.

20. Quinn, "Ibsen and Herne," p. 157.

21. Julie Herne, "James A. Herne," p. 722.

22. Quinn, "Ibsen and Herne," p. 145.

23. Garland, *Roadside Meetings*, pp. 395–96.

24. Donald Pizer, ed., *Hamlin Garland's Diaries* (San Marino, California: Huntington Library, 1968), p. 200.

25. *Washington Post*, January 17, 1899, p. 3.

26. John Chapman and Garrison P. Sherwood, eds., *The Best Plays of 1894–1899* (New York: Dodd, Mead and Company, 1955), p. 251.

27. W. D. Howells, "A New Kind of Play," *Literature*, I (1899), p. 265.

28. Archer, *Play-Making*, pp. 254–55.

29. Quinn, "Ibsen and Herne," p. 160.

30. John Corbin, "Drama," *Harper's Weekly*, 43 (February 11, 1899), p. 139.

31. Howells, *Criticism and Fiction*, pp. 14, 21.

32. John Corbin, "Drama," *Harper's Weekly*, 43 (March 1, 1899), p. 213.

33. *Ibid.*, p. 139.

34. *Players Weekly*, February 11, 1899.

35. Howells, *Criticism and Fiction*, pp. 47, 48.

36. Quinn, "Ibsen and Herne," pp. 345–46.

37. *Ibid.*, p. 143.

38. John D. Barry, *The Literary World*, 30 (1899), p. 57.

39. *New York Dramatic Mirror*, February 11, 1899, p. 16.

40. Quinn, "Ibsen and Herne," pp. 141, 143.

41. *New York Dramatic Mirror,* February 11, 1899, p. 16.

42. *Brooklyn Daily Eagle,* July 29, 1900, p. 15.

43. Lewis C. Strang, *Famous Actors of the Day in America* (Boston: L. C. Page and Company, 1900), p. 19.

44. "James A. Herne," *The Conservator,* 12 (June, 1901), p. 55.

45. Hapgood, *Stage in America,* p. 65.

46. *London Tribune,* May 26, 1906, p. 2.

47. William Archer, *Pall Mall Magazine,* January, 1900, p. 37.

48. *London Morning Leader,* December 22, 1900, p. 9.

49. *London Tribune,* May 26, 1906, p. 2.

50. *New York Dramatic Mirror,* January 4, 1896, p. 2.

51. Barry, *The Literary World,* p. 57.

52. *New York Dramatic Mirror,* January 4, 1896, p. 2.

53. *Boston Journal,* February 23, 1893, p. 10.

54. Richard Moody, *America Takes the Stage* (Bloomington: Indiana University Press, 1955), p. 166.

55. Howells, *Criticism and Fiction,* p. 52.

56. Ormsbee, *Backstage with Actors,* pp. 173–74.

57. Edwards and Herne, "James A. Herne," p. 124.

58. Mario Tiempo, "Workers at Work: James A. Herne in 'Griffith Davenport,' " *The Arena,* 22 (1899), p. 377.

59. *Ibid.,* p. 380.

60. *Stamford Daily Advocate,* May 15, 1899, p. 1.

20 A Descendant of Aaron

1. George C. Tyler and J. C. Furnas, *Whatever Goes Up* (Indianapolis: The Bobbs-Merrill Company, 1934), p. 150.

2. Garland, *Hamlin Garland's Diaries,* p. 199.

3. Julie Herne, "James A. Herne," p. 748.

4. Pearl Sieben, *The Immortal Jolson, His Life and Times* (New York: Frederick Fell, Inc., 1962), p. 32.

5. Tyler and Furnas, *Whatever Goes Up,* p. 150.

6. *Washington Post,* June 23, 1901, p. 27.

7. Julie Herne, "James A. Herne," p. 749.

8. *Washington Post,* September 18, 1899, p. 7.

9. *New York Dramatic Mirror,* September 23, 1899, p. 12.

10. Abraham Cahan, "Zangwill's Play, The Children of the Ghetto," *The Forum,* 28 (1899–1900), p. 503.

11. *Washington Post,* September 19, 1899, p. 7.

12. Winter, *David Belasco,* p. 453.

13. Cahan, "Zangwill's Play," p. 510.

14. *Ibid.,* p. 506.

15. Maurice Wohlgelernter, *Israel Zangwill* (New York: Columbia University Press, 1964), p. 89.

16. Cahan, "Zangwill's Play," p. 511.

17. John Corbin, "The Ghetto & The Children of the Ghetto," *Harper's Weekly*, XLIII (October, 1899), p. 1011.

18. "The Drama," *The Critic*, 35 (November, 1899), p. 1049.

19. "Drama," *The Athenaeum*, MDCCCXCIX (July–December, 1899), p. 844.

20. Winter, *David Belasco*, p. 451.

21. Hapgood, *Stage in America*, pp. 334–35.

22. Tyler and Furnas, *Whatever Goes Up*, p. 162.

23. *Ibid.*, p. 164.

24. M. J. Landa, *The Jew in Drama* (Port Washington, New York: Kennikot Press, Inc., 1968), p. 222. For an analysis of Zangwill's later plays see: Elsie Bonita Adams, *Israel Zangwill* (New York: Twayne Publishers, Inc., 1971), pp. 107–32.

25. Glenn Loney, "The Heydey of the Dramatized Novel," *Educational Theatre Journal*, 9 (1957), p. 198.

26. Julie Herne, "James A. Herne," p. 786.

27. *Ibid.*, p. 787.

28. W. C. Cawley Collection, New York Public Library at Lincoln Center, (undated clipping).

21   The Poet of the Poor

1. Letter from James A. Herne to Julie Herne, September 29, 1898, Arthur Hobson Quinn Collection, University of Pennsylvania Library.

2. The Players Collection, New York Public Library at Lincoln Center, (undated clipping).

3. James Fenimore Cooper, *The Sea Lions* (New York: W. A. Townsend and Company, 1960), p. 14.

4. Chrystal Herne, *I Remember Me*, p. 71.

5. *New York Dramatic Mirror*, July 29, 1900, p. 15.

6. *New York Times*, September 30, 1900, p. 19.

7. *Ibid.*

8. Lionel Barrymore, *We Barrymores* (New York: Appleton-Century-Crofts, 1951), p. 55.

9. The Players Collection, New York Public Library, (undated clipping).

10. *Boston Traveler*, October 25, 1899, p. 5.

11. *Boston Globe*, October 25, 1899, p. 5.

12. *Boston Herald,* October 25, 1899, p. 9.

13. *Boston Sunday Journal,* October 29, 1899, p. 2.

14. *Boston Sunday Post,* October 29, 1899, p. 11.

15. *Boston Daily Advertiser,* October 25, 1899, p. 2.

16. *Boston Journal,* October 25, 1899, p. 3.

17. Mrs. James A. Herne, "Shore Acres," p. xxvii.

18. *Boston Herald,* October 25, 1899, p. 9.

19. *New York Dramatic Mirror,* October 6, 1900, p. 16.

20. John Bouve Clapp and Edwin Francis Edgett, *Plays of the Present* (New York: The Dunlap Society, 1902), p. 237.

21. Julie Herne, "James A. Herne," p. 763.

22. Mrs. James A. Herne, "Shore Acres," pp. 180, 199, 195.

23. Theatre Collection, New York Public Library at Lincoln Center, (undated clipping).

24. Theatre Collection, New York Public LIbrary at Lincoln Center, (undated clipping).

25. Julie Herne, "James A. Herne," p. 776.

26. Garland, *Daughter of the Middle Border,* p. 162.

27. Julie Herne, "James A. Herne," pp. 780–81.

28. *Ibid.,* p. 797.

29. George Blumenthal and Arthur H. Menkin, *My Sixty Years in Show Business* (New York: Frederick C. Osberg, Publishers, 1936), p. 663.

30. Vincent Sheean, *Oscar Hammerstein I* (New York: Simon and Schuster, 1956), p. 56.

31. *New York Dramatic Mirror,* September 29, 1900, p. 17.

32. *New York Times,* September 29, 1900, p. 14.

33. *New York Times,* September 23, 1900, p. 17.

34. Winter, *David Belasco,* pp. 51–52.

35. Chrystal Herne, *I Remember Me,* pp. 63, 64.

36. *New York Times,* September 28, 1900, p. 5.

37. *The Commercial Advertiser,* September 28, 1900.

38. Tyler and Furnas, *Whatever Goes Up,* p. 103.

39. Theatre Collection, New York Public Library at Lincoln Center, (undated clipping).

40. Chrystal Herne, *I Remember Me,* p. 67.

41. Julie Herne, "James A. Herne," p. 800.

42. Garland, *Hamlin Garland's Diaries,* pp. 145–46.

43. Julie Herne, "James A. Herne," p. 801.

44. "James A. Herne," *The Conservator,* 12 (June, 1901), p. 54.

45. *Ibid.*

46. Theatre Collection, New York Public Library at Lincoln Center, (undated clipping).

47. Theatre Collection, New York Public Library at Lincoln Center, (undated clipping).

48. Gloucester *Daily News,* June 3, 1901, p. 4.

49. *New York Dramatic Mirror,* June 15, 1901, p. 8.

50. *Ibid.*

51. *New York Times,* June 3, 1901, p. 7.

52. Letter from John Herne to Richard Moody, August 21, 1960, Richard Moody Collection, Indiana University Library.

53. *New York Times,* June 21, 1901, p. 7.

54. Helen M. Gardener, *An Unofficial Patriot* (Boston: Arena Publishing Company, 1894), p. 351.

55. *New York Times,* February 9, 1943, p. 23.

index